AFRICAN PRESENCE
in the
AMERICAS

AFRICAN PRESENCE IN THE AMERICAS

General Editor: Dr. Carlos Moore

Editors: Dr. Tanya R. Saunders
Ms. Shawna Moore

A Publication of the
AFRICAN HERITAGE FOUNDATION

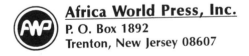

Africa World Press, Inc.
P. O. Box 1892
Trenton, New Jersey 08607

Africa World Press, Inc.
P.O. Box 1892
Trenton, New Jersey 08607

Copyright © 1995 by African Heritage Foundation
First Printing 1995

Book Design: Krystal Jackson
Cover Design: Carles J. Juzang

Library of Congress Catalog Card Number: 91-70747

ISBN: 0-86543-232-5 Cloth
        0-86543-233-3 Paper

The AFRICAN HERITAGE FOUNDATION dedicates this work to all of those—known and famous, unknown and anonymous—who brought all of us here, out from our own Holocaust.
THE HOLOCAUST OF HOLOCAUSTS.

CONTENTS

PART II
RACISM IN THE AMERICAS: CASE STUDIES

PART IV
THE AFRICAN WORLD AND THE CHALLENGES
OF THE 21ST CENTURY

AIMÉ CÉSAIRE (1913–   )
Man of Letters, Philosopher, Pan-Africanist and Political Activist

PREFACE

T HIS BOOK comprises selected and edited proceedings of the First Conference of African Communities in the Americas, held in Miami on February 26-28, 1987 around the theme: "Negritude, Ethnicity and Afro Cultures in the Americas." The Conference, dedicated to the Caribbean poet, philosopher and statesman, Aimé Césaire, was convened by Dr. Carlos Moore at Florida International University (FIU).

The proceedings of the Conference were edited by Dr. Tanya Saunders-Hamilton and by Ms. Shawna Moore. Dr. Carlos Moore acted as general editor. Dr. Saunders-Hamilton's editorial services, with supporting staff, were secured through an agreement between Dr. Moore and Florida International University's Center for Multilingual and Multicultural Studies. Ms. Shawna Moore graciously donated her services as editor. Dr. Moore likewise donated his services as general editor. Dr. Saunders-Hamilton donated personal time. Dr. Antoine Aguste also assisted in the editorial process in a lesser capacity.

A contractually agreed percentage of the proceeds of this book shall go to The African Heritage Foundation, sole proprietor of all of the Conference's audiovisual and written proceedings. The

Foundation, a non-profit entity derived from the conference, with headquarters in Miami, is the parent body of the following entities: Institute for the Cultural Integration of the Caribbean; Institute for the Development of African Cultures in Central and South America; Center for the Cooperation of African Universities, Colleges and Institutes in the Americas; Center for the Analysis and Management of Ethnic and Racial Relations.

ACKNOWLEDGEMENTS

THE AFRICAN HERITAGE FOUNDATION wishes to acknowledge the contribution made by the following institutions towards the organization of the conference on "Negritude, Ethnicity and Afro Cultures in the Americas" (February 26–28, 1987), and/or towards the editing of the proceedings and videotaping thereof: Florida International University, Florida Memorial College, Miami Dade Community College, Lincoln University, Atlanta-Clark University, the University of the West Indies, Metropolitan Dade County Board of County Commissioners, the National Endowment for the Arts, The Dade Community Foundation, the State of Florida Arts Council, the Florida Endowment for the Humanities, the National Black Arts Festival (Atlanta), the Caribbean Cultural Center (New York), The Miami Times, The Miami Herald, Essence magazine, WPBT-Channel 2 (Miami), Africa World Press, the City of Miami, the City of Philadelphia, the City of Atlanta, Pan American World Airways, Air Jamaica, Citicorps Savings, Holland and Knight, the Adolph Coors Company (Atlanta), and the Human Resource Department of Dade County.

The contribution of the following individuals stand out from among the hundreds of persons who, in one way or another, made the conference a tremendous success, and/or whom helped to process its proceedings: Tanya Saunders-Hamilton, Shawna Moore, Francena Thomas, Claude Lise, John Warford, Lisandro Perez, Jessica Lisovsky, Marlene Alba, Betty Ferguson, Carrie Meek, Frank Scruggs, Barbara Carey, Lucrecia Granda, Kassahun Checole, Marta Vega Moreno, Wilkie Ferguson, Rudolfo Cortina, Mohamed Hamaludin, Eugene Shy, Eugene Jackson, Barbara Edwards, Olga

Garay, Peter Bailey, Toni Gary, Uva Clavijo, Myriam Rivera, Dominik Bernard, Lula Rodriguez, Pamela Douglas, Rose Watson, Sharon Lowery, Ted Schmidt, Willie Robinson, Molefi Asante, Modesto Maidique, Esther McClaude, Ester Juste, Tony Maingot, Greg Reeds, Jeanine Paul, Mark Rosenberg, Michelle Lamarre, Maria Cristina Finlay, Jacqueline Menendez, Elvira Fins, Diana Zayas-Bazan, Ghilsaine Mazarin, Garth Reeves, Susan Taylor, Alex Haley, Ulric Haynes, Maya Angelou, Antoine Auguste.

INTRODUCTION

FAMILY ALBUM
OF A GRAND SITTING

IVA E. CARRUTHERS

ONE MAY initially approach this work as a volume of conference papers which documents a special event and moment in time: a time of intellectual gathering; a time of celebration and homage to Aimé Césaire and Léopold Sédar Senghor; a time for historical reflection; a time for future agenda setting. This work portends all of this, but there is an African proverb which says, "Events are linked to one another like the days of the week."

We must introduce these works of the Conference on Negritude, Ethnicity and Afro Cultures in the Americas as the fruit of the aged baobab tree whose roots run deep, whose taste is constant and whose nectar can be felt. This tree and its fruit are the *Pan African ideal and tradition*—a longing to return home; a struggle against the forces of slavery and oppression; a quest for African unity, independence and dignity. And because this Conference was rooted in the Pan African ideal and tradition of the past, it was transcendental. Transcendental, not only for the

African world representatives who gathered, but for the global village which observed and reacted to it as a significant gathering. The two living legends of Pan Africanist tradition, in the form of "Negritude," Léopold Sédar Senghor of Senegal and Aimé Césaire of Martinique, embarked to Miami to entrust their legacy to future generations and give their final public statements on Black and Pan African consciousness as an instrument against racism and Eurocentricity.

The world took notice for this was no ordinary meeting. This was attested to by the national and international media coverage given the voices of the Conference, from *The New York Times* to China's news agency, *Sinhua*. And as was further attested to by the more than fifty messages addressed to the gathering from leading international personalities. Those of Errol Barrow, Prime Minister of Barbados, and Françoise Mitterrand, President of France and Head of the European Community, stood out.

Reflecting the deep feelings of gratitude and respect Africans of the diaspora and Africa have for Aimé Césaire, Barrow praised him as "the force behind the reawakening of Black consciousness in the Twentieth Century." President Léopold Sédar Senghor read to the gathering the letter from President Mitterrand, which reflected both an understanding of the significance of the gathering and a discreet admonition on behalf of the European world. Mitterrand's statement, insightful and mindful of the events of the past, said:

> From the Negritude of the 30s to the 'Afro' cultures of the 80s, from Paris to Miami, in both space and time, a long road has been travelled which runs through emancipated Africa, from Dakar and Abidjan to Lagos and Kinshasa....Yesterday Negritude was the banner of the African intelligentsia, a slogan, a password for decolonization and a symbol of the freedom that African people have now retrieved. Negritude resurfaces today,

more pertinent than ever, as the ferment of a humanistic thought, as we face the great challenges that must be confronted at the end of this twentieth century.

Mitterrand went on to say that he personally saw three possible avenues in which Negritude could evolve "usefully" in the near future. He detailed these as follows:

Negritude as a manifestation of *solidarity between continental Africa and Africa in exile.* Negritude as a coming into consciousness and as an *affirmation of cultural identity.* Finally, and above all, Negritude as a quest for a real *dialogue and mixture between the cultures of Africa and those of the West.*

In a real and figurative sense, the statements of these two heads of state, Barrow and Mitterrand, mirror the differences between the varieties of Negritude as expressed by Senghor's plea for *accommodation* and Negritude as expressed by Césaire's call for relentless *struggle.* These two positions contextualize the historical and future challenge of Pan Africanist thought and action in the world. It should be noted, however, that the thought of both elders of the Negritude movement did rest on a sense of Pan African *unity between Africans of the world* and the reclamation and declaration of African *cultural identity* as prerequisites to a healthy reaching out to other civilizations and cultures.

Giving homage to Aimé Césaire and Léopold Sédar Senghor, a prospective dialogue and international summit unfolded. The life and spirit of this Conference, and the summit feelings which flowed, were derived from the collective remembrances of a people's resistance to slave ships and their continuing struggle and longing for freedom and independence. This Conference's life and spirit began in the womb of the early Negro Convention Movement, was nurtured by the Pan African Congresses, the Universal Negro Improvement Association (UNIA) conventions and Garveyism; and ultimately birthed by the forces of the

Negritude Movement and its World Congresses of Black Artists and Writers of the late 1950s, and the Black Power Movement of the 1960s and 1970s.

The repatriate themes debated in the Negro Convention Movement between 1830–1850, and throughout the late 1800's, led by such men of the U.S. and Caribbean as Paul Cuffee, John Russwurm, Edward Blyden, Henry H. Garnett, Martin Delaney and Henry McNeal Turner, had nurtured the embryo of a Pan Africanism still to come and gave impetus and vision to Henry Sylvester Williams, W.E.B. DuBois, Ras T. Makonnen and George Padmore.

In 1897, Sylvester Williams founded the Pan African Association whose goals included "to secure [for] Africans and their descendants throughout the world their true civil and political rights, to ameliorate the condition of our oppressed brethren on the continents of Africa, America, and other parts of the world, by promoting efforts to secure effective legislation, to encourage our people in educational, industrial and commercial enterprises."

Williams convened the First Pan African Congress in 1900 in London. Some 30 delegates attended from the U.S., Canada, Ethiopia, Haiti, Liberia, Sierra Leone, Gold Coast and most of the British West Indies. W.E.B. DuBois drafted the final statement of the First Pan African Congress, entitled "Address to the Nations of the World."

Williams died in 1911, so in 1919 W.E.B. DuBois spearheaded and was pivotal to what was once again termed the First Pan African Congress, held in Paris. This was followed by four other Pan African Congresses: London, 1921; London and Lisbon, 1923; New York, 1927; and Manchester, 1945. The Manchester Pan African Congress eclipsed the others in that the leadership was more inclusive of the African world and included many who emerged as leaders of the African independence movements. The list of participants included Kwame Nkrumah, Blaise Diagne, Jomo Kenyatta, George Padmore, Ras Makonnen, Nnamdi Azikiwe, C.L.R. James, Peter Abrahms and Amy Ashwood Garvey. Also, this Pan African Congress closely paralleled and reflected strong links and convergence of thought and action between the DuBois Pan Africanist movement, the Garvey Pan Africanist movement and the Negritude movement.

Under the leadership of Marcus Garvey another strand of Pan African initiatives also emerged through the unprecedented mass-based organization of the Universal Negro Improvement Association (UNIA). A strong Pan African consciousness enfolded the UNIA Conventions which were held in 1920, 1921, 1924, 1926, 1929, and 1934. The 1920 Convention gathered 25,000 participants who met at the old Madison Square Garden the entire month of August and is reported to have had to turn away another 30,000 would-be participants.

Another major impetus for Pan African thought and action was embodied in the Negritude Movement of the 1930s led by Aimé Césaire, Léopold Sédar Senghor and Léon Gontran Damas. This movement of French-speaking Africans was connected to the "New Negro Movement," or Harlem Renaissance, spearheaded by writers and intellectuals such as Langston Hughes, Mercer Cook, Claude McKay and Countee Cullen. Coined by Césaire in his 1939 poem "Cahier du'un Retour au Pays Natal" (*Notebook of The Return to the Native Land)*, the term "Negritude," expressed the continuum of ideas and actions reflective of the cultural, political and economic alienation of Africans dominated by European colonialism.

From its inception, the vitality of the Negritude Movement was characterized by Senghor's position that the movement was cultural and that Africa's contribution to a world dominated by Europeans and European values could be a humanizing transformation which would lead to a "Universal Civilization." Césaire, on the other hand, saw Negritude more as an expression of resistance, cultural *and* political, to the forces of European domination and oppression. It was through this prism of Pan African debate that the force of the Negritude Movement and its collectivity was truly actualized. Thinkers such as Jean Price-Mars, Cheikh Anta Diop, Frantz Fanon, Alioune Diop and Jacques Rabemananjara were central to that debate.

The progenitors of the Negritude Movement convened the World Congresses of Black Artists and Writers. The first was held in Paris in 1956 and the second in Rome in 1959. These Congresses, summits of the Negritude Movement, brought together the intellectual and creative spirits of the African world which forged and undergirded the African independence movements. Likewise, these Congresses and the Negritude Movement were inextricably wedded to the 1958 All African Peoples Conference in Accra, Ghana, convened by Kwame Nkrumah.

The continuing cycle of Pan African energy in the world was sparked by the assassination of Patrice Lumumba in 1960 and Malcolm X in 1965, as well as the Black Power Movements of the 1960s and 1970s. The Sixth Pan African Congress held in Dar Es Salaam, Tanzania, in June 1974, echoed the consciousness of the past. Consider the magnitude of this 1987 Conference by the revelation of Abdias do Nasciamento of Brazil that he was the only South American delegate to the Sixth Pan African Congress in 1974!

Thus, it is the Pan African ideal and tradition which link this Conference on Negritude, Ethnicity and Afro Cultures in the Americas the historical movements and congresses of the past. It is from this Pan African ideal and tradition that the Conference on Negritude, Ethnicity and Afro Cultures in the Americas claims its unique and prophetic agenda for African people in the next millennium. This Conference symbolized the coming together for the first time of Africans from South and Central America, North America and the Caribbean; the coming together of the various strands of the Pan African movement. The elders of these movements, people such as Abdias do Nascimento of Brazil and Manual Zapata Olivella of Colombia, John Henrik Clarke of the USA, Jan Carew of Guyana, Aimé Césaire of Martinique and Léopold Sédar Senghor of Senegal, engaged and met with one another in the tradition of eldership and kindred spirits. Most importantly, the elders felt a sense of entrusting their legacy to a future generation of scholar-activists from around the African World.

Forging its rites of passage and linked to the tradition bearers that had gone before, the Conference on Negritude and Afro Cultures in the Americas, its summit feelings and works, will claim its space and place on its own generational terms and context, daring to address the critical issues facing African people in the Americas in the third millennium. It is indeed propitious that this volume is being released at the time of the 500th Anniversary "celebration" of Columbus "discoveries."

In convening a conference of this magnitude, the African tradition of *A Grand Sitting*—a gathering of community to discuss and debate—was necessarily required. Only that special someone with the generational energy, sensibilities, understanding and respect of community could make an effective call for such a gathering. Such a call, to be successful had to resonate with the perception of the community for the need to gather and forge an agenda. It was truly no accident that the voice and experiences of Carlos Moore legitimated the call for the Grand Sitting. In many ways, Carlos Moore's state of personal exile has mirrored the internal exile and alienation of Africans in the Americas. Thus, as a personification of our collective experience, Carlos Moore could summon us together and charge us to be empowered by the truth of our varied yet same experience.

Of equal importance, this call was in special homage to the works of contribution of Aimé Césaire, poet, scholar, statesman and Father of the Negritude Movement. This rightful acknowledgement of our African elder from Martinique was appropriate to this Grand Sitting in the Americas. And we were further honored by the presence of his close friend, President Léopold Sédar Senghor of Senegal, the poet. Mindful of the fact that Léon Gontran Damas died in 1983, it should be understood that this Conference, this historic Rite of Passage, brought together the two last surviving founding elders of the Negritude Movement. "I wish future generations well on their millennial journey. As for us, we did what we could," said Senghor to a group of students as he obliged with autographs. Césaire's presence at such a gathering was the first since the 1959 Congress in Rome. "This is my farewell," said Césaire softly with customary shyness. This conference witnessed the passing on of their legacy and heard their last statements to the African generations of the 21st century.

As you engage in dialogue with these essays of *African Presence in the Americas,* be mindful that they are all borne of the continuity of African world tradition and experience; of a *Grand Sitting*, a representative conference symbolized by the Sankofa bird's look backwards in order to see forward. This work, and the Conference which gave it birth, was legitimized from beginning to end by its convener, its mission and its form.

In hearing the call, they came! They came from all over the diaspora. To speak truth. To listen and converse. They came in the tradition of presenting self as an extension of the communities they represent. They came to affirm what Cheikh Anta Diop referred to as the "profound organic cultural unity still alive beneath the deceptive appearance of cultural heterogeneity."

Despite the contextual and experiential differences, the collective works of the Conference are transcendental and fuel the unifying ideas of the African experience which has defied time, space, language and circumstance. *African Presence in the Americas* speaks with authority and is encyclopedic in character. It is bound by the continuity of African dialogue between generations and across disciplines. The individual essays presented here are seminal in content and form, opening new vistas of understanding through which to examine the past, present and future of African people. They exude passionate intellectualism characterized by academic and cultural integrity. They echo the unceasing drumbeats, daring truths and urgencies of the African communities in the Americas.

Aimé Césaire's "What is Negritude To Me?" anointing the stage and setting the standard for the presentations that follow, affirms the bittersweet joy for what he/they/we have done and what he/they/we could hope for in the future. Césaire's intellectual genius, strength and humility punctuate this historic essay and posit him as the celebrant of the hour. Léopold Sédar Senghor's essay in personal presentation attests to the deep commitment and kindred spirit he holds for Negritude and his friend Aimé Césaire. In his retrospective view, he shares the mood, personages and poetic songs of Negritude. He emphasizes the significant influence and role of English speaking theorists and writers in fashioning the

Negritude Movement. As he looks toward the future, he summons Africans of the Diaspora and Continent to the building of the "Civilization of the Universal." A civilization to be made rich and human by virtue of its African foundation, African infusion and the transforming power of African intercession.

Richard Long's essay, "Aimé Césaire: Interfaces with the Past and the Present," provides a bibliographic and personality foundation for understanding the Negritude Movement and chronicles the work of Césaire. For all of us Long celebrates Césaire as "a poet and intellectual, a pilgrim of Africa, and a man of action who has been, for our health and our solace, a mentor, a master and a benefactor." "The Aesthetics of Negritude: A Metaphor for Liberation," by Rex Nettleford, sees Negritude as a tool against oppression and central to the concept of power. A most befitting celebration of Césaire was offered by Nettleford's reflection that Negritude created visions of liberation, redemption and hope, prerequisites for revolutionary action.

Edward Greene's examination of "The Political Economy of Negritude," identifies the need to understand the nexus of culture, power and economics. He poses questions about the lack of *economic dominance* in our communities and argues for a world economy driven by a "global Black ethnicity" and its self-interests.

The untold story of Africans in the Americas unfolds startlingly in the essays which are country specific. Abdias do Nascimento's essay, "The African Experience and Negritude in Brazil," addresses the role and power of language to facilitate the drumbeats of our conversations with one another. Nascimento unapologetically calls for an international African language. Documenting the Brazilian experience, he declares Negritude to be "a force beyond the literary," a force which creates space—meaning space for "simultaneous expression of Africans' specific identity, humanity and struggle for liberation in all corners of the world where we are present. "Brazil's story, since it is the country where the largest number of Africans of the diaspora resides, provides an appropriate backdrop for the essays which follow.

Jose Carlos Luciano Huapaya's work, "The African Presence in Peru," addresses the dynamics of Black/Indian relationships and the evolution of the myth of racial democracy. Quince Duncan's essay, "The Race Question in Costa Rica," outlines the economic contribution Africans have made to that country. That contribution, he explains, has been mostly exploited and veiled by the myth of a racial democracy. This theme is repeated in "The Life of Blacks in Ecuador," where Antonio Preciado Bedoya speaks of the illusory history of free Blacks which obviates the painful reality of oppression and racism in Ecuador. Justo Arroyo's essay, "Race Relations in Panama," positions African peoples at the crossroad of the Americas, also victim of the illusory racial melting pot. Arroyo sees the common thread of Africa weaving the will, strength and joy as the binding force of the "multiple Negritudes" present in the experiences of Africans in the Americas.

The essay by Bassette Cayasso, "Afro-Nicaraguans Before and After the Sandinista Revolution," parallels and connects with Carlos Moore's "Afro-Cubans and the Communist Revolution." This unique view of African communities caught up in Marxist revolutionary struggles profoundly revisits and shadows the challenges of African liberation everywhere. Guevara Arzu's "The Garifunas in Honduras," sheds new light on a people he identifies as "the only non-enslaved black group in the world." Undergirded by the "will of Negritude," Jean Crusol examines the potential for the development of "Black Business" in the French West Indies.

Nothing is more dramatically provocative than the issue of necessary symbiosis and synergy of Black men and women as exalted by Maya Angelou's live presentation and essay titled "Together". In her inimitable style (and inspired by Toni Cade Bambara's pivotal question: "What are we pretending we have forgotten?"), Maya Angelou reminds us that our survival fundamentally depends upon our ability to *remember* that"...from the slave trappings to the hatches of slave ships, to the auction blocks to the plantation, before sunrises and sunsets, we were Together." Black men and women must/will come to peaceful reconciliation, she insists, adding that either we will survive together or die together. The poems and prose of Black women inform the world that they have never abandoned the Black man despite perceptions to the contrary. Angelou reminds Black men that "our strength is your endurance."

Lelia Gonzalez' essay, "The Black Woman in Brazil," affirms the "togetherness" and absorption in spirit and action of the Black woman into the Black man-led struggle for racial dignity and freedom. More often than not, the Black woman is also fighting the incongruency of the White feminist movement. Ultimately, Gonzalez' essay brings the Black woman center stage to the national ideology of Brazil's illusory racial democracy and "*blanqueamiento*" or whitening. She identifies the Carnaval ritual and the "*mulata* enterprise" as the ultimate in objectifying and symbolizing the multiple oppression of Black women in Brazil. Adrienne Shadd's, "A History of Black Women in Canada," adds a significant missing link to our shared understanding of Africans in America. Through the history of African women in Canada, she unveils additional insights into the historical and cultural connections between African communities of the Diaspora.

The African American woman's "fall from grace" and the challenges of "together again" are examined by Betty Parker Smith's "The Continuing Saga of Black Women in America." Through the literary prism of novelist Alice Walker's women, this exacting essay appropriately outlines the complexities of African male/female togetherness in and out of fiction. Mari Evans', "Chaos and Change in the African American Family," forthrightly uncovers the crisis of the Black child and the challenges of parenting. Her thesis is that increased absence of order and positive love in a colonized oppressive environment, can only lead to greater internal disintegration for the African American family. Evans argues that the African American community cannot afford not to claim full ownership and responsibility for the destiny of its children.

Val McComie's discussion on "The Crisis of Identity in the Americas," reflects upon the contextual and conflictual struggle in the search for self. He argues that "there is no such thing as an African culture in the Caribbean," but rather *many* varied ethnic and cultural influences. He regards African cultures as the legacy or springboard for the emergence and affirmation of a distinct national Caribbean identity. My own essay on the changing environment of racism, "The Evolution of Racism into the 21st Century," addresses critical issues about the use of science and technology and "new knowledges" as they relate to race definitions and access to the tools of power. This essay outlines a need for additional Afrocentric considerations in the creation of world human sciences. Ruth Simms Hamilton's essay, "Conceptualizing the African Diaspora," outlines geosocial factors of displacement and oppression upon the processes of "peoplehood" formation and transformation. She further looks at the double-edge blade of race and class in the cumulative processes of developing community consciousness and collective self-actualization.

Manual Zapata Olivella's "The Role of Black Intellectuals in Forging Black Unity," summons Black intellectuals to hold fast and remain vigilant, "never pretending to forget" the 100 million Africans constrained by the slave trade. At the 500th year mark since Columbus' ship arrived on American shores, Black intellectuals must use the science of human knowledge, and the power of ideas and language, to evoke ethnic and cultural unity for action and liberation. Olivella reaches back to remembrances of the first transpacific migrations of Black people and the recurrent creativity henceforth which has molded our survival despite the alienating forces of slavery and colonialism.

John Henrik Clarke's essay, "African Cultural Responses to Slavery and Oppression in the Americas," brings us in harmony with the Sankofa bird, that mythical African symbol referred to earlier which instructs us to go forward to the future informed by the past. Clarke reminds us of the communities of *Cimarrones*, (Maroons) and *Quilombo* and their unyielding quest for human dignity and freedom which they fought to protect. Too, he reminds us that from these communities came generations of men and women who have dared to claim their *Africanity*, using the ink of redemption, repatriation, Pan Africanism and Negritude in the "building of a concept of a world union of African people and the bringing into being of a new humanity."

A *Grand Sitting.* Together. Remembering. Never Pretending to Forget. Celebration. *African Presence in the Americas* is but a watershed of the prolific presentations made at the Conference on Negritude. It cannot and does not adequately reflect all that emanated from the *Grand Sitting.* There was much said and not included in this volume; there was much felt and not heard; there was much seen and not captured. In all that was, is and is to be, the remembrances and evidences of time and space shared by the conferees have already shaped a new African consciousness throughout the world. As Rex Nettleford noted: "The conference on Negritude mounted in February 1987 at Florida International University may well be seen as a re-affirmation of faith in the intellectual, creative and artistic resources at the command of Africans all over the globe—who, in the continuing battle against a persistent humiliation, must utilize such inner reserves for their eventual liberation."

To those fortunate enough to have gathered there, a special debt of gratitude is owed to Carlos Moore, for sending forth the Call to the *Grand Sitting.* And forever bonded, we will remember this celebration of the life and works of Aimé Césaire and Léopold Sédar Senghor, as well as their presence among us.

Like creating a family album, we have prepared this volume in the spirit of love and joy, with some sadness and frustration, melded by an empowering vision. May it serve to further whet and nourish your appetite for truth and liberation.

PART I

NEGRITUDE, OR THE ESSENCE OF BLACK AWARENESS

AIMÉ CÉSAIRE: INTERFACES WITH THE PAST AND THE PRESENT

RICHARD LONG

THE AFRICAN Diaspora is the primary demographic and cultural product of the present world system, now five hundred years old. Indeed, while plans for celebration of the epitomizing event, the Columbian Discovery, are advancing, it is well to call to mind what indeed is being celebrated: nothing less than the abrupt rearrangement of millennial geopolitical patterns and the imposition by arms and fiat of the first planetary super polity.

The dizzying sequence of events following hard upon the conquest of Granada and the expulsion of the Jews from Spain in 1492 is instructive. The voyages of Columbus, the voyages of the Cabots, the voyage of Cabral to Brazil, and the eventual circumnavigation of the globe by the expedition of Magellan provided the basis for seafaring exploitation of the globe by Christian Europe, an exploitation whose rewards were arrogated to the maritime powers. The maritime explosion, itself made possible by the magnetic needle, is situated between two cultural events of the greatest importance, one technological, the other ideological, namely the development of printing from movable type and the

Protestant Reformation. These two events interact in a fundamental manner with the maritime expansion that provided the modern world system, providing important means of communication and documentation on the one hand and an added incentive to frenetic rivalry on the other.

Within a century of the Columbian Discovery, the indigenous empires of Mexico, Yucatan, Colombia, and Peru had been transformed into dependencies of the Spanish crown; Portugal had captured Goa, monopolized trade with India, and Jesuits were established in Japan under the protection of emergent military chieftains. While the European presence was thus being extended globally, in Europe itself this century experienced not only the Reformation and the counter-Reformation, but the rise of the Dutch Republic, the Defeat of the Spanish Armada, the Massacre of St. Bartholomew, and the beginning of the Conquest of Ireland occurrences some of which resonate until the present hour.

It is important to note that this century also saw the development of a special relationship between Europe and Africa. While the enslavement of captives from Africa and their utilization in the Iberian peninsula preceded the Columbian Discovery, the need for labor in relatively underpopulated areas of the new Atlantic domains provided the motivation for a radical increase in the slave trade from Africa, a trade which was conducted, however, without any profound penetration of the African continent, a process which was to be delayed for centuries.

The situation of the Caribbean, and eventually the tropical and semitropical areas of North and South America, is particularly interesting. It is in these areas that a quantitative and qualitative change in exploitation was to occur in the second century of the new planetary order, namely an expansion of the plantation system primarily for the production of sugar, creating an insatiable demand for slave labor and transforming the trans-Atlantic slave trade into one of the major economic enterprises of the globe, with tentacles in Africa, Europe, and the New World.

Of the many demographic consequences of this enhanced slave trade, beginning in the latter half of the 17th century, the most profound was the creation of a new inter- and intra-ethnic society, the overwhelming proportion of which was black, spread through the Caribbean archipelago, with analog societies in coastal North and South America. Thus the Greater African Diaspora, an increasing subject of mediation, enters the stage of history.

With enormous vicissitudes, plantation society dominated the New World for two centuries and provided the major focus of European imperialism. However, with the onset of the Industrial Revolution in Europe, the conditions for a new imperialism were created, one that required not merely the coastal exploitation of the African continent, but rather its penetration and subjection. This historical process is epitomized by the partition of Africa at the Berlin Conference of 1884-85, followed by the scramble for Africa according to the rules of play devised at Berlin. A coy appendage to the high deliberations creating this new order was the call for the suppression of the slave trade, but not of slavery, within the African continent.

Within a period of 20 years, Africa was territorially invaded by the various European powers, and the full colonial period may be said to extend from 1902 to the end of World War II. However, it is precisely concurrent with this period of full colonialism in Africa that we perceive the maturation of African revindication manifested by the terms Pan-Africanism, Harlem Renaissance, and Negritude, the interrelations of which are now classic, but which we must sketch lightly in order to more fully appreciate the status and stature of Aimé Césaire.

The name of William Edward Burghardt DuBois (1866-1963) is virtually inseparable from the term Pan-African, for he was both a Pan-African scholar and Pan-African activist, whose public career as a Pan-Africanist extends from the dissertation, *The Suppression of the African Slave Trade to America* in 1896, to his death in Ghana in 1963 while editing the *Encyclopedia Africana*.

Not precisely hidden, but also not especially singled out from among DuBois' many works, is a book whose significance and importance has been underestimated by students of the Diaspora, namely *The Negro* which appeared in 1915. Its significance lies in the fact that, succinct though it may be, it is the first Pan-African history worthy of the name. Its importance is that it was indeed read by and deeply influenced most black intellectuals of the first quarter of the present century. It is this book which underlies the better-known but still relatively underappreciated book by DuBois, *The World and Africa*, which appeared in 1947. But already in 1915, in the existence of *The Negro*, we have the scholarly basis and orientation for DuBois' advocacy of Pan-Africanism in the *Crisis* and for his organization of Pan-African Congresses in the 1920s.

DuBois's Pan-Africanism was one of several strands of consciousness which interacted to form the swiftly eddying tide of revindication that we now call the Harlem Renaissance, though it is of historiographical importance to remember that the term applied to this self-conscious movement by its contemporaries was either Negro Renaissance or the era of the New Negro. The latter term was the phrase of choice for Marcus Garvey whose vision was the objective correlative of the sensibilities and aspirations of large numbers of black people in the United States, as well as elsewhere in the western hemisphere. In Africa, *The Negro World*, journal of the Universal Negro Improvement Association, was banned as seditious by the colonial powers who followed Garvey's fortunes with the greatest interest.

The signature piece of the New Negro movement is that complex and dense artifact, much more than a mere anthology, entitled *The New Negro*. In the title essay Alain Locke says,

> The pulse of the Negro World has begun to beat in Harlem. A Negro newspaper carrying news material in English, French, and Spanish gathered from all quarters of America, the West Indies, and Africa has maintained itself in Harlem for over five years. Two important magazines, both edited from New York, maintain their news and circulation consistently on a cosmopolitan scale....Three Pan-African congresses have been held abroad for the discussion of common interests, colonial questions and in terms of the race question as a world problem, the Negro mind has leapt, so to speak, upon the parapets of prejudice and extended its cramped horizons.

The newspaper Locke refers to is *The Negro World*, the magazines, *Crisis* and *Opportunity*. DuBois had founded *Crisis* in 1910 and edited it from that date. *Opportunity*, founded in 1923 and edited by Charles S. Johnson, had been profoundly shaped by Locke himself. His essay, "Apropos of Africa," an important statement of the need for Africa consciousness among Afro-Americans, appeared in *Opportunity* in 1924.

The New Negro provided both testament and promise of a new awareness, anchored in the black American experience but extending throughout the black world. The compendium contains, notably, poetry by Claude McKay, Jean Toomer, Langston Hughes, and Countee Cullen; essays by Jessie Fauset, J.A. Rogers, Arthur Schomberg, and James Weldon Johnson; of special interest to its larger compass are the essays by Locke himself, by W.A. Domingo, and the magisterial essay by DuBois, "The Negro Mind Reaches Out," which closes the volume. *The New Negro*, whose unique crafting is a consequence of Locke's sensibility, intelligence, and commitment, became a major counter in the revindication of the black world.

It is a curious fact that in *The New Negro* the republic of Haiti is hardly mentioned since, in fact, Haiti, then occupied by a U.S. military force, was very much in the consciousness of Afro-Americans. One of the contributors of *The New Negro*, James Weldon Johnson, had visited Haiti on a fact-finding mission some years before and published a series of articles, collected as *Self-Determining Haiti* (1920). Other contributors to *The New Negro* who were to have close connections to Haiti include Zora Neale Hurston, John Matheus, Langston Hughes, and DuBois. In 1943, Locke himself gave an important series of lectures in Haiti under the title, *Le Role du Nègre dans la Culture des Amériques*.

To the two books which we have especially noted, DuBois's *The Negro* and Locke's *The New Negro*, we must now add a third which completes, in my view, the tableau of precursors of Negritude, *Ainsi Parla L'Oncle* of Jean Price-mars (1876–1969). In this work which appeared in 1927, Price-Mars, after elaborating a definition of folklore and folk belief, provides an extended survey of the African background, including religion, and then proceeds to an exposition of Haitian folk belief and of the sparse representation of it in Haitian literature. The conjunction of a scientific account of the African background and its active presence in Haiti constituted a near revolutionary intellectual act in the Haitian milieu and provided the impetus for what has since been called the Haitian School of Ethnology. In 1959, on the nomination of President Léopold Sédar Senghor, the University of Dakar conferred an honorary degree upon Price-Mars, then 83 years old. Speaking of this event, Léon Damas, in his essay on Price-Mars says:

> In honoring him, the new Africa, which remembers its own past and which still desires to give full force to its dispersed values, honored the master of present-day thought whose message undoubtedly made possible the flowering of original works of high quality...—works violent and passionate; tender and robust; works at the disposal of all the countries and races from which they drew and continue to draw their inspiration.[1]

In his *Manuel de Négritude,* a book of over three hundred pages, the learned and prolific Haitian scholar René Piquion sketched a tableau of the Negritude movement examining its history, its themes, its origins, and its major figures. He reviews rapidly the facts of the early life of Aimé Césaire, his birth in 1913 in humble circumstances in Martinique, characterized by its own particular variety of Antillean colonialism; his studies there and subsequent move to Paris to continue his studies; his encounter in Paris with others from the colonized world, notably with Senghor and Damas.

Piquion then describes Césaire as a man of three aspects: the intellectual and poet, the Martinican patriot, and the pilgrim of Africa. This happy formula can, I believe, provide us with a framework for appreciating the achievement of Aimé Césaire. But, it is important to understand that these three aspects are in no sense stages of development, but rather concurrent and intersecting elements providing the basis for the consideration of Césaire's accomplishments and stature. The first historical action of Césaire and his companions in Paris in the early thirties was the establishment of *L'Etudiant Noir,* which is a key event in that pattern of revindication of the black world of which we have spoken. *L'Etudiant Noir* drew self-consciously on the example of the Harlem Renaissance, which had already been directly introduced to a francophone public in *Le Monde Noir* edited by Paulette Nadal.

Like his companions on the team of the short-lived *L'Etudiant Noir,* Césaire continued his studies during the turbulent thirties and like them he wrote poems. Toward the end of the thirties he began the vast poetic project which the world was to know fully only years later as *Cahier d'un Retour au Pays Natal* and which was destined to become, as no other work has, a thematic poem of the black world, creating a new genre compounded of lyric, saga, and epic; lyric in its personalism, saga in its breadth, and epic in its assertion. Excerpts only of the poem appeared in 1939, before Césaire's actual return to Martinique on the eve of World War II. A text of the poem was published in 1947 after the war. By the time of the definitive *Présence Africaine* edition of 1956, the poem had become for much of francophone Africa at once a "cri de coeur" and a "cri de guerre."

While the poem draws technically on Césaire's predisposition for surrealism, it does not fall fully in the category of the surrealist *oeuvre* of Césaire produced between 1940 and 1949 and represented by collections *Les Armes Miraculeuses* (1946) and *Soleil Cou Coupé* (1948), later republished in part as *Cadustre* (1961). Two other collections appeared following the surrealistic ones, namely *Corps Perdu* (1949) and *Ferraments* 1959). But as a poet Césaire had already begun to move from the study to the theatre and, with the dramatic work *Et Les Chiens se Taisaient* (1956), we find the poet seeking the larger public who had responded to *Cahier.* That public was to be captured by the two dramas which followed, namely *La Tragédie du Roi Christophe* (1963) and *Une Saison au Congo* (1967), one work treating the Antillean past, the other the African present, both setting forth in stark dramatic and barely palatable form the agony of African redemption. In a subsequent drama, Césaire draws back, in a sense, from direct confrontation with history and, using *The Tempest* of Shakespeare, the first drama of colonialism as a source, composes a drama of colonialism for a black theatre in *Une Tempête* (1969). In this drama, played by actors wearing masks, Césaire re-employs the characters of Shakespeare with two supplemental precisions, Ariel is a mulatto slave, Caliban, a black slave, and a supplementary character is invoked, the Yoruba trickster god, Eshu, noted for his unaccommodating etiquette.

It is significant that in these dramas, mature works of the imagination, Césaire invokes continually the question of colonialism which he has treated as historian, as political theorist, as polemicist, and as active politician. For it is colonialism that has been the defining reality of the *pays natal* of the black man whether in the Antilles, the American continents or in the African homeland.

In 1955, the *Discours sur le Colonialisme* with its trenchant analysis of colonialism established Césaire as one of the most searching and eloquent critics of the varieties of colonialism devised for the inflicted upon the African world. Emergent nationalism in the colonial context is analyzed in the essay "Les Antilles et le Probléme Antillais" which appears as a preface to *Les Antilles Decolonisées* by Daniel Guérin. These two essays, together with the *Lettre à Maurice Thorez* which announced Césaire's disaffiliation with the French Communist party, are inextricably connected with Césaire's political life. Elected to the French Assembly following World War II, he has embodied Martinique in its successive relations with metropolitan France for over four decades. As mayor of Fort-de-France in that same period, he has brought his immense prestige to the development of civic consciousness in the capital of Martinique. Césaire is the outstanding statesman and political spokesman of the French Caribbean.

As an intellectual, he has brought his powers of analysis to the shaping of a post-Columbian episode of West Indian history, namely the Haitian revolution. In his *Toussaint L'Ouverture*

(1961), the subtitle "La révolution française et le problème colonial" indicates the orientation of his work not as a stilted foray into the past, but as a dynamic commentary on the modern world whose central economic and social conflicts have not wandered far from those so dramatically thrown into relief by the cruel and calamitous events which then ravaged the still tortured soil of Haiti. What Césaire found in Toussaint and his travail he summarizes as follows:

> When Toussaint L'Ouverture came, it was to take literally the declarations of the rights of man, it was to show there was no pariah race; that there is no marginal country; that there are no people who are to be excepted. It was to incarnate and particularize a principle; one might say to vivify it....The struggle of Toussaint L'Ouverture was the struggle for the transformation of legal rights into actual rights, the struggle for the recognition of humanity and therefore he is inscribed, and the black slave revolt of Haiti is inscribed, in the history of universal civilization.[2]

Césaire thus proposes Toussaint as exemplar and model to the Antillean world, to the black world, to humanity. In his own life and practice, Césaire has exemplified the vision of Toussaint. A poet and intellectual, a pilgrim of Africa, and a man of action, Aimé Césaire has been, for our health and our solace, a mentor, a master and a benefactor.

NOTES

1. Quoted from Berrian and Long, *Negritude: Essays and Studies* (1967), p.37.
2. Quoted from Césaire, *Toussaint L'Ouverture* trans. R.A. Long.

WHAT IS NEGRITUDE TO ME*

AIMÉ CÉSAIRE

I CONFESS to not always liking the word negritude even if I myself, with the complicity of others, contributed to inventing and promoting it.

But even if I do not revere the term, I affirm that the word negritude fits a visible reality and fulfills an undoubtedly profound need.

What is this reality?

An ethnic reality, some would say.

But the word ethnic should not confound us.

In fact, negritude is not essentially of a biological nature. Beyond immediate biology, it obviously refers to something deeper; more precisely, to a sum of lived experiences which have defined and characterized one of the forms of human condition made by history. Its common denominator is not skin color as such but the fact that we all belong in one way or another to a people who has suffered and continues to suffer, a people who is marginalized and oppressed.

I shall never forget the day I saw in a bookstore window in Quebec a book whose title bewildered me: *We the White Negroes of America (Nous Autres Nègres Blancs D'Amérique)*. Of course

I smiled at the exaggeration, yet I said to myself: "Well, this author may be exaggerating, but at least he has understood negritude."

Yes, we do constitute a community, but a community of a very particular type, recognizable for what it is and for what it has been. First, it is a community forged out of suffered oppression, imposed exclusion and discrimination. And to its honor, it is also a community of continued resistance, of stubborn struggle and of indomitable hope.

At least, that's what negritude was to us then as young students. There was Léopold Senghor, Léon Damas, myself, Alioune Diop and other fellowmen who met at Présence Africaine. Negritude is still all of that to the surviving members of that group. Discredited, misused and distorted, the term negritude continues to be difficult to apprehend.

Negritude is not a philosophy.

Negritude is not metaphysics.

Negritude is not a pretentious conception of the universe.

It is a way of living a history within history; the history of a community whose experience is indeed unparalleled with its population deportations, its forced migrations of men and women from one continent to another, the wreckage of slaughtered cultures and remnants of long forgotten beliefs.

How can this coherence not constitute a specific heritage?

What more is needed to create an identity?

Who cares about chromosomes?

I believe in archetypes.

I believe in the value of all that is buried in the collective memory and even in the collective unconsciousness.

I don't believe that we come into the world with an empty brain in the same way that we come with empty hands.

I believe in the virtue of accumulated and secular experiences conveyed by cultures.

I have never been able to believe that the thousands of Africans that the slave trade transported to the Americas could have had no other importance than that of their animal strength—an animal strength similar to and not necessarily superior to that of the horse or the ox—and that they did not impregnate the new civilizations with a certain number of essential values, these new societies being potential carriers.

That is to say, that negritude in its initial stage can be defined as a sudden awareness of difference, as a collective memory, as loyalty, and last, as a form of solidarity.

Negritude is not only passive suffering and enduring.

Nor is it pathetic or painful.

Negritude arises from an active and aggressive attitude of the mind.

It is a sudden reawakening.

It is refusal.

It is struggle.

It is revolt.

But then—you may ask—revolt against what?

I believe that negritude has historically been a form of revolt against the world cultural order as it was constituted over the last centuries, characterized by a number of prejudices and presuppositions that led to a very strict hierarchy. In other words, negritude has been a revolt against what I would call European reductionism. I want to talk about this system of thought, or rather of the instinctive inclination of an eminent and prestigious civilization to abuse even its own prestige in order to make a void around itself by abusively reducing the notion of universal to its own dimensions; that is, to think of universality from the point of view of its own assumptions and categories.

We have seen all too well the consequences this has wrought to cut man off from himself, from his roots, from the universe, from his own humanity and, as a result, to isolate him in a suicidal pride when not in a rationalistic and scientific form of barbarism.

But—you will tell me—a revolt which is only a revolt constitutes no more than a historical dead end.

If negritude has not been a dead end, it is because it was leading somewhere. Where? It was leading us to ourselves. After a long experience of frustration, we managed at last to seize our own past and, through the imaginary, grasp the intermittent flashing of our potential being.

A revolution of concepts, a cultural earthquake; all metaphors are possible here. The essential is that negritude spawned the rehabilitation of our values by ourselves; the plumbing of the depths of our past by ourselves; of our own re-rooting in a history, a geography and a culture; the whole given meaning not by an archaic dwelling on the past but by a reactivation of the past in order to leave it behind.

Literature?

Intellectual speculation?

Undoubtedly. But neither literature nor intellectual speculation is innocent or harmless.

When I think of African independence in the 1960s, when I think of this surge of faith and hope which raised up, at the time, an entire continent, it is true, I think of negritude. I think negritude had something to do with that; it played its role, perhaps a major one, since it played a role of catalyst.

This reconquest of Africa by itself has not been easy. The exercise of this new independence has required many transformations and sometimes many disillusions. But it would take a guilty ignorance of the history of humanity, of the history of the birth of nations in Europe itself and elsewhere, not to understand that inevitably Africa also had to pay its dues at the moment of this great mutation.

But that is not essential. The essential is that Africa has turned the page of colonialism and, by turning that page, it has contributed to inaugurating a new era for all mankind.

In regard to the American phenomenon, it is neither less extraordinary nor less significant, even though here it is a question of internal colonialism and of silent revolution (the best of all revolutions, by the way).

Indeed, when I see the remarkable progress accomplished recently by our Afro-American brothers; when I see the number of large cities administered in the United States by black mayors; when I see in schools, in universities, the ever increasing number of young blacks; when I view this great progress—to use the American word: "advancement of colored people"—I cannot help but think of the work done in this country by Martin Luther King

Jr., your national hero to whom the American nation has justly consecrated a national holiday.

I also think of others, in particular of that host of writers, essayists, novelists, and poets who, after World War I, constituted what was called the "Black Renaissance." Men like Langston Hughes, Claude McKay, Countee Cullen, Sterling Brown, Richard Wright, to mention only a few. It must be remembered that it was here in the United States that negritude was born, the first negritude was the American negritude. We have a debt of gratitude to those men that we must remember and proclaim.

In every political readjustment, in every rebalancing of society, in every renewal of morals there is always a precondition which is cultural. At the beginning there is always an intellectual and moral reform or, if you will, a cultural revolution.

You may wonder how all this affects the notion of "ethnicity" that was listed as one of the reasons for this conference and that I was asked to reflect upon.

As far as I'm concerned, I would gladly replace "ethnicity" by another, more or less synonymous word but one devoid of the confusing connotations that the word "ethnicity" entails.

Rather than say ethnicity, I would say "identity." Identity clearly designates what is meant: that which is fundamental, that on which all the rest is built; the hard and irreducible core; that which gives a man, a culture, a civilization its own shape, its style and its irreducible singularity.

Since I have spoken of a cultural precondition which is indispensable to all political and social awakening, I will say that this cultural precondition itself (this cultural explosion which generates all the rest) has its own precondition which is nothing less than the release of long-thwarted, oft times denied and finally liberated identity which, in liberating itself, affirms itself in order to be recognized.

Negritude has been all this: the search for our identity, the affirmation of our right to be different, the appeal to all to recognize this right and to respect our collective personality.

I know very well that this notion of identity is challenged nowadays if not fought by some who pretend to see in our identity-obsession a sort of annihilating and paralyzing self-complacency.

Personally, I think of an identity not as paralyzing and self-devouring but as devouring the world, that is, seizing all of the present in order to better re-evaluate the past and, even more, to prepare the future.

Because, in the final analysis, how can we measure the road travelled if we do not know where we come from nor where we are going. We have *long ago* struggled against deculturation and against acculturation. To turn our backs on the notion of identity is to go back to what we fought against and to surrender ourselves disarmed to alienation.

We can renounce our patrimony.

We can renounce our heritage.

But do we have the right to renounce the struggle?

Some people wonder about negritude from time to time. But in reality negritude is not the question today. The question is *racism*; the resurgence of racism worldwide, the flames of racism that again and again light up here and there. It is especially the great torch of South Africa and of apartheid.

Is this the moment to lower our guard and disarm ourselves?

The present moment is a very serious one to us because a question is being asked: either to get rid of the past as an embarrassing and unpleasant burden that could only hinder our evolution or to assume it courageously, to have it assist us in our continued march forward.

We must decide.

We must choose.

For us, the choice is made. We are those who refuse to forget.

We are those who refuse the method of amnesia.

This is neither orthodoxy nor fundamentalism, even less a foolish dependence.

We are simply on the side of loyalty.

Yes, to sowing!

No, to uprooting!

Some are obsessed by the noble ideal of the universal and reject what seems to them a prison or a ghetto, if not a limitation. As for myself, I do not have this straight jacket conception of identity. The universal, yes. But it has been a long time since Hegel showed us the way. The universal, of course. Not as negation but rather as a deepening of our own *singularity.*

To insist on identity is not to turn our backs to the world or to separate ourselves from the world or to sulk about the future or to sink into community solipsism and resentment.

Our commitment has no meaning unless it means not only a rerooting but also a blooming, an overcoming and the conquest of a new and broader fraternity.

NOTES

*   Translated by Shawna Moore.

NEGRITUDE AND THE CIVILIZATION OF THE UNIVERSAL

LÉOPOLD SÉDAR SENGHOR

IN ESSENCE, Negritude is nothing other than the set of human values of Negro-African civilization. This is what Aimé Césaire, creator of the word, would tell you in his own style. Having said this by way of introduction, I would like to explain now how we started the Negritude movement, what its objectives were and what are, for the moment, its results.

It was in Paris, in the Latin Quarter, that a few Black students—that is, students from the West Indies, Guiana, and Africa—founded the Negritude movement. It began with the launching of *L'Etudiant Noir*, a newspaper directed by Aimé Césaire. It was in the 1930s. The leaders of the movement were Aimé Césaire from Martinique, Léon Damas from Guiana, and myself from Senegal. I should also add another Senegalese, Alioune Diop, who would later establish a publishing firm in Paris called *Présence Africaine*. I should be careful not to forget Paulette Nadal from Martinique, who had previously started the *Revue du monde Noir*, financially supported by Doctor Sajous, a Haitian.

I must also point out the preponderant role that the Americas played in the birth of this movement: The West Indies, Guiana, South America, but also especially North America with the New Negro or Negro Renaissance movement, whose theorists were Alain Locke and Dr. William Edward Burghart Du Bois. However, since we all read English quite well, it was really the texts of the Black American writers, rather than the texts of the theorists that we read: Countee Cullen, Claude McKay, Richard Wright, James Weldon Johnson, but first and most important, Langston Hughes, whom I knew personally. The other day, while going through my library, I was astonished to find out that I had many essays and novels by Negro Renaissance authors in their French translations, even more than I thought I had. This should give you an idea of how much the echoes of this American movement were heard in France and in Francophone Africa.

It seems, however, that it was in France, at least since the Franco-Prussian War, if not since the 1848 Revolution which abolished slavery in the French colonies, that *Black art*, in the generic sense, had begun to interest men of culture, in particular, artists and writers. Soon, with what I call the "1889 Revolution," this art was going to invade Europe and America. It is in this atmosphere, and I will come back to it, that certain Black students, in the 1930s, next became interested in the phenomenon and tried to go back to its origin to *Mother Africa*.

This was the situation for Léon Damas and myself. Thus, while pursuing a degree in liberal arts at the famous Sorbonne, we were at the same time taking classes at the Paris *Institut d'Ethnologie*, which was directed by Paul River, founder of the *Musée de l'Homme*. In particular, we were interested in Negro-African languages and oral literature. And it so happens that Aimé Césaire and the other students who were not taking these courses were buying not only the texts and translations of Negro-American writers that I mentioned above, but also works from the new French literature of Black inspiration. Among others, I'm thinking about Apollonaire, Blaise Cendrars and, in a general way, the surrealist poets. I shall come back to these, as well.

As for Negro-American literature, we were especially interested in poetry. We found certain affinities between this poetry, whether popular or learned, and the Negro-American poetry. As for me, when I began to prepare a complementary doctoral dissertation on popular poetry from my native Senegal, the reasons for this relationship soon became clear to me. I refer you to my work entitled *Liberté I,*[1] in particular to the two lectures entitled "Negro-American Poetry" and "Negro-African Language and Poetry."

Let us get to the heart of the problem by trying to understand *Black poetry*. After this, it will be easier to return to the idea of Negritude, not in order to define it, which we have done, but to better understand it, in this year of grace, 1987. I define Black poetry, either popular or learned, as an "image or set of images that are analogical, melodious, and rhythmic." It is the first thing that one notices in Blacks, wherever they live and whatever they do: they all speak in images. Whether the image is a simile or metaphor, it is always, even beyond the form, an identification with substances, elements, something that we learn about in philosophy or, even better, in Negro-African religion. Such is the case of the following popular poem, "Danse Africaine," by Langston Hughes, which evokes the life of Negro-African blood in the veins:

> The low beating of the tom-toms
> The slow beating of the tom-toms,
> Low . . . slow,
> Slow . . . low—
> Stirs your blood.
> Dance!

And it is Aimé Césaire who echoes him to proclaim the dynamic presence of Africa in his innermost self:

> With my heart,
> I took out the ancient flint and the old amadou,
> placed by Africa in the depths of my being.

Our Caribbean poet could not have said it better. And, as I said before, to fully understand the phenomenon, I too had to go back to the source, to Mother Africa, to the popular poetry of my native village. Here are a few lines of one such Serere poem, in which a young woman proclaims her joy in being imprisoned by the love she has for Mayaye, her fiance:

> Everything that is from Mayaye pleases me:
> The prison I longed for I have.

Thus, in Africa, alive with poetry, one is living constantly and beyond the identification of substances, in the reality of life that is to say, in the emotion of the soul, the music of analogical or, if you want, symbolic images.

In fact, the second quality of black poetry is melody, which naturally becomes song. After all, in most Negro-African languages, we use the same word to mean both song and poem, as for example *gim* (*kim* in the plural) in my native tongue. I recall here the case of *kim ndyom*- or "battle songs," which enchanted my childhood. These are songs which young women from good families compose to sing praise to their slender, black loved ones. In fact, to be considered handsome at Senegal's latitude, you must be tall (at least 5'8"), slender and ebony black. These poems are either sung in a polyphonic chorus, recited or, better, chanted like psalms. In this latter case, each line has the same number of accented syllables, as in Germanic poetry. For me, this is the moment to insist upon the fact the plain-chant and polyphony are of Negro-African origin. One of the best proofs is that the black slaves transported from Africa to America kept their plain-chant and their polyphony. Thus, it is not by chance if Negro Spirituals are sung in polyphonic plain-chant.

From this heritage, the French black poets, like the American ones, inherited the taste for melodious poetry. It is so true that the poem by Langston Hughes which I quoted earlier (The heavy beating of the tom-toms . . .) conserves its melody even in the French translation ("ce lourd roulement des tam-tams"). I still keep in mind the poem, "The Negro Speaks of Rivers" by the same poet, which ends like this:

> I've known rivers:
> Ancient, dusky rivers.
> My soul has grown deep like the rivers.

I'm reciting this from memory. You will have noticed that the repetition of the sound *ou* in the second line, with soul and grown, translates well with the mysterious depths of the rivers.

And here we have, once more, Francophone poets of Negritude reviving, so to speak, the melody of African poems, as in this lament by the poet Léon Damas:

> SINCE
> how many ME's
> have died
> since they came that evening, when the
> tom
> tom
> beat out
>   from rhythm
>   to rhythm
>   the frenzy
> of eyes
> the frenzy of hands the frenzy
> of statue feet.

You will note once more the song-like quality of this lament, with all its alliteration, especially in the last four lines, where the hissing of *f* and *z* imitates the frenzy of the rhythm of Negro bodies.

Thus, from melody we have gone naturally to rhythm. So much so that in Black poetry, the three elements of song-analogical imagery, melody, and rhythm—form a symbiotic relationship; they influence each other. It is the rhythm, "the repetitions that do not repeat," as I like to say, which characterizes Negritude the best. That is why I'll start here by reciting the beginning of an African poem, translated from a Bantu language and entitled "Fire Song":

> Fire, fire, fire in the hearth below, fire in the hearth
>   above;
> Light that glitters in the moon, light that glitters in the
>   sun,
> Star, that sparkles in the night, star that cracks open the
>   light, shooting star
> Spirit of thunder, brilliant eye of the tempest,
> Fire of the sun gives us light,
> Fire, it is you I call to make amends, fire, fire!

It is precisely this rhythm that the Negro-Americans would inherit, whether it be poems in dialect or learned poetry. Just listen to James Weldon Johnson reliving, in his turn, the "Crucifixion" of Jesus:

> Jesus, my lamb-like Jesus,
> Shivering as the nails go through his hands;
> Jesus, my lamb-like Jesus,
> Shivering as the nails go through his feet.
> Jesus, my darling Jesus,
> Groaning as the Roman spear plunged in his side;
> Jesus, my darling Jesus,
> Groaning as the blood came spurting from his wound.
> Oh, look how they done my Jesus.

Before looking at the problem of Negritude in depth, I would like to return to Aimé Césaire. It wasn't by chance that you Americans invited him, along with the senior person that I am, to this conference in Miami. In fact, his masterpiece, his epic poem, "Notebook of a Return to the Native Land," sums up marvelously the three qualities of black poetry that we talked about:

my Negritude is not a stone, its deafness
thrown against the clamour of the day
my Negritude is not a speck of dead water
on the dead eye of the earth
my Negritude is neither a tower nor a cathedral

it thrusts into the red flesh of the soil
it thrusts into the warm flesh of the sky
it digs under the opaque dejection of its rightful patience

Eia for the royal Kailcedrat!
Eia for those who invented nothing
for those who have never discovered
for those who have never conquered

but, struck, deliver themselves to the essence
of all things,
ignorant of surfaces, but taken by the very
movement of things
not caring to conquer, but playing the game
of the world

truly the elder sons of the world
porous to all the breath of the world
fraternal space of all the breath of the world
bed without the drain of all the waters in the
world
spark of the sacred fire of the world
flesh of the flesh of the world
panting with the very movement of the world

You will notice the double alliteration in the last lines and also the liberty that Aimé Césaire takes with punctuation marks, a particularly touchy matter for French grammar.

Having tried to show you how the Negritude movement was born and what were and still are its major elements, I would like now to say something about the future. I leave Europe once more, without forgetting about the United States of America and the more and more decisive role it is playing in the *Civilization of the Universal*, that the philosopher and the paleontologist Pierre Theilhard de Chardin, in the middle of the 20th century, predicted for the dawn of the 21st century. And you know that we are nearly there.

Now, at the time that we launched the Negritude movement, our models were the French poets, Charles Peguy, but especially Paul Claudel, whose centennial we celebrated last year, the centennial of what he called his "conversion." I could not do anything better to explain this paradox than to quote the following lines of Claudel, an excerpt of a text entitled "My Conversion:"

> I had completely forgotten about religion and in this respect had a savage ignorance of it. The first glimmer of truth came to me through an encounter with a great poet, who played a predominant part in the formation of my thinking and to whom I owe an eternal debt, Arthur Rimbaud. Reading *Illuminations,* then a few months later, *Une Saison en Enfer* was for me a capital event. For the first time, his books opened a crack in my materialistic servitude and gave me a vivid and almost physical impression of the supernatural. To this I must add the "Clairvoyant's Letter."

But what did Rimbaud reveal to the young Claudel? Well, it is precisely, before its time, the esthetics of Negritude, which would provoke what I call the "Revolution of 1889." Let us listen then to Rimbaud. In the "Clairvoyant's Letter," he advocates a "long, immense, and rational disordering of all the senses," which gives birth to analogical images. But here's the essential, which is found in *Une Saison en Enfer:*

> Yes, my eyes are closed to your light. I am a beast, a Negro, but I can be saved; you, you are false Negroes...I will enter the true kingdom of the children of Cham...I invented the color of the vowels....I ordered the form and

movements of each consonant and, with instinctive rhythms, I flattered myself on inventing a poetic verb, accessible, one day or another, to all of the senses.

One can see that after the analogical images, Rimbaud borrowed from the Negro-Africans not only their melody, but also their rhythm, consisting of, once again "repetitions that do not repeat." It is from this that the Revolution of 1889 would be born. We will stop a bit to explain the influence of Black art first in France, but also in the United States, and finally on the entire surface of our planet Earth.

1889 is the date of the French philosopher, Henri Bergson's "Essay on the Immediate Notions of Consciousness," where he gives back to sensibility, to intuitive reason, if you want, its rightful place in mankind, i.e., first place. It is also the date of Paul Claude's first play *Tête d'Or*. They say that for the staging, he had specified: "with the accompaniment of drums or tom-toms." That's to say that he was thinking about Africa, about Negritude. Even better, in his play *Le Soulier de Satin,* which was just made into a successful film, the Negress Jobarbara sings and dances in the nude to the light of the moon.

In truth, Claudel was reacting against French intellectualism: against the *cogito, ergo, sum,* the "I think, therefore I am" of Rene Descartes. And thus he returned to the ideas of the Greeks, founders of Albo-European civilization. So much so that they borrowed a lot from the Egyptians, whom Herodote, the father of History, in his *Histories* described as having "black skins and crinkled hair." Thus, in his *Ethics to Nicomaque,* Aristotle, the disciple of Plato, but the true founder of Greek philosophy, explains to us that there are three faculties that permit us to know and transform nature. They are sensibility *(aisthesis),* reason *(nous)* and desire *(orexis).* But here we have the French philosopher, Rene Descartes, taking the Greek formula, reversing the order of the words, and giving us the formula of "thinking, wanting, and desire." In truth, he did more by hardening the words *nous* (reason) and *orexis* (desire), and making them "thinking" and "wanting." The most grave result is that Descartes led philosophy, and consequently culture, even French poetry, toward what was going to be in the 19th century "positivism," or "realism" of "the stupid 19th century," to use the words of Leon Daudet.

It is from the revolution of 1889 that was born the literary, but also artistic trend—the cultural trend if you will—that would expand the 20th century with Surrealism and Cubism. Surrealism, whose principal founders were Andre Breton and Paul Eluard, without forgetting my friend Tristan Tzara of Romanian descent, had succeeded in liberating itself from the tyranny of discursive logic. The Surrealist poets gave way to inspiration mixed with sensibility and intuitive logic, with the *anima* and the *animus*, with the vital breath of the soul, as Claudel would say. It is precisely this symbiosis that is the basis of Negro-African animism and that the Senegalese Wolofs translate by *fit*, "soul." Consequently, one understands how the doctoral dissertation of a French professor from Dakar could be significantly entitled "The Black Model." One understands also how the School of Paris" or Cubism could be inspired by *Black art*. And we can define this Negro-African poetry: "an image or set of images that are analogical, melodious, and rhythmic."

One equally understands why, at the same time and perhaps even before, a similar revolution was taking place in the United States. Because it was taking place under the influence of Blacks, imported from Africa. These men and women were arriving in the New World with their hidden riches—their music and songs, their dances and, let's not forget, their popular poetry. I have often noted, but without surprise, that during the music and dance festivals organized in Europe in the summer, there is often jazz among other Black contributions.

Before concluding, I would like to say a few words about this, namely Black music. I discovered the other year, the plain-chant and polyphony, which played such an important role in Medieval European music and song, are of African origin, of Negro-African origin to be more correct. I know we sometimes read in the music manuals that the Arabs brought plain-chant and polyphony to Europe by way of Andalusia. This fact is true, but as we know, the Semites, when they arrived in the Near East and in Africa, had a monodic song, a type of psalmody. It is in Arabia, in the land of the Queen of Saba, and then Africa that they found both plain-chant and polyphony. The proof, among others, is that the black slaves, deported to the Americas since the 16th century, brought with them in their apparent nudity, their interior cultural riches, which once again included the plain-chant and polyphony found in Negro Spirituals. This is the occasion to point out another richness, still in music. While in European polyphony, accompaniment is comprised of 4ths and 5ths; in Negro-African polyphony, it is done with 4ths and 3rds. And if one points out that the 3rd constitutes a sensual disquieting accompaniment, I would answer: "Certainly, it is the rich accompaniment, because by appealing to the senses it becomes fundamental, truly complementary."

Before concluding, I would like to point out that in Black Africa, as in the cultural revolution of 1889, the Negritude movement, which started in poetry, spread out to art, music, and dance. The phenomenon started in Senegal, where Andre Malraux, the great French writer, told me during one of his visits, "you have five or six painters who are worth the greatest artists of the world." In time, this encouraged me to organize the first "World Black Festival of the Arts" in Dakar during the 1960s. Since then, the Senegalese government has organized other art expositions in many European capitals. Better still, in Washington, during the 1970s, the President of the United States and I inaugurated an exposition of contemporary Senegalese art, which traveled around the United States. I still recall what an American critic wrote for the Washington exhibit: "The French claim that the Senegalese artists imitated those of the School of Paris. We must not reverse the roles, because as we know, the French artists are the ones who imitated Black art."

I would like to conclude by returning to the role the United States played in the building of the Civilization of the Universal. Not only did they create new Black poetry, music, and dance, not to mention song, but they did better. In reality, they inserted all of these creations, not exactly into the traditional English civilization, but into a new civilization, more rich and consequently, more human. As I said at the beginning of this talk, the Greek and Latin

Humanities are playing a different role in this new civilization, but so are the Francophone Humanities, nourished with the contributions of "upright Negritude," as Aimé Césaire would say.

NOTES

*   Translated by Peter Machonis.

1.   Editions du Seuil: Paris. 1964.

THE AESTHETICS OF NEGRITUDE: A METAPHOR FOR LIBERATION

REX NETTLEFORD

T HE VERY title of this paper betrays the problems of Black existence as part of the human condition in the lopsided world of today. It is useful to note that the notion of Black aesthetics, as against a supposedly white aesthetics, comes out of the conceptual configurations of a white world that is used to conquest, domination, and superordinate status with Europe (presumably a homogeneous civilization and a cohesive state of mind underpinning a particular culture-sphere) as Conqueror, Overlord and Mother Superior while the rest remain at the base of a power pyramid on the basis of certain laws of nature and the Law of God.

The idea of Black aesthetics is very much a European invention, as part of a power apparatus devised to keep large masses of humanity in subjugation and to deny to them any innate sense of order, interior logic or consistency in all of the varied acts of intelligence that are the product of the collective or individual intellect and imagination of those people. Such preferred patternings of the Black experience as are deliberately misrepresented and discounted, have pushed the Blacks (in Africa and the Diaspora) into dialectical defense, for survival and *beyond.*

Africans have long turned the weapons of their denigration against their oppressors and so to many people of African ancestry, Black aesthetics takes on positive meaning in the fight against such denigration. Yet one can be sucked into arguments that are shaped by European experience about self-worth and about the credit-worthiness of this or that work of art created out of the experience, worldview(s), or ontological configurations of people of African ancestry.

The temptation to be sucked in is indeed great especially when the Black man functions in an environment of power over which he has no control. Hence, the adoption of the terms and attitudes of a tradition of aesthetic description/evaluation or criticisms coming out of European experience characterizes efforts to find and present that irreducible kernel that makes the life of the African what it distinctively is in all its varied manifestations, both in Continental Africa and throughout the communities of exiled Africans in the rest of the world.

It was from an exiled African, Aimé Césaire[1] of Martinique, that the world received the gift of a new and resonant designation for the quest for Blacks for the ideal, form and purpose they knew to reside in their African heritage. It came at a time when that heritage was facing the threat of enfeeblement from assimilationism in the case of the Francophones and from counterpart afflictions which had been the target of assault by men like Marcus Garvey and William DuBois among the Anglophones.[2]

Then 30 years ago Léopold Senghor, one of the founding apostles of this grand attempt at the rejection of Black humiliation offered a seminal essay entitled "African-Negro Aesthetics."[3] The essay could have been easily dismissed as being sucked into Eurocentric traditions of studies in aesthetics.

Indeed, 13 years later, a younger generation found a spirited spokesman in the person of one Stanislas Adotevi[4] who at the Pan African Cultural Festival held in Algiers in 1969 took not just the aesthetics of Negritude but all of Negritude to task for being too fey to deal seriously with the harsh reality of armed struggle and the technological modernization of a slothful society. Both of these duties had by then become to many the only mean-ingful ones in response to the very humiliation that Negritude had sought to address but failed to destroy. Adotevi, with the anguish and anger of youthful impatience and the thirst for less poetic resistance against an affliction of ages, declared as follows: "Today, this humiliation is still apparent and the problem posed by negritude remains." Literary assertions of "the values which distinguish the Black world from that of the white man," Adotevi graciously acknowledged as "the first moment of present-day requirements...(and as) one of the possible forms for the struggle of emancipation, especially in the realm of artistic creation." Negritude to this young and ardent critic even represented the "courage...needed to dare protest against the humiliation of the thirties." But the new generation, according to Adotevi, found this wanting. And in the spirit of the times (Black Power and the ideas of Fanon were in the ascendancy) Negritude was all but substituted by what the critic called "Melanism."[5]

At the heart of this stirring mission statement was a sense of history with its chronic humiliation starting with the slave trade to be avenged by the recognition of a state of war seeking affirmation in positive action. For the immediate task, according to the revolting young, was not to decorate the torture of history "with trophies conquered from shame"—in reference, no doubt, to Negritude's aesthetically acceptable literary expressions in the torturer' lexicon and complete with Eurocentric notions of the perfection of line, harmony, metric logic, truth and beauty. The immediate task was, rather, the addressing of such issues as the methods of modernization, the liberation of Africa from the old structures of the past, the rational use of technology, the attainment of equality within African societies, the allocation of place and human purpose to Black women and the young in society, a realistic approach to tribalism, and getting into perspective the role of traditional religions in modern African society.[6]

Besides such harsh evidence of existential reality in the late sixties, the primary involvement of Negritude with literary concerns, aesthetic sensibilities, the characteristics of a poem, dance, song or carving seemed irrelevant and insipid. "Negritude, hollow, vague and inefficient as an ideology" insisted Adotevi.

"There is not further place in Africa for literature other than that of revolutionary combat," he declared. "Negritude is dead," he pronounced. The literary indulgences of Negritude are here seen as too far divorced from the ordinary activities of the humiliated Africans, from what Adotevi referred to as "the daily problems which must be solved immediately."[7]

Yet, part of Senghor's claims for the aesthetics of Negritude was that "literature and art [to the Africans] are not separable from men's generic activities, particularly from the artisan's techniques." The functionality of art, with man at the center of the process of creation, affirms man's "individual essence." But African literature and art are also collective, taking on meaning through the participation of the "anonymous masses who sing, dance, carve and paint." By their very nature, functionality and collectivity in turn commit the persons involved both as individuals and as members of the community, precisely because, according to Senghor, literature and art for the Africans "are techniques of essentialization."[8]

Negritude is in this sense a search for essences. The now classic dismissal of the movement as an exercise in futility since the "tiger does not concern itself with its tigritude"[9] raises questions about the Black man's own claim to full and unfettered membership in the human race. For his irresistible claim lies in the fact that he, as Man, is able to *think* and follow through to action on the basis of his thought(s). To equate him with a tiger in any literal sense is to fall prey to assumptions about the Black man's legendary location outside the very species that sets great store by the gift of culture in the creative exercise of his imagination and intellect—something reportedly not within the reach of living organisms like tigers. The tiger is not concerned about his tigritude indeed. But that may well be why Man is able to cage him and not he Man. And when Man attempts to deprive the tiger of his natural habitat, the tiger fights back, which may well be that animal's way of asserting his tigritude. Well, if with the tiger, let alone with the human being? Deprivation of self and society has never failed to attract resistance from, and assertion of self-preservation by, the human being. Man is by nature concerned with the essence of himself: it made sense that men like Césaire, Senghor and Léon Damas would approach their liberation from this angle. The Gallic concerns with things ontological would have been part of the apparatus of assimilationist education meted out to French-speaking Africans to whom the search for essences would come more naturally than to their Anglophone counterparts, whose Anglo Saxon education often eschews such essays into what Edmund Burke, the English philosopher, might well have dismissed as metaphysical nonsenses.[10]

As if in anticipation of a future generation's cry for armed resistance, in preference to cultural affirmation through artistic creation, Senghor implies that in the aesthetics of African artistic products are values (of functionality, collectivity, commitment or engagement) which are critical to any program of action leading to the acquisition of political and economic power. These different types of activities are not mutually exclusive. All art is social in any case. Negritude aesthetics has nothing to do with art for art's sake. The intrinsic qualities of the artistic product are not divorced from the social reality by which it is mediated. George Lamming, the Caribbean novelist and essayist, put it another way: "the material base of our existence must always be supported and informed by a native cultural vision which has absolute confidence in human worth."[11]

Armed resistance without such native cultural vision will be worth little in the wake of victory when the harnessing of revolutionary enthusiasm and the maximization of benefits from the spoils of war become critical to the consolidation of freedom and the reinforcement of bulwarks against further humiliation and the obscenities of oppression. The aesthetics of Negritude, insofar as it serves to define the native cultural vision for Africans, is integral, rather than opposed, to the totality of the struggle against the denigration of things African, so endemic to Western world-view(s).

Senghor's essay went further, even if not far enough in conscious opposition to the stereotypes to be found in Western assessment of Black artistic creation, ontology and lifestyle. He repeats and elaborates on what is often said, namely that "the

Negro is a man of nature....He is first of all sounds, odors, rhythms, forms and colors...he is touch before he is sight, unlike the white European. He feels more than he sees: he feels himself. It is within himself, within his flesh, that he receives and senses the radiations that any existing object emits. Aroused, he responds to the appeal and lets himself go, moving from subject to object, from me to thou, on the waves of the Other. He dies within himself to be reborn in the Other. He is not assimilated: he assimilates and identifies himself with the Other, which is the best way to know him."[12]

A careless reading of this passage could lead, and probably did lead, many an insensitive critic to a frame of reference that places the artistic/intellectual work of the African artist and intellectual in the noble savage mold or the "I *feel* therefore I am" Cartesian formula, parodied. The performing arts are particularly vulnerable here. A dance performed by a West African dance ensemble, a Caribbean dance company or an Afro-American Modern dance troupe is likely to be hailed for its high energy and for the vigor of African sensuality and never for the thought that may have gone into that dance. The naturalness of the Black African is lauded for being uncomplicated, ritualistic and unimpeded by cerebration. The "jungle" is celebrated, primitivism is exalted. Innocence is preserved against the debilitating rationality of the decadent West which is supposedly what is attractive to imitative, pretentious and "uppity" Blacks. Black aesthetics is neatly and subtly safeguarded within the parameters of "backwardness"—economics, social, and political. Europe approves of the jungle with tinsel, yearns for black talent "in the raw," applauds bare-breasted authenticity, and extols lush and rotund spontaneous prose from writers with soul.

But Senghor had news for the adoring patronizing West. He follows the passage quoted above immediately with the following: "this is not to say that the Negro is traditionally devoid of reason as one would have me believe. But his reason is not discursive; it is synthetic. It is not antagonistic but sympathetic. This is [merely] another path to knowledge....White reason is analytical through use. Negro reason is intuitive through participation"[13] So much for Gallaic logic and the symmetry of stylistic balance.

The opposition of such polarities may be nothing more than means to clarification of essences. But Senghor is here vulnerable in the eyes of a younger generation better educated and more complex than the descriptions above suggest. They might well have seen Senghor setting up a static state of affairs between the master and the subjugated, with the master in the ascendary, rather than the dynamic dialectical reality of the defiant African in contact with the West for hundreds of years, and especially throughout the last half of a millennium when the encounters culminated in the trans-Atlantic trade in slaves and the creolization process in the Americas where Africa and Europe met on foreign soil. Those encounters were to give to the Western world new dimensions of human relationships, new challenges to aesthetic sensibilities, and a reordering of priorities with respect to creative artistic activity, patterns of kinship, novel orientations in divine worship, distinctive attitudes to political authority and variations on the modes of production, distribution and exchange.

The cultural memory of ancestral hearths sustained the so-called New World as it affirmed its aesthetic mooring with eyes back on the African continent. And Senghor's further claims for such essential African features as the moral basis of *beauty* (beauty is goodness, good is beautiful), the power of *imagery* (the Word is flesh in both the rich oral literature of the African and the African-derived scribal expressions outside of the mainland), and the all pervasiveness of *rhythm* in African life and art, all find empirical verification in the games at which the Blacks excel (football, soccer, cricket, boxing, athletics), the performing arts (dance and music especially), the writing which has emerged over the past years from the experience of Blacks (poems, novels, plays, lyrics) and the plastic arts and crafts (sculpture, painting, ceramics, textile and basketry).

To Senghor and many others of the movement the pheno-menon of rhythm is not restricted to "the poem"—Senghor's generic designation for all artistic products. Rhythm in Senghor's own words "is the architectural structure of our being, the internal dynamism that gives us form, the network of undulations, that others receive from us, the pure expression of the vital force."[14] A later generation thirsting for blood rather than for righteousness need not be scandalized by the thought that even the making of revolution requires rhythm. Revolution may indeed be technical (rather than poetic) as Adotevi declared in his essay but the science of planning the combat is nowhere devoid of that sense of rhythm.

Sartre's account of Negritude as being "not a state but an attitude" was understandably worrying to the young Adotevi. For the philosopher's further description of it as "an act which ignores the world, which does not tend towards transforming the wealth of the world [but] is a matter of existing in the midst of this world...of an appropriation which is not technical,"[15] suggests a misunderstanding of the African's consciousness of his presence in the world. Functionality and participation through the collective in the creation of a work of art are themselves an expression of the existence of Man in his world. And the artistic form as well as the craft underlying the object produced are not separable as Senghor took pains to state.

Rhythm is similarly not restricted to the artistic creative process. If Sartre chose to interpret the existence of repetition in African art and Negritude's celebration of such "repetition" as central to rhythm by sanctifying the coital act with "the sexual pedal pressed right down"(as Adotevi, employing Africanesque imagery, describes one of Sartre's "enormities"), too bad for Sartre who was quite capable of misplaced enthusiasm on the matter of Black liberation. Adotevi's desire to free the Blacks from the stereotype of poetic romanticism is not unjustified. Yet the technical revolution, after which his generation hankered, could still have benefitted from the articulation by Negritude of the intrinsic qualities and values that have long served the African in his every endeavor at home and abroad. The notion that the avenging Black is all muscle and soul without imagination and intellect is no basis on which to stake a revolution. Nor is the obverse true.

Negritude has been denounced for not being a philosophy of action. But insofar as it saw liberation, redemption and hope in the creation of literature and art, it could lay claim to genuine capacity for action. Many an African or Afro-American artist without the benefit of training in gun marksmanship would regard what they do *as a form of action*, as engagement with social reality rather than flight from real issues, as functional and not esoteric, as being *in* the world and not outside it even while retaining the elements of what would be claimed to be universally "artistic."

To dismiss the founders of Negritude and their epigones as fugitive offenders retreating from the reality of mandatory revolutionary activism into safe and sheltered harbors of black culture, of self-indulgent poetry, dance or music, is to fail to appreciate the intrinsic merits of the modality of resistance offered by artistic creativity which has long been accessible to and utilized by the marginalized and the oppressed. And these include the Africans at home and abroad. How, otherwise, could one explain the power of the impact on their societies and the wider world of a Fela of Nigeria, a Sparrow of Trinidad, and a Bob Marley and the Rastafarians of Jamaica?[16]

Ironically, the fault lies in part with the original thrust of Negritude in its vulnerable failure to see or to focus sharply on the organic relationship that exists between the undoubted excellences emerging from the creative imagination of the African peoples on the one hand, on the other, the hands-on struggle for power as basis of the control one must have over one's own destiny to be really alive; the relationship between the creative tension that inheres in the act of creating on the one hand and the dialectical dynamics of the political process on the other. But the true artist, following the African principles of functionality, collectivity (participation), engagement (commitment), imagery and rhythm, will grasp with little or no difficulty the energy needed for and challenges implied in the task of shaping a modern society out of a humiliating past—a modern society that will be able to take the lethargy out of an inefficient government bureaucracy, to decrease unemployment among the mass of the population, to narrow the gap between town and country, to provide proper health care, nutritious food and potable water, to effect rational structural changes in an ailing and sluggish economy, to avoid the misuse of the educated manpower on the ground, and, in the language of the eighties, to emancipate an entire society from the debt trap.

These, Adotevi and his generation, would have regarded as *human,* not Negro problems. So Negritude as the expression of one's negroness was deemed to be superfluous, "African Negroes all know they are Negroes," Adotevi declared.[17] But is it as simple as this? Do all Negroes always know that they are Negroes?

Does the wider world with which he is forced to interact (and millions of Africans have been doing just this for half a millennium in the Americas and elsewhere) afford the Negro the freedom of enjoying his self-awareness? Is not the fact of the "African catastrophe" (Adotevi's description of the parlous state of persistent underdevelopment) a function, at least in part, of the denial of the Africans' sense of self and of that ancestral right to be somebody and on his own terms—a right that all men claim? Is not the relegation of that very "negroness" to a state of non-Being part of the apparatus of a continuing domination over an old economic order and, by extension, over a corresponding old international cultural order? Is not the restoration of that sense of self, if even through the aesthetics of negritude, a valid component of total struggle towards Black liberation?

The fiery necklace around the necks of nonconscious Blacks (called traitors) in the armed and violent struggle against apartheid in South Africa may well be the peril that awaits those who merely wish to deal with "today's tasks" (Adotevi again) at the expense of a medium term or a future that spells liberation. Blacks have had in their repertoire of struggle armed resistance, technocratic planning for serious social transformation, Garveyite radicalism, the civil disobedience of a Martin Luther King Jr., the rhetoric of violence of a Malcolm X, and the commitment to the arts of the imagination as forms of action in the process *à la* Fela, Bob Marley, the Rastafarians, Wole Soyinka, and Negritude's apostles Aimé Césaire and Léopold Senghor. Are all these several paths to the Africans' freedom mutually exclusive? The experience since the Black Power and refreshingly militant days of the late sixties gives a loud resounding "no" as answer. Both Senghor and Césaire have after all gone on to run governments—national and municipal. They are politicians besides being intellectuals and poets.

Still, there is need to invest any investigation into the aesthetics of Negritude with the deepest understanding of the centrality of considerations of *power* to the definition of self and all actions that flow from such definition. For this is critical to a firm grasp of the underlying sources of energy to be found in any initiative taken by Blacks to establish command over the conduct of their lives through the productive creative exercise of imagination and intellect. For the African intellectual elite working out of Paris in the thirties owned little of the means of production other than their imagination and intellect. The 21st century with its information-oriented and knowledge-intensive sectors will reaffirm this fact which has been known for centuries to the oppressed Africans in their encounters with the West.

In this, Marcus Garvey was no different from the early apostles of Negritude though formal contact with Oxbridge or the Sorbonne was not part of his dossier. His preachings were no less the product of a highly active intelligence and a fertile imagination. He was a man of action as well, with a program of projects to be worked on and developed by Black men and women whose economic liberation he saw as integral to their political and cultural redemption. And so it was with all the movements that followed Negritude in the fight against the humiliation of Africa—whether it is a politico-religious upsurge of feeling manifest in the Rastafarian faith and embodied in the Malcolm X of the Black Muslims, or whether it is the armed struggles in Black Africa and the Marxist experiments towards fundamental social transformation in parts of the Black Third World.

Not even Castro's Cuba could escape for long the fact of the unique Black experience and its importance to the socialist Cuban revolution. His repeated declarations of Cuba's Afro-Latinity was conscious surrender to the demands of cultural and political legitimacy in the Caribbean. And his more recent cry to have the Cuban Communist Party hierarchy reflect, *inter alia*, the ethnic realities of Cuba (more Cubans are of African ancestry than is often admitted) speaks to the presence of the indelible stain of Africa in the blood of the Caribbean and much else that goes by the name of Plantation America.[18]

Negritude in its primal assertion of an ancestral logic and cultural consistency among people of African ancestry is therefore not dead, the patricidal yearnings of a later generation notwithstanding. But by the same token it lost much of its appeal over time for not going far enough beyond the specificity of the Black experience into the universal realms of freedom and active struggle.

Any indication of its potential to do just this will guarantee the movement a valid place in a plurality of options, singly and in varied combinations, open to African peoples in their struggle to have control over their environment—physical, social, political, economic and cultural.

It is by no means justified to accuse Negritude of failing to grasp the potential of art as a vehicle of protest and change. To dismiss Negritude's seeming preoccupation with metaphors as escape from facing the live issues of the day is to miss the power of the mask in the life of the African in fighting his battles not only with Nature and the Gods but with material dispossession and real-life oppressors. To dismiss the use of literature and art as weapons in the struggle is to underestimate the tradition of political artistry common to all on the planet and particularly appropriate for the marginalized in an overwhelmingly domineering environment as the apostles of Negritude undoubtedly were in metropolitan France of the 1930s and as the millions of African slaves were on the plantations. They, too, wore masks preserved in the rich oral literature, music, dance and religious rituals of Black America and the Caribbean.

Perhaps men like Senghor, Césaire and Léon Damas wore their masks too well. For polemical texts were hidden beneath the deceptive fidelity to conventional European canons of literary creation by these alienated souls writing in the language of their masters. Never mind the beat of the tom-tom, the polyrhythmic contours, the tonal qualities and imagery of Africa surreptitiously enlivening the poetry of these men. They are still regarded by many as French poets, by those who wish to celebrate the assimilationist successes of French imperialism and by others who wish to prove that "we" are as good as "they."

Yet Negritude was no less an indictment of Western society than Marcus Garvey or the Harlem Renaissance had been or Black Power and Rastafarianism were to be. But its historical significance aside, it was difficult for many to pin down. The cynics doubted whether Africans could fight the war that was needed to be fought with rose petals for bullets. Not even the Russian revolution tarried on nice and beautiful thoughts. Did Lenin not say the revolution was the power of the Soviets plus electrification?[19] Negritude to the energetic lacked gumption and muscle.

But those were the days when the place of cultural reality in the development process and strategies for change were given short shrift, if considered at all. It was a misperception that art and aesthetics had no bearing on programs of African liberation. It was a brash conceit indulged by half of a generation and it has left its scar. It is now better appreciated that Black people had better learn to *think* and to continue to create work out of the imagination or remain the hewers of wood and drawers of water even after robots will have been programmed to do these chores.

Hope springs momentarily in the invocation by the present generation of Marcus Garvey whose centenary is being celebrated in 1987, of William DuBois, Claude McKay, Langston Hughes, Countee Cullen, Jean Price-Mars, Alioune Diop, Cheik Anta Diop, Léon Damas, Léopold Senghor and Aimé Césaire. The conference on Negritude mounted in February 1987 by Florida International University may well be seen as a re-affirmation of faith in the intellectual and creative artistic resources at the command of Africans all over the globe who in the continuing battle against a persistent humiliation must utilize such inner reserves for their eventual liberation.

The need to do this is no less urgent today than it was in the early 1940s when the young Francophone Blacks from West Africa and the Caribbean knocked heads together in poetic assertion of their personhood, or in the late sixties when impatience, anger and disillusionment gripped young Blacks more impatient with the barriers to dignity, self-respect and, above all, to *power*. In 1987, the phenomenon of Howard Beach and Forsyth, Birmingham and Brixton, Johannesburg and Pretoria and the declining economies of Black Africa, Black America and the Caribbean are all forcing people of African ancestry to reassess realistically their gains and to reassert their Beings.[20]

The structuring of their intellectual shape, of new forms of social ordering, and the relationships to freedom as well as the creation of institutions to service Black development are now high on the agenda. Meanwhile, erstwhile masters adopt every means possible to maintain white cultural dominance over Black powerlessness. Despite the advantageous position they continue to hold in their control of technology and their grip on science, former masters are desperate because of the uncertainty at the end-of-century about the future. The intransigent facts of the human condition are, in the circumstances, defiant of any known vocabulary adequate enough to communicate meanings and explanations.

So much of what is taken to be "rational and the bearer of truth is in fact rooted in domination, subjugation, the relationship of forces—in a word power," according to the French historian Michel Foucault.[21] The aesthetics which so many Diasporic Blacks proudly declare to have no racial, national or geographical boundaries, does not yet exist! To the conquerors of the world beauty and truth, believed to be the principal components of aesthetics, are universal only on their terms. If this were not so, why would Blacks want to declare black is beautiful in self-defense against a world that judges beauty by Eurocentric standards whether what is to be judged is a beauty queen, a spatial design in dance, the tone/pitch/form of music, a stanza of poetry, the denouement of a novel, or the structure of an idea. It was enough to have the rebels against Negritude insisting that until African peoples have power, their arts and aesthetics will mean nothing. The apostles of Negritude could well reply that the arts and aesthetics will mean nothing. The apostles of Negritude could well reply that the arts and aesthetics are as much a source of and means of power as are the guns blasting their way to epic victory. In any case, an enfeebled sensibility is the worst enemy of the revolution.

Those intellectuals knew then, as we should know now, that texts on aesthetics were little more than Eurocentric configurations of ideas about human sensibility or of operational frameworks for assessment of human achievement. Aesthetic truth was to become little more than a scholarly artifact in the maintenance of European cultural ascendancy. And Negritude was clearly not prepared to accept this product of incestuous intellectualism in the service of racial and cultural conceit. Yet many of the once colonized spend their lives striving to attain the standards set them by their colonizers.

Not even the great United States, when it perceives itself as an extension of Europe, escapes the trap. If what happens at the Metropolitan Opera House is still deemed to be artistically superior to what takes place in Basin Street, then this is a signal of the aesthetic myopia of a still culturally dependent America. The pointless debate as to whether "West Side Story" is an opera or a musical or whether Gershwin is a classical composer or something less than that, is part of the lack of certitude for an otherwise powerful nation.[22] In the end the cultural establishment in and around the Met gave in. After fifty years and without a change of note, Porgy and Bess" graced the stage of the Met. It is hardly necessary to remind the reader that the Porgy and Bess story is about Black folks in the American South.[23]

The contradictions are everywhere in the Black world. The very ones who gave us Negritude confused their contemporaries and many who came later, for being "black Frenchmen" even while they yearned for their nativeland and their native selves.[24] Many Trinidadians still wish to have the steel pan, play Tchaikovsky or Handel to prove the instrument's artistic legitimacy. And one is tempted to ask why should the steel pan or the drums of Africa for that matter, wish to sound like violins, violas, cellos or French horns? And why if the corot of Guinea, Mali and Senegal give off sounds that strike responsive chords in the ear of the Westerner, should its origin be suddenly placed somewhere in Europe? The oppressive nature of traditions of outside cultural bombardment is all pervasive. Duke Ellington could not be allowed a reputation rooted in his black reality: he had to have come to aesthetic legitimacy through one Delius as mentor. A suave and urbane black actor like Sidney Poitier is described as a black Cary Grant—a white actor who once reigned as Hollywood's icon of debonair Anglo-Saxon masculinity.[25]

Bach, it is often said, is the father of jazz. The fact that ordinary creative souls of New Orleans and many a black ghetto in the United States could invent or discover for themselves point and counterpoint, the fugue or the complex duple, is yet to be accepted by those who still see a master-culture providing the norm while everything else constitutes an aberration. The powerful speak *languages* while the powerless talk *dialects*. The Caribbean, that rich laboratory of living, native-bred and native-born creole languages is fighting hard to invest its indigenous tongues with the status of languages through careful research. And though the mass of the population hold tenaciously to their native tongues, the standard languages (English, French, Spanish, Dutch) remain the passport to individual progress and upward mobility in Caribbean societies.

A black director of a black American dance company is reported as saying that European classical ballet is standard and all other dancing is dialect. This ill-conceived and inaccurate statement all but relegates to aesthetic illegitimacy the dancing millions living in India, the South Pacific, Africa south of the Sahara and its dispersed offspring in the USA, the Caribbean and Latin America—all places where dance, as means of communication and expression of a people's aesthetic, abounds. Black writers, black dancers, black painters, black sculptors and black scholars all over the Americas want to be *writers, dancers, painters, sculptors and scholars* without the ethnic adjective—some no doubt in genuine assertion of the universal validity of their output, others in urgent need to be accepted on the criteria set by the mainstream society even when it is antithetical to the Black experience. The powerless are often humored, tolerated even patronized in such a situation.

The aesthetic of Negritude sought to change this, to put into the control of African peoples the opportunity to determine the criteria of aesthetic evaluations of artistic creations, of cosmologies and their architectonic manifestations rooted in the realities of the Black experience. The cry for a tradition of criticism that could appropriately serve the realities of literature produced by African writers or of the arts that emerge from the African-based cultures especially in the Americas has been a constant one ever since Negritude staked its claims for African authenticity.

Out of the Afro-Saxon Caribbean where cultural definition and artistic discovery have long been part of the social dynamics of a process of decolonization and socioeconomic transformation has come a schematic formula for expression of arts. The contributor is the poet-historian Edward Kamau Brathwaite.[26] Caribbean dance theatre, for example, should be organized (and assessed) around six crucial elements, he suggests. The elements are (i) *rhythm* one of the basic elements of African life: Senghor spent several paragraphs in his 1956 essay on this most critical of elements affirmed as such by many Black artists. A Caribbean man of letters has no doubt about the centrality of rhythm to the aesthetic sensibility of Black people. "We dance babies," he mused, "conveying to the child almost from the moment of that primal scream rhythmic possibilities which are used in a variety of ways as is evident in how we make love, how we perform jazz, how we toil in field and factory, how we worship, how we play sports...;"[27] (ii) *kinesis* which Brathwaite describes as the special use of energy evident in Caribbean drama, in poetry, music, sex and gospel, (iii) *possession*, the dominant power of the mind that transcends boundaries; (iv) *icon,* or the creation of a recognizable Caribbean image; (v) *nommo*, which is the ability to find one's own vocabulary to describe not only individual realities but also the universality of human experience; and (vi) *nam*, Brathwaite's "irreducible kernel" that holds the essence of Caribbean culture or any emerging culture.

That much of Brathwaite's scheme bears strong resemblance to the elements of African life and art, outlined in the Senghor essay of 1956, is no surprise. In the Caribbean cultural certitude turns on the distillation of essences out of the complex phenomena forged in the encounters between Africa and Europe and later between both of these and latecomers India and China.

For this reason, the work of those who have exercised their creative imagination and intellect is taken seriously as part of the process of nation building. Hence, the significance of the calypsonians, reggae artists, writers (poets and novelists), performing artists (dancers and choreographers, actors and playwrights) and plastic artists (painters and sculptors and ceramicists) with popular appeal and national recognition.

Independence came to most of the Caribbean by negotiation rather than by armed resistance. So while the struggle continues in the efforts to achieve fundamental social transformation, neither Bob Marley, Jimmy Cliff nor Peter Tosh in their unrelenting assault against the hypocrisy and endemic ills of the post-colonial order, has fired a shot. Nor have Sparrow and the calypsonians in the Eastern Caribbean where a calypso commenting on the advance of American militarism into the region attracted banning by one government.[28]

All the aesthetic elements of functionality, collectivity, commitment, imagery and rhythm, as Senghor described them, are here used by the sons and daughters of Africa against political oppression (threatened and real) and to keep the native heirs to the British raj on their toes. Creative and dynamic use of intellect and imagination are critical to any hope of lasting liberation, growth and development. Not even Karl Marx, a patron saint to many who would eschew Negritude, denied to Man the necessity of being able to create spiritual products as well as material ones.

Could it possibly be the fullest understanding of this fact which prompts a seeming resistance to now widespread notions that alongside the cry for a new international economic order must come a new international cultural order? The view is a logical outcome of the position taken by Negritude some fifty years ago. And it is no wonder that one of its greatest advocates in the eighties is Léopold Senghor himself.[29]

That new international cultural order is, for me, predicated on a fundamental change, on the part of the world at large, of their belief in an indefensible hierarchy of artistic culture arbitrarily segmented into classical at the apex and everything else including ethnic this or that at the base of an immovable pyramid. I have long spoken of another cultural reality, which if taken seriously could affect, for the better, perceptions of aesthetics and the arts in general.[30]

The view replaces the static Western rationalist hierarchy with a dynamic interplay of modes of artistic cultural expressions, such modes severally described as the ancestral/traditional, the contemporary/popular, and the classic. They exist simultaneously, together and apart, now reinforcing each other, now rejecting each other, sometimes overlapping and producing, in fine, a rich tapestry of possibilities which serve as sources of energy not only for further artistic creation but in the quest for appropriate designs for social living that will guarantee to a future generation justice and the classic freedoms from hunger, disease, ignorance and fear. It matters little in the final analysis how many ballistic missiles or nuclear warheads are in the arsenal if such freedoms are not in place or are not likely ever to be attained.

Perhaps, deep in the suffering and survival of the exiled African, or in the complex configurations of the ancestral life of mainland Africa, or in the contemporary existential realities of a still denigrated race of people in the world, lie some of the crucial answers for that tolerable future of which Negritude dreamt.

If this is at all possible in the smaller ways, then Negritude with the metaphors of existence it celebrated, the aesthetics it uncovered, the hope of redemption it indicated, is of renewed relevance to the struggle which continues.

NOTES

1. Aimé Césaire, was born in Martinique in June 1911, and educated in Paris, France where he met Léon Damas of French Guiana and Léopold Sédar Senghor of Senegal. Together they became the "legendary founders of the Black Awareness Movement known as Negritude." A foremost thinker of the 20th Century's Black Consciousness Movement, Césaire is a practicing politician in his native Martinique besides being an acclaimed poet, playwright, literary critic, and philosopher.

2. Francophone black awareness had its forerunner in (a) the Garvey Movement led by Jamaican visionary and activist, Marcus Mosiah, Garvey founder of the Universal Improvement Negro Association (UNIA) who worked out of Harlem and influenced liberation movements among Blacks all over the Americas and in colonial Africa itself, and (b) the Harlem Renaissance in which the scholar and a leading intellectual William DuBois was a major figure. Dr. DuBois is considered one of the fathers of Pan-Africanism, a movement that saw Africans and peoples of African ancestry outside the African continent joining forces for effective political action to fight racism and African denigration.

See: The *Marcus Garvey (and UNIA) Papers* edited by Robert Hill, UCLA Press.

Marcus Garvey: Anti-colonial Champion by Rupert Lewis (Karia Press, London, 1987).

Philosophy and Opinions of Marcus Garvey. edited by Amy Jacques Garvey (Athenaeum, New York, 1969).

Dusk of Dawn: An Essay Toward an Autobiography of a Race Concept, Harcourt, Brace and World, N.Y. 1940) and *Souls of Black Folk* (Fawcett, N.Y. 1965) by W.E.B. DuBois and *W.E.B. DuBois: A Study in Minority-Group Leadership*, by Eliot N. Rudwick (University of Pennsylvania Press, Philadelphia, 1960).

3. Senghor, Léopold S: "African-Negro Aesthetics", *The Ideology of Blackness* (Edited with introduction by Raymond Betts, D.C. Heath & Co., Lexington, Mass., 1971) pp. 110-125 and reprinted from *Diogenes* No. 16 (Winter 1956) pp. 23-38.

4. Adotevi, Stanislas: "The Strategy of Culture" in *The Ideology of Blackness* (Edited with Introduction by Raymond Betts, D.C. Heath & Co., Lexington, Mass., 1971) pp. 186-196, and reprinted from *The Black Scholar*, November 1969.

Dr. Adotevi, who at the time of writing of his essay was Commissioner General for Culture and Youth in Dahomey (later Benin), presented his paper at the Pan-African Cultural Festival, held in Algiers in the summer of 1969. That Festival was reportedly organized as a rejoinder to the Festival of Negro Arts held in Dakar in 1966, in celebration of Negritude. The Adotevi contribution was enthusiastically received as one of the more forceful interventions in the conference which sought to discredit Negritude as a meaningful ideology for modern Africa. Nathan Hare reported on the Algiers Conference in *Black Scholar I*, 1 (1969) pp. 2-10.

5. Adotevi, S: *op cit* p. 192.

6. Adotevi, S: *op cit* p. 189.

7. *Ibid.*

8. Senghor, Léopold: *op cit* p. 114-115.

9. The pun is attributed to the poet-playwright and Nobel Laureate Wole Soyinka of Nigeria.

10. Attributed to the English philosopher, Edmund Burke in his objections to the natural rights claims made by protagonists of the French Revolution. See Burke's *Reflections on the Revolution in France*, in *Durham University Journal*, Vol. XIV, No. 3, June 1953, and *The Moral Basis of Burke's Political Thought* by Charles Parkin (Cambridge Univ. Press, 1956), Chapter II.

11. Lamming, George: "Jamaica's National Dance Theatre—A Celebration: An Artistic Work of Excellence," *Caribbean Contact*, September 1985, p. 13.

12. Senghor, Léopold: *op cit* p. 110.

13. Senghor, Léopold: *op cit* p. 111.

14. Senghor, Léopold: *op cit* p. 120.

15. Adotevi, Stanislas: *op cit* p. 188.

16. Fela Anikulapo is the popular Nigerian musician and artist of protest; the Might Sparrow is the leading Trinidadian calypsonian and social commentator; the late Bob Marley flourished throughout the seventies as a leading Jamaican reggae composer, songwriter and performer universally know as a artist of protest advocating black dignity and liberation; the Rastafarians from whom Bob Marley *et al* drew inspiration are the adherents of a Jamaican-born black consciousness movement that declares the divinity of Haile Selassie I of Ethiopia and seeks redemption in repatriation (physical and/or psychological) to Black Africa in general and Ethiopia in particular. For further reading on the above, see Carlos Moore's *Fela* (Allison and Busby, London 1982); Gordon Rohlehr's essay "Calypso and Social Confrontation in Trinidad, 1970 to the Present" (unpublished); and *Report on the Rastafarians of Jamaica* by M.G. Smith, F.R. Augier, Rex Nettleford, (ISER, UWI, Kingston 1960); *Bob Marley, Reggae King of the World*, by Malika Whitney & Dermott Hussey, (Kingston Publishers, Kingston 1983).

17. Adotevi, Stanislas: *op cit* p. 189.

18. See reports on 1986 conference of the Cuban communist Party held in Havana.

19. Quoted by Adotevi *op cit* p. 193.

20. The references are to (a) the tragic death of a Black American of West Indian Parentage who was chased to his death from a passing car by white youths in Howard Beach, New York in January 1987; (b) the racist demonstrations against Blacks who tried to march to Forsyth County, Georgia, on Martin Luther

King Jr.'s Day, 1987; (c) riots by Black youths at different times in 1986 in Birmingham and Brixton against police brutality and (d) the escalating violent resistance by Black South African youths against apartheid in South Africa.

21.   Quoted by Harold Davidson in an essay in *Foucault: A Critical Reader*, edited by David Roy (Basil Blackwell: New York, 1986), and reviewed in *The New York Times Book Review*, Jan. 18, 1987, p. 31.

22.   Crutchfield, Mel: "West Side Story States Its Case as a Splendid Opera" *New York Times*, Sunday, April 20, 1985, pp. 22-23.

Crutchfield reported that "Marcel Praway of the Vienna Staats-opera asked a critics' panel some years ago for one good reason why 'West Side Story' is not an opera, and though an answer was attempted in these pages on whose basis a third of the standard repertory could be swept from the operatic canon at a stroke, *"the real answer is that there is none"* (my emphasis).

23.   "Porgy and Bess," the Gershwin classic was actually presented at the Metropolitan Opera in New York for the first time in 1985 after fifty years of doubt among the Operatic Establishment in the USA as to its status as "serious music."

24.   This alludes to Aimé Césaire's famous *Notebook of a Return to the Native Land* ("Cahier d'un retour au pays natal"), his 1939 classic in which the term Negritude was used for the first time.

25.   The references in this and the ensuing paragraphs are common examples of Black achievement being assessed on criteria for excellence set by the white world. The sometimes unwitting absorption of Black creative artists into the scheme is part of the dilemma plaguing the quest for cultural definition and artistic confidence in the Black Diaspora.

26.   Brathwaite, Edward K.: "Caribbean Perspective: Historical Frame-work," paper presented at the Caribbean Dance Seminar, December 6-8, 1979, sponsored by the Organization of American States and the Jamaica School of Dance at the Cultural Training Center, Kingston, Jamaica.

27.   Comment by Dr. Cliff Lashley of the College of the U.S. Virgin Islands, St. Thomas, in an interview with author.

28.   The calypso entitled "Government Boots" by The Mighty Gabby (Tony Martin) was banned by the Barbados Government in the 1980s.

29.   See *The Courier* No. 100, November-December 1986, pp. 13-14. Interview with Senghor in Liege (September 1986), when he presided over the 15th Biennale Internationale de Poésie, the two-yearly poetry festival.

30.   See my *Caribbean Cultural Identity: The Case of Jamaica*, (CAAS, Latin American Publications UCLA, 1979), Chapters I & II.

TOWARDS A POLITICAL ECONOMY OF NEGRITUDE

J. EDWARD GREENE

O NE OF the major cultural features of the present century is the awakening of racial consciousness and pride among Africans and people of African descent. The literary expression of this racial awareness, though not limited to one language or part of the world, is most commonly referred to as negritude. This complex ideology was derived from a number of related themes in Caribbean literature of the 19th and 20th centuries. It developed specifically out of the *indigenist* movement in the former French colony of Haiti where the initial *prise de conscience* of the negro living in a white world took place. American occupation of Haiti between 1915 and 1934 fostered a rejection of European culture by black intellectuals and a spirit of reverence toward the most primitive aspects of the local culture and folklore, including voodoo. Yet it was not in the Caribbean but rather in Paris that the specific literary movement associated with negritude took shape in the 1930s.

It is significant that the three principal architects of negritude were all poets who later became politicians: Aimé Césaire of Martinique, Léopold Sédar Senghor of Senegal, and Léon Damas of French Guiana. Through their influence, negritude emerged as a literary style, a complex of racial attitudes, the affirmation of a negro cultural essence and as a possible instrument of liberation. At the same time, an interesting observation by David Caute, negritude was almost wholly divorced from the African Continent; its appeal and inspiration almost exclusively limited to the most "advanced" and assimilated regions where the sense of uprooted- ness created a combination of nostalgia for African primitivism, political radicalism and intellectual sophistication.[1] It was, therefore, always questionable if negritude could ever be a solution to the fragmentation of the black world. Fanon, for example, disagreed with Senghor that African history provided viable living ideologies. He accordingly wrote that to believe that it was possible to create a black culture is to forget that niggers are disappearing just as those people who brought them into being are seeing the break up of their economic and cultural supremacy.[2] This paper seeks to establish the relationship between negritude and ethnic diversity and between these two and economic dominance. What emerges is more or less indicators toward a political economy of racism. It demonstrates the theoretical distinctions between race and ethnicity but admits to the overlap in the scope and functions of both phenomena. It provides illustrations from the plural society model as it relates to the Caribbean and to the system of apartheid in South Africa as extreme forms of ethnic segmentation and racism, respectively. Finally, it offers a possible agenda of research that needs to be undertaken in order to fully comprehend the origins and prospects of international racism.

CONTEMPORARY VARIANTS OF NEGRITUDE

Black writings in the colonies seem to have evolved in three phases. First, there was the general attempt to *assimilate* the occupying culture. Second, there was the emphasis on *negation* or withdrawal and a search for an authentic local identity. Third, a revolutionary literature emerged whereby the writer goes to the people, identifies with their struggle, and inspires them. Negritude represents the second phase. A similar distinction in the Latin American experience is drawn by the negrista poets of Afro-

Cubanism, between *Negrismo*[3] and *Negritude.* While *negrismo* perpetuated myths and stereotypes, in *negritude,* there appears to be a conscious deliberate preoccupation with the destruction of myths and stereotypes. In this regard, it has been suggested that the *Afro-criollo* movement in Cuba relates to the Africanist movement's search for a primitivistic utopianism in the early 20th century.[4] At the same time, the black presence in Cuba demanded attention because of the widespread presence of racism and racial discrimination and their unsettling effects. The influx of black workers from neighboring islands in the late 19th and early 20th century to work on the plantations as cheap labor created a considerable black phobia. There was, of course, the example of the Haitian revolution which provided a possible role model for black liberation struggles everywhere. This phobia in the mid-19th century led to a massacre of blacks following the worst racist incident in Cuban history.[5]

The representation of Cuba's Nicolas Guillén as a poet of neg-ritude simultaneously portrays him reacting to the marginalization of Cuban blacks and in particular to the historical legacy of racism in Cuba. The literary critics have shown that from his early works, *Motivos de Son,* 1930; *Sonqoro Consongo,* 1931; and *West Indies Limited,* 1934, Guillén confronts the painful wretchedness of his historical legacy, both personal and national. According to Ronald Bush:

> Consistent with the Francophone poets' concern for their brothers who share the same fate in Guadeloupe, W.I., we find the poet looking across the waters of the Caribbean to focus on the exploitation of Blacks: *Los Negros trabajando / junto al vapor. Los árabes vendiendo, / los Franceses, paseando y descansando, / y el sol ardiendo,* and in "Cana" looking at his own Cuba where the Spanish slavery has been replaced by the Yanqui.[6]

The concept of negritude sought to invoke the spirit of black African civilization. It was opposed to the dependency relationship between colonized and colonist and provided a foundation for winning back African identity. As an ideology, it encountered first Pan-Africanism and more contemporary international responses to racism which were responsible for the Black power movement and the Anti-Apartheid movement.

Pan Africanism arose at the beginning of the 20th century among English-speaking Blacks. The first Pan African Conference was organized in London in 1900 by Henry S. Williams, a Trinidadian. After World War I, it was expanded on the initiative of George Padmore, also a Trinidadian, and W.E.B. DuBois. This movement was committed to the view that there must be a collective struggle against colonialism. Negritude, the intellectual strand, and Pan Africanism, its political variant, converged on two issues of principle: first that all Africans had a common civilization and, second, all Africans should fight together. Marcus Garvey provided yet another political lobby in the struggle for African awareness. As C.L.R. James so aptly wrote: "Two black West Indians using the ink of negritude wrote their names imperishably in the front pages of the history of our time. Standing at the head is Marcus Garvey."[7]

As a function of race, negritude assumes greater meaning in the contemporary world. Race has replaced religion as the international status group category. It explains why, in the 1970s, the Black Power Movements in the Caribbean directed their attacks against all black governments on the grounds that these governments functioned as allies to North American imperialism. By comparison, in the U.S.A., the wealth of studies on the Black Power era illustrate that the complexity of motivations stemmed essentially from Black dispossession. At the heart of the struggle in all of these strands—Negritude, Afrocriollo, Pan Africanism and Black Power—the objective is to reduce social and economic inequalities, to ensure freedoms and justice, as well as to erode the amorality of systems of exploitation that reinforce racism.

NEGRITUDE AND THE PERSISTENCE OF RACISM

Negritude is the first in a series of intellectual and political responses to the expansion of European racism and Western capitalism. Western capitalism more than any other brand developed a flourishing mythology and ideology. In the era of the enlightenment, the belief was that both the physical and social environment were greater influences on human behavior than was heredity. Racist thinking in the Anglo-Saxon world was on the ascendancy in the 1830s and 1840s. It became rooted in the natural and social sciences in the second half of the 19th century. In folklore, as well as in literature, racism became deeply ingrained in the *Western Weltanschauung*. Its advocates included poets like Rudyard Kipling; philosophers, as revealed in Arthur Gobineau's *Essai Sur l'Inégalité des Races Humaines* (1855) and Stuart Chamberlain's *The Foundations of the Nineteenth Century*; and statesmen like Hitler, Theodore Roosevelt and Verwoerd.

Three factors relevant to this discussion and which help to explain the genesis of Western racism are:

1. the prevailing forms of capitalist exploitation, notably illustrated by slavery in the New World and incipient colonial expansion in Africa.
2. Social Darwinism which dovetailed with the economic liberalism of the late 19th century. Liberal utilitarians like John Stuart Mills legitimized *laissez-faire*, which in turn was re-interpreted as a mandate not to interfere with any form of human inequality and suffering. It literally reflected the Platonic ideal which would have supported the view that Negroes were slaves as a result of natural selection.
3. The paradox of the egalitarian and libertarian ideas spread by the American and French revolutions which both conflicted with and consolidated racism. Hence, the dichotomy between "the Civilized" and "the Savages." The need to preserve the profitable forms of discrimination and exploitation as well as the

> democratic ideology made it necessary to deny
> humanity to the oppressed groups.[8]

The overriding implication of negritude and its variants is their role and function in understanding race and racism in the international context. If each national case of racial conflict were discrete and logically separate, the function of race would not be so pervasive. But the national cases are not discrete and logically separate. Status and prestige in the national system are intricately linked to status and rank in the world system. When Africans deny that the conflict between lighter-skinned Arabs of Northern Sudan and dark-skinned Nilotes of Southern Sudan is a racial conflict, they are reserving the term *race* for a particular international social tension. That type of conflict, though formally similar to, is politically different from that between blacks and whites in the United States or Africans and Europeans in South Africa. Racism, according to this argument, is an act of maintaining the existing international social structure.

This need not necessarily be the only model of racism which may become institutionalized on a national scale. For example, Guyana and, to a lesser extent, Trinidad and Tobago portrayed, especially in the 1960s and 1970s, deep social cleavages which parallel the racial identification of East Indians and Africans in voting behavior. Patterns of political organization and responses to ethnic leadership, according to several studies, blurred the lines between race as a cultural ideology and as a function of status-group consciousness. Ethnicity is, therefore, a function of race. In the case of the latter, it seems appropriate to classify the phenomenon as ethnic segmentation leaving race as a general classification for differentiating the international social structure. Whatever the rigors of the theoretical distinction between these two concepts, race and ethnicity, most authors admit to an overlap, both in their conceptualization and in their application to reality. Two illustrations are given focusing on the Caribbean and South Africa, respectively.

ETHNICITY AND ECONOMIC DOMINANCE IN THE CARIBBEAN

Taking the Caribbean experience as a point of reference, there has been much debate among scholars about the efficacy of the *Plural Society Model* for properly characterizing the relationship between ethnic segmentation and economic dominance. M.G. Smith's thesis was that the fundamental differences of beliefs, value and organization that connote pluralism required monopoly of power by one cultural section as precondition for maintaining the total society.[9] Critics of the model point essentially to its failure to demonstrate how ethnic segmentation can be attenuated by economic conditions, social mobility and political participation. These reservations notwithstanding, the value of the plural society model is in highlighting the impact of ethnic identification as a discernible factor in social and political life in the Caribbean, a phenomenon which has not been demonstrably replaced by class identification.

The structural break up of the plantation system after emancipation imposed, generally, a competing economic sector comprised essentially of *local peasants* while the ruling class was intent on maintaining control in several ways. In Barbados, for example, the white planter class was able to perpetuate the subjugation of the Blacks by legislating and enforcing the *Master and Servants Acts* in 1840. This made the ex-slaves perpetual tenants and serfs at the disposal of the estate managers. In Antigua, the planters imposed a similar dependency relationship on the slaves. In Jamaica, Guyana, Grenada, and Trinidad and Tabago, the ex-slaves quit the plantations and established villages and the planters used government revenues to import Chinese, Portuguese and Indians under the indenture system.

The persistence of ethnic segmentation and the correlation between color and class are important features of social stratification in the Caribbean. It embraces both the notions of creole and plural society. It explains in part how order and stability were maintained due to the recognized authority of the colonial powers, whose rule in the period of Crown Colony Government reinforced the social and economic dominance of the Imperial state in Britain. This coincided with modifications to the plantation system through the consolidation of large foreign estate ownership such as Booker Brothers (in Guyana), Tate and Lyle in Jamaica, and Geist (in St. Lucia). It explains also that even after the 1960s when "black intellectuals came to power," economic dominance remains in the hands of the white minority. Two recent studies illustrate how economic dominance is reinforced through inter-marriages and interlocking directorates within a circulating elitism. Stanley Reid[10] shows how the corporate elite in Jamaica in the 1970s comprised essentially 21 families drawn almost exclusively from the white minority. This situation was linked to a strategy involving the old alliance of land ownership and sophisticated corporate structure, on the one hand. On the other, there was the presence of families whose wealth was derived from industrial activity and who subsequently became landowners either to diversify their investments or to enhance their economic base. In another study, Barrow and Greene[11] examined the origins and persistence of a white elite in Barbados. It demonstrated that the planter elite on that island not only owned most of the property (land and slave), but also had virtually remained on the spot to dominate political affairs until the mid-19th century. Unlike most of the other islands, absentee landlordism in Barbados was relatively low and the resistance to foreign ownership, in the same period, relatively strong. Hence, what emerged was a strong agro-commercial elite reflecting similar patterns of circulating elitism as in Jamaica.

These two studies reinforce the findings of an earlier one on occupational mobility in Trinidad and Tobago in the later 1960s which identified the persistence of black dispossession.[12] There has been a degree of flexibility in the economic systems in so far as blacks have risen in the economic hierarchy but the extent of black dispossession is widespread. This refers to those who are inher-ently the landless poor.

A question that requires analysis is why even today the subsidiary economic elite is more likely to be the once indentured Chinese, East Indian or Portuguese or why 150 years after emancipation, the Afro-Caribbean remains marginalized in terms of economic dominance.

The question is pertinent because unlike the case of Afro-America, which comprises ten percent of the population of the United States, the Afro-Caribbean accounts for approximately eighty percent of the total population in the region as a whole. The notable exceptions are in Guyana where they are less than 50 percent and in Trinidad and Tobago where they are just over 50 percent. In addition, with very few exceptions, political power resides in the hands of the blacks in the Caribbean. One explanation—an unsatisfactory one—is that the special complex of cultural identity and habits we classify as ethnicity has always proved elusive in modern 'creole' society. Black ethnicity becomes ambivalent in form and precarious in meaning. The architects of negritude were sensitive to the fact that it is the only ethnic configuration that has to be perpetually retrieved, fought for and fabricated from issue to issue and epoch to epoch. It probably helps to explain why in the black diaspora—whether in Jamaica, Haiti, Brazil, Suriname or in the United States—it is difficult to translate black ethnicity into principles of sacrifice, altruism and group tenacity for long run goals.

THE CASE OF APARTHEID

A different type of experience manifests itself in the case of South Africa but leads to similar conclusions. Apartheid is an extreme version of race and racism, with implications for the political, economic, sociocultural, legal and moral bases by which individuals interact in such a system. Apartheid is specific to South Africa. Whatever the mix of motivations that may be involved, however, South Africa is an integral part of the Western, predominantly Christian, culture. Among many other issues, the apartheid regime of South Africa characterizes its opponents as Marxists or Communists. As one writer aptly puts it, South Africa "espouses the broad ethical values and standards of our Western Christian society. It can be argued, therefore, that it has to be judged on Western Christian ethical and moral standards."[13] The only contemporary society in which racial discrimination is officially institutionalized and enshrined in its constitution is in South Africa.

Given its history, developments and their implications, apartheid is generally a reflection of Western morality and the strategic stakes of Western imperialism. Apartheid originated, like slavery, in settler colonialism. It transformed a rural African economy and subjugated it to the capitalist mode of production. Racial segregation in South Africa, dating back to 1913, reinforced white monopoly on political power and provided cheap and coercible black labor for industry and development. Hence, as one writer puts it, "the extraordinary growth of the South African economy in the post-war period not only rested on apartheid but reinforced it."[14] Apartheid is not only a form of super-exploitation but a function of imperialist expansion since 1945. More specifically, direct foreign investment in South Africa has played a critical role in mobilizing international credits without which the apartheid regime could not persist. One-third of the growth in South Africa's domestic product over the past two decades has been attributed to foreign investment. According to the UN Commission on Transnational Corporations, America's strength in South Africa's growth and technologically advanced sectors is reflected in its control of 40 percent of the oil market, 33 percent of the car market, and 70 percent of the computer market.[15]

When to these examples is added the role of Western capital in the expansion of military and mining operations in South Africa, then it can be more readily appreciated how important apartheid has been in the post-war expansion of Western capital. It is, therefore, essential to study thoroughly such an extreme system of international racism. This makes it necessary to focus on the political economy of apartheid and its implications for human resources, human rights, family life and the role of women, and aspects of cultural revival or subordination.

THE POLITICAL ECONOMY OF APARTHEID

An increasing number of studies are addressing the interrelations of South Africa and the world economy, the patterns of trade, foreign (direct) investment, economic interdependence and the political implications of this interdependence. Coordination of research in this area would require in-depth studies of the nature and persistence of these interrelations. Identification of sources of investment, levels of trade, actual goods and services, forms of bilateral aid to and from South Africa indicate some of the critical factors that should be addressed. This brings into sharp focus other specific concerns: To what extent may South Africa be viewed as a middle power in international relations? How do its fortunes compare with other states so designated and what are the main reasons for (dis)similarities? These questions, in turn, raise other important issues relating to South Africa's military power. Hence, its ability to impose sanctions on its neighbors through its strategic control of the transportation network and port facilities. What is the real extent of the vulnerability of Botswana, Lesotho and Swaziland? What is the impact on destabilization policies on SADCC economies? What are the options facing these states?

THE DEVELOPMENT/UNDERDEVELOPMENT OF HUMAN RESOURCES IN SOUTH AFRICA

In order to establish the magnitude of the underdevelopment of human capital among blacks, it is necessary to sustain an ongoing directory of demographic information on vital aspects of activity in black homelands and townships, for example:

- patterns of migration within and between the homelands, etc.
- patterns of mobility through employment,
- levels of unemployment,
- opportunities for basic education and levels of literacy,
- opportunities for technical and vocational training.

The Dynamics of Human Rights: Basically, this theme was the major concern of the report of the Commonwealth Group of Eminent Persons. The wealth of information gathered by the group should be further explored to elaborate on one of the major issues concerning the inalienable rights and freedoms of citizens of a democratic state. In this regard, studies need to examine:

- How human rights can be manifested in the establishment of political freedom.
- What are the implications of the continued denial of political freedom for the persistence and/or escalation of violence.
- What are the prospects for negotiating a reasonable solution with the white minority government in power.
- Which are the main interest groups—how are they aligned in the political system, what are the prospective alignments under a reformed or dismantled system?

Apartheid Family Life and the Role of Women: While some information is available, there is apparently a lack of in-depth analyses based on systematic study. It would be useful to embark on family life studies especially to establish:

1. the effects of apartheid on the consolidation or decay of the family as a vital social institution,
2. the possibility of the re-establishment of family life/patterns from which may evolve social norms for the reconstruction or sustaining of viable societies.

A related issue is the role of women in the struggle for survival. How does this role differ qualitatively from that of women in other parts of the world? Does apartheid have more disruptive consequences on male/female relations than other systems in the western system?

CULTURAL REVIVAL OR ATROPHY

Cultural viability is manifested in several ways including folklore, art, drama, music, dance, writings, and other non-traditional forms. It is also sustained through religious practices and other social manifestations that consolidate group, ethnic, national or regional identity. Especially in the face of economic adversity and during civil or international conflict, a vibrant culture is essential to the survival of the community spirit. It will, therefore, be useful to examine the development and persistence of various cultural expressions and to ascertain whether they exemplify resistance or recapitulation to the apartheid regime.

There is need to document systematically the forms of art and craft, the content of songs and chants, the style of music and, in general, the influence, meaning and changes that accompany these forms. The main issue is whether the consequences of apartheid have been so far reaching as to erode and/or destroy the creativity of a deprived and alienated people. This obviously requires some comparison with the existence and development of cultural support systems afforded black South Africa. Indeed, it is possible that the atrophy of cultural vitality in black South Africa may cause repercussions contributing to the diminution of a South African Culture.

CONCLUSION

The research agenda suggested for the study of apartheid is intended to indicate the vast amount of work still required to be done in order to comprehend more fully the fundamentals of racism. It seems reasonable to form some tentative conclusions to the effect that the failure of blacks to assert economic dominance is partly because of the structural factors in the world economy and partly because of a major failure to consolidate a Global Black ethnicity. Marcus Garvey attempted such a consolidation by developing an international organization of black people under the banner of African Redemption, anti-colonialism and civil rights. As Rupert Lewis puts it:

> He had to find his own way in a colonized world where the odds were against him in one sense but in which the historical process which he envisioned and which most could not comprehend was moving toward the realization of his ideas.[16]

While the Garvey Movement failed to institutionalize a global form of ethnicity, it left a ritualistic approach to transnational issues that is of critical importance to the political economy of racism. As we have indicated, underlining a political economy which should draw its impetus from the globalization of black ethnicity are issues relating to human resources and human rights, family life and the sexual division of labor, cultural identity and unity.

For scholar intent on advancing the work of the architects of negritude, it is important to take a critical stand: one that insists on the requisites of a first world order; not necessarily one whose aim is to redress the brutalities of the past (As Rex Nettleford so aptly pointed out in all reality, we do not have the kind of ammunition to win that kind of war). In trying to comprehend the disjuncture between ethnic differentiation and economic dominance, the black scholar must accept the burden of moral scrutiny and confront the perversions of newly acquired power by black rulers. Wole Soyinka, Nigerian poet, playwright and Nobel Laureate did so courageously during the Nigerian Civil War. So, too, did my friend and colleague, the late Walter Rodney, Guyanese historian, who put his intellect to the service of human rights, sacrificing his life in the process.

The relevant question is whether negritude is a sufficiently concrete operational tool to help to explain what essentially is *the political economy of racism*. To do so, negritude must address the issue of *race* by establishing it, in a most fundamental sense, as a particular form of status group in the contemporary world. As racial conflict becomes acute, status group lines tend to coincide with class lines. Ethnic rivalries, though inevitable, are an impediment to the wider issues inherent in international racism. At the same time, what the architects of negritude fully underscored is the need to abort the catharsis of simplistic nationalistic—racial or ethnic—sentiments. To do so, as Kilson[17] correctly points out, is to prop up black power elites who may be pretenders, who squander national resources, squash political opposition and trample human rights. It would indeed be a negation of the principles, as well as of the hopes and aspirations, to which the life and works of Aimé Césaire and Léopold Sédar Senghor have been dedicated.

NOTES

1. David Caute, *Frantz Fanon* (NY: Viking Press, 1970), Chapter 2.

2. Frantz Fanon, *The Wretched of the Earth* (New York: 1965), p. 188.

3. Fanon, ibid.

4. Richard Johnson, "The Afrocriollo Movement Revisited," *Afro-Hispanic Review*, January 1984, 5-12.

5. Lloyd King, "Nicolas Guillen and Afrocubanismo," in Burce Kind and Kolawale Ogun-Besa, eds., *A Celebration of Black and African Writing,* aria and Ibadan, Nigeria, Ahmadu Bello University Press.

6. See Ronald E. Bush "Cuba's Nicolas Guillen as Poet of Negritude," *Afro-Hispanic Review* (May and September 1985), 5.

C.L.R. James, *Black Jacobins*, Vintage Pub., 1963, p. 396.

8. Pierre L. Vanden-Berge, *Race and Racism: A Comparative Perspective* (New York: John Wiley, 1967).

9. M.G. Smith, *Culture, Race and Class in the Commonwealth Caribbean*, Department of Extra-Mural Studies, U.W.I., Kingston, 1984.

10. Stanley Reid, "An Introductory Approach to the Concentration of Power in the Jamaican Corporate Economy and Notes on its Origin" in Carl Stone and Aggrey Brown, eds., *Essays on Power and Change in Jamaica* (Kingston: Jamaican Publishing House, 1977), pp. 115-44.

11. Christine Barrow and J.E. Greene. *Small Business in Barbados: A Case of Survival* (Barbados: ISER, 1979), Chapter 2.

12. Acton Camejo.

13. Stuart Harris "South Africa: The Australian Perspective" *Current Affairs Bulletin*, Vol. 62, No. 10 (March 1986), 4-13.

14. Raymond Lotta "The Political Economy of Apartheid and the Strategic Stakes of Imperialism."

15. Commonwealth Secretariat Mission to South Africa, Report of the Commonwealth Group of Eminent Persons appointed under the Nassau Accord, 1986.

16. Rupert Lewis, *Marcus Garvey: Anti-Colonial Champion* (London: Kama Press, 1987), p. 12.

17. Martin Kilson, "What is Africa to Me: Dilemmas of Transnational Ethnicity," *Dissent* (Fall 1984), 433-440.

PART II

RACISM IN THE AMERICAS: CASE STUDIES

AFRICAN CULTURAL RESPONSE TO SLAVERY AND OPPRESSION IN THE AMERICAS AND THE CARIBBEAN

JOHN HENRIK CLARKE

AFRICAN CULTURAL response to slavery and oppression in the Americas and the Caribbean began on the shores of West Africa when captured Africans tried to take African soil in their hands and sometimes in their mouths, onto the slave ships as a last desperate struggle to hold onto a piece of Africa. Slavery was a war. A war against African culture, especially against the structure of the African family. This war has not ended.

THE SUSTAINING FORCE OF AFRICAN CULTURAL CONTINUITY

In the fight against the worst aspects of slavery and oppression, the African's most effective weapon was cultural continuity, maintained to a large degree in spite of the fact that African families were broken up and scattered. Somehow, they remembered their African past and drew strength from it. It was this culture that sustained the Africans during the holocaust of the slave trade and the ensuing colonial system. African culture, reborn on the alien soil, became the cohesive force and the communication system that helped to set in motion more than 300 slave revolts in the Americas and the Caribbean.

The Africans were brought into South America and the Caribbean Islands to replace the Indians as a labor force. Under the first impact of the European presence, the Indians had either died or been killed in large numbers. The Europeans did not treat the Africans much differently. During the course of the first 100 years after the beginning of European settlement, most of the Indians in the Caribbean Islands became extinct and the Indian population of South America drastically declined. In the meantime, in spite of the brutality they suffered, the number of Africans increased in both places. They made a partial adjustment to their environment and waited for an opportunity to revolt against it. In large areas of South America and the Caribbean Islands, these opportunities began to come before the end of the first half of the 16th century. There was a major slave uprising in what is now Santo Domingo in 1522 and another one in Cuba in 1550. The uprising in Cuba was the first of a series of slave revolts by the Africans who had escaped from the plantations and had set up rough-hewed government structures of their own. They were the first of the Africans in the so-called "New World" to use African cultural continuity to pull and hold their revolts together.

The plantation system was a natural incubator for the slave revolts that the system was established to contain. In many ways the plantations were small autonomous states. The plantation owners and their overseers had complete authority over the lives of the Africans. Very often their attempt to break the spirit of the Africans set the thought pattern of revolt in motion. Although there was a concerted effort to do so, the rebel spirit of all the Africans could not be broken. The newly arrived Africans were the most effective in these early slave revolts. They were closer to their African culture and had not adjusted to the new way of life.

The spread of the plantation system in the Americas and in the Caribbean Islands required more Africans. The increase in the slave trade also meant an increase in African cultural input into the system. Africans under different European slave masters revolted against slavery and oppression in many subtle ways that the Europeans did not understand, mainly because they did not recognize that the Africans had a culture and a spirituality.

When Europeans emerged from the Middle Ages and projected themselves once more onto the broader world, they not only colonized most of the world, they colonized information about the world. They denied that the people whom they had enslaved had anything worthy of being called history or culture. This is the basis of the conflict that we as scholars now confront. As Professor Ivan Van Sertima has stated, African history and culture "was locked into a five-hundred year room." Our mission as African scholars of the world has been, since the 18th century, to liberate African history and culture from the bind of European misconceptions and from the figurative 500 year room. In approaching this subject it is therefore necessary, at least briefly, to establish the fact that African culture is not only a part of world culture, but may well be the basis of world culture. Thus, contrary to a lot of clever propaganda writings on this subject, African cultural traits were never completely destroyed. African culture borrowed from and gave to the cultures of the Indians and, in turn, contributed to shaping the regional forms of western culture in the Americas.

The papal bull of 1455 authorized the Portuguese and the Spanish to, "reduce to servitude all infidel people."[1] Since most Europeans in the slave trade considered African people to be infidels, a people without a spirituality or a culture, outside of humanity, they were not mentally prepared to deal with African culture as a factor in the revolts against slavery and oppression. Slavery was a moral and philosophical problem to the Europeans. They wanted to present themselves to the world as Christians. They also wanted to continue in the business of slavery, which was antihuman and, therefore, anti-Christian. The teaching of the Christian church, which said that all men were equal in the sight of God, was a dangerous doctrine under the circumstances. The African perception of man and his relationship to the world had no parallel in western perception. This fortunate circumstance frustrated the planters' attempt to use religion as a form of social control. They did not understand the Africans' religions and when the Africans were converted to Christianity, this religion did not mean the same thing to the Africans as it did to the planters. Because African religious concepts left no room for fatalism, these concepts helped to sustain

African cultural continuity, the cohesive force in nearly every slave revolt?[2]

In the slave revolts in the Americas and in the Caribbean Islands, African cultural traits were the main sustaining ingredient. It is necessary to look at African culture in the Americas systematically in order to see how it manifested itself under different slave systems and colonial rulers, beginning with the Spanish and the Portuguese.

In South America and in the Caribbean Islands, the slaves outnumbered the planters. The Europeans had to develop methods of coercion in dealing with the Africans who were now threatening the existence of the plantation system. These methods of coercion forced the slaves in South America and the Caribbean Islands to develop patterns of revolt based on prevailing conditions in the developing plantation systems. The early method of buying and distributing slaves indirectly helped maintain African cultural continuity. Slaves were bought in large numbers and generally kept together. Some of the plantation owners thought that, in this way, the Africans could communicate with each other and more work could be accomplished. They did not seem to realize that communication is the best way to perpetuate a people's culture. With the drums and a common language that most of the Africans understood because they came from the same general area within Africa, communication systems were developed that would later serve to facilitate slave revolts. Another aspect of cultural continuity was that the African family was not broken up in South America and in the Caribbean Islands with the same casual ruthlessness of the slave systems in the United States.

I do not mean to imply that the slave systems in South America and the Caribbean Islands were benevolent, quite the contrary. They differed from the slave systems in the United States only by method and degree. In the English colonies the slave system rested upon the legal concept of property. In the English colonies, more than others, the policy of the planter was to demoralize the slave and to divorce him from any knowledge of his former cultural and social heritage.

From its inception slave society was punctuated with slave uprisings and rebellions. The planters' search for a way to put down these uprisings created another dilemma. To let the Africans keep their own religion and way of life was to facilitate the uprisings; to convert them to Christianity would make them turn against slavery as their Christian duty. The dilemma of how to control the slaves marked each period of slavery and of the slave trade and continued into the first half of the 19th century. The iniquities of slavery forced the Africans to take refuge in mountains and in woods. Here African culture played a major role in holding these bands of runaway slaves together; here they planned the strategy of their survival.

SLAVE UPRISING AND THE QUEST FOR FREEDOM

The Spaniards called the fugitive slaves *Cimarrones* and the French adopted the word to their language and made the name *Maroons*. Flight was the slaves' goal because it signified liberty, however temporary. In the jungles and virgin forests, protected by the lush tropical growth, some of these Africans developed self-contained communities and for years avoided re-enslavement. Sometimes, according to Fernando Ortiz in his book, *Los negros esclavos (Black Slaves),* fugitive slaves banded together and settled in hidden spots, such as mountains where access was difficult, in order to become strong and live independent lives. Sometimes they were successful in developing farms similar to those they had known in Africa. The future of these small African colonies depended mainly on the number of women that were persuaded to join them. The slaves in this state of rebellion were called *apalencados* and their retreats were called *palenques*.

According to José Luciano Franco:

> The first recorded black slave insurrection took place in Santo Domingo on December 26, 1522, in the sugar mill of Don Diego Colon, Admiral and Governor. The rebels

fought the Spaniards valiantly but were subdued. The Admiral had most of the surviving black mutineers hanged. In 1529 black mutineer slaves destroyed Santa Marta. In 1531, in Panama, disturbances arising from the continuing protest of the slaves were recorded. In 1537, in Mexico, the first slave slaughter occurred, provoked by European settlers who were frightened by the rebellious attitude and the numbers of Africans, and simply quartered a few dozen whom they suspected of thinking rebelling. "From the first days of the colonization and conquest of the island of Cuba, the Indians and black slaves rebelled against the servitude imposed on them by the bloodthirsty and cruel Europeans. In 1533, Governor Manuel de Rojas went from Santiago de Cuba to Bayamo, and from there went two squads to the mines of Jababo in the province of Cueyba to subdue four blacks who had hidden there and who fought to their death."

The Africans used every opportunity to avenge themselves against their oppressors. African slaves under Spanish rule often joined with and fought with the enemies of Spain. In 1538, when the French corsairs or pirates attacked the city of Havana, the African slaves helped them in their systematic destruction of the city.

José Luciano Franco further states that:

In Cuba, for several centuries, the Palenques were the single example of nonconformity to the colonial regime, the virile protest against the infamies of slavery. The cleverness and the skill of the *Cimarrones* as guerrillas, their knowledge of how best to use the topography of the mountainous areas, the jungles, and the swamps where they had cultivated their little farms and established their refugee homes, permitted them to confuse their persecutors and, sometimes, destroy those same regular troops and militia that were hunting them.

In Brazil, some Africans worked for the Portuguese, some worked against them and others ran away from the towns and the plantation and established purely African states, mainly Palmares and Bahia. These states and their fight to survive represent the best examples of African cultural continuity in the New World. There were nine revolts in Bahia between 1807 and 1835. These revolts involved several African cultural groups such as the Hausa, Yoruba and Kwa-speaking groups, as well as the Ogboni Society and Muslim *Glufas*, a forerunner of the Back-To-Africa Movement. The Portuguese declared total war against these communities of escaped slaves. These wars lasted for more than a hundred years. According to an assessment by R.K. Kent:

> Nothing, however, in the annals of Brazilian history compares with the "Negro Republic" of Palmares in Pernamuco. It spanned almost the entire seventeenth century. Between 1672 and 1692 it withstood, on the average, one Portuguese expedition every fifteen months. In the last *Entrada* against Palmares, a force of six-thousand took part in forty-two days of siege.

Palmares was Brazil's classic *Quilombo* or slave settlement. Early writers on Brazil attributed the establishment of this slave state to the Portuguese-Dutch rivalry over Pernambuco, from which slaves profited by escaping in groups.

The site of this unusual slave community was in a mountainous region that became a natural fortress for its inhabitants. The many fruit trees gave easy sustenance to those who knew where they were. The timber-yielding trees served various industrial uses. In time, the Africans made this a self-contained community. They cleared some of the forest and developed small farms. This, with fishing and hunting, made their food supply ample. The settlers created a government using what they remembered from Africa and what they had learned since their arrival in Brazil. Murder, adultery, stealing and desertion demanded death as a penalty.

The Portuguese did not easily sit by and permit the continuous existence of Palmares. Fifteen expeditions were sent against the

Republic, including that of Zenobio Accioly de Vascocallos in 1667 and Bandirante Domingos Jorge Velho together with Sevasrian Dias and Bernardo Vieira de Melo in 1695. In campaigns against Palmares that lasted over 50 years it is possible that other unrecorded expeditions were sent against Palmares.

North American historians, with few exceptions, have ignored the long tradition of resistance to slavery that the Africans established in South America and in the Caribbean Islands. They contend that the slave seldom revolted and, when he did, his motive was more hatred for the whites than a desire for freedom. Any serious study of the states of Bahia and Palmares in Brazil alone would contradict this point of view.

There were several competing slave systems in South America and the Caribbean. Important, though sometimes neglected by historians on the subject, is the slave system started by the Dutch and the nature of resistance to this system. According to Sir Harry H. Johnston:

> The Dutch were hard taskmasters; as slaveholders they were disliked more than the British or British Americans. They threw themselves into the slave trade and the establishment of slave-worked plantations with a zest exceeding that of any other nationality.[3]

The Dutch established their first South American colonies in Guyana and in northern Brazil. African reaction to the harsh Dutch rule started on the Dutch ships bringing them from Africa. The best known slave revolts against the Dutch are the revolt of the Surinam Maroons, 1715-1763, and the Berbice revolt in 1763. These revolts threatened the very foundation of an economy based on slavery. The pattern of revolt differed only by degree in the Caribbean Islands. It can be said with almost absolute justification that these revolts and the personalities involved were the Caribbean and South American antecedents of the 20th century New World black radical. The present-day resistance movements among blacks in South America, the Caribbean, and the United States can best be understood against this historical background.

The closeness in time of the Berbice uprising to the "Bush Negroes" movement in Surinam and Jamaica and to the revolu-tions in Haiti and North America reminds us that they took place in a period of world convulsions, when the established order stood in hourly jeopardy–apparently to remain so eternally. The spirit of man, after the refinement of the Renaissance and the nationalism of the Reformation, had been made extremely vigilant by the self-centered individualism of the bourgeoisie. Now, it was in quest of liberation. So it was too in the West Indies, a main-spring of the Industrial Revolution.

The war of the Maroons of Jamaica predated the Berbice rebel-lion and is better known in history. The word, "Maroons," once spread terror along the skirts of the blue mountains of Jamaica. There were times when the Maroons swept down, unsuspectedly, upon the outlying European plantations. According to an official statement of that day, the Maroons endangered public credit, civil rights and the prosperity, if not the very existence, of the island co-lony of Jamaica. The Maroons have been compared to the Euro-pean rebels called the Circassians. The difference is that while the white mountaineers numbered 400,000 and only defied Czar Nic-holas of Russia, the black mountaineers numbered less than 2,000 and defied Cromwell of England. The Circassians, after years of revolt, were finally subdued. The Maroons, on the other hand, whose revolt started in 1655, were never completely conquered.

The revolt of the Maroons, both in Jamaica and in Surinam, helped to create the condition and attitude that made the Berbice revolt in Guyana possible. These revolts collectively helped to cre-ate the condition and attitude that went into the making of the most successful slave revolt in history, better known as the Haitian Re-volution. This revolt was brought into being by three of the most arresting personalities in Caribbean history: Toussaint L'Ouver-ture, Jean-Jacques Dessalines and Henri Christophe. The distin-guishing feature of this revolution is that it achieved what the others were not able to achieve–nationhood.[4] This is only part of the story. The slaves in Jamaica fought longer and harder than the slaves in Haiti but did not achieve nationhood because they fought under different political circumstances.

The news of these revolts reached the United States, partly through slave sailors on ships between the Caribbean Islands, South America and the United States. This was part of the stimulant that helped to set in motion the massive slave revolts early in the 19th century in the United States.

In a speech, "The American Negro and the Darker World," delivered in New York City in April 1957, the African-American scholar, Dr. W.E.B. DuBois, summarized the position of the Africans in the United States:

> From the fifteenth through the seventeenth centuries, the Africans imported to America regarded themselves as temporary settlers destined to return eventually to Africa. Their increasing revolts against the slave system, which culminated in the eighteenth century, showed a feeling of close kinship to the motherland and even well into the nineteenth century they called their organizations "African" as witness the "African Unions" of New York and Newport, and the African churches of Philadelphia and New York. In the West Indies and South America there was even closer indication of feelings of kinship with Af-rica and the East.

The 19th century black militants, and some before them, were saying essentially the same thing in different ways. The fight against the distortion and suppression of the true history of Africans and African Americans was started long before the Civil War by "free negroes" and escaped slaves who had learned to read and write.

THE FORMATIVE YEARS OF THE BACK-TO-AFRICA MOVEMENT IN THE U.S.

The Back-To-Africa idea has been a recurring theme in the lives of African Americans for more than a 100 years. The thought was strong during the formative years of the colonization society and some of the most outstanding black men of the 18th and 19th centuries came under its persuasion. In the mid-19th century, while the issue of slavery was being debated in most of the country, the feeling for Africa among American blacks was growing stronger. Publications like *Freedoms' Journal* and *Douglass Monthly,* edited by Frederick Douglass, called attention to the plight of the people of Africa as well as to that of the African Americans.

As far back as 1882, the renowned scholar and benefactor of West Africa, Dr. Edward Wilmot Blyden, speaking on the occasion of his inauguration as President of Liberia College, sounded the note for the organized teaching of the cultures and civilizations of Africa and decried the fact that the world's image of Africa was not in keeping with Africa's true status in world history. I quote from his address on this occasion:

> The people generally are not yet prepared to understand their own interests in the great work to be done for themselves and their children. We shall be obliged to work for some time to come not only without the popular sympathy we ought to have but with utterly inadequate resources.
>
> In all English-speaking countries the mind of the intelligent Negro child revolts against the descriptions of the Negro given in elementary books, geographies, travels, histories ....
>
> Having embraced or at least assented to these falsehoods about himself, he concludes that his only hope of rising in the scale of respectable manhood is to strive for what is most unlike himself and most alien to his peculiar tastes. And whatever his literary attainments or acquired ability, he fancies that he must grind at the mill which is provided for him, putting in material furnished by his hands, bringing no contribution from his own field, and of course nothing comes out but what is put in.

The great human drama that was called "The Black Revolution in the U.S.A." has long historical roots and cannot be fully understood until it is seen in this context. In the United States every attempt was made to destroy the slave's memory of Africa and what it meant to him. This attempt failed. The image of Africa in the mind of the slave took many forms, but it did not disappear. In the reestablishment of the connection with Africa and in the search for a more enlightened image of that continent and its people, the early African-American writers in the United States soon learned that Africa was an important factor in world history and that, in the great human drama of the rise and fall of nations, Africans had played every role from saint to buffoon.

These writers, preachers and self-educated men of affairs referred to themselves mainly as Africans–not "coloreds," or "Negroes," or "Blacks," but *Africans!* Nearly all their organizations bore the name "African" and they thought of themselves as an African people. This small group of black freedmen and escaped slaves that began to develop during the latter part of the 18th century were by the end of that century being heard as petitioners, anti-slavery speakers and pamphleteers. Their writings and their place in history are well recorded in a recent book by Dorothy Porter, *Ear & Negro Writing, 1760-1837.* Referring to some of these organizations, their leaders and their program objectives, Mrs. Porter observes that:

> the pioneer colonization projects of Paul Cuffe and Daniel Coker in Sierra Leone reflect the African-American's world view of race and race destiny for the blacks as they established communities overseas. Many African Americans had significant connections with African, Haitian, and other black communities abroad. The stimulus of the British anti-slavery movement served to enhance African American prospects for emigration to lands where their people might be free.

THE REPATRIATIONIST MOVEMENT IN THE U.S.

While Paul Cuffe's ideas for African colonization had been expressed in his writing during the closing years of the 18th century, he did not succeed in taking any African Americans back to Africa until the early part of the 19th century. Thirty-eight black settlers arrived with Paul Cuffe as he landed his ship *Traveller* in Freetown, Sierra Leone, on the morning of February 3, 1816. In many ways, his was the beginning of the African colonization movement. The Back-To-Africa idea, and Africa as a subject for African American writers, would prevail for the next 100 years and would reemerge in the 20th century. Paul Cuffe was one of the paramount figures who helped give birth to this idea.

The Free African Society was organized by the Black Methodists in 1787. This society, under the leadership of Richard Allen and Absalom Jones, brought into being the independent black church in the United States – the African Methodist Episcopal Church. The early black churches were more than religious organizations. They performed the services of social agencies, publishers, community centers and, occasionally, hiding places for escaped slaves. The first historical protest and literary writings of the black freedmen in the New England states found an outlet in the church or in organizations affiliated with the church. In the "Essay on Freedom with Observations on the Origins of Slavery," written by a member of the Sons of Africa Society formed in 1798, the writer outlined some of the difficulties blacks were encountering in seeking freedom and expressed appreciation to the people of the city of Salem, Massachusetts, for showing signs of its "approbation of the Africans' freedom." These pamphlets, broadsheets and monographs would continue to appear throughout the first half of the 19th century and their writers would help to establish the early black press in the United States. Some of these writers became editors of such papers as: *Freedom's Journal, The North Star and The Anglo-African Magazine.*

The subject of colonization and migration to Africa was debated in the pages of these publications. Many blacks who were sure about Africa being the homeland of their people were not sure about returning to Africa. Others saw the return to Africa as the only solution to their problems. The plans of the American Colonization Society, strongly influenced by whites, included returning only free blacks to Africa. The black press, in the main, saw this as an attempt to protect the institution of slavery by removing a very active abolitionist group. This insight into a then prevailing situation did not deny their deep cultural ties to Africa. The colonization movement, literally started by Paul Cuffe, continued concurrent with the fight of African people to enjoy complete citizenship status in the United States.

The spiritual and cultural return to Africa is reflected in the names of early black institutions, especially in the churches. In his book, *The Redemption of Africa and Black Religion*, Professor St. Clair Drake draws this picture of the black church during its formative years. He says:

> Black people under slavery turned to the Bible to "prove" that black people, Ethiopians, were powerful and respected when white men in Europe were Barbarians. Ethiopia came to symbolize all of Africa; and throughout the nineteenth century, the redemption of Africa became one important focus of meaningful *activity* for leaders among New World Africans. "Ethiopianism" became an energizing myth in both the New World and in *Africa* itself for those pre-political movements that arose while the powerless were gathering their strength for realistic and rewarding political activity. Its force is now almost spent, but "Ethiopianism" left an enduring legacy to the people who fought for black power in the twentieth century, and some of its development needs to be understood.

Black churches sprang up wherever black people lived: First African Baptist Church, Savannah, Georgia (1788); African Baptist Church, Lexington, Kentucky (1790); Abyssinia Baptist Church, New York (1800); Free African Meeting House, Boston, Massachusetts (1805); First African Baptist Presbyterian Church, Philadelphia, Pennsylvania (1809); Union Church of Africans, Wilmington, Delaware (1813); First African Baptist Church, New Orleans, Louisiana (1826); First African Baptist Church, Richmond, Virginia (1841). These institutions and their congregations kept alive the African connection. Some of them, independently of the

American Colonization Society, went back to Africa to preach, teach and live out the rest of their lives.

The vision of Africa that began to develop during the 18th century was enhanced by the organizations using the word "Africa" or "African" in referring to their objectives. While they addressed themselves mainly to the plight of African people in the United States, they emphasized that they belonged to a universal people, with land, history and culture. This, of course, did not settle the matter. The historian W.E.B. DuBois tells us that:

> There was, during the 18th century, strong agitation a-mong certain groups of black people in America for a return to Africa. This agitation was found mainly among groups of "Free Blacks" because of the uncertainty of their position as freed men in a slave-holding society.

One can see it late into the eighteenth century. Dr. DuBois explains in his book, *Dusk to Dawn:*

> when the Negro Union of Newport, Rhode Island, in 1788, proposed to the Free African Society of Philadelphia, a general exodus to Africa on the part of at least free blacks.

The Back-to-Africa idea had been a recurring theme in African American life and thought for more than a generation now. This idea was strong during the formative years of the American Colonization Society and succeeded in convincing some of the most outstanding black men of the 18th and 19th centuries, such as John Russwurm, editor of *Freedom Journal,* and Lott Carey, the powerful Virginia preacher. The men who were against the program of the American Colonization Society were equally outstanding, and they included Frederick Douglass. Some contended that it was a philanthropic enterprise; others considered it a scheme for getting rid of the free people of color because of the seeming menace they were to slavery.

In the year 1829, two events occurred that brought radical change, and much debate, to the black movement in the United

States. John B. Russwurm abandoned his opposition to the American Colonization Society and announced that he had been convened "to the view that the free negro could help himself and his race best by giving strong support to Liberia." The establishment of this state on the west coast of Africa was a historical turning point in the African Americans' attempt to return, in body as well as in mind, to their African homeland. The other event was the publication of a document now best known as "David Walker's Appeal."

In Liberia, John B. Russwurm moved to a position that today would be called Black Nationalism. He established another newspaper, *The Liberia Herald*, and served as Superintendent of Schools. He further distinguished himself as Governor of the colony of Cape Palmas that was established in Liberia by the Maryland Colonization Society.

As a result of "David Walker's Appeal," the debate over the destiny of African Americans was lifted to a new level of consciousness. It has been said that "if any single event may be said to have triggered the Black Revolt, it is the publication of 'David Walker's' Appeal, to the colored citizens of the world, in September 1829." The slave-holding South saw in it only incitement to rebellion and went to fantastic lengths to suppress it. Even in the North, where slavery was, generally, opposed in principle, moderates insisted that the time for its abolition had not yet come and agreed that the pamphlet was inappropriate and incendiary. With the appearance of the "Appeal" a more militant fight against slavery was born. In calling for slaves to take up arms against their master, David Walker went beyond nationalism and saw slavery as a crisis affecting African people everywhere.

In the years between 1830 and 1850, the debate over the plans of the American Colonization Society continued. The society was still white-dominated and held in suspicion by a large number of African Americans. In his article, "Pan-Negro Nationalism in the New World before 1862," Professor Hollis R. Lynch has pointed out why men like Paul Cuffe and John B. Russwurm gave their support to the American Colonization Society despite having some misgivings about some aspects of their program. "Whatever the motive of the Society's leaders and supporters," professor Lynch says, "the society was creating a Negro state in Africa."

In 1851, John B. Russwurm, a pioneer editor and freedom fighter, died in Liberia and, in the same year, Edward Wilmot Blyden went to Africa and established himself in Liberia. He was destined to become the greatest black intellectual of the 19th century. He concerned himself with the plight of African people the world over and eventually built a bridge of understanding between the people of African origin in the West Indies, the United States and in Africa. More than anyone else in the 19th century and during the early part of the 20th century, Edward W. Blyden called upon the black man to reclaim himself and his ancient African glory. The concept now called "Negritude" started with Blyden.

In the decade that led to the Civil War, a new renaissance of interest in Africa by African Americans was reflected in the black press and in the speeches of a growing number of black men of affairs, mainly Martin R. Delany was proud of his African background and of the Mandingo blood that flowed in his veins. He was one of the leaders of the great debate following the passage of the fugitive slave act of 1850. He was the spokesman for the black people who felt that the bitter climate in America had made life unbearable for them. Delany was the strongest voice in several conventions of free blacks to discuss plans for emigrating to Africa. In 1859, he led the first and only exploratory party of American-born Africans to the land of their forefathers. In the region of the Niger River, in the area that is now Nigeria, Delany's party carried out scientific studies and made agreements with several African kings for the settlement of emigrants from America.

Martin Delany was accompanied on this expedition by Robert Campbell, a Jamaican, who had been director of the Scientific Department of the Institute for Colored Youth in Philadelphia and a member of the International Statistical Congress in London. His account of the expedition can be found in his book, *A Pilgrimage To My Motherland, An Account Of a Journey among the Egbas and Yorubas of Central Africa in 1859-1860*. About his report, Robert Campbell said,

after what is written in the context, if I am still asked what
I think of Africa for a colored man to live and do well in, I
simply answer, that with as good prospects in America as
colored men generally, I have determined with my wife
and children to go to Africa to live, leaving the inquirer to
interpret the reply for himself.

What needs to be remembered about this mid-19th century Back-
to-Africa movement is that, to a moderate degree, it was successful. There was, of course, no mass exodus to Africa. Individual
families, however, did go to Africa at regular intervals for the next
50 years.

General interest in Africa continued through the pre-Civil War,
although emigration efforts to establish an autonomous nation for
African Americans did not succeed. The Civil War and the promises to African Americans that followed lessened some of the interest in Africa. Pat Singleton started an internal settlement
scheme, his plan being to settle blacks in the unused areas of
America — mainly, at that time, the state of Kansas. He hoped to
establish free separate black communities.

The betrayal of reconstruction and the rise of lynchings and other atrocities against black Americans made a new generation of
black thinkers and freedom fighters run to Africa again. New men
and movements entered the area of struggle. The most notable of
the new personalities was Bishop Henry McNeal Turner. In his
book, *Black Exodus*, Edwin S. Redkey gives this view of Bishop
Turner's importance to the history of this period. He says:

Bishop Henry McNeal Turner was, without a doubt, the
most prominent and outspoken American advocate of
black emigration in the years between the Civil War and the
First World War. By constant agitation he kept African
Americans aware of their African heritage and their disa-
bilities in the United States. Turner possessed a dominating personality, a biting tongue, and a pungent vocabulary which gained him high office and wide audiences,
first in Georgia's reconstruction politics and later in the

African Methodist Episcopal (AME) Church. In his bitter disappointment with the American treatment of Blacks, the Bishop had an all-consuming nationalism which demanded emigration to Africa. To understand his forceful agitation in the years following 1890, one must know Turner's background and the nature of his vision of Africa.[5]

NEO-REPATRIATIONISM AND THE STRUGGLE FOR DOMESTIC CIVIL RIGHTS IN THE U.S.

The Black American entered the 20th century searching for new directions, politically, culturally and institutionally. New men and movements were emerging. The Niagara Movement, under the leadership of W.E.B. DuBois and Monroe Trotter, was born in 1905. Some of the ideas of the Niagara Movement went into the making of the NAACP in 1909. The African-American interest in Africa continued, but was abated by the burden of troubles at home. The end of the first world war brought no improvement to the lives of African Americans. The then prevailing conditions made a large number of them ripe for the militant, Africa-oriented program of Marcus Garvey.

In the appendix to the second edition of his book, *The Black Jacobins*, the Caribbean scholar C.L.R. James observes that two West Indians, "using the ink of Negritude, wrote their names imperishably on the front pages of the history of our times." Professor James is referring to Aimé Césaire and Marcus Garvey. He places Marcus Garvey at the forefront of the group of 20th century African American radicals whose ideas and programs still reverberate within present-day liberation movements. Marcus Garvey was a man of his time who, in retrospect, was ahead of his time. This is proved by the fact that his ideas have resurfaced and are being seriously reconsidered as a major factor in the liberation of African people the world over.

Professor James further reminds us that Marcus Garvey, an immigrant from Jamaica, is the only black man who succeeded in building a mass movement among African Americans. He advocated the return of Africa to the Africans and to people of African descent. He organized, maybe too hurriedly and with a shortage of competently trained people, the institutions and enterprises that would make this possible. His movement began to develop an international framework around 1921; but by 1936, the structure of the movement was shaken by internal strife and power-hungry personalities fighting for control. This in-fighting led, in part, to the arrest, trial and subsequent deportation of Marcus Garvey. This is the bare essence of the situation; C.L.R. James extends the explanation in this way:

> But Garvey managed to convey to Negroes everywhere (and to the rest of the world) his passionate belief that Africa was the home of a civilization which had once been great and would be great again. When you bear in mind the slenderness of his resources, the vast material forces and the pervading social conceptions which automatically sought to destroy him, his achievement remains one of the propagandistic miracles of this century.

After the deportation of Marcus Garvey and the beginning of the Great Depression, interest in Garvey and the Back-to-Africa idea declined and was not rekindled until the Italian-Ethiopian War (1935-1936). This war and its implications for African people at home and abroad stirred the latent African consciousness in the African communities in the West. In the period of the Italian-Ethiopian war, the streets of Harlem were open forums, presided over by master speakers like Arthur Reed and his protege, Ira Kemp. Young Carlos Cook, founder of the Garvey-oriented African Pioneer Movement, was on the scene, also bringing a nightly message to his street fellows. Part of every message was about Africa. The Blyden Society, the Ethiopian World Federation and other organizations attracted a number of African supporters, some of them students like Nkrumah. After the second world war, Africa consciousness was reflected in the literature and activities of the Civil Rights movement. Black newspapers began to pay more attention to items about the developing crisis in Africa concurrent with their interest in personalities like Martin Luther King Jr. The coverage of news about Africa accelerated with the rise of independent movements on the continent. This acceleration reached some kind of ceremonious plateau of excitement in March 1957, the week the West African nation called the Gold Coast gained its independence and took the ancient name, Ghana. Dr. Kwame Nkrumah, the first Prime Minister of Ghana, became a national hero to African Americans. The African freedom explosion had been set in motion.

Named "Pan Africanism" in the late 1800s and early 1900s, this international movement affected African people everywhere. The antecedent of this movement was the 16th century struggle against slavery and oppression in Africa, the Americas, and the Caribbean Islands. This struggle, in turn, led to the African independence explosion, the Caribbean movement for independence and federation, and the civil rights movement in the United States for complete citizenship. The next logical step will be the building of a concept of a world union of African people and the bringing into being of a new humanity.

The response in the Americas of African descendants to slavery and oppression has been and continues to be persistence in retaining African cultural expressions and in returning to or developing ties with Africa.

NOTES

1. Eric Williams, *Capitalism and Slavery* (New York: Capricorn Books, 1966), pp. 3-4.
2. Gonzalo Aquirre Beltrán, "African Influences in the Development of Regional Cultures in the New World," in *Plantation Systems of the New World* (Washington, D.C., Pan-American Union, Organization of American States, 1959, pp. 64-70.

3. Ibid, pp. 32-37.

4. George Padmore, "Back to Africa Movements" in *Pan-Africanism or Communism* (New York: Doubleday), pp. 1-16.

5. Edwin S. Redkey, *Black Exodus* (New Haven: Yale University Press, 1969).

6. Eric Williams, *Capitalism and Slavery* (New York: G.P. Putnam), pp. 3-30.

BIBLIOGRAPHY

Slave and Citizen, The Negro in the Americas, by Frank Tannenbaum. Vintage Books, Random House, New York, 1946, 3-5.

Slave Trade and Slavery, edited by John Henrik Clarke and Vincent Harding, Holt, Rinehart & Winston, Inc. New York, 1970, 1-7.

The Horizon History of Africa, edited by Alvin M. Josephry Jr., American Heritage Publishing Co., NY, 1971. See Chapter Nine, "Time of Troubles," by John Henrik Clarke, 363-365.

"Slavery and Slave Revolts: A Sociological Analysis of the First Maroon War, 1665-1740," by Orlando Patterson, in *"Maroon Societies,"* edited by Richard Price, Anchor Books, NY, 230-246.

Black Revolution, by Wenworth Higginson, Arno Press, New York, pp. 4-37. (date)

The Myth of the Negro Past, by Melville J. Herskovits, Beacon Press, Boston, Mass. 1958, pp. 5.1-85.

Social Control in Slave Plantation Societies: A Comparison of St. Cuba, by Gwendolyn Midlo Hall, The Johns Hopkins Press, Baltimore, MD, 1971, pp. 52-53.

"Palmares: An African State in Brazil," by R.K. Kent, in Maroon Societies, edited by Riehard Price, Doubleday Anchor Books, New York, pp. 169-190. (date).

The Negro in the New World, by Sir Harry H. Johnston, Methuen and Co., Ltd., London, 1910, pp. 38-1.1.

The Man Who Stole a continent, by Hohn M. Weaterwax, Bryant Foundation, Los Angeles, California, 1963, pp. 1-30.

The Negro in the New World, pp. 77-93.

Journal of African History, vol. No. 2, 1965. Cambridge University Press, New York & London, pp. 161-166.

"Numbi and the Republic of Palmares," by Irene Diggs. *Phylon Magazine,* First Quarter, 1953, pp. 62-70.

Negroes in Brazil, by Donald Pierson, Southern Illinois University Press, Carbondale, III, 1967, pp. 3-70.

"Some Neglected Aspects of Yoruba culture in the Americas and in the Caribbean Islands," by John Henrik Clarke, *The Proceedings of the Yoruba Civilization,* University of Nigeria, July, 26-31, 1976.

"Black Power and Black History," by John Henrik Clarke, *Negro Digest,* February, 1969, Chicago, Illinois.

"Afro-American Image of Africa," by John Henrik Clarke, *Black World Magazine*, February, 1974, Chicago, Illinois.

Black Nationalism: A Search for an Identity in America, by E.U. Essien-Udom. Laurel Edition, Dell Publishing Co., New York, 1964.

"The Origin and Growth of Afro-American Literature", by John Henrik Clarke, *Black Voices*, edited by Abraham Chapman, New American Library, Mentor Books, New York, 1968. pp. 632-645.

How Europe Underdeveloped Africa, by Walter Rodney, Bogle-L'Ouverture Publications, London, 1972, pp. 40-83.

Review of Walter Rodney's Book, *How Europe Underdeveloped Africa*, by Arthur Nurse, in *Shango, The Magazine of the Caribbean*, Vol. I, No. 3, Summer 1973, p. 22.

"The African Roots of War (1915)", by W.E.B. DuBois, in Meyer Weinberg, Harper and Row, NY, 1970 pp. 360-371.

Early Negro Writing 1760-1837, by Dorothy Porter, Beacon Press, Boston, Mass., 1971, pp. 1-86.

Paul Cuffe: Black America and the African Return, by Sheldon Harris, Simon and Schuster, NY, 1972, pp. 13-26.

The Black Press 1827-1890, edited by martin E. Dahn, G.P. Putnam Son's, New York, 1971, pp. 236-245.

The Redemption of Africa and Black Religion, by St. Clair Drake, Third World Press, Chicago, Ill, 1971, pp. 11-15.

"The Attitude of the Free Negro Toward African Colonization", by Louis Mehilinger, *Journal of Negro History*, July 1916, pp. 275-301.

"Pan-Negro Nationalism in the New World Before 1862", by Hollis R. Lynch, Boston, *University Press Papers on Africa*, Vol. II, African History, edited by Jeffrey Butler, 1966, pp. 149-179.

"David Walker's appeal in the Colored Citizens of the World, but in particular, and expressly, to those of *Black Brotherhood, Afro-American and Africa*, edited by Okon Ed. Uya.

The Black Jacobins, by C.L.R. James, Vintage Books, Random House, Second Edition, Revised 1963, pp. 396-397.

"The New Afro-American Nationalism", by John Henrik Clarke, *Freedom-ways Magazine*, Vol, I, No. 3, Fall, 1961.

THE AFRICAN EXPERIENCE
IN BRAZIL*

ABDIAS DO NASCIMENTO

T HE PAST few decades witness a moment in history when African[1] peoples in the Americas, more specifically in South and Central America, have increasingly claimed their rightful place at the conference tables of the African world. The first difficulty we confront, of course, is language. International events carried on in French and English, and sometimes Arabic, exclude those millions of Africans who speak Spanish and Portuguese, or limit seriously their ability to participate fully. For this reason we support, as a long-term goal, the establishment of an international African language to be taught our children the world over.

Beyond this linguistic isolation, the specific nature of racism in South and Central America and our people's destitution obstructed our presence at most *Pan-African* encounters until very recently. The very concept of Diaspora was essentially linked in the minds of many, and certainly in the practice of international gatherings, to Africans in the United States and the Caribbean. I remember insisting, at working sessions of the Encounter on African Alternatives in Dakar, 1976, that members of the United States delegation take care not to monopolize the hemisphere by referring to themselves exclusively as "African Americans." And I remember, also, the heroic efforts of C.L.R. James, during the organizing process of the 6th Pan-African Congress held in Dar-es-Salaam in 1974, to see that the event have a solid and significant representation from Brazil, due to its demographic, historical, geopolitical and economic importance in the African world. His efforts brought forth few real fruits: I was the sole South American delegate at the 6th PAC.

Racist oppression in South and Central America is reflected in the general habit of referring to the area as "Latin America." This phrase linguistically brings to fore the racist attitude of the ruling classes, almost exclusively of European origin, who force their cultural and ethnic identity on the very definition of the region itself. Reference to "Latin America" has been legitimized in progressive and "Third World" circles, in a show of insensibility or ignorance of the great majority of the region's people who are not "Latin" at all, but African and/or Native American (Indian). Conventional eulogies of *"mestizaje"* or *"morenidade,"* the process of race-mixing, ignore both the sociohistorical origin of that mixture and the fact that, mixed as their ethnic origin may be, the identity of these populations is forcibly defined as "Latin" while their Native American and/or African heritage is repressed or despised. In the course of this essay, we will examine some details of this process as it takes place in Brazil. However, it is safe to say that basically the same ideological impositions are suffered by our neighbors in Colombia, Ecuador, Costa Rica, Peru, the Dominican Republic, Haiti and other countries of the region. Their forms and minutia may differ from one context to another, but the essentially racist nature of these social structures is common to all.

My initial observation would be that to speak of the African "presence" in Brazil is to understate the question from the start, for history shows that Brazil is demographically and culturally an African country. Africans arrived there soon after the territory's so-called "discovery" by Pedro Alves Cabral in 1500. By 1535, the African slave traffic was a normal, organized activity. This date is simultaneous with the establishment of colonial Brazil itself, i.e., the subjugation and murder of its native people and the sacking of its resources by bands of greedy Portuguese bent on milking the land to its last *escudo*. It was this enterprise that laid the country's economic and infrastructural foundations, and Africans were brought in chains to Brazil not to help others build the country, but to build it themselves. Given the more advanced state of metallurgy and agricultural technologies in Africa at the time, it was most often the slaves who taught their masters.

From the beginning, the agro-industrial policy of monoculture for export condemned the nation to a process of dependency and foreign debt culminating in today's infamous standing as world champion of insolvency. Sugar was the colony's first industry, feeding the European craving for newly-discovered sweets. In today's states of Bahia and Pernambuco, sugar plantations sprang into action so fast that by 1587 Bahia alone had 47 mills. Africans, the majority population all over the colony, were clustered there for about two centuries, while the sugar industry dominated the economy. Later, cotton was king, and concentration of the slave population moved north to Maranhao. Discovery of diamonds and gold in the 18th century, in Minas Gerias state, moved slavery's focal point south. This process repeated itself in the first half of the 19th century, with falling productivity in the mines and the beginning of the coffee cycle. Plantations of this object of European vice were found in Rio de Janeiro and Sao Paulo. It is virtually impossible to pinpoint the number of Africans who arrived in Brazil. This fact is due not only to the vagueness and unreliability of statistics, when available, but especially to Finance Minister Rui Barbosa's infamous decree of May 13, 1891 which ordered the destruction, by fire, of all historical documents and archives related to slavery and the slave trade. Estimates are extremely precarious. One, which seems to me lower than reasonable, suggests that four million Africans were imported live, with approximately 38% going to Rio de Janeiro, from where some were sent to Minas and Goias; *25%* to Bahia; 13% to Pernambuco; *12%* to Sao Paulo state; 7% to Maranhao and 5% to Para.[2]

If statistics on the total number of Africans to arrive in Brazil are unworthy of credit, even worse are those that pretend to locate their places of origin in Africa. Ethnologists of European origin confuse ports of embarkation with ports or areas of origin, names of places in Africa with those of sovereigns, and so on. This branch of white "scholarship" was dedicated in Brazil largely to the proposition that slaves it designated "Sudanese" were "culturally more advanced" and generally more docile than those inferior ones they labelled "Bantu."[3]

What we do know about the enslaved Africans is that they never stopped fighting for their freedom. The list of *quilombos* (maroon societies) is long and incomplete (Nascimento 1979, Moura 1972). Their perennial consciousness and untiring struggle inspired my proposal of Afro-Brazilian social and political organization, based on our specific history: *Quilombismo* (Nascimento, A. 1980, 1980A).

Constant rebellion and uprisings like those of the Males, the Tallors, the Balaio and countless others, were the true and conventionally unrecognized historical agent of slavery's abolition. Brazil was the last country in all the Americas to abolish slavery, with a decree signed on May 13, 1888. Next year, the nation commemorates abolition's centennial. Africans in Brazil can only say that one hundred years of civic lies and official hypocrisy do not deserve celebration.

The Black movement has long since rejected May 13 as a day of celebration for our community. In the late 1970's we instituted National Black Consciousness Day on November 20, the anniversary of elected king Zumbi's death in defense of Palmares. This *quilombo* was in fact the first free republic in the Americas, which fought off armed colonial aggression for more than a century (1594-1696), defending a pluri-racial, anti-racist African state in the lands of Serra da Barriga (today in Alagoas). Each year, on that day, the Zumbi Memorial, virtually a federation of Afro-Brazilian organizations, sponsors a pilgrimage to Palmares' site. Conventional histories omit the Africa-Brazilian heroes of the abolitionist cause. Among them the giant is Luiz Gama, along with his mother Luisa Mahin. Poet and precursor of *Negritude,* Luiz Gama's exceptionally lucid African consciousness was his main weapon, wielded in various forms: he was poet, lawyer, orator, writer and militant. His legacy to the contemporary African community in Brazil is one of inspiration and example. Abolition of slavery brought no real benefits to Africans in Brazil. Now labelled "free," they were left to the streets without work, education, health care, housing or land. Others stayed with former masters on the latter's imposed conditions. Black women were doubly victimized by this process, in which they became at once the last on the social scale and the mainstay of their families and community.

In a process of social engineering based on the most crass assumptions of racial Darwinism, the European elite promoted mass immigration of white people in order to "improve the nation's racial stock." The ruling class was in panic over the Africanness of this newly-declared citizenry, and hurried immediately to deny it suffrage by instituting in the 1891 Constitution, for the first time, the literacy requirement for voting. This done, it went about subsidizing European immigration to saturate the labor market, leaving Africans destitute, and simultaneously inculcating in the national consciousness a social compulsion to "marry white." The idea was to eliminate the African presence entirely, hopefully by the end of this century. This campaign and its racist rationale are examined in depth in Thomas Skidmore's work (1974).

Brazilian intellectuals, writers and "scientists" who created a complex network of sophistries idealizing the whitening of the Brazilian "race" are among those most often translated into English and other languages. Two major examples are Gilberto Freyre and Jorge Amado. Both contribute enormously to foreign readers' misinformation, depicting race mixture as a true index of ethnic harmony and racial "democracy"in Brazil. The truth, however, is just the opposite. Applied to Afro-Brazilians' living reality, the concept of "racial democracy" operates as one more tool used to perpetuate the ruling minority's domination over Brazilians of African origin.

The architects of the immigration/Aryanization campaign entertained their hopes in vain. When we say that Brazil is demographically an African country, we refer to the historical and contemporary failure of these policies designed to wipe the "Black stain" from the population. According to available statistics, in 1600 there were 20,000 Africans in Brazil, twice as many as there were Europeans. Native Americans counted 35,000.[4] In 1798, the proportion remained constant for Africans and Europeans, while the "discovery" of more Native Brazilians brought their count to

250,000.[5] By 1822, the artifice of counting *pardos* (mulattoes) separately from *pretos* (Africans) was already being used in the attempt to diminish the official number of Africans. The sum of the two categories (2,456,000) is almost two and a half times the number of whites listed (1,043,00). In 1872, we have: whites, 3,787,289; *pretos* and *pardos.* 6,143,279 (Nascimento 1968: 19, 31).

In spite of European immigration, Africans remain a numerical majority, even according to these statistics, through 1890, when they represent 56% of the population. At this point, the white population begins to increase relatively. By 1940, according to the Brazilian government, it represents *63.47%* of the Brazilian people. It then declines until, in 1980, we have 54.77% white and 44.34% African *(preto* and *pardo)* presence in the country's populace.[6]

This rough statistical outline must be qualified by the fact, widely cited by demographers and statisticians, that racial ideology in Brazil distorts them highly in favor of the white category. Mixed-blood people obviously of African descent, questioned by the census taker, almost invariably declare themselves white or *pardo,* in a process in which "... the Black group loses a great deal, the *pardo* group gains much more than it loses, and the white group gains a lot and loses nothing."[7] If we add to this the fact that Africans are disproportionately represented among those groups that the census does not reach (isolated rural communities, poverty pockets, shantytowns and so on), it becomes more than clear that Africans represent much more than 44.3% of Brazilians. We have more than enough reason to state that Africans make up a majority of Brazil's people.

In this distortion of statistics we come upon a cornerstone of "Latin" racism: the psycho-social whitening of Africans in these societies. The compulsion to identify with European values, aesthetics and criteria of personal beauty create various negative psychological complexes which are nothing new to students of Frantz Fanon or Albert Memmi. What distinguished the "Latin" situation is that, rather than being seen as one of racism's many faces, this compulsion to whiteness is presented, ironically, as proof positive of "Latin" anti-racism! Thus we have the following declaration by a member of the Brazilian military dictatorship's delegation to the Second World Festival of Black and African Arts and Culture (Festac 77, held in Lagos):

> the predominance of the white portion [in the population] is evident, since in Brazil, even those of mixed race who have a small or large amount of Black or Indian blood, but without one of these group's physical traits, are considered white. Which demonstrates the absence of any discrimination of racial nature, in terms of the person's ethnic origin.[8]

This author assumes unchallengeable, as do most Brazilians, that Africans and Native Americans yearn to be honored with the exalting title "white." Condescension to this desire, a magnanimous gesture, is a certain sign of the Brazilian elite's non-racism. It never seems to occur to these writers that the extolling of whiteness as a virtue is in fact the essence of white supremacism. Nor do they recognize the absurdity of accepting as valid the statistical contusion of whites' "predominance" in the population despite the distortions they themselves so enthusiastically expose.

With authors like Nina Rodrigues and Oliveira Vianna in the forefront, this kind of "scientific reasoning" has furnished major justifications for post-abolition racial discrimination (Nascimento 1979). A whole body of literature was authored by whites or mentally Europeanized Afro-Brazilians, crystallizing the idea of a "Black problem" in Brazil. Yet if Africans are the main element of the nation's demographic, economic, cultural and social stock, we can hardly be legitimately seen as a problem. It is much more pertinent to define racist whites, creators of the "Black problem," as the real dilemma of Brazilian society. Afro-Brazilian sociologist Guerreiro Ramos correctly identifies the true nature of these sophistries:

> To ensure exploitation, the ruling minority had recourse not only to force and violence but also to a system of

pseudo-justifications, stereotypes and processes of psychological domestication.

Dogma such as the excellence of whiteness and the
aesthetic degradation of blackness formed one of the psychological pillars of exploitation. (1957:175).

Another branch of white scholarship in Brazil spent enormous
energies on the proposition that Brazilian society entertained a
certain color prejudice *(preconceito de marca)* described as
"purely aesthetic" because it discriminates on the basis of pheno-
type as opposed to racial origin. In the name of "science," these
writers dissociate the rejection of Black people's physical features
from their African origin and invent a purely gratuitous aversion
in order to proclaim Brazilian prejudice "more benign" or "less
serious." (Nascimento, E. 1980: 17-19). That this "aesthetic" aversion to Blackness is a function and product of white supremacy
could be the suggestion only of a heretic or a racist.

These ideas are popularized to an extent probably unprecedented for academic theories. In a discussion with almost any Brazilian, race mixture will be extolled as a positive value in itself and
a proof of non-racism. In many cases, "Marxist" class analysis will
have led the person to idealize the ultimate amalgamation of races
in a universal *cafe au lair* mass as the automatic solution to racism
and the road to unity of the proletariat. Long discourse will follow
on the fact that in the United States (where racism really exists),
one must discern whether someone has one thirty-second part
African blood in order then to refuse him or her a place on the bus
or train. The argument usually culminates in the Brazilian, almost
invari-ably a mulatto of more or less obvious African descent, pro-
claiming: "If this were the United States, even I would be
considered Black!"

Ghanaian scholar Anani Dzidzienyo, of Brown University,
comments:

Because the extent of racial mixture is considered to have
resulted in large-scale intermingling, it is sometimes argued that racism cannot be said to have marked Brazilian

society in ways similar to the United States of America. Nonetheless, even this Brazilian complexity, which provides a much more complex range of definitions between blackness and whiteness, is based upon prejudice directed against nonwhite. (1984: 13)

The "aesthetic prejudice" theory and its popular corollaries fly in the face of statistics on race discrimination in Brazil. The 44.34% of Brazilians we define as Africans in the 1980 census represent the sum of two categories: *preto* (Black) and *pardo* (roughly the equivalent of "brown," except that most browns class themselves as whites). Only 5.89% classify themselves as *pretos*. But statistics on employment and education show that the 38.45% who call themselves *pardos* suffer the same kinds of discrimination. Among men classed as *pretos,* for instance, 46.7% have one year of schooling or less, while about half that percentage (24.3%) applies to whites. And *pardos?* Their situation is worse than that of pretos: 48.2% have one year's education or less. Whites have 6 times more chance to complete 12 years' education or more. In terms of income, the situation is not much different. Among white men, 17.8% earn minimum wages or less, while among *pretos* the percentage is 33% and among *pardos,* 32.5%. 6.5% of white men earn more than minimum wages while only 0.4% of *pretos* and 1.1% of *pardos* earn that much. Among women, the situation of double discrimination is evident. 14.6% of white women earn minimum wages or less, while twice that many *pretas* (28.5%) and 19.8% of *pardas are* in that situation. These data reflect the only significant advantage held by mixed-bloods. The vast majority of *pretas (preto* women) are to this day exploited as domestic servants at less than poverty wages. Some mulatto women have a greater chance of escaping this trap. On the other hand, they do not do much better than pretas on the high end of the income scale: 0.8% of white women earn more than minimum wages, while 0.03% of *pretas* and 0.09% of *pardas* are in that bracket.

These statistics, as a whole, render useless the "mulatto escape hatch" theory in which some sociologists posit that greater social status conferred upon mixed-bloods creates an outlet through which potential protest is neutralized by the possibility of social ascension through miscegenation.[9]

In contrast to the image of "racial democracy," these data show a clear racial hierarchy in terms of income and educational opportunity: at the top, white men; next, white women; third, Black men and lastly, Black women (Gonzalez 1985). Between 1980 and 1982, this situation worsened.[10]

Nevertheless, to this day, Africans who raise the question of racism in public as a political issue are still dismissed with the allegation "That's not race discrimination, it's a class question. Here we have poor whites and poor Blacks, but not racism." This in a country where, even according to distorted official statistics,[11] about 50% of whites as opposed to more than 75% of Blacks live on or below the poverty line.

The most sinister effect of this racial ideology is that the victims themselves become convinced that racism does not exist. Thus, the Black movement expends enormous energies trying to "prove" to its own people that their situation is due to race. Continuously, we must answer the question "Does racism really exist?", turning our energies away from the real questions of our struggle. Indeed, if Brazilian racism is effective from the statistical point of view, keeping Africans well "in their place" socioeconomically, its real achievement lies in this capacity to curb the growth of African consciousness and the community's protagonism on its own behalf.

This is not to say that Afro-Brazilian resistance abated after abolition. On the contrary, the present century has witnessed from the start an active vanguard of Black consciousness. Most often, this consciousness is expressed in non-political forms such as Catholic religious brotherhoods, African religious organizations, mutual aid societies, recreational clubs, samba schools and so on. Even at the turn of the century, there existed a proliferation of these organizations with the name "Quilombo" or "Palmares," in direct reference to the military struggle carried out by our ancestors. An active Black press also existed, with foreseeable problems and lack of continuity due to the community's destitution. In the 1930s, the Brazilian Black Front, led by Jose Correia Leite and others, sponsored mass demonstrations against discrimination in Sao Paulo state, where Jim Crow policies were common. The focus on African identity and cultural values was introduced by the Black Experimental Theater (TEN) founded by this author in Rio de Janeiro in 1944. The TEN organized the National Black Convention (Rio de Janeiro and Sao Paulo, 1945 and 1946) and the First Congress of Brazilian Blacks (Rio de Janeiro, 1950), among many other similar events. The National Black Convention of Rio, in 1945, was responsible for presenting to the National Constituent Assembly a series of measures which were, predictably, rejected under the allegation that no discrimination existed in Brazil. Characteristic of Brazilian power relations and Black alienation is the fact that among more than 300 members of the Assembly, only one was African: Claudino Jose da Silva of the Brazilian Communist Party. He voted against the Afro-Brazilian community's proposal.

During the military dictatorship of the sixties and seventies, mere discussion of race questions was banned by the National Security Law. Nevertheless, the Black movement grew, particularly during the latter half of the seventies. In 1978, a major demonstration against racism was held in Sao Paulo. Black organizations, in various forms and branches of activity, appeared all over the country.

During the 1982 elections, several Afro-Brazilians ran for legislative office. While few of these were successful, the political weight of the movement did increase. In Rio de Janeiro, three Africans were appointed to first-line posts in Leonel Brizola's state government. In Sao Paulo, the state government created its Council for Black Community Development and Participation. With the civilian government of Tancredo Neves, substituted by Jose Sarney before actually taking office, an Afro-Brazilian advisory council was created in the federal government's Ministry of Culture.

As a protagonist and/or witness of almost all these events, I can attest to the *Negritude* movement's importance for Afro-Brazilians. To us in Brazil, the expression *Negritude* refers not only to a literary movement, but is one of the words that encapsulates the essence of our struggle and that of Africans worldwide: the fight for our dignity and the courageous statement of our humanity in the face of those who deny it. After centuries of dehumanization and systematic humiliation, it is natural that we sometimes disagree over the details of the identity we are working to recapture. Beyond these disputes, however, lies that essence which we call *Negritude,* among other names: the humanness, in its unique forms, of our people and their civilizations. In this sense, *Negritude* for us transcends the definitions conceived by the formal movement's first founders, Damas, Césaire and Senghor. It represents African consciousness, from Zumbi and Benkos Bioho to Queen N'Zingha and Ottobah Cuguano; from Martin Delany and Edward Wilmot Blyden to Garvey, DuBois, Nkrumah, Malcolm, and Lumumba; from Cheikh Anta Diop to Karenga and Asante; from Agostinho Nero to Ivan Van Sertima and Steve Biko. Eventual disagreements with the literary movement's protagonists should not lead us to reject *Negritude* itself outright, for its historical importance is undeniable. Its role in mobilizing the process of African independence is a fact, and its repercussions in African communities outside the Continent, including Brazil, are undeniable. In reference to our own history, we must deem it unjust and unacceptable when certain Brazilians condemn *Negritude,* invoicing the tired and tattered cliche of "reverse racism."

Césaire himself identified three elements of *Negritude:* identity, fidelity and solidarity. This solidarity is universal and antiracist, repudiating hatred and aggression. Even independently of this dialogue with others, however, African liberation is intrinsically a humanist proposal because it contributes to the liberation of humanity as a whole, whose qualitative existence is defective as long as Africans or any other people are deprived of their identity, human dignity and historical, cultural and social protagonism.

To those who cry "reverse racism" at the mention of *Negritude,* we would posit that racial consciousness is not the same as racism; only if I learn to love myself, indeed, may I love and interact with others. Yet Africans are exhorted, taught and brainwashed not to love themselves, internalizing white supremacist ideas of history, aesthetics, religion and sociology with which they are daily bombarded by the mass media. This problem is perhaps more acute in Diaspora communities, but Africa is by no means immune. Her foreign reserves are still used, in part, to import cosmetics, wigs, skin creams, foodstuffs, beverages, clothing and so on, sustaining the urge to whiteness created by racist propaganda. This urge, one of neo-colonialism's major mainstays, is no longer a monopoly of monied elites, but even penetrates the African masses (Kabengele 1986).

We must agree with Wole Soyinka: the tiger has no need to proclaim his tigritude. But this is because there has never been a worldwide campaign, orchestrated by the rich and powerful, to remove him from the forest, demote him to the status of cockroach and forcibly impinge upon his cubs that new identity. In the Afro-Brazilian context, the tiger's pounce in Soyinka's metaphor is what we mean by *Negritude*. It could also be called Black Consciousness, Afrocentricity, Kawaida or *Quilombismo*. All denote the same search for liberation on the basis of our own history, identity and self-definition. In the Brazilian context, there is no doubt that this need is felt by the masses, who have expressed it through countless movements like "Black Mad," "Black Rio," "Soul," "Rastafari" and others.

The major difference between Brazil and most other African communities in the Americas is that, as the majority democratic force, a unified Afro-Brazilian community, in defining and determining its own destiny, is implicitly responsible for the nation's as a whole. Thus, *Quilombismo* as a proposal for Afro-Brazilian social and political organization is a proposal for global organization of Brazil as a nation-state, based on our own history and values (Nascimento, A. 1980). This fact simply takes to its logical conclusion the idea that racism is not a dilemma of the Black community alone, but of the society as a whole in a multi-racial state and of humanity as a whole in the world context.

Finally, it is worthwhile also to underline the universal value of *Negritude* in the cultural and literary sense. There exists a tendency to dismiss it as simply a reaction, a defense strategy against white supremacism, without whose previous existence *Negritude* could not itself exist legitimately. This is to deny the legitimacy of the African world itself, for all peoples have their unique expressions of universal values. Love, hate, life, death, human relations, family unity and breakdown, all these themes are dealt with in languages, manners and styles specific to the culture from which the literature or other manifestation arises. To deal with them abstractly is to engage in philosophy, and philosophies are also culturally specific. If one can speak of Oriental, Western, Judeo-Christian or Amerindian culture and philosophy without raising protests of "reverse racism," why must this occur when we speak of an African culture and philosophy distinct from that of the Arab world? *Negritude,* in our definition, is one expression of that specificity, repressed for centuries from the world's consciousness and our own. The argument that no such specific culture exists, only ethnic tribes and customs, has long since been put to rest by authorities from Frobenius to Diop (1978), and so many others (Asante and Asante 1985). However ideologically correct it may seem to some, as Wole Soyinka has observed, one cannot simply program out of existence this reality of *enia dudu, meedidzii, baike mutane,*[12] for "... the fact remains that in usage and consciousness, our societies have recognized this particularist reality of our ethnic consciousness, one that has not, in *our* histories, bred racism." ("The African World and the Ethnocultural Debate," in Asante and Asante 1985: *16).*

This is not to say that we accept one or two men's definitions of our culture and philosophy as correct; nor does any other people. All civilizations engage in healthy debate over the concepts and priorities of their collective art, thought and social/political practice. The difference is that we Africans have been led to believe that we have none, and that to entertain any such pretension is to indict ourselves for the crime of reverse racism. *Negritude's* great contribution has been to help throw off that yoke.

To disagree with the *Negritude* movement's founders and spokesmen, however, is in no way incoherent with a due recognition of its inherent value and positive role in our civilization. We cannot accept, for example, exaltation of the French language as a unifying element among African peoples. One of my last memories of Léon Damas, just before his death, is a long argument over this question, in which I defended universal adoption of an African language as vehicle for our mutual understanding. Obviously, this is a long-term goal, but certainly preferable to expending our energies upon a choice among the languages colonialism imposed on us. Likewise, we must be careful in our definition of Césaire's first principle, identity, not to incorporate uncritically qualities as they are attributed to us by white supremacism. Depiction of Africans as a people who do not invent or explore is belied by our own history as architects of the first scientific civilization, that of ancient Egypt, and as travellers of the Americas and the world long before Diogo Cao, Columbus and their cronies (Diop 1974, Sertima 1976, 1985, 1985A).

Yet we must also maintain some historical and human perspective when we raise these questions. For the *Negritude* writers, fiery young men studying in Paris, to turn into positive values the very stereotypes used against Africans and throw them back in the face of their deprecators, was an aggressive form of self-defense, a sort of ideological boomerang. Senghor characterizes it as "... a weapon of defense and attack and inspiration rather than a tool of construction" (1965: 99).

In Brazil, the stereotype of the *malandro,* roughly equivalent to the ghetto dude, with his street wisdom and ability to dupe the man, is often flouted in the face of white society in the same spirit. Exu, who represents the devil according to Catholic interpretation, is represented as *malandro* in the Umbanda religion. Called Exu Pelintra, he opens the doors to survival and victory for the Black community.

In certain critiques of *Negritude* we find some of our colleagues judging by European yardsticks the values we consider in our reflections on self-apprehension. Thus, objections raised to Seng-hor's polemical argument that emotion is African too often focus on its supposedly racist tenor, when it is clear that its author is dealing not with genetics or biological chemistry but with civiliza-tion and cultural values. To reject emotion automatically as a pejorative quality is to accept unquestioningly a European value judgment not necessarily applicable to our peoples' experience. Whether it is in fact, for us, a "mode of knowledge" or a "higher state of consciousness" (Senghor 1965: 33-35) is the question that should concern us, and it is not to be dismissed, I think, as patently absurd or unworthy of discussion.

We can also question the postulation of a "universalist civilization" as the ultimate goal of anti-racism. In the first place, this goal seems contradictory to *Negritude's own* most essential contribution. Rather than eliminate the differences among human beings and cultures, so enriching to our existence, by amalgamation in one great cultural "melting pot," the goal should be to end transformation of those differences into inequalities and motives or rationale for oppression. It should be to respect and demand respect for ourselves as human beings with a specific history and identity, and to live in peace with others, respecting their specific identities as well.

It seems to me that the concept of "universalist civilization" runs the risk of endorsing certain distorted forms of similar abstractions. Perhaps this was the case with the "Luso-Tropicalism" of Brazilian white supremacist writers like Gilberto Freyre and Jorge Amado, which became so seductive to certain leaders of the *Negritude* movement. Unfortunately duped by Brazilian mystifications about race mixture and "social democracy," it seems, certain African leaders welcomed and honored these and other spokesmen at international cultural events, apparently unaware of the fact that they built their careers and prestige at the cost of rationalizing Afro-Brazilians' continued exploitation and marginalization.

As we discussed earlier in this paper, perhaps the most effective element of Brazilian racism is its very self-denial, and the myth that race mixture led inexorably to non-racist social relations is the pillar of that strategy. Gilberto Freyre is the master of this reasoning:

> The cross-breeding so widely practiced here corrected the social distance which otherwise would have remained enormous between plantation mansion and slave quarters. What the large landholding slaveholding monoculture produced in the way of aristocratization, dividing Brazilian society into classes of masters and slaves, with a piddling and insignificant middle section of freedmen

sandwiched between the two antagonistic extremes, was in great part neutralized by miscegenation's social effects. Indian and African women, at first, then mulatto women, the yallers, octoroons and so on, becoming the white master's domestics, concubines and even legitimate wives, played a powerful role in Brazil's social democratization. (2969: 34).

Freyre is a prolific creator of mirages, coining phrases like *metarracial brunettism* and others in his attempt to depict Brazilian racial harmony in the rosiest hues possible. He even metaphorically harnesses Africans to the sinking ship of colonialist illusions by characterizing Black Africans, "despite their condition as slaves, as co-colonizers of Brazil, with considerable acculturating influence over the Amerindian, who was less culturally developed than the African Negro." (1976: 8).

The preposterous suggestion that a people who were conquered, hunted, captured and kidnapped from their home in chains of bondage could be called "colonizers" of a land where they were held in captivity shows to what lengths the Brazilian ruling class go to convince itself of its supposed non-racism. In this same text (distributed at the Second World Festival of Black and African Arts and Culture--Festac '77, in Lagos), Freyre contrasts his "metarracial brunettism," symbolizing for him the ultimate eradication of racism through cross-breeding, against what he considers two patently racist ideologies: Aryanism and *Negritude* (1976: 19). Thus, the very theories which seem to fascinate certain proponents of *Negritude* condemn their movement as racist.

Freyre is not the only writer espousing these ideas in the African world. I have elsewhere analyzed the depressing spectacle of Pierre Verger pontificating, at faculty seminars at the University of Ire, Nigeria, on Afro-Brazilians' contemporary "acceptable social status" and on the marvels of Brazilian slave society, where the masters' sons were "sexually initiated" in the fields with docile and "hot" adolescent Black girls (Nascimento 1979: 144, 61-70).

Such hypotheses ignore the racist cornerstones of miscegenation in colonial society. Sexual abuse of African women in slavery is a form of the same rape and pillage inherent in war, with the added dimension of dehumanization supplied by white supremacism. Mulatto populations are the logical product of this violence in any slave society, and their existence is more likely to prove racism's presence, justifying this collective rape, than its absence.

Stereotypes involving African women's sexual abandon are part and parcel of white supremacism, and represent the continuation of this systematic rape from colonial times. Scholars like Teofilo de Queiroz (1975) and David Brookshaw (1983) agree that Jorge Amado is a master at nourishing and developing these stereotypes, applying them particularly to Afro-Brazilian religion. Doris Turner (1975) shows how, in his novel *Jubiaba, African* religion *(candomble)* is portrayed by Amado in terms of buttocks, thighs, breasts and "foaming sex." The African protagonist is described as "pure as an animal, his only law his instincts." The aggregate of images used to create the vision of *Jubiaba's Candomble* manifests implicitly a denial of the Afro-Brazilian religion as religion, rendering it a wild emotional manifestation of primitive sensuality and eroticism (Nascimento 1979: 121-125).

I would like to end on a note of appeal to our brothers and sisters in the rest of the African world: heed Aimé Césaire's call to solidarity! Be careful with seductive slogans and pretty mirages designed to obfuscate and perpetuate Afro-Brazilians' domination. "Racial democracy" has too often succeeded in presenting to the African world, as "spokesmen" for the Black community, precisely those who provide racism's intellectual sustenance in Brazil. Another classic example is Clarival do Prado Valladares, General Coordinator of the Brazilian Government's delegation to Festac '77, who wrote upon returning from the First World Festival of Black Arts (Dakar 1966):

> Whites did not hunt Blacks in Africa, but bought them peacefully from Black tyrants.... Thus it is not surprising that the best understanding and analysis of Africa is not to be found among Africans, [because] in historical terms, there seems to exist a certain inferiority complex that is

African. This is why there is no historical text running parallel to those of Western countries (1966:4).

This is an extreme example, and more subtle positions are the more dangerous. But the fact remains: on the whole, white "spokesmen" more often represent Brazil at international gatherings on African culture than its own protagonists. (Nascimento 1966, 1977, 1979).

Here I want to pay tribute to Aimé Césaire for his practice of solidarity. In the middle sixties, at a UNESCO-sponsored event held in Rio, at the Ministry of Foreign Relations, the usual white "representatives" of Afro-Brazilian culture were pontificating and interested Afro-Brazilians barred from speaking. At the request of this author and of Marietta Campos, a courageous Black militant who later married Léon Damas, Césaire protested to the plenary against this situation. And we know that, when protest is articulated, a new value is being implicitly created. In this case, Negritude's intrinsic value as simultaneous expression of Africans' specific identity, humanity and struggle for liberation in all comers of the world where we are present.

Axe!

NOTES

* Collaboration and translation by Elisa Larkin Nascimento.

1. In this paper, the term "African" is used in the wider sense, including Africans and their descendants in the Diaspora around the world. The words "Afro-Brazilian" and "Black" are used, in the Brazilian context, interchangeably with "African."

2. Thales de Azevedo, *Democracia Racial: ideologia e realidade* (Petropolis: Editors Vozes, 1975), p. *16.*

3. Nei Lopes analyzes this phenomenon in his essay "0 saber e 0 Espirito entre os Bantos," *Afrodiaspora: Journal of Black World Thought,* nos 6-7 (Rio de Janeiro: IPEAFRO, April-December 1985).

4. Luis Vianna Filho, 0 *negro na Bahia (Rio* de Janeiro: Jose Olympio Editors, 1949), p. 45.

5. Thales de Azevedo, "Os grupos negro-africanos," *Histotis da Cultura Brasileira* (Rio de Janeiro: Ministry of Education and Culture, 1973), p. 87.

6. Census data published by the Brazilian Institute of Statistics and Geography (IBGE) (Rio de Janeiro, dates cited).

7. Giorgio Mortars, "O desenvolvimento da populacao preta e pards no Brasil," *Contribuicoes pars o estudo da demofrafia no Brasil* 2nd ed. (Rio de Janeiro: Instituto Brasileiro de Geografia e Estatisticas--IBGE, 1970), p. 458. See also Remulo Coelho, "A composicao da Populacao segundo a cot no Brasil ... em 1950," in the first edition of this work (Rio de Janeiro: IBGE, 1961).

8. Manuel Diegues Junior, A Africa na vida e na cultura do Brasil, published by the official Brazilian delegation to Festac '77 and distributed in book form at the Festac Colloquium.

9. Carl Degler, *Neither Black nor White* (New York: MacMillan, 1971).

10. National Survey Based on Domicile Samples (PNAD) (Rio: IBGE, 1982).

11. National Survey Based on Domicile Samples (PNAD) (Rio: IBGE, 1976).

12. In the text cited, Soyinka points out that the Yoruba peoples use the term *enia dudu,* the Ga *meedidzii,* and the Hausa, *baika mutane,* the black peoples, to refer to "themselves and to others with whom they experience an affinity of being, including their descendants wherever they are."

BIBLIOGRAPHY

Afrodiaspora: Journal of Blade Worm Thought, ed. by Abdias do Nascimento (6 Vols., 1983-85). Rio de Janeiro: IPEAFRO - Afro-Brazilian Studies and Research Institute.

Asante, Molefi Kete (1980). *Afrocentricity.* Buffalo: Amulefi Publishing Company.

Asante, Molefi Kete and Kariamu Welsh Asante, eds. (1985). *African Culture: the Rhythms of Unity.* Westport: Greenwood Press.

Brookshaw, David (1983). *Raca e Cor na Literatura Brasileira. Rio* de Janeiro: Editora Mercado Aberto.

Diop, Cheikh Ann (1978). The *Cultural Unity of Black Africa.* Translation Presence Mficaine. Chicago: Third World Press.

— (1974). *The African Origin of Civilization: Myth or Reality.* Ed. and trans. by Mercer Cook. New York/Westport: Lawrence Hill.

Dzidzienyo, Anani (1984). *Nascimento and his Times: The Socio-Political Context of Afro-Brazilian Writing and Activity.* (Unpublished manuscript.)

— (1971). *The Position of Blacks in Brazilian Society.* London: Minority Rights Group, Report no. 7.

Fernandes, Florestan (1972). 0 *negro no muundo dos bancos.* Sao Paulo: Difusao Europeia do Livro.

Freyre, Gilberto (1976). "Aspectos da influencia Aricana no Brasil." *Cultura,* Vol. VI, no. 23, October-December. Brasilia: Ministry of Education and Culture.

—(1969). *Casa Grande # Senzala,* 14th ed. Rio de Janeiro: Jose Olympio Editora. Gonzalez, Lelia (1985). "Mulher Negra." *Afrodiaspora, no. 6-7 (April December).*

—(1984). "The Black Woman's Place in Brazilian Society." Presented at *1985 and Beyond: a National Conference,* sponsored by the African-American

Women's Political Caucus in Conjunction with Morgan State University (Baltimore, August 9-11).

Journal of African Civilizations, ed. by Ivan Van Serdma (1979-86). New Brunswick.

THE AFRICAN PRESENCE IN PERU*

JOSÉ CARLOS LUCIANO HUAPAYA

> "Because the last recourse of the
> colonized is to defend his person-
> ality against his equal"
>
> —FRANTZ FANON

THE PRESENCE of the Black man in Peru goes back to the arrival of the Spaniards in Tumbes (north of present day Peru) in 1527; from that time, we Blacks have been an integral part of the social reality of Peru, as much for the colony as for the republic.

We arrived as prisoners of war. Therefore, we fulfilled a specific function, that of serving, supporting and defending the Spanish colonizer. It was as Black "*ladinos*" that, at first, we fulfilled the function of "*colonizer by force*" or "compulsory conqueror" and generated profound wounds, not yet healed, on the indigenous Incas. The objective vision of the Black conqueror—aggressor in spite of his slave condition—arises precisely at this moment in which the Black man, in order to survive, must necessarily attack, kill and destroy, given the fact that he formed part of the invading Spanish forces.

A second moment is the bringing of strong contingents of slaves to fill the need for labor that, by genocidal depopulation, the

Spaniards had generated. In this way, the Black man gained spaces in the rural and urban zones that the few members of the Incas nation had abandoned in order to resettle themselves in the Peruvian mountain range; thus the coast became a place where the workforce was comprised predominantly of slave laborers. Worse still, the few members of the Inca nation that remained on the coast were placed under the responsibility of the Black overseers who, in order to insure completion of specific work functions, dominated by means of physical aggression, strengthening the negative feelings that the indigenous peoples had of the "compulsory conqueror." Thereby, the Spaniard succeeded in strengthening a slave duality.

The Spanish conquerors, once the invasion was stabilized, implemented a series of laws intended to separate the ethnic groups and to strengthen their own *ruling mentality*; for this reason racial mixing or sexual relations between individuals or different ethnic groups was condemned, the formation of castes and brother-hoods was promoted, and the presence of the Catholic religion at all levels, particularly in the life and daily acts of the Blacks, was required. The struggle on the part of the Spaniards to distance the Incas from the Blacks was constant and permanent until the great agricultural crisis of the 17th century. During this period, the power of the lords weakened, the incidence of fugitive slaves increased to alarming proportions, and fugitive slave villages ("*palengues*") were formed (for example, the "*palengues*" of Huachipa, 1710-1713). The Black man began to carry out functions that were not permitted previously and, therefore, entered into greater contact with the descendants of the Incas. This contact and the deterioration of the living conditions of the Black and Andean populations in the rural areas would determine the presence of Antonio Obiltas, a Black, in the armies of Tupac Amaristas, the Indian Resistance leader. It was precisely this latter national hero who proposed the liberty of the Blacks so that they might fight against the oppressor.

A third moment is the formation of the Republic, for which a gathering of Creoles, imbued with the new liberal European ideas and with a vital necessity to dominate the economy of the colony, generated an independence movement. However, we Blacks were not considered at first in the proposal; it was the dynamism and necessity for men of war which obliged the inclusion of liberty for the Black man in the plan for independence. Thus, San Martin offers liberty to all Blacks who join his army and, after having consolidated independence, decrees the pseudo "liberty of the womb." This was subject to the "trustees," which implied the right of the former owners to guardianship of the newborn being until the age of 24 for males and age 20 for females; a rule which later, in 1839, was extended to age 50. Once the Republic was established, the Black man continued in slavery until 1854, during which year Ramon Castilla negotiated the riches produced by the "guano" (manure) on islands with slave owners, paying enormous sums for the liberty of Blacks.

However, the new governors of the Republic were the same rulers from the colonial epoch or their descendants; their ruling mentality did not change and their conception of society as divided into castes or races persisted. As a result, they employed many mechanisms to preserve the feudal lord scheme that Spain imposed as a faithful exponent of European dominion. Thus, in spite of the new egalitarian ideological pattern that the situation required, the new rulers of the Republic did not include in plans the recognition of the value and contributions of distinct ethnic groups that formed the nation; for this reason the Andean people and the descendants of Africans came to be members of a society that denied, from the beginning, their presence as beings who contributed to the formation of our nationality.

All of this rubbish is inherited and reflected in the educational system in which education and the dominant caste were synonymous; Blacks and Indians were not participants in education. We were objects of study. In this way, all values and cultural contributions were made invisible; education, far from being a cohesive element for the distinct groups forming the new nation, served to perpetuate privileges and to distance one group from another, perpetuating and strengthening prejudices which, with the passage of time, were internalized by all of the social strata and, therefore, were perceived as unquestioned facts not protected by any law, not openly manifested, but present in daily life, and which unconsciously break apart a conscious desire for the search for a national identity.

INTEGRATION OF THE BLACK MAN INTO THE COLONIAL ECONOMY AND SOCIETY

The process of integrating Blacks into the colonial economy and society constitutes one of the most important chapters for understanding the later process of acculturation and group disintegration among Blacks in colonial society. This integration into colonial economic life was favored by factors that were inserted into the nature and type of society imposed by the Spaniards. But these circumstances are also explained by the peculiar socio-cultural characteristics which were brought by the native African directly imported, on the one hand, and, on the other, the special talents possessed by the "*ladino*" Black.

Differing from other colonial powers of the epoch which found themselves in full mercantile expansion and at the beginnings of the industrial revolution undergoing very important changes in ways of thinking, Spain had only recently succeeded in leaving behind 800 years of domination by the Moors and begun to restructure the power of the nobility, although on a base of absolute monarchy. These two situations made the spirit and the mentality it carried not that of the Anglo Saxon or French pioneer, in the entrepreneurial sense, but rather that of the impoverished vagabond or the predatory adventurer, both with aspirations of grandeur and a feeling of noble and independent means with respect to work and society. These causes, which are at the very root of the European economic and social structure and of the process of differentiating and creating the nation states of Europe, permit us to understand the reason for the Spaniard's abandonment of productive practices, for his absenteeism from the estates and his inclination for a soft and luxurious life. The Blacks, as has been shown above, came from African societies where the high level reached in agriculture, mining, and manufacturing, afforded them a rapid adaptation to the western system of production which the aboriginal populations, due to their collective sense of property and work, to their cultural resistance and other factors, were reluctant to perform. On the other hand, the long contact between *"ladinos"* and Spaniards had facilitated the adaptation of the Black man to Spanish habits and customs and to the assumption by the Spaniards of many African techniques and practices, a process initiated in Spain itself.

Within this context, the integration of Blacks into colonial economic life was rapid and decisive. In fact, many diverse productive labors fell to the Blacks and to their descendants in the colonial economy. One of the productive sectors which depended almost completely on slave labor was that of agriculture. Along the breadth and width of the Peruvian coast, agriculture rested on the work of African slaves who, due to their knowledge of African agricultural techniques, sustained its functioning, although, one must add, because of the characteristics of the colonial economy, the techniques and process of productive organization in the countryside were performed on a basis of western techniques. In that sense, three agricultural products (imported by Europeans) acquired special emphasis: sugar cane, the grape vine and the olive. These demanded a constant influx of African slaves and constituted the essential elements of agricultural production on the *haciendas* (estates). Agriculture, a labor oriented to satisfying the subsistence needs of the vice-royalty, did not acquire a monoculture character although, upon developing, it tended to regional specialization. Thus, from the narrow valleys of the north coast to Chancay, they specialized preferably in the cultivation of sugar cane; meanwhile, in the valleys of the central coast, those of Canete, Chincha and Ica, was developed the basic production of the grape vine (very tied to the winemaking industry); more to the south, the cultivation of olives was prevalent.

But, agricultural production was not circumscribed only to labor on the large estates. In the city, there was an important development of products of *"panllevar"* and fruits from orchard gardens and small family farms, all private property. A peculiar aspect of coastal agriculture was the work carried out by the Jesuits who organized important agricultural enterprises on the monastic lands under their control. It was on these large estates that the work of the slaves bore its best fruits. Many times the work of the slave became cloaked with the characteristics of day workers, given the absenteeism of the estate owners, the practical handing over of the administration of the estate to black stewards and the handing over to the slave of family parcels of land for his own subsistence. This impressed on slavery in the countryside distinct and very special nuances. However, here it is necessary to state an important caveat. The living conditions of the rural slave were totally precarious and subhuman; he found himself in conditions worse than those of the rest of his brothers in the cities. The subsequent crisis in coastal agriculture and the resultant deepening of the worst living conditions of the slaves in these zones explain in great measure the significant presence of rural slaves forming part of "*palenques*," bands of runaways, and even their integration into the great Andean resistance movements and the later independence movements of the Creoles. Finally, one of the factors intimately tied to this agricultural crisis was the increase in the demand for Black slaves which resulted in increased prices for slaves and the depreciation of land property. In addition, at the height of the 18th century, the agricultural slave became indispensable for the cultivation of alfalfa for the feeding of herds of horses and mules. With respect to cattle raising, the number of Black slaves was very large. The north was dedicated to the raising of goats, in the central area to raising pigs, and in Lima to horses and cattle.

In the cities, Blacks assumed many functions. In industry, they were prominent in the construction of temples, houses, hospitals, and convents. Equally, the presence of the Black man in the craft industries, like shoemaking, pottery, leather work, was systematically increasing. In the area of services, he participated as dock worker, sailor on ships, herder, watchman, militiaman, water vendor, etc. It was especially in domestic service that he was outstanding for his own special touches; above all, the Black woman was important for her role as acculturator and as transculturator. We will return to this point later.

In retail commerce also the slave was successful in making strong inroads. Black food sellers and street vendors were able, through these activities, to introduce to our Peruvian popular cuisine tasty dishes of African origin. In medicine and pharmacy, the Black slave was nurse, "latin doctor," etc. These multiple opportunities for advancement and social mobility were a detriment to the integration of Blacks as a group even though they opened doors for personal mobility.

Seen globally, colonial society presents itself as a society of noble outline with marked characteristics of slavery which followed the general model and pattern of Hispanic societies in America; thus we will avoid the troublesome road of dredging up the model for state division and for the castes which derived from that division; instead, we will proceed with issues of greater interest.

In Peru, one's attention is drawn to the growing number of freemen and emancipated slaves which will gradually come to equal the number of slaves. On the other hand, the increasing opportunities for employment permitted the entrance of a significant number of Blacks–along with indigenous people and poor whites–to the middle class, with such prestigious professions as medicine, cabinet-making, and others.

But undoubtedly, racial mixing and massive acculturation were the two distinct characteristics of colonialism in Peru, due to their depth and their consequences. It is sufficient to see the explosive increase, in the census, in the so-called mixed or cross-breeds in order to have an idea of its magnitude.

Racial mixing was a fact to be combatted at the official level but was, in real terms, even impelled by the conqueror himself. Let us not forget that the conquest was a military enterprise of men, such that the coming together of the white man and the native woman, especially the Black woman, came about spontaneously and increasingly. In the same way, the disproportionate number of men in the Black population pushed the African male towards the native woman, although many times these relations were clandestine and with much fewer prerogatives than those of the white conqueror. Because of its extra-legal nature, interethnic sexual relations were principally under the condition of concubinage; thus racial mixing made it difficult to define the limits which separated one person from another and made possible rapid social mobility for the Black and his consequent acculturation. In this process of acculturation and racial mixing, the Black woman fulfilled a prominent role and served as a courier for transmission between the Blacks and whites of the values of both groups. This fact awakened in them strong affective ties which emanated from similar cultural characteristics. A key issue to point out is that motivated by distinct sociophysical causes, Spaniards and Blacks tended towards rapprochement. The conquest had united them, asymmetrically, in a "common" military enterprise that undoubtedly contributed to forging these ties. But contributing also to this result was the paternalistic mentality of the white man and the irresistible desire of many Blacks for social ascendancy, a situation that accentuated their servility and faithfulness to whites. Finally, these situations were influenced as well by feelings of inferiority on the part of Blacks and of superiority on that of whites.

This institutional picture would be incomplete if we did not add the strict control of the social and affective life of the Black by the conqueror. By means of many ordinances, documents and legal mechanisms, the most minor detail of Black life was regulated. The feelings of insecurity among the Spaniards in the face of a possible Black uprising, of an Indian-African rebellion, or an alliance among Blacks, corsairs, pirates and overseas enemy powers tormented them. Thus the existence of our Black ancestors took place between work and the most absolute social rigidity, between the whip and sermons.

One of the most important accomplishments of colonial society was having wisely combined reward and punishment, fidelity and betrayal, deceit and authority; these ideological and psycho-social resources were their preferred weapons of social control, weapons which through time have demon-strated their efficacy.

Because of these circumstances the presence of the descendants of Africans was marked by the systematic violation of his most basic rights and by the permanent rupture of the individual from the group, from self-affirmation and esteem, with the consequent disintegration of the foundations of his personal and group identity. Faced with these conditions, we had to develop different forms of response according to the existing historical conditions and the resources we had at hand. Thus, our ancestors employed different forms of resistance, be they active or passive, active and passive in the face of ferocious persecution of his beliefs and cultural practices, of group disintegration and the nullification of his liberty. During all this period there appeared and developed runaways, bandits, palenqueros, militiamen, independents, etc. who, with the use of violence, proposed to recapture their lost freedom. This option, however, was the option of a minority of Blacks, since the majority made passive resistance their principal weapon of struggle. It camouflaged their religious beliefs, it imbued music and coastal dance with the African spirit; with its empiricism it changed medicine and popular cuisine, and made of the instability of the family a life style which extended itself in society. The greatest act of resistance by Blacks is to have impregnated with their values a society that discriminated against them, thus making a contribution to the new culture of our country. We could call it the Black cultural contribution, a contribution from resistance. This resistance was a collective action; brotherhoods and councils were its purest expression.

INDEPENDENCE AND EMANCIPATION

In spite of the Black man having been one of the protagonists of national independence obtained in 1821-1824, his situation did not change. His fight for liberty was of greater dimension than the national struggle: having a nationalistic content, the fight of the Black man related more to the struggle for social democracy. The establishment of the Republic and the abolition of slavery did not change the placement of the Black man in the social pyramid. The scarce possibilities for advancement and a series of prejudices and racial stereotypes continued to befall him, for the reasons we have summarily outlined. In the social sphere, this was expressed in that the Afro-Peruvian continued to carry out the same activities as in the previous period. If before we were coachman for the owner, we came to be, during the Republic, the chauffer of white or mestizo patrons. We were bricklayers, street vendors, unskilled labor, domestic servants, etc. In the cities, we continued to reside in alleys and hovels and, finally, in periferal districts, districts which in accordance with the euphemism launched by the military reformism of "*velasquismo*" were baptized as "youth towns." In the countryside, we lived in the most depressed and backward zones, laboring as peons, muleteers, estate cooks, etc. In the cultural sphere, our traditions were termed "negroid" folklore, separating it from the new emerging national culture. In the educational field, we continue to form the majority portion of illiterates in the country.

In this frame of institutionalized repression, the Black had to redefine his response strategies, denying itself as a group, directing his aggression against himself, consolidating the process of depersonalization. Group disintegration began during colonial times; Blacks opted for racial mixing as a means to "whitening" and social ascendancy. Thus transfigurated and changed into one more amongst the "citizenry," his existence began to be denied by the entire society and by the Black man himself. The myth of racial democracy took shape. Since the 1930s and, even more, since the second world war, the situation began to change. In the cities, especially in Lima, arose some partial experiences which are nevertheless important: The group "Harlem de la Victoria" appeared as well as the nucleus of the "*melamodernos*"–greatly influenced by the important efforts to organize among Blacks in other countries (USA, Brazil, etc.); in the rural zones, Black towns and communities appeared and began to value their local identity upon perceiving themselves as communities of African descendants; such is the case of Yapatera (Piura), Zaña (Chiclayo) in the northern zone; of Aucullama and Cañete on the central coast and that of Chincha in the southern zone.

In Lima, little by little, these experiences began to lead to a certain "benevolent tolerance" in the face of "rowdiness" and

"Black crudity." The resistance of Blacks had achieved some victories, but the struggle continues. It continues because the same pressures and characteristics that typify their daily experience in the country continue. The old judgements of prejudice and discrimination continue and the Black man himself is not capable, neither individually nor collectively, of going beyond the limits of integration and participation that society has assigned to him. Towards the 1960s, Lima was the scene of a series of attempts tending to visualize in the best manner the contributions of the Black to Peruvian society and culture. An important movement was consolidated for the revaluation of the Black contribution to national folklore, especially the coastal folklore, headed by Nicomedes and Victoria Santa Cruz. Although on a small scale, the studies of Blacks carried out by doctors Emilio Hart Terre and Fernando Romero were disseminated. Novels were read where Black characters were beginning to appear, in the papers and magazines were published works like those of Juan Jose Vega, Luis Millones and others.

The margins of participation in universities and educational centers had been broadened such that, at the end of the decade, the cultural Association of Black Peruvian Youth arose. This entity is formed by young Afro-Peruvian university students who propose to carry forth activities for the benefit of the Black race. The ACEJUNEP proposes as well to carry out a diagnosis of the social historical and cultural reality of the Black in Peru.

Thus, after 450 years, we find ourselves forming part of a country and a continent that still refuses to recognize that in us Blacks their own future is in large measure determined. If at one time we were "compulsory conquerors" ("*a palos*"), today we are "America in Tears."

NOTES

* Translated by Tanya Saunders Hamilton.

BIBLIOGRAPHY

Aguirrre Beltrán, Gonzalo. *Cuijla. Esbozo etnografico de un pueblo negro.* Fondo de Cultura Economics. Mexico, 1958.

Bastide, Roger. *Las Americas Negras.* Las civilizaciones africanas del nuevo mundo. Alianza Editorial, Espana, 1969.

Bowser, Frederick. *El esclavo africano en el Peru colonial (1524-1650.)* Siglo Veintiuno Editores S.A., Mexico, 1977.

Carrera Damaas, German. "El dominador cautivo." *Revista Nacional de Cultura,* Caracas, Venezuela, 1985.

Millones Santagadea, Luis. *Minorias etnicas en el Peru.* Pontificia Universidad Catolica del Peru. Lima 1973.

Montoya, Rodrigo. *Capitalismo y no capitalismo en el Peru. Un estudio historico de su articulacion en un eje regional.* Mosca Azul Editorial, Lima, 1980.

Moreno Fraginals, Manuel. *Africa en America Latins.* Compilador Siglo Veintiuno Editores S.A., Mexico, 1977.

Moreno Fraginals, Manuel. *El Ingenio,* Tomos I, II, III, Editorial de Ciencias Sociales, La Habana, 1978.

Rocca Torres, Luis. "La Otra Historia" (Memoria colectiva y canto del pueblo de ana). Instituto de Apoyo Agrario Editores, 1985.

UNESCO. *Introduction a la cultura africana en America Latin.* Compilador, Salvador Bueno, Organizacion de las Naciones Unidas, para la educacion, la ciencia y la cultura. Belgica, 1979.

Urfe, Odilio. "La musica y la danza en Cuba." *En Africa en America Latina.* Compilador, Moreno Fraginals, Manuel. Siglo Veintiuno Editores S.A., 1977. Zahar, Renate. *Colonialismo y Enajenacion. Contribucion a la teoria politica de Frantz Fanon.* Siglo Veintiuno Argentina Editores S.A., 1969.

THE RACE QUESTION IN COSTA RICA

Quince Duncan

THIS PAPER should be understood as a tentative reflexion on race relations in Costa Rica. It preludes ongoing studies undertaken by my colleague, Lorein Powell, and myself on the situation of the Blacks in Costa Rica. It is about racism in my country. I am totally aware that a large number of Hispanic Costa Ricans may not share the views consistently expressed by Powell and myself. So bear in mind that this is a look from the inside: that is, from the point of view of people who have suffered discrimination. For this I do not apologize whatsoever.

I

We have said elsewhere that racism is an ideology. It is the problem of the Black race. To say it another way: racism is the stumbling block in our way. Our other problems are not very different from those of other human groups. What is very specific (although not exclusive) about our struggle the world over is the question of color.

There is only one racism. But in our modern world, this phenomenon differs in the way it expresses itself from one context to the other. We have pointed out seven basic forms, but we must bear in mind that in no place does racism appear in only one form.

The classification then is basically methodological, a matter of emphasis.

Racial genocide is one of the forms in which racism expresses itself in our world. We are talking here about the massive assassination of Amerindians in Latin America, in many cases disguised as a struggle against subversion, and terrorist action against Black individuals and their families, as is the case of the National Front in England or of the Ku Klux Klan in the United States.

Racist ethnocide is another form. Practiced the world over, it consists of the systematic destruction of Black and other oppressed cultures. White culture is considered superior in every way and nonwhite cultures are stigmatized as "pagan," "savage," "primiive," "backward," and so on.

Regional segregation is another way in which racism is practiced. In Costa Rica, for example, the most depressed areas of the country are those populated by local indigenous groups and Blacks. Of course, since the basis of this regional segregation is racist, the tendency is to blame the victims. The fact is, whether it is in Latin America or in Australia, in Europe or in the United States, as a general rule, one finds proportionally more depressed non-white communities where the basic services of the state are faltering.

Psychocide is another well-extended practice of racism. It consists of the systematic degradation of the racially oppressed. Starting in the schools, by assertion or by omission, the victim is made to believe that he and his kin are "good for nothing," or "only good for" whatever that may be (sometimes sports, music, but never highly prestigious scientific fields).

Cultural segregation is another form. Adopting sometimes a very patronizing attitude, anthropologists, missionaries and tourist boards assume the "defense" of a racial minority, without consulting the people affected, on the grounds that they have the sacred right to preserve their culture. The outcome, of course, is that the university students have a source for developing research, missionaries whom to preach to, and the business men curiosities to offer.

Two other forms have been identified: *reflexive racism,* that is, a racist reaction from the interior of the racially oppressed, which sometimes, as a matter of self-defense, serves out the same dish. And *residual racism,* that is, racism which, for a number of reasons, survives in a society after revolutionary changes that were supposed to abrogate it.

II

The Caribbean Coast of Central America, or "Costa Atlantica" as Central Americans like to call it, extends from Port Barrios in Guatemala to Port Colon in Panama. As a cultural area it cuts across the political boundaries of five countries: Guatemala, Honduras, Nicaragua, Costa Rica and Panama.

Historically, one can distinguish five basic characteristics that make the area unique: the process of hispanization led by the Spanish Empire was incomplete; the population is multiracial and multiethnic; the area has a very specific form of relationship with the world market; the population ascribes by means of linguistic and other cultural traits to non-Latin cultural spheres; and the area has been subjected to segregation by the national states.

In the case of Costa Rica, the Spanish invaders and colonizers established themselves mainly on the Pacific Coast and in the Central Valley. They never completely dominated the Limon area which is on Costa Rica's Costa Atlantica. Spain never succeeded in transforming the Amerindian population into true *"mestizos."* The difficulties of the Spaniards in coping with Limon's very hostile nature and the lack of important economical stimulus, such as abundant precious metals, converted the area into a refuge for indigenous groups that settled on the Talamanca mountain and coast. This led to the survival of Amerindian culture. In evident contrast with the Central Valley, the population of Limon is racially and culturally heterogeneous. Amerindian groups share the province with Chinese, Mestizos and Afro-Caribbeans.

Another important historical factor that helps to shape the area is the specific relations that Limon has maintained with the world market. Foreign companies moved into the area, during the late

19th century, to build the railroad and to plant bananas, cacao, and other produce. The economical and social relation that developed out of this plantation economy is very specific. For example, the second world war meant immediate depression for the national economy of Costa Rica, owing to the fact that the country lost its European coffee markets (England and Germany). For the "*limonenses*" it meant prosperity, as they produced rubber and "*abaca*" fiber for the American Army.

Taken as a whole, the Costa Atlantica has a culture of its own, distinct from that of the rest of the country. In some ways, there is much more in common between a "*limonense*" from Costa Rica and a "*costeno*" from Nicaragua than there is between a "*limonense*" and his San Jose countryman.

III

This reality presents us with the first problem in considering the race question in Costa Rica: what portion of reactions observed can be blamed on racism and what portion is a product of ethno-centrism?

On the one hand, we have a fairly well defined population in the interior of the country: the white mestizo is culturally Hispanic. Outside of Limon, the hispanization process was successful.

As mentioned above, Amerindians took refuge in the Talamanca mountains to avoid or minimize the effect of Spanish conquest and so managed to hold on to their culture. The Blacks and Chinese were later brought in to build the railroads and to grow bananas, plantains and cocoa. The Chinese came mainly from Canton, while the Blacks were predominantly Jamaican.

There was a moment when more than 50 percent of the Limonese population was West Indian. In Limon, Jamaicans repro-duced rural Jamaica and abided by the laws of their homeland, except when forced by the local government to do otherwise. Although Limon was officially under the rule of Costa Rica, for all practical reasons, it was a British colony. For example, Black babies were registered by their parents with the British Consulate as late as the 1940s. The Jamaican population made very little effort to learn Spanish, which they contemptuously considered "bird language" because of the more frontal articulation of that language in comparison to English.

The school system was British. Books were imported from England and teachers from Jamaica as late as the early 1950s. The dominant religion was Protestant while the rest of the country was predominantly Roman Catholic. Black people in Limon considered themselves to be Jamaican even if they were born in the very capital of Costa Rica.

Since in Costa Rica, for more than a 100 years, schooling has been obligatory, Black children were hidden when the local authorities took the annual census to enroll them in Spanish schools. Local Hispanic culture was looked down upon and the local population was termed by the immigrants as "Spanish" or, scornfully, as "*pana*" (pania). So, although the Caribbean Coast has always been an Hispano-Afro-Indo-Oriental combination, the dominant culture was Black with close ties to the British Empire and to the American economy; the area was basically a plantation economy enclave, with its "Northern Railway Co. of Costa Rica," "United Fruit Company," and so on.

The national state, as well as national public opinion, was non-sympathetic to Blacks. As early as 1862, the law of "Bases y Colonias" prohibited the colonization of the country by Chinese and African "races," while establishing a fund of 100,000 pesos yearly to stimulate the immigration of white Europeans (La *Gaceta:* 11.8.1862).

Although the lack of sufficient labor supply forced the Costa Rican Government to authorize the introduction of Chinese and Blacks, racist policy continued consistently. Antonio Maceo, the Cuban mulatto national hero, while living as a refugee in Costa Rica, solicited and received authorization from the Costa Rican government to introduce 100 Cuban families into the Nicoya region. The first article of the contract said that the immigrants should be of the white race and that only with specific authorization from the government could he do otherwise (Contrato VIII, 5.13.1891).

These restrictions were constantly ratified in Costa Rican legislation. As late as 1942, migration legislation expressly established a list of forbidden subjects, among these:

> Raza negra, chinos, arabes, sirios, gitanos, coolies... delincuentes, profugos o impedidos mentales ... (Decreto Ejecutivo N.4 4.26.1942. Article 41).[1]

In 1936, the Municipality of Limon prohibited the use of a public pool by the Black population. The justification given was that the presence of the Blacks reduced rentability, because "white" people would not use it if Blacks were around.

Along with legislation went social discriminatory practices. Paula Palmer in her folk history of Costa Rica's Talamanca Coast, *What Happen,* registers testimonies of elder Jamaicans about discrimination in hotels and public places. Although discriminatory laws were abolished by the Revolutionary Government headed by José Figueres in 1948, as late as 1966, there was an attempt to prevent the Black Carnaval Queen from entering one of Limon's hotels to attend an invitation for dinner with the President of Costa Rica.

IV

Anti-Black articles constantly appeared in the national newspapers. One of the most overt was published in 1930 by *La Tribuna.* Signed by José Guerrero, a former congressman, the article calls the attention of Costa Ricans to the problem of the growing Black population. According to him, Costa Rica had progressed because of its racial unity.

> El negro es la sombra del banano. La extracion del oro verde no puede prescindir de ese elemento humano pot razones de lengua, de sumision y de obediencia ... propia de una raza primitiva como en realidad es; por ausencia de un ideal etico e historico que no pone en el inquietudes de

libertad y dominio que se reemplaza por actitudes religiosas, supersticiones y diversiones infantiles (8.13.1930).[2]

What Guerrero omitted is that it was with Black labor that Costa Rica built its important railway to the Caribbean Sea, boosting the country's coffee exportation which, even today, is the main produce. He also forgot to say that the other two main Costa Rican products, banana and cacao, were then produced by Black labor. One could extend this list to include ecological preservation of the region, in contrast to the typical devastation by peasants of the interior, and many other contributions of the Black people who Guerrero so ardently despised. But, the point here is to illustrate the strong anti-Black ideology that was shared by large sectors of the Hispanic population.

Now and then in the Costa Rican press, one can read articles that are clearly racist and ethnocentric. For example, in La Nacion, Ing. José Montero Gomez expresses his concern over the possibility of acceptance by the Costa Rican government of Indochinese refugees. A good Costa Rican, he says, should defend the purity of "our" white race.

> un buen costarricense no debe pensar jamas en desmejorar nuestra raza blanca, sin rasgos negroides, orientales o indios (1.13.1979).[3]

There were some reactions to his article in the Hispanic community. Lic. Oscar Cruz Salazar reacted in *La Nacion,* a few days later, (1.21.1979) in defense of the Black community's contribution to Costa Rica, while ridiculing Montero Gomez's racist comments.

And in October of 1986, another of the main newspapers of Costa Rica, *La Republica* in a section called "Aprendamos," directed to children in the school system, published an article which one would dare to affirm is a vulgarization of 18th century Linneo or 19th century Chamberlain. The article sustained that white people are much more intelligent than Blacks because of their larger brains. This is the sort of vulgar racism that one would not expect to come across these days. But what is much more troublesome is the fact that La *Republica* simply ignored my protest. No rectification was ever made.

V

Literature was one of the sources used to propagate racist stereotypes. Lic. Lorein Powell has demonstrated in her licenciatura dissertation the degree to which racist ideas are entrenched in Costa Rican fiction. Comparing William Faulkner's *Sartoris* with Carlos Luis Fallas' *Mamita Yunai* and Joaquin Gutierrez's *Cocori,* she points out eleven derogatory stereotypes commonly associated with the Black race. Table 1 illustrates her findings.

TABLE 1

STEREOTYPE	BOOKS		
	Cocori	Sartoris	Mamita Yunai
Primitivism or bestiality	X	X	X
Lust	X		X
Perversity	X	X	
Cowardness	X		X
Submisiveness		X	X
Stupidity		X	X
Buffoonery	X		X
Servility	X	X	X
Non-aesthetic		X	
Laziness		X	X
Identity crisis		X	
Totals	6	8	8

Source: Powell, Lorein, 1985

As observed, *Cocori* rivals *Sartoris* in the number of stereotypes used to describe or refer to Black characters or to speak about Black people. The results may not seem too surprising when one becomes aware of the fact that both Costa Rican books were written during the 1940s. Therefore, it is tempting to say that in Costa Rica, at least in literature, racism is a thing of the past. But, unfortunately, racism continues to be a part of the national ideology. Lorein Powell's more recent work provides evidence of similar racist overtones in such books as Roberto Rivera Mena's *Costa Atlantica,* a collection of short stories published in 1980. The author, claiming himself to be a Limonese, uses the same old myths in his fiction. *Costa Atlantica's* performance is shown in Table 2.

TABLE 2

STEREOTYPE	Costa Atlantica
Primitivism or bestiality	X
Lust	X
Perversity	X
Cowardness	
Submisiveness	
Buffoonery	
Servility	
Non-asethetic	
Laziness	X
Identity crisis	
Drug addition	X
TOTAL	5

Source: Powell, Lorein, 1985. Unpublished.
It is interesting to point out that Riveria
includes a new element: drug addition.

VI

At present, there are no discriminatory laws in the country regarding Black citizens. After a petition was made by Congress, the current government cut off diplomatic relations with South Africa. Costa Rica takes pride in its democratic ideology based on such things as free elections, social security, political purality. The Matron of the Country, Our Lady of the Angels, sprung out of the Black-Hispanic tradition of "*pardos*" of Cartago, one of the main cities, and is proudly and very popularly referred to as "*Negrita*," which is an affectionate term for Black woman or Black girl.

Discrimination is practiced on the basis of class in some exclusive private clubs. But, there are very few Blacks in the higher class, not enough to really test the system. In the daily life of the common people, while one can identify a degree of racial prejudice, there is no social prestige in being overtly racist and there is no evidence that mixed children suffer any particular stigma.

But in two other areas this ambiguity vanishes to give way to strong racist feelings: one is regional discrimination against Limon. Although the Black population in the province is no longer the majority, because of Latino immigration and Black migration, Limon is still considered to be the Black man's territory. It is the most depressed area in the country, although it produces a huge part of the national income.

The other area is related to competition for certain positions. There are numbers of testimonies to support the assertion that people are apparently non-racist until a Black person gets the key job. Some years ago, when a prominent Black university professor ran for Rector of the University of Costa Rica, a number of his colleagues openly said that they did not vote for him because they feel that "Black Costa Ricans are not quite ready for the job," in spite of the fact that the candidate has a Ph.D. from a very prestigious university in the United States.

So, I think it is safe to say that while there is no evidence of racial genocide, all other forms of racism are actively present in Costa Rica.

NOTES

1. "Blacks, Chinese, Arabs, Syrians, gypsies, coolies ... delinquents, fugitives or the mentally impaired ..." (Executive Decree, Number 4 4.26.1942. Article 41).

2. "The black man is the shadow of the banana tree. The extraction of green gold cannot do without that human element for reasons of language, submission and obedience ... characteristic of a primitive race which in reality it is; due to the absence of an ethical and historical ideal which does not imbue him with concerns for liberty and power but is replaced with religious attitudes, superstitions and childish diversions" (8.13.1930).

3. "A good Costa Rican should never think of damaging our white race with negroid, oriental or Indian characteristics" (1.1 3.1979).

BIBLIOGRAPHY

Powell, Lorein, *Lectura (en crisis) de ires obras racistas.* (licentiatura dissertation). Heredia, Costa Rica: Universidad Nacional, 1985.

Palmer, Paula. *What Happen. A Folk History of Costa Rica's Talamanca Coast.* San Jose: Ecodesarrollos, 1977.

Adler, Elizabeth, Quince Duncan and others. *Justice for Aboriginal Australians.* Geneva: Programme to combat racism, 1981.

Duncan, Quince and Carlos Melendez. *El Negro en Costa Rica.* San Jose, Costa Rica: Editorial Costa Rica, 1987.

Duncan, Quince. "Identicos o diversos. Factores de etnia, raza y nacion en la construcion del pueblo latinoamericano." In Raul Vidales y Luis Rivera Pagan, editores, *La esperanza en el presente de America Latina.* San Jose, Costa Rica: Dei, 1983.

Duncan, Quince. "Apuntes para una teoria general del racismo" and "Racismo, Iglesia y Teologia." In, Quince Duncan and others, eds., *Cultura Negra y Teologia.* San Jose, Costa Rica: Dei, 1986.

CONSIDERATIONS ON THE LIFE OF THE BLACKS IN ECUADOR*

ANTONIO PRECIADO BEDOYA

T HERE DOES not exist among those who study the subject definitive agreement concerning certain aspects of the life of the Black man in our country. The discrepancies, especially with respect to certain details of an historical nature, frequently expressed in writing and at conferences, give rise to the permanent currency of those old dissensions.

In the brevity of these pages the various divergent discussions will not fit. These concern the arrival of the Black slaves to what is now Ecuadorian territory; the exact locations in Africa with respect to anthropological peculiarities and socioeconomic circumstances occurring during the colonial and republic periods; and, above all, the passionate discussion between those who maintain that in Esmeraldas, the coastal province which constitutes the principal seat of negritude in Ecuador, contrary to what happened in many other places in the mountain range, there was no slavery during Spanish domination because the Blacks ran away and set up in the dense jungles of Esmeraldas a kingdom of liberty which never could be conquered, and those who allege the existence of numerous slaves in various gold mines and plantations of the region. In summary, for many long years the rumor has prevailed, repeated in other American countries, that a slave ship was wrecked on the Esmeraldas coast, a circumstance of which the slaves took advantage in order to escape to the dense jungle and to found a kingdom they knew how to preserve, repelling the constant attacks of the Spaniards.

To this very much spread about version has been opposed the reasoning that the shipwreck is just a story. This pejorative reasoning hides the zeal of always, in this case as in other countries where it is maintained without the support necessary for credibility, to negate tendentiously the capacity of the Black man to organize and take appropriate and opportune decisive actions in order to achieve his liberty.

Generally, it has been accepted, with proof from irrefutable documents, that the kingdom of free Blacks existed in a part of the province of Esmeraldas. Without ignoring or obscuring this traditional source of pride for the people of Esmeraldas, a symbol of the turbulent and completely free character of our people which has been effectively confirmed in subsequent important moments in Ecuadorian history, young Black researchers, among whom Juan Garcia stands out, have succeeded in proving that especially in the northern zone of Esmeraldas territory, towards the boundaries with Colombia, a considerable number of Blacks were apportioned among slave holdings and subject to the most inhuman oppression. However, the controversy concerning this matter persists. To those representing the new position, the denial of this important aspect of our past reality by those who already know of the supporting documents that have been rescued with great conscientiousness and who plead for the triumph of something which cannot be sustained implies an eagerness to affirm a false *integrity,* illusionary on this point. Concomitantly, this distances us from truthful judgements of our past reality which are useful for a more objective interpretation of the present and for the consequent derivation of accurate operational judgements needed today. Concerning which, Juan Garcia writes:

The black understood that his greater or lesser social acceptance depended, in great measure, on the degree of acceptance and assimilation that he himself demonstrated in his relations with other groups of people. It became obvious for the blacks engaged in this process of whitening that they would not secure any benefit by publicly acknowledging their former social condition, since the remembrance of slavery was a hindrance to their objective, and any person with social ambitions, by all means possible, would distance himself from any act that might associate him with the memory of slavery and with his African heritage.

With respect to the places of origin of the Black slaves brought to Ecuador, according to the census carried out by the Royal Tribunal of Ecuador in 1780, there were 18,000 slaves; recent studies of cultural parallels indicate with high probability that our forebears were exiled to these lands from the regions of Zaire, Ruanda and Angola.

It would be pointless to refer here to the well known fact that the emancipations which took place in some American countries in no way meant a substantial change in the fate of the Black man; he continued to be oppressed with almost identical violence by the classes which inherited political and economic power after the wars of independence in which the Black man also perseveringly participated.

Independence was proclaimed in Ecuador on the 24th of May in 1822. Thus was initiated the slow process of decolonization, a process entangled in a cultural continuity in the Spanish style inherent in almost everything: institutions, customs, tastes, aesthetic preferences, the overwhelming weight of religious pressures and, among other things, the sustained estimation of the Black man as cheap labor.

That continuity, the successive interlinking of forms of domination adapted to new historical circumstances for the purpose of achieving the material and psychological effects desired, the invariable placement of the Black man in the most backward economic sectors, the oppressive overlapping of pains and frustrations accumulated during more than a century after independence, resulted in establishing for the Black man, as an unconscious collective fate, an undoubted sense of inferiority which still has not disappeared. In those individuals belonging to the smaller populations of Blacks located in the two small warm valleys of the inter-Andes region, this circumstance has always been more apparent, more visible, more observable; the Black people of these places are to this day silent, bowing, and submissive in the face of contempt and mistreatment from the white man. As a community, *"comunitariamente,"* they live in a gregariousness closed in upon itself, impenetrable even for those of us Blacks who are not from these communities, that is, the Blacks from Esmeraldas who have different characteristic features, greater pride, and more easy and joyful communication. Perhaps the attitude of the mountain Blacks can be explained as a response to the so different and asphyxiating cultural and environmental pressures with which their lives have been enclosed and as a form of gathering in solidarity in the face of a painful and growing impoverishment.

If in Esmeraldas the situation has not reached the stage described in previous lines with respect to other places in the country, I cannot affirm that we Blacks (in Esmeraldas) have lived without socioeconomic and cultural problems. On the contrary, these problems have been always very serious, only they have acquired a special configuration which relates to ecology, historical antecedents, and a facade of permanent joy which has covered up during the course of years the basic dramatic situation of our existence.

The majority of the Black Ecuadorian minority is from Esmeraldas, a province in the northwest of Ecuador, a verdant land with lush vegetation and beautiful landscapes. Esmeraldas fundamentally defines that which is Black in Ecuador.

During colonial times, Alonso Sebastian de Yllescas, from Cabo Verde, became the first Black leader of the originating group and succeeded in completely imposing his authority and domination on the natives of the region. In 1589, the priest Juan de Salas entered the Esmeraldas jungles and found that the Blacks there lived in a permanent state of aggressiveness and that their ferocity was such, as noted an historian, that they called their land "land of war." It would take time to recount the history in which the Black from Esmeraldas appears ardently defending his liberty throughout colonial times or to try to reevaluate here our contribution to the social and political struggles to rescue and maintain that liberty.

During the entire republican epoch, our province has been kept by all the succeeding governments in the most apathetic abandonment, in spite of its great natural resources, and exploited within a typical framework of agricultural exportation. Products of the jungle like rubber, ivory nut, balsa wood, etc. were exported for a long time to Europe and to the United States. During the decade of the 1950s and the first quarter of the 1960s, the great banana bust took place when great extensions of the fertile cultivated land were dedicated to the sole cultivation of that fruit. Sudden drops in demand in the international markets caused the ruin of hundreds of peasants who had dedicated all of their efforts to this product and had indebted themselves to state credit organizations.

THE GREAT YEARS

It was when they told us
that this one was the paradise reserved
for when the rains
exhausted the heavens.
And more rains fell,
and more rains,
and in the midst of the rains we waited
absorbed,
indecisive,
with open mouths,
as if perhaps God, in the rain,
were crying.
It was the words that rained on us,
and the words that flourished,
and they told us that we had
the most blossoming land of the universe,
as if even from each tomb

new cemeteries would germinate.
Thus we were overwhelmed with words,
thus abundance gave us a sudden shock,
and at the precise time,
the moment at the height of nausea,
they spoke of the banana tree,
of destiny,
of a full belly,
of a contented heart,
and we swallowed the lie green,
and our dreams turned green,
green the voice,
green what was said,
green the banana grove green the time,
and green was the pain of the peasant,
green was the naive
anonymous finger that he placed
at the foot of outrage.
Black are my fears,
green are my memories
now that the land insists on my throbbings,
each time much closer
like the premonition
that I am one of those who understand
all they have truly done to us.
The land in me does not cease
and, palpitating,
turns and turns again inside me.
Therefore I have land at my side.
Therefore, I want to be more at its side,
and one of these days, my heart,
I sow the seed of my self.

This crisis in the agricultural sector has been the motivation in recent years for a large migration of the peasant population towards urban centers, in large part towards Guayaquil, the most populous city and the principal commercial center of the country;

but especially towards the city of Esmeraldas, capital of the province, where that great offer of labor has not been able to be absorbed. The consequence is a tremendous picture of unemployment and misery.

The major occupation of the peasants today is the exploitation of the forests rich in fine woods, by which they turn themselves into victims of exploitation by the great purchasing companies who pay insignificant prices; in addition, little by little, they are being dispossessed by the large concessions to powerful wood enterprises which oblige them to become salaried farm workers, poorly paid by the nearby estates.

POEM OF SOLIDARITY

The mountain, in the distance,
almost is remotely imaginary,
something like the countryside
which the clouds sketch in the sky.
Roughly and in passing
vaguely one knows
that, everything up above, the trees are good,
and thus no longer is a rubber tree shade,
and the whitish laurels hang,
like phosphorescences,
from the placid moons of memory.
So far away are things,
a hard knock is only an echo,
the weeks rot in the land for no one,
no ax blow pursues his dream,
because so much in the distance
and only roughly and in passing
the woodcutters are not seen in the background.
But let's get to the point
with women,
with children,
brothers,
cousins,

> uncles,
> and then,
> for example, put yourselves in my place
> and fuck life
> in the noon sun that falls on the violent
> greenness,
> guiltless,
> without involvement,
> on edge,
> no matter how uselessly one turns to verse,
> to see if in this part of the poem one doesn't
> get splinters,
> and whether so close, a true pain doesn't hurt
> you along with me.

In general, the Esmeraldas peasant has always exploited the environment through individual physical strength or social cooperation. The people live within an oppressive subsistence economy with forms of cooperation and reciprocity that are formally inscribed. As much in the rural environment as in the outskirts of the city, made up primarily of persons of peasant extraction, social cohesion has transferred the traditional habits from the rural communities. It is based on the gregarious strength of kinship and in productive activities since, of necessity, the people form nuclei in which ties of mutual assistance function.

The joy of a Black from Esmeraldas, evident in a compensatory festive spirit, does not really hide the gravity of the drama that is not dance but suffered. Among us, unemployment and poverty have been tied to the effects of a poorly disguised discrimination practiced for a long time by the non-Black minority, the owners of the principal means of production, possessors of political power, privileges and supposedly worthy values. Traditionally, richness has been identified with the white man; poverty, the most menial jobs, that which is despicable are identified with the Black man.

This caused a collective psychological picture which has involved even the desire to escape his real and objective human condition. That history, that subtle current of inferiority has been frequently expressed by Black women upon saying: "I want to improve the race," referring to the advantage of having children by a white man, in the subconscious desire to avoid the self, to approximate oneself to that which is valued in society, in the illusionary search for a personal source of pride, for another status. Nevertheless, the Esmeraldan Black has never accepted verbal aggression, physical abuse or any type of personal humiliation arising from color.

In recent decades the composition of the Esmeraldas population has experienced important changes with the presence of many Blacks from other provinces of the country and, to a lesser extent, from abroad. Those from the country of Ecuador are generally poor, small farmers or businessmen, artisans and under-employed workers who share the fate of the majority of Blacks. Thus they have created ties based on class, trade or family solidarity, since inter-ethnic unions, whether matrimonial or free, are more frequent; and if before, at the extreme of contradiction, that which was poor and inferior was identified solely with Blacks, these categories have been expanded today to embrace those new marginalized sectors which are joining with Esmeraldans in a broad current of active participation in the common fight for popular recovery.

The creation and operation of the University of Esmeraldas, and the attendance of youth from the broadest popular sectors, generated a movement which has obliged the redefining of the foundation of social prestige. Concomitantly, there has been growing strength in the recovery and affirmation of our cultural identity, a lively collective sentiment of human dignity that impels us to demand that to which we feel we have the right.

The thought that is becoming fixed with penetrating analytical power confronts the penning of our people in arbitrary concepts, convenient to the interests which weigh down our pain. This thought of young intellectuals pokes around in the duplicities of our reality and shapes theoretical proposals that aim for the recuperation and revaloration of all that has been swindled from us, in the clarifying light of the truths recently revealed, and animates the youth with the ferment of the ages, drunk suddenly now from our own profound springs.

Of course, throughout the time of the republic we have been the object of waves of acculturation and of deculturation; but we have found desperate handholds of cultural survival which have permitted us to safeguard a good part of our values, from food uses to artistic expression like the music of the marimba, an instrument similar to the African "*rongo*," which is played accompanied by other percussive instruments like the "*bombo*," the "*cununo*" and the "*guasa*" and produces a vertex of ecstatic warmth.

Anonymous, popular, oral poetry, the "*decima*," continues to express in witty and brilliantly improvised octosylables that un-learned secular root of our people in different thematic streams that go from verses of erotic impishness to those of political content, covering a rich gamut of subjects and circumstances.

The practice of religious syncretism, in which are inextricably unified that which is Christian with ancestral elements appropriate to negritude, has been evident in Esmeraldas. Typical examples of that symbiosis are the "*arrullos*" and the "*chigualos*," songs in which are mixed religious sentiment and the condensations of oral poetry in order to praise the baby Jesus [arrullo] or say goodbye to a dead child [chigualos], all sustained by an overwhelming emotion.

Longtime cultural interactions, aggressions and defenses contributed to a sedimentary mixture in which we are an "indelible stain," in the sense of our contribution to the integrative process which today is conceived of as that plural unity of crossbreeding in a multinational and multicultural country such as ours. Within this plurality fits the visible and secretive micro-world that is particularly our own, but also part of a greater reality which contains it and to which it finds itself inextricably united, to the historic moment which today all of us here live; and it obliges us to gather together, to look at each other through the transparency in which we coincide, and to move forward together. We carry all that is ours to that encounter. We carry grandparents, dust from the road, drums, blood, pains and joys. We go with open arms. We already have embraced those who are known. We have a presentiment of those unknown.

In the midst of the oppressive reality that we live, I believe that we should be cohesive and not divisive, to the extent that objective reality with all its implications permits. I think that one can, being oneself and without denying oneself, leave one's parcel of land for the necessary encounter with others, with whites, Indians, those of mixed race, with all men who suffer and make up the mass of anonymous beings who raise their inseparable voices with their unmistakable reasons. We, the Blacks, contribute drums so that the world always may perceive its definitive resonances.

NOTES

* Translated by Tanya Saunders Hamilton.

RACIAL THEORY AND PRACTICE IN PANAMA*

JUSTO ARROYO

In PANAMA, a country with high racial mixing, the degrees of discrimination have been refined into gradations that approach infinity.

Writers, philosophers and singers have tried to define the Panamanian. Philosophers like Diego Dominguez Caballero, novelists like Joaquin Beleno and popular singers like Ruben Blades and Pedro Altamiranda have all tried to reach the essence of the Panamanian. What distinguishes us? What makes us distinctive? What makes us Panamanians and not Cubans or Mexicans? Could it be religion, language, race, the geographical position of the isthmus? Our gastronomic, musical, or artistic preferences? Our powerful vocal cords? Our deafness? What? What defines the "*homo panamensis*"?

Panama, because of its position in the center of America, has traditionally been a crossroad, one which acted in favor of a great religious, ideological and racial tolerance. Each of us has "passed through" Panama; therefore, all of us have a right to life. Then, with the separation from Colombia in 1907 and the construction of the inter-ocean canal, travelers began to stay. Individuals from all parts of the world began to settle down, attracted not by the climate, the history or the traditions of the country, but by a fast dollar. At that time, as in the rest of America, there were indigenous Indians, descendants of the conquistadors, descendants of Black slaves and their respective mixtures. The Indians were there, the Spaniards came voluntarily, and the Blacks were brought in chains. With the Canal came the North Americans, with their apartheid type of discrimination (but more of that later), Asians (Chinese and Hindus), Europeans, and more Blacks, the latter from the Antilles, thus giving substance to our "racial melting pot" and to our complacency with the seeming harmony of the races. But, does racial harmony truly exist in Panama?

If racial harmony is the absence of violent confrontations between the races, then the answer is yes. But if harmony is the forced and angry acceptance by one group, the Blacks, of the worse living, educational, and working conditions, the acceptance of their invisibility in 99 per cent of the activities of daily life, then the conclusion is that Panama's "racial harmony" is but an illusion. I am sure that out of five Panamanians questioned, four would be surprised even at the pertinence of the subject. "Don't we all go to any restaurant?" "Don't we all live wherever we like?" "Don't we buy in any store?" They would be surprised if the answer to all these questions were "no."

The illusion could prompt us to pose the problem as one of *class* rather than of color or race. The illusion could tell us that the Black man occupies the base of the pyramid as a result of the social system. Of course, the government of General Torrijos, with its reformist activities, would point out Black faces in the ministries and other positions of importance. But even those token Blacks who succeed in penetrating the exclusive citadels of power can be counted on one hand. The reality, however, is that in Panama Blacks are not discriminated against because they belong to a low social class. Rather they belong to a low social class because they are discriminated against.

THE WEST INDIAN "OUTSIDER"

In 1903, upon the birth of the Republic, the United States under-took the construction of the Canal. By means of a despicable treaty, they secured rights to practice a "socialist dictatorship" in the so-called Canal Zone. The United States, the great anti-communist power, considered it a perfect system wherein everyone worked for the government and lived in government houses, while all public services (electricity, water, telephone, transportation, schools, recreation) belonged to Big Brother. Discrimina-tion/apartheid obtained the name Gold Roll for the North Americans and Silver Roll for those who were not North Ameri-can. Thanks to this invention, they justified separate schools for Blacks and whites; separate water fountains for Blacks and whites. A teacher myself, for a time in the Silver Roll schools (euphemis-tically called later "Latin American" schools), I had in my hands the initial "courses" of these schools for Blacks, with their attrac-tive *Sign Painting, Window Washing and Shoe Shining*. These schools were attended by the children of West Indian immigrants, the second wave of Black Panamanians.

Upon completing construction work on the Canal, these West Indians remained in Panama and as the opportunities for employ-ment diminished, they found themselves in a sort of existential limbo between a dying system and an hispanophile republic. Some opted for the United States, others for the peripheral neighbor-hoods of the capital. The West Indian from Jamaica, Trinidad and Barbados differed from the so-called "colonial" Black in language, religion and customs. The "colonial" Black arrived on the isthmus 400 years ago, speaks Spanish, is Catholic and is "integrated" into Panamanian life. The West Indian Black arrived scarcely 80 years ago, by and for the Canal. He speaks English, is Protestant, and is "integrated" into the "socialist" system of the Canal zone. Indica-tive of the great work of the colonizing metropolitan cities–Madrid and London–is the mutual distrust and distance between these two groups of Blacks who inhabit Panama, in spite of the fact that their ancestors left the Island of Goree, in Senegal, in the same boat, under the same wretched conditions.

In Panamanian literature, three novels by Joaquin Beleno stand out for their insistence on the Black theme: *Gamboa Road Gang, Luna Verde* and *Curundu Lane*. Beleno, a Black writer, shows, as a "colonial" Black, how the distrust and distancing mentioned above produces a form of internal racism. In his novels, the colonial or hispanophilic Black appears as a "legitimate" Panamanian, while the "Canal" Black–the Anglophilic–is the upstart, the stranger, the second class citizen; in one word, the *"chombo."* In these novels, the whites, Indians, and mestizos, along with the colonial Black, defend themselves against the *"chombo"* with the armor of language. Because of his English, the "Canal" Black stops being a like fellow. He is the *outsider*.

Rogelio Sinan, perhaps our most accomplished writer, has recourse in *La Isla Magica* to the myth of the Black as a sexual superman, using the stereotypes that were clinically proven false by Frantz Fanon. The rest of the national literature[1] reserves its epic for the white, the Indian or the mestizo in an attempt to form a bridge with the Hispanic metropolis and as a defense against acculturation by the "yankee" presence and influence.

Those who conform with appearances and are complacent before the racial illusion, with its Caucasian advertisement the repeated use of the Greco-Latin prototype for beauty in all ads, are clearly espousing the image which most Panamanians wish to project: that of a dark-skinned Caucasoid country! In recent years, organized groups of Blacks have directly challenged that absurd notion and have achieved a refreshing level of consciousness. Sometimes, however, their reasoning is frankly surprising. For instance, to the insistence on white carnival queens, they responded with an original competition to select what they called "The most Panamanian Black Queen." (For what it is worth, I have noted that the Miss Panama who achieved the highest classification in the Miss Universe competition was a Black woman).

The sort of racial tolerance existing in Panama undoubtedly favors the rise of more and more Blacks to influential positions in the economic, political and cultural world, positions whereby they can make their voices heard and influence events. It is to be expected that these Black voices will also denounce the treatment of the other great victim of racism in Panama: the Indians.

RACIAL SELF-AWARENESS

Because the creative Black brings long centuries of research in Eurocentric models, as distinct from Oriental cultures with their millenary continuity, Black cultures have had to overcome the standards imposed by the colonizing metropolis in order to find some characteristic of their own which distinguishes and redefines them. The restrictions imposed by colonization and slavery closed the way to Black self-appreciation, fostering alienation. The Greco-Latin model, inherent to Europe, projected itself as the model to be revered by the captives. For the Black man, the result was confusion, self-laceration and self-hate. Confronted by a foreign concept of beauty, of the "ideal," and by the aggravation of its imposition, the colonized had no choice but to withdraw from the game or render homage to the model, in negation of his own personality and essence.

Black society, upon coming in contact with that of the European, suffered the trauma of exploitation, plunder and ruin. Physical domination was followed by economic and cultural domination. Subjugation by force to the dictates of the metropolis brought about, as a consequence, the imposition of all the values of the colonizers. Thus, through the irreplaceable expedient of language, the colonized were bound to the habits and customs of the colonizer. Large linguistic groups, with their own literature and traditions, were forced into silence by the requirement of Portuguese, Spanish, English or French. The Black man was permitted to express himself, but only in a rudimentary manner and always in the language of the conqueror. This served as an excellent means for achieving psychological submission as well as the most basic dependency, not producing dignified human beings but representations of children, no matter how adult they might have been, ready to obey.

The social pyramid distributed the work between the domineering and the dominated, reserving positions of power and prestige for the European. The Black was the proletarian, the resigned. The rumors of liberationist actions undertaken by the colonized reached Blacks in diluted, adulterated and terribly fragmented form. It was not intended that Blacks should become enlightened. To the contrary. The idea was to keep them in their state of intellectual virginity such that they would obey without question. Exploitation thus implied mental castration.

Not even the greatest imaginative effort could give us an approximation of the helplessness that must have resulted from the abandonment of a language and the necessity to capture fragments of another, such as must occur in the mind of an animal, anxious to respond to the grunts which his master calls language. All Black creation, art and literature, was destroyed, plundered or subject to ridicule in comparison with the western model. Great Black creations, monuments, temples and sculpture were denied in the face of the need to maintain the myth of white superiority. And the Greco-Latin model, time and time again, was put forward as the only valid pattern to follow.

If we look at Oriental civilizations, we see that Asians maintained their artistic continuity during thousands of years because they were not subject to the degree of destruction suffered by African arts. We appreciate Chinese, Japanese and Korean arts for the continuous thread they have maintained during millenia. Such is not true for African civilizations that were wrecked to their foundations by European invasions. One must search for African art beneath the ruins, in metropolitan museums, or in private collections. With the end of slavery and with African independence, the cultural thread, interrupted by displacement and invasion, was again taken up. The Black in Africa could gather the pieces and emphasize his cultures, his religions as old as Christianity, take up again his traditional clothes, customs and his art. The Black in the Americas faced a greater problem. He was no longer African. Everything had to be invented. The Black in Africa could initiate the sifting of the immediate past, that of the colonizer. He analyzed the convenience or not of foreign languages, integrated them into his relationships, emphasizing in passing the national languages. He carried out, in synthesis, the adaptation of the salvageable elements of colonization.

In the Americas, the process of elevating the Black was long and painful. At the end of slavery, Blacks found themselves still dependent, unable to read or write, discriminated against, set apart. They had to face unheard of adversities in order to survive. Far away from Africa, captive in a hostile land, without his own language or the means to learn it, the existence of Blacks in the Americas constitutes a miracle and their presence today is the best testimony of their intelligence, courage and will.

PLURAL NEGRITUDE

Already, in the 1920s, a Black woman named Josephine Baker, in Paris, defined the cry of the 1960s, Black is Beautiful. That which now distinguishes the statement is its political and economic meaning. Negritude cannot be viewed in isolation as the mere accumulation of Black characteristics in the culture of a country but as a force towards the achievement of the highest positions in all walks of life. Thus is explained and justified that negritude does not confine itself merely to the United States but embraces a plurality.

There is not one negritude, but various, multiple negritude, from Africa to Europe, from North America to Patagonia. It is a question of the infinite forms in which are expressed the personal experiences of the colonized, of negritude as the great fan which gathers the sadness of the blues and the harmony of the spiritual, the rage of the Black Panthers and the delicateness of James Baldwin, the strength of Paul Robeson or the joy of the Latin "salsa"and the magic of Jorge Amado. In all these variants of negritude, we find a thread leading to mother Africa. A thread with three segments: will, strength and joy. These segments, a while ago, stopped imitating in order to exercise free creativity with their own models. It is no longer a question of copies but of the surmounting of models and the opening of roads: Miles Davis after Harry James; Winston Marsalis after Miles Davis.

Free at last, the Black man has much to contribute to other cultures. (In Latin America, the whites have no idea of how Black they are: their manner of speaking, their way of walking, their manner of laughing; it is a "colonizing corporal negritude.") As equal to equal, he can select and integrate that which is considered pertinent. As equal to equal, he can place himself in the human mosaic: valued, respected and influential, even for the same eurocentrics of the past who, in this manner, benefit from the contributions of negritude.

NOTES

*Translated by Tanya Saunders Hamilton.

1. The author, in his novel *Dejando atras al Hombre de Celofan,* also treats the theme of the Black West Indian in the Canal zone.

THE AFRO-NICARAGUAN BEFORE AND AFTER THE SANDINISTA REVOLUTION

BASSETTE CAYASSO

T HE HISTORICAL and ethnic realities of the Atlantic Coast of Nicaragua are understood in depth by very few Nicaraguans and by only a small number of foreign academic researchers. World media coverage is limited to superficial reporting on the events in this little known area of Central America and there is a distinct lack of awareness and understanding by world Black academicians of the African-ancestry ethnic groups of this region.

The sparsely-populated Atlantic Coast of Nicaragua, home of the Black Creoles, Garifunas, Mestizos, and the Miskito, Sumo and Rama Indians, is of vital importance to the future of the Nicaraguan revolution. It is presently in turmoil and in a state of transition as the Marxist-Leninist FSLN *(Frente Sandinista de Liberacíon Nacional)* revolutionary state interacts with the Black and Indian inhabitants of this frontier region.

Of paramount importance for the success or failure of Marxist Leninist doctrine in Nicaragua, and in Latin America, is the question of indigenous and minority rights within a revolutionary national state, and the compatibility of Marxism-Leninism and the demands of the revolutionary national state with the aspirations, belief systems and traditional lifestyles of indigenous peoples and national minorities.

These fundamental questions have been brought into sharp focus on the Atlantic Coast of Nicaragua, a region which has never been successfully incorporated into the national life of the country due to historical factors, geographical isolation, and the presence of Black and Indian peoples with cultures fundamentally different from the Nicaraguan Hispanic mestizo culture of the Pacific region of the country.

THE HISTORICAL CONTEXT

Research work undertaken and books and reports published over the years concerning the Atlantic Coast of Nicaragua have mainly focused upon the Miskito Indians and the examination of indigenous cultures. There has not yet been published a comprehensive in-depth analysis of the Afro-Nicaraguan experience, which includes not only the African-ancestry ethnic groups of the Atlantic Coast of Nicaragua, but also the Afro-Nicaraguans of the Pacific region.

Prior to the revolution of 1979, there was an impetus in Nicaragua, primarily located among the Black Creoles of Bluefields, to search out the roots of the Black experience and to examine the impact of Afro-Nicaraguans on Nicaraguan history and culture. This awakening of Black pride, search for ancestral roots, and celebration of African heritage was the central focus of the SICC (Southern Indigenous Creole Community) movement, founded in 1977. While this awakening of interest in negritude, ethnicity and culture was occurring among the Black Creoles of Bluefields, the Miskito and Sumo Indians of the northern Atlantic Coast zone were developing an activist indigenous rights movement. The ALPROMISU (Alliance for the Progress of the Miskitos and Sumos) had already been founded in 1973.

In the period during which SICC and ALPROMISU were developing and expanding their activities and influence on the Atlantic Coast of Nicaragua, the Nicaraguan revolution was moving steadily towards its violent climax in the Pacific region under the leadership of the FSLN. Due to the isolation of the Atlantic Coast of Nicaragua from the Pacific region, there was very little revolutionary activity or violence in the eastern region leading up to the overthrow of the Somoza regime. However, the consensus of opinion among the Costeños was that there was a necessity for profound social change in Nicaragua, and they looked towards the Nicaraguan revolution in a positive manner, believing that it would usher in a new era for the Atlantic Coast of Nicaragua and its peoples.

The historical perspective in which the events on the Atlantic Coast of Nicaragua have unfolded since 1979 is the central theme of this paper. The story of how this hope for the future was destroyed and the Black and Indian peoples of the Atlantic Coast of Nicaragua found themselves in confrontation with a new and unfamiliar system of revolutionary doctrine and state control which impacted negatively upon their beliefs and traditional ways of life is presented here.

THE SETTING OF THE ATLANTIC COAST OF NICARAGUA

The Atlantic Coast of Nicaragua, which includes the Department of Zelaya and the eastern part of the Department of Rio San Juan, is a vast region encompassing approximately half of the Nicaraguan national territory.

Within the Atlantic Coast is found a variety of terrain, from mountainous regions in the northwest to pine savannahs in the interior and hot humid lowlands along the Caribbean coast. Numerous rivers, among them the Rio Coco, Rio Grande de Matagalpa, Rio Escondido and the Rio San Juan, serve as waterways for transportation and commerce and most of the villages of the Atlantic Coast are located along the banks of rivers. The principal population centers are Puerto Cabezas in the north and Bluefields in the south, both located on the coast itself.

The Atlantic Coast of Nicaragua was in the past, and continues to be, the frontier of Nicaragua, a vast isolated region rich in natural resources and development potential (e.g., mining, forestry, agriculture, fisheries, hydro-electric power). In the past, the natural resources of the Atlantic Coast of Nicaragua were subject to exploitation by western Nicaraguans and foreign interests, mainly from the United States, with little benefit accruing to the Black and Indian peoples of the region, whose rights and interests were supposedly guaranteed by treaty in the 19th century. In the 20th century, it was primarily the foreign missionary church groups which brought high quality schools and hospitals to the Atlantic Coast of Nicaragua. It was only in the period immediately prior to the Sandinista revolution that the Nicaraguan government instituted a comprehensive development program for the Atlantic Coast, which included the building of a new hospital in Bluefields, new airports, television facilities, direct-dial telephone system, and a fleet of boats to improve the transportation system on the Atlantic Coast rivers. Some of these projects were completed prior to the revolution and others were completed after 1979.

The population of the Atlantic Coast has been estimated recently to be between 240,000 and 276,000 out of a total Nicaraguan population of approximately 2,600,000. The present-day population figures for the Atlantic Coast and for Nicaragua are difficult to determine due to the exodus of hundreds of thousands of Nicaraguans of all socioeconomic levels and ethnic groups since 1979. Large numbers of Nicaraguan refugees and exiles are located in Costa Rica, Honduras and the United States, and considerable numbers are scattered in other countries throughout Central America and the Caribbean.

THE ORIGINS AND DEVELOPMENT OF THE SIX ETHNIC GROUPS OF THE ATLANTIC COAST OF NICARAGUA

Prior to dealing with the present-day ethnic groups of the Atlantic Coast of Nicaragua, it is necessary to define the following terms:

Costenos. This modern-day term is used to refer to all the ethnic groups of the Atlantic Coast of Nicaragua (Black Creoles, Garifunas, Mestizos, and Miskito, Sumo and Rama Indians). It refers to any person born on the Atlantic Coast of Nicaragua, encompassing the Department of Rio San Juan. There are estimated to be between 240,000 and 276,000 Costenos in total, including those who are refugees and exiles in other countries.

Afro-Nicaraguans. This term includes the Costenos of African ancestry and also those Nicaraguans from the Pacific region who are of African ancestry but who have the Hispanic mestizo culture of western Nicaragua and speak Spanish as their principal language. Afro-Nicaraguans from the Pacific region, who are located mainly along the coast and in Managua and Nandaime, are not considered to be, and do not identify themselves as, Creoles or Black Creoles. The term Creole or Black Creole is used only to refer to English speaking Afro-Nicaraguans of Afro-Caribbean culture from the Atlantic Coast of Nicaragua. Most modern reference books estimate the Afro-Nicaraguans to comprise between 9 to 10 per cent of the total Nicaraguan population of approximately 2,600,000.

Sumu Indians. War-like, Indian tribes of the Chibcha culture of Colombia who migrated northwestward along the Caribbean coastline of Central America in the period between 1000-1300 A.D. and settled in the eastern regions of Panama, Costa Rica, Nicaragua and Honduras. "Sumu" is a collective name for linguistically and culturally related subtribes which once included, in eastern Nicaragua, the Twahka, Panamaka, Ulwa, Kukra, Bawihka, Yusku, Prinsu, Boa, Silam and Ku (Conzemius 1929 a:64; 1932:15; 1938:936). The Twahka, Panamaka and Ulwa are today known as the Sumo Indians, the Bawihka were transformed biologically and culturally into the Sambos, whose present-day descendants are found in the Miskito Indian and Black Creole ethnic groups, and the Kukra, Yusku, Prinsu, Boa, Silam and Ku lost their identities through contact with the Sambos, Black immigrants and slaves, Europeans and others, and were transformed biologically and culturally into Miskito Indians. The present-day descendants of these latter Sumu subtribes can also be found in the Black Creole ethnic group.

Sambos or Zambos. The Black-Indian people formed by the union between the Bawihka Sumu subtribe of the Cape Gracias a Dios region and the African survivors of a Portuguese slave ship wrecked on a reef off the northeastern coast of Nicaragua in 1641.

Historical accounts claim that the African slaves revolted and took over control of the slave ship on its way from the west coast of Africa to Colombia and, as the liberated slaves did not know how to sail the ship, it drifted onto a reef off Cape Gracias a Dios on the northeastern coast of Nicaragua. The several hundred African male survivors made their way to the mainland where they joined with the Bawihka Sumus. The Sambos became the dominant people of the eastern regions of Nicaragua and Honduras from the mid-17th century to the early 19th century and formed an alliance with the Sumu Indian subtribes living along the Nicaraguan coast immediately to the south, who came to be known as Miskito Indians. The Sambos were a mixture of Africans and Bawihka Sumu Indians with some European blood (mainly British) and had predominantly African features. The Sambos apparently spoke their own language and English and took up British customs and surnames through contact with British buccaneers, log cutters, sailors, settlers and Caribbean blacks. Although they were the dominant people of the eastern regions of Nicaragua and Honduras from the mid-17th century into the early 19th century, and the majority of the kings of the Kingdom of the Mosquitia were Sambos, by the mid-19th century the Sambos had lost their identity in Nicaragua as a distinct people. This was likely due to a number of factors, including the lack of knowledge on the part of outsiders concerning Sambos, Miskitos and Creoles and the prevalent use of inexact terminology to refer to the various ethnic groups of the region. Books and historical accounts on the Honduran and Nicaraguan Mosquitia regions written in past centuries refer to the Sambos as the "Mosquito men" and as the "Mosquito Indians," and later as "Miskito Indians." The Treaty of Managua of 1860, the Mosquito Convention of 1884, and the Harrison-Altimorano Treaty of 1905, all important historical documents concerning the Nicaraguan Mosquitia region and its inhabitants, refer only to "Mosquito Indians" and the Harrison-Altimorano Treaty of 1905 also refers to "Creoles." There is no mention in these documents of Sumus, Sambos, Miskitos, Sumos or Ramas. It is reported that there presently exists a Black-Indian people called Sambos living in an isolated region of eastern Honduras, but this information has not been verified, and it is not known what relationship, if any, there is between this group and the Miskito Indians of eastern Honduras.

Sambo-Miskito alliance. This alliance was formed in the mid-17th century between the Sambos and Miskitos, both Black-Indian peoples derived from the Sumu subtribes, and functioned effectively into the early 19th century, enabling the war-like Sambo-Miskitos to dominate the eastern regions of Nicaragua and Honduras and to prevent the Spanish colonization of these regions. Through this alliance, and with the use of weapons obtained from the British, the Sambo-Miskitos subjugated the Sumu subtribes of eastern Nicaragua and Honduras, driving them into remote interior regions and exacting tribute from them. The British sponsored the establishment of the protectorate of the Kingdom of the Mosquitia in the late 17th century in order to further their colonial designs in the Central American region. Within the alliance, the Sambos dominated the Miskitos, who were under the jurisdiction of the Sambo king. The Sambos and Miskitos were commonly referred to as the "Mosquito Indians" by the British and others during the 17th, 18th and 19th centuries.

The breakdown of the 240,000 to 276,000 Costenos into the 6 ethnic groups of the Atlantic Coast of Nicaragua is subject to considerable variation depending upon who is making the calculation and according to what criteria (race, culture, language, location) are being used. The following figures have been used recently by various sources:

a) as publicized by the Miskito Indian leadership, using a Costeño population of 275,000:			
Miskito Indians	55.0%	or	151,250
Black Creoles	22.5%	or	61,875
Mestizos	15.0%	or	41,250
Sumo Indians	5.0%	or	13,750
Rama Indians	0.5%	or	1,375
Others	1.0%	or	2,750

b) from Luis Carrion, Representative of the National Leadership of the FSLN for the Atlantic Coast, in a speech entitled "The Truth about the Atlantic Coast" made at the Conference of Latin American Intellectuals in Managua on March 7, 1982, using a Costeno population of 276,000:

Miskito Indians	25.0%	or	70,970
Black Creoles	9.74%	or	26,933
Mestizos	62.0%	or	172,000
Sumo Indians	1.64%	or	4,202
Rama Indians			530
Garifunas	0.35%	or	967

c) by the FSLN National Commission for Autonomy for the Atlantic Coast in 1985, using a Costeno population of 240,300:

Miskito Indians			80,000
Black Creoles			30,000
Mestizos			120,000
Sumo Indians			8,000
Rama Indians			800
Garifunas			1,500

d) Bernard Nietschmann, who has done extensive research on the Miskito Indians and their culture, estimated the Miskito Indian population of the Atlantic Coast of Nicaragua at 35,000 in 1969 with an annual growth rate of 3.3%.

There is reason to speculate that the Black Creole population may be underestimated, as western Nicaraguan professionals with extensive experience working for the Nicaraguan government on the Atlantic Coast have reported that the Black Creoles number between 80,000 and 100,000. However, this difference of opinion may be partly due to the fact that many of the Costenos classified as Miskito Indians have predominantly African features. The *Area Handbook for Nicaragua* prepared for The American University by Johnson Research Associates in 1969 states *up to 50% of the Miskito Indians have Negroid physical characteristics.* If racial origin were the sole criterion used, it would appear then that the majority of the Costenos are of African ancestry, including in this calculation all of the Black Creoles, Garifunas, Miskito and Rama Indians and a sizeable percentage of the Mestizo ethnic group. Only the members of the Sumo Indian ethnic group would not be included.

PRESENT-DAY ETHNIC GROUPS OF THE ATLANTIC COAST OF NICARAGUA

Creoles or Black Creoles. The Black Creoles are a diverse group of Costenos who have in common African ancestry, an Afro-Caribbean culture, and the speaking of English (e.g., Creole English) as their principal language. The Black Creoles speak Spanish and those from the northern region of the Atlantic Coast also speak the Miskito language. The Black Creole ethnic group includes the following:

- recent Afro-Caribbean immigrants from Jamaica, San Andres, Grand Cayman, and other Caribbean islands, and from Honduras and Panama.
- descendants of the formerly termed "Mosquito Indians" (e.g., Sambos and Miskitos).
- descendants of all the other Costeno ethnic groups (Sumos, Ramas, Garifunas and Mestizos) who intermarried through the centuries with Sambos,

Miskitos and Caribbean Blacks and took up the Afro-Caribbean culture and the speaking of English as their principal language.

The term Creole appears to have been used on the Atlantic Coast of Nicaragua in the late 19th century to distinguish between the Black-Indians who had an Afro-Caribbean culture and the Black Indians (e.g., "Mosquito Indians" or Sambos and Miskitos) who had an Indian culture. In general, the Creoles can be thought of as the Black-Indians (e.g., "Mosquito Indians") who took up the values of the outside world with its different economic systems and social responses, while the Miskitos were the Black-Indians who retained the traditional Indian ways of life and followed Miskito customs and social responsibilities. The members of the present-day Black Creole ethnic group exhibit a wide variety of racial features, from African to Indian to European.

The Spanish translation of Black Creole is *Criollo Negro,* which is often used to mean a black person born in the Americas or, in this case, in eastern Nicaragua (e.g., the Atlantic Coast). However, this use of the term does not adequately describe the Black Creole people, most of whom are of mixed African, Indian and European origin. The majority of the Black Creoles can properly be classified as indigenous due to their Indian ancestry. At times, the Miskitos use the term *Criollo Negro* in a way that appears to deny the indigenous ancestry of the Black Creoles. The Afro-Caribbean Creole culture is predominant in the southern region of the Atlantic Coast of Nicaragua, from the Rio Grande de Matagalpa south to the Rio San Juan, and is also centered in Puerto Cabezas, the principal population center of the northern region, which has a large Black Creole presence.

In general, it can be stated that the Creole culture is one of the two principal cultural forces, the other being the western Nicaraguan Hispanic mestizo culture, which impact upon the Miskito, Sumo and Rama peoples and their Indian cultures. In books and studies published in recent years, Bernard Nietschmann and other researchers have referred to the advance of the Creole cultural frontier northward on the Atlantic Coast, while the western Nicaraguan Hispanic mestizo culture steadily expands its influence westward with the immigration of large numbers of western Nicaraguan Mestizo campesinos into traditionally Miskito and Sumo Indian areas and the recent increased western Nicaraguan presence in the major population centers of the Atlantic Coast. This increase in Hispanic cultural pressure from western Nicaragua has accelerated since the 1979 revolution as a result of FSLN policies and programs and is a source of friction between the Black and Indian Costeño ethnic groups and the western Nicaraguans.

The Black Creoles are one of the more highly-educated ethnic groups of the Atlantic Coast of Nicaragua and from their ranks have come many of the Costeño professionals. The Black Creoles are mainly Protestant (Moravian, Anglican, Baptist, Adventist, Pentecostal). Traditionally, they have had strong cultural ties to Jamaica and more contact and experience with foreigners, mainly North Americans, due to employment in the past with foreign-owned enterprises and travel abroad to study and to work as seamen.

Miskito Indians. The Miskitos, an Indian-African- European mixture, originally developed on the Atlantic Coast of Nicaragua in the region immediately to the south of the Sambos. There are two theories concerning the origin of the aboriginal ancestors of the Miskitos. The first is that their aboriginal ancestors were from the Sumu subtribes of the Chibcha culture of Colombia who migrated northwestward along the Caribbean coastline of Central America in the period between 1000 and 1300 A.D. and settled on the northern coast of the Atlantic Coast of Nicaragua. The second is that their aboriginal ancestors originally settled in the Pacific lowlands of Nicaragua and were subsequently displaced and forced to move to the northern coast of the Atlantic Coast of Nicaragua prior to the Spanish Conquest. Historical accounts written in the 17th and 18th centuries state that many of the Miskitos tended to have predominantly Indian features at that time, as they were less mixed with Negros than were the Sambos. In the present day, a wide variety of racial features can be seen among the Miskito people, from Indian to African to European. Various researchers have reported that as many as 50% of the Miskitos have Negroid physical characteristics. The Miskitos are the result to the intermarriage of their aboriginal ancestors and Sambos, Caribbean Blacks, Europeans, Mestizos (Spanish-Indian mixtures from western Nicaragua) and others.

The Miskitos are mainly Protestants (e.g., Moravians) through the missionary work undertaken on the Atlantic Coast of Nicaragua since 1859 by the Moravian Church, which has reshaped much of the outlook and inter-relations among the Miskito. The Miskito speak their own Indian language and Spanish; most do not speak English. There are the Miskito coastal dwellers and riverine Miskitos in Nicaragua. There are also the Miskito Indians of eastern Honduras. Bernard Nietschmann reported in 1969 that most of the Miskitos no longer lived on the coast, but occupied river locales formerly inhabited by the Sumu subtribes. Nietschmann estimated in 1969 that approximately 30% of the Miskito population resided on or near the coast. He also observed that the coastal Miskito were usually much larger in body size than the riverine Miskito, attributing this to the higher Negro admixture and the superior diet of the coastal Miskito.[1]

In the early 1970s the Afro-Caribbean Creole culture, which represented the modern world and its different value systems, was exerting increasing influence upon the traditional Miskito culture. As Miskitos became "Creolized," particularly those living along the coast and south of Rio Grande de Matagalpa, many Miskitos developed a defensive posture and resentment against Black Creoles who, they felt, had not remained in solidarity with them.

In the socioeconomic hierarchy on the Atlantic Coast prior to the 1979 revolution, the Hispanic Mestizo elite (e.g., government officials, administrators, professionals, merchants, etc.) occupied the highest level, with the Black Creoles in the middle, and the Indians (Miskitos, Sumos, and Ramas) and the Hispanic Mestizo campesinos at the lowest levels. In general, the Black Creoles occupied a higher socioeconomic level than the Miskitos due to their better education, the greater economic opportunities available to them, and their greater adaptability to changing market forces and to the influences of the outside world. The traditional Indian culture of the Miskitos, their strong attachment to the land, and the recent emergence of an Indian rights awareness and activism are the principal factors that, since the advent of the 1979 revolution and its resultant turmoil, have enabled the Miskitos to maintain a considerably greater degree of group cohesiveness than the Black Creoles, who tend to be more individualistic.

Sumo Indians. The Sumo Indians are the amalgamation of several of the original Sumu subtribes (the Twahka, Panamaka and Ulwa) who were driven into the interior regions of the Atlantic Coast of Nicaragua by the Sambos and Miskitos in past centuries. The Sumo villages are located in remote, mountainous interior regions in the northwestern Atlantic Coast. The Sumos have maintained a tradition of discouraging intermarriage with outsiders and thus are a relatively purer Indian strain with predominantly Indian features. The Sumos have an Indian culture, speak their Sumo Indian language and Spanish, and do not speak English. The historical enmity between the Sumu subtribes, today represented by the Sumo Indians, and the Sambo-Miskitos has continued to the present time. The small-stature, sturdy Sumos mainly keep to themselves in their isolated villages and restrict their interaction with the Miskitos, who tend to discriminate against them.

Rama Indians. The Ramas, an Indian-African-European mixture, are the descendants of one of the smaller Sumu subtribes of the southern region of the Atlantic Coast. Most of the Ramas live on an island on the coast to the south of Bluefields called Rama Cay. The Ramas have an Indian culture and speak their Rama Indian language and Spanish. Some speak English.

Garifunas or Black Caribs. The Garifunas, a Black-Indian people, originated on the Caribbean island of St. Vincent, where they were the result of the union between escaped African slaves and the Carib Indians of the island. The Garifunas were deported from St. Vincent by the British in 1797 after an unsuccessful revolt and were transported to the Honduras island of Roatan. They subsequently made their way to the Honduras mainland and established small villages along the Caribbean coast. Two Garifuna villages, Orinoco and La Fe, were established on the Atlantic Coast of Nicaragua to the north of Bluefields in the late 19th century.

The Garifunas have been able to retain their own culture and language. The Garifunas also speak Spanish and English.

Mestizos or "Spaniards." The Mestizos, who are also referred to as Ladinos, include recent immigrants of European-Indian origin and Hispanic culture from western Nicaragua and those Costeños of Hispanic culture whose ancestors came to the Atlantic Coast in the 19th and 20th centuries, mainly after the Reincorporation of the Mosquito in 1894, bringing with them the western Nicaraguan Hispanic mestizo culture and the Spanish language. Most of the Mestizo Costeños are campesinos who live in the western and interior regions of the Atlantic Coast, but their numbers also include local government officials, administrators, profess-ionals, and workers. Through the years, Mestizos have spread to all regions of the Atlantic Coast and many have intermarried with members of the other Atlantic Coast ethnic groups. The Mestizo Costeños have the western Nicaraguan Hispanic mestizo culture, speak Spanish as their principal language, and are mainly Catholic. There are African ancestry Costenos in the Mestizo ethnic group, including those who live along the western part of the Rio San Juan; they are sometimes referred to as "Black Spaniards." The increasing migration to the Atlantic Coast of western Nicaraguan Mestizos, including thousands of campesinos who have settled in traditional Miskito and Sumo Indian areas and encroached upon Indian lands, has increased inter-ethnic tensions on the Atlantic Coast in recent years. Also, the Black Creoles and the Indian peoples of the Atlantic Coast have resented the political dominance of the Mestizos, or Ladinos, in the years since the loss of autonomy by the Atlantic Coast (e.g., the Mosquito Reserve) in 1894.

LIFE ON THE ATLANTIC COAST OF NICARAGUA PRIOR TO THE SANDINISTA REVOLUTION

Nicaragua can be visualized as having two geographic regions, one in the west and the other in the east, each having its own distinct history, ethnic groups, and cultural development. The isolation of the eastern region from the west acted as a barrier, impeding communication and genuine understanding between the peoples of the two regions. However, it also allowed the Black and Indian peoples of the Atlantic coast to preserve their cultural autonomy and resist the process of cultural homogenization into the western Nicaraguan Hispanic mestizo mainstream.

In the decades prior to the 1979 revolution, life on the Atlantic Coast had reverted to a peaceful and tranquil existence after the severe social and economic disruptions caused by the 1909-1910 and 1925-1927 revolutions and Sandino's guerilla activities. The local police and Nicaraguan National Guard, as a rule, did not bother to carry firearms in the conduct of their duties on the Atlantic Coast. There was no repression of the Black and Indian peoples by the National Guard.

The missionary churches had continued with their programs to establish high quality schools on the Atlantic Coast. There were government schools but each of the churches operated its own schools. In general, the Atlantic Coast school system was under local control. Many of the teachers in the church schools were highly qualified foreigners. A school education up to high school graduation was available to all who wished, but it was necessary to travel to the Pacific region for a university education.

The Moravian Church established a church-school- hospital-nursing school-sanatorium complex at Bilwaskarma in the northern Atlantic Coast region. This hospital was of the highest quality in Nicaragua, equipped with the latest medical technology. The doctors stationed there were able to perform surgical operations unobtainable in Managua. Medical care in the Atlantic Coast hospitals was free to all who required it.

The Roosevelt highway, which was under construction for over 20 years with funding supplied by the United States government, was completed in the 1960s and linked the Pacific region with the river port of Rama, located at the upper end of the Rio Escondido. Communication was greatly improved between the western and eastern regions, although the final part of the journey to Bluefields had to be made by river boat on the Rio Escondido. Prior to the completion of this highway, transportation from the Pacific region to Bluefields was a long trip by way of Lake Nicaragua to the Rio

San Juan and then up the coast. The completion of the highway increased the migration of western Nicaraguan mestizos of Hispanic culture to the eastern region and also put an end to the duty-free importation of goods into Bluefields from foreign countries.

Food was in plentiful supply on the Atlantic Coast and there was a tradition among the Black and Indian peoples of sharing surplus food among kin, neighbors and others in the community.

For years, the Somoza government had adopted a policy of benign neglect towards the Atlantic Coast. It was only in the period immediately prior to the 1979 revolution that it instituted a comprehensive development program for the region. Somoza had shrewdly followed a policy of not causing governmental interference in the traditional life styles of the Black and Indian peoples. They were basically left alone to live their lives in their isolated eastern region. When Somoza visited the Atlantic Coast, he came without armed bodyguards and spoke to the Black Creoles in English and to the Miskito Indians in Miskito.

The Atlantic Coast peoples lived a life of almost complete freedom, coming and going as they pleased, working when they had to, taking what they needed from the sea and the land. The Black Creoles and Miskitos worked on fishing boats and in the fish processing factories and agricultural, forestry and mining enterprises. Much of the commercial activity was dominated by Mestizo Costreños and western Nicaraguan Mestizo businessmen and merchants, Chinese shopkeepers, and a few white North Americans, although Black Creoles and Miskitos did own fishing boats. Black Creole men also worked abroad as seamen on freighters and cruise ships in the Caribbean, sending money home to their families.

Religion was highly important to the Black Creoles and Indian peoples, who tended to have a conservative outlook upon life. Religious leaders in the communities had considerable influence over the Black Creoles and Indian peoples.

In general, the Black Creoles and Indian peoples were not involved in national political life and held a skeptical attitude towards the political process. Their political participation was minimal due in part to the political domination by the western Nicaraguans and their mistrust of politics. Revolutionary activity and violence was minimal on the Atlantic Coast in the period leading up to the overthrow of the Somoza regime. The Costeños followed the course of the revolution by listening to radio broadcasts. The Black Creoles and Indian peoples expected that the revolution would bring a democratic form of government similar to that of Costa Rica and were totally unprepared for the authoritarian Marxist-Leninist policies and programs of the FSLN *(Frente Sandinista de Liberacíon National)*.

The interaction between the ethnic groups on the Atlantic Coast of Nicaragua in the period immediately prior to the 1979 revolution can be summarized briefly. A small elite of Mestizo Costeños and western Nicaraguan Mestizos, which occupied the highest socioeconomic levels and was made up of professionals, businessmen, and government and business administrators, felt superior to the Black Creoles and the Indian peoples. The members of this elite were usually active in politics. A tiny group of Chinese were merchants, shopkeepers and businessmen and exerted considerable influence upon local commercial activity.

The Black Creoles, who were usually to be found in the middle levels of the socioeconomic spectrum, in general were more highly educated than the Indian peoples and thus were able to obtain better employment and higher social status. Many of the Costeño professionals were Black Creoles. The Black Creoles tended to feel superior to the Miskito, Sumo and Rama Indians, who were considered to be backward and disadvantaged as they clung to the old traditional Indian ways and mainly lived in small interior villages. The Black Creoles resented the political and economic domination of the elite Mestizo Costeños and western Nicaraguans. Many of the Black Creoles felt that the "Spaniards" had a racist attitude towards them.

The Mestizo campesinos, including Costeños and recently-immigrated western Nicaraguans, were poor farmers located mainly in the interior and western regions of the Atlantic Coast. Their encroachment upon traditional Indian lands caused tensions with the Miskito and Sumo Indians. The increasing migration of western Nicaraguan Mestizos of all socioeconomic levels, bringing with them their Hispanic culture, steadily exerted cultural pressure upon the Black Creoles and the Indian peoples, and also resulted in increased competition for scarce jobs in the labor market.

The Miskito Indians mainly lived in small interior and coastal villages and worked as subsistence farmers, hunters, fishermen and laborers. Prior to the 1979 revolution, there had developed a small elite of university-educated and professional Miskitos. In recent years, there had arisen resentment among some of the Miskitos towards the Black Creoles. These Miskitos felt that the Black Creoles had received better educational and economic opportunities than the Miskito people, thereby achieving higher socio-economic status. They also felt that the Black Creoles had chosen to distance themselves from the Miskito people instead of remaining in solidarity with them. The Miskitos recognized the capabilities of the Black Creoles and resented them, but also feared that the Black Creoles would choose to forge ahead on their own and leave the Miskito people behind to fend for themselves.

Whatever material progress had come to the Atlantic Coast in the 20th century had not signinificantly benefited the majority of the Miskito people. They felt themselves disadvantaged and discriminated against by the western Nicaraguans. In the mines, the most difficult, dangerous and lowest-paying jobs were performed by the Indian peoples. In general, the Miskitos felt themselves to be in an inferior socioeconomic position and without political influence in their ancestral homeland. The Miskitos were increasingly concerned over protecting their traditional Indian culture, indigenous rights and ancestral lands.

The Garifunas were being steadily assimilated into the Creole culture and, as a result, were losing their distinct cultural identity. The Sumo Indians mainly kept to themselves in their remote interior villages in the mountainous northwestern Atlantic Coast. The Sumos were mainly subsistence farmers and hunters, and some found work as laborers in the mines. The Sumos had benefited little, if at all, from material progress on the Atlantic Coast and occupied a lower socioeconomic level than did the Miskitos. In general, relations between the Sumos and the Miskitos were not friendly or cooperative, the legacy of the historical enmity between the Sambo Miskitos and the Sumu subtribes in past centuries. The Sumos were feeling pressure from the migration of the western Nicaraguan Mestizo campesinos into their areas and, like the Miskitos, were also concerned over protecting their traditional Indian culture, indigenous rights and ancestral lands.

The Rama Indians mainly lived on a small island on the coast to the south of Bluefields and had relatively close ties to the Black Creoles. Their small community had also experienced a lack of material progress and they occupied the lowest socioeconomic level with the other Indians of the Atlantic Coast. The Ramas had virtually no contact with the Miskito and Sumo Indians of the northern Atlantic Coast region.

THE CONFRONTATION BETWEEN THE AFRICAN-ANCESTRY ETHNIC GROUPS AND THE SANDINISTAS AND THE DEVELOPMENT OF RESISTANCE MOVEMENTS ON THE ATLANTIC COAST

In 1973, ALPROMISU (Alliance for the Progress of the Miskitos and Sumos) was formed as the indigenous rights movement for the Miskito and Sumo Indians of the northern zone of the Atlantic Coast of Nicaragua. The Moravian Church assisted in the formation of ALPROMISU and initially its goals were fairly conservative, involving the defense and promotion of the traditional Indian cultures, languages and indigenous rights, and the protection of the ancestral Indian lands. The leadership of ALPROMISU was dominated by the older, conservative representatives of the Miskito Indian communities. In the late 1970s, the youth wing of ALPROMISU, led by university -educated Miskito Indians, Steadman Fagoth and Brooklyn Rivera, began to develop an activist political orientation due to contacts with Marxist professors at UNAN, the national university.

In 1975, UCCOD (United Committee for Community Development) was formed in Bluefields as a cultural and ethnic awareness organization for the Black Creole youth of Bluefields. Its goals were to promote leadership among the youth, to search out the ancestral roots of the Black Creole people, and to celebrate

Black music and art and African heritage. The various activities of the young members of UCCOD stimulated an interest in the Black experience and promoted Black culture in the Bluefields community.

In 1977, an annual Caribbean festival was inaugurated in Bluefields, which included a parade of historical floats. Two of the floats, which moved the Black Creole people to an outburst of great emotion, were those commemorating General George Hodgson and General Naman Connor, heros of the Black Creole people whose exploits had been kept hidden from public display for many years. The orientation of UCCOD was seen to be too limited in its scope to serve the needs of the Black Creole people and, therefore, a new movement called SICC (Southern Indigenous Creole Community) was formed in Bluefields in November of 1977 as an indigenous rights and multicultural and ethnic awareness movement for all the ethnic groups (Black Creole, Garifuna, Indians and Mestizos) of the southern zone of the Atlantic Coast of Nicaragua, encompassing the region from the Rio Grande de Matagalpa south to the Rio San Juan. SICC had a multiethnic orientation in recognition of the common heritage and blood ties (African and indigenous) and shared history of the Atlantic Coast ethnic groups. The development of the Creole culture of the Atlantic Coast of Nicaragua had resulted from contributions through the centuries by the African, Indian and European (mainly British) cultures. The goals of the SICC movement were:

1) To prevent the assimilation and obliteration of the distinct cultures of the Black Creoles, Garifunas and Indian ethnic groups of the Atlantic Coast by the western Nicaraguan Hispanic mestizo culture.

2) To promote, preserve and revitalize the Creole and indigenous cultures, traditional values and languages through research and

3) To search out the ancestral roots of the Black Creoles and the other Atlantic Coast ethnic groups.

4) To defend the rights of the indigenous peoples of the Atlantic Coast of Nicaragua.

5) To promote and develop leadership within the Atlantic Coast ethnic groups, particularly among the youth. The youth were to be prepared to assume leadership positions on the Atlantic Coast.

The SICC movement was divided into two age groups, youth and elders. The youth were involved in historical research, the compilation of historical documents, and the interviewing of the older members of the community in order to gain knowledge of their history and cultures. The community elders had a clearer vision of the African and indigenous ancestry of the Atlantic Coast ethnic groups and the young people lacked this knowledge. The youth were trying to define the meaning of Black and Creole and, as their knowledge of the historical and ethnic realities increased, their feelings of self-confidence and identity grew. The SICC movement eventually had approximately 200 active members in the Bluefields area.

Unfortunately, the goals and projects of the SICC movement would come to be regarded as subversive by the FSLN, which waited until the opportune moment to destroy the movement. The lack of political experience and historical perspective of the SICC members was to lead to the movement's demise as a social and cultural force inside Nicaragua. When the movement deviated from its original goals and became enmeshed in political activities, it gave the FSLN the opportunity to act against it. The SICC movement did not establish an accommodation with the FSLN, which might have assured its continued survival, as its goals and projects were not compatible with the Sandinista Marxist-Leninist policies and programs on the Atlantic Coast of Nicaragua. In the period immediately after the revolutionary triumph, the promotion of the Black Creole people was not one of the policy objectives of the FSLN.

A meeting was held in 1978 at Punta Arenas, Costa Rica, between the FSLN and the Miskito leaders of the youth wing of ALPROMISU (Steadman Fagoth, Brooklyn Rivera and Hazel Lau). An agreement was reached on mutual assistance and cooperation and a plan was developed whereby the leaders of the youth wing would gain control of ALPROMISU from the conservative founding leaders with financial assistance supplied by CEPAD (Centro Evangelico por Asistencia y Desarrollo). The FSLN began developing a plan to introduce its revolutionary policies and programs in the Atlantic Coast through the Indian peoples, who occupied the lowest socioeconomic levels, with the Miskito people having the leadership role. The scenario that was developing for the Atlantic Coast in revolutionary Nicaragua was markedly similar to that leading up to the Mosquito Convention of 1894, in which the western Nicaraguan government was able to manipulate the separation of the Mosquito Indians from the Creoles and Caribbean Blacks in order to further its interests on the Atlantic Coast. However, the FSLN underestimated and misinterpreted the Miskito commitment to pursuing an activist indigenous rights orientation. This miscalculation lead to ill-conceived FSLN policies and programs which soon created confrontation and armed conflict with the Indian peoples in revolutionary Nicaragua.

In July 1979, the broad-based coalition of revolutionary forces of the Nicaraguan people, with FSLN playing the vanguard role, succeeded in overthrowing the Somoza dictatorship. The revolutionary forces had signed agreements beforehand stipulating that the new revolutionary Nicaragua was to be pluralistic and democratic. After the revolutionary triumph, the Marxist-Leninist FSLN then moved to consolidate its control over the Nicaraguan revolution with the assistance of Soviet Bloc, Cuban and other international political, economic and military advisors. It soon became clear that the Sandinista party intended to exert its influence and control over all aspects of Nicaraguan life.

There had been very little revolutionary activity or violence on the Atlantic Coast of Nicaragua in the period leading up to the overthrow of the Somoza regime. The Black Creoles and Indian peoples had no indication that the triumph of the Nicaraguan revolution would bring drastic national government intervention and control over their traditional ways of life. They initially expected that they would be given the opportunity to meaningfully participate in a democratic system of government structured upon the pluralistic model of Costa Rica. The Black Creoles and Indian peoples had never been given the opportunity to gain political experience and had no familiarity with democratic institutions or with political ideologies and concepts. The idea of communism was repugnant to them as it attacked the foundations of their societies, their traditional lifestyles and belief systems. They had been able to live a very free and independent lifestyle on the isolated Atlantic Coast of Nicaragua with little, if any, interference in their daily lives by previous national governments. In general, the Black Creoles and Indian peoples did not harbor anti-American sentiments, but rather looked upon the national government and the western Nicaraguans as the historical sources of their problems. Although there were resentments and differences among the ethnic groups of the Atlantic Coast, there were still the fundamental underlying unifying factors of common heritage and blood ties and shared history. The present day Creole and Indian cultures are both the result of the interactions, through the centuries, of the African, Indian and European (British and Hispanic) cultures on the Atlantic Coast of Nicaragua.

Since the 1979 revolution, the Marxist-Leninist policies and programs of the FSLN have interacted with the Creole and Indian cultures and have caused continual conflict and confrontation. The FSLN has adopted a strategy of indoctrination of the Black Creole and Indian school children in Marxist-Leninism in order to create their revolutionary socialist human being. Thereby, it fundamentally alters traditional belief systems, attitudes and life styles for the creation of a new generation of Nicaraguan Marxist-Leninist revolutionaries on the Atlantic Coast. The effect of these Marxist-Leninist policies and programs has serious implications for the continued survival of the distinct Creole and Indian cultures and is viewed by the majority of Black Creoles and Indian peoples as a form of ethnocide.

For several weeks after the revolutionary triumph, Bluefields was in a state of limbo with no central government authority and with the leaders of the local "Spaniard" and Black Creole ethnic groups jockeying for power. The "Spaniards" took control of the municipal government offices and denied access to the Black

Creoles who, thereupon, set up their own municipal government and military command in the Black Creole neighborhood of Beholden. For a period of time, the jurisdiction of Bluefields was split between the "Spaniards" and the Black Creoles. Tensions between the two groups rose dangerously and on several occasions came perilously close to armed violence. Several leaders of the Black Creole community then travelled up the Rio Escondido by river boat to Rama to make contact with the FSLN and request that they send officials down to take control of Bluefields. They returned with a small contingent of western Nicaraguan FSLN troops and the Black Creoles handed over the police and military installations in Bluefields to FSLN control. In late August of 1979, Comandante Lumberto Campbell, a Black Creole, arrived from Managua to try to mediate the power struggle between the two ethnic groups in Bluefields. Additional tensions had arisen when Marvin Wright ("Kalalu"), a Black political activist from Limón, Costa Rica, arrived in Bluefields immediately after the revolutionary victory; he was soon deported by the FSLN as a result of his political activities among the Black Creoles.

Initially, the Black Creoles and SICC members cooperated enthusiastically with the FSLN, but they soon discovered what the FSLN intentions were for the Atlantic Coast. The initial optimism of the Black Creoles turned to pessimism when the FSLN began instituting policies and programs which intervened in all aspects of traditional life on the Atlantic Coast. The attitude of the "Spaniards" (i.e. the western Nicaraguan FSLN political and military cadres), who were in control of the Bluefields municipal government, was that the Black Creoles had not earned the right to be in positions of authority in the new revolutionary order as they had not participated in the revolutionary sacrifices and struggle. The Black Creole young men soon became demoralized and disenchanted by the discriminatory attitude displayed towards them by the western Nicaraguan FSLN cadres and they soon drifted away from participation in activities involving the FSLN.

As the FSLN steadily introduced its Marxist-Leninist policies and programs to the Atlantic Coast and exerted increasing control over all aspects of life, SICC members participated in meetings which discussed armed action to overthrow the FSLN on the Atlantic Coast. It was generally believed by the SICC members that there was a strong possibility that Great Britain would intervene on behalf of the Black Creoles and Indian peoples in the event of a confrontation with the FSLN, due to the treaties signed in the past between Great Britain and Nicaragua concerning the Mosquitia. However, the discussions never resulted in concrete plans for military action against the FSLN as the Black Creoles were not experienced in political organizing and military preparations and had no contacts with foreigners who had the ability to supply weapons. The SICC movement continued with its cultural and research programs in Bluefields and set up cultural survival groups.

It is arguable whether the western Nicaraguan FSLN and its leadership had an in-depth understanding of the Black Creole people and the historical and ethnic realities of the Atlantic Coast. On the one hand, the FSLN simply may not have had any real interest in the Black Creoles due to perceiving them as lacking in revolutionary potential as a people. On the other hand, the FSLN may have viewed the Black Creoles as a dangerous element and a potentially subversive obstacle to the implementation of their Marxist-Leninist policies and programs on the Atlantic Coast.

The research work and studies on the Atlantic Coast undertaken by sociologists and other foreign researchers and academicians working with the FSLN has been concentrated on the Miskito Indians and the MISURASTA indigenous rights movement. The information made available on the Black Creole people and the SICC movement has been extremely limited. In general, the information that has been publicized on the Black Creoles has contributed to a stereotype of this Black people as being basically poorly educated and illiterate, except for a small elite of highly-educated intellectuals and professionals, and as having an inordinately high percentage of criminal elements, or lumpenproletariat, in their Black society. An excerpt from a research study by Philippe Bourgois reprinted in the publication "*Nicaragua in Revolution*," which is entitled "The Problematic of Nicaragua's

Indigenous Minorities," is illustrative of this stereotype attitude towards the Black Creole people:

> The class composition of the Afroamericans concentrated in southern Zelaya is different. Within the black population, in addition to a disproportionately large lumpenproletariat, there exists a local petit bourgeoisie with a relatively high representation of North American-educated intellectuals and professionals.

Research studies and articles on the Atlantic Coast and its ethnic groups written after 1979 usually refer to the pre-revolutionary lack of educational and health-care facilities and to the high rate of illiteracy among the Atlantic Coast population. This does violence to the facts. The relevant facts concerning the actual conditions on the Atlantic Coast prior to the revolution were:

- The Black Creoles, as a people, had the highest literacy rate in Nicaragua, almost twice the national average.
- The private schools on the Atlantic Coast, which were operated by the various churches, were available to all who desired an education. Every village on the Atlantic Coast had at least one church and a primary school. Many of the schools on the Atlantic Coast had highly-qualified foreign teachers.
- The Moravian hospital at Bilwaskarma in the northern Atlantic Coast region was the highest quality medical facility in Nicaragua and was equipped with the latest medical technology. Medical procedures and surgical operations unobtainable elsewhere in Nicaragua could be performed at this hospital. The medical treatment at this hospital was free, as it was at the other hospitals on the Atlantic Coast.
- The Black Creoles were a deeply religious, conservative and law-abiding community. Prior to the

revolution, the police and National Guard did not carry firearms on the Atlantic Coast in the normal conduct of their duties, due to the low incidence of crime and violence.

THE GROWING CONFLICT

In November of 1979, an Assembly of the Miskito and Sumo Indians of ALPROMISU was held in Puerto Cabezas with the attendance of high FSLN government officials, including Daniel Ortega. Several representatives of the SICC movement were invited to the Assembly by the youth wing of ALPROMISU, with the expenses paid by CEPAD. The events leading up to and during this Indian Assembly bore certain important similarities to the events surrounding the Mosquito Convention of 1894. A brief summary of the important events that took place at the historic Indian Assembly is in order. At the insistence of the FSLN, the name of ALPROMISU was changed to MISURASATA (Miskitos, Sumos, Ramas and Sandinistas All United). MISURASATA was to be the officially-sanctioned representative movement of the Atlantic Coast indigenous peoples. Although the Ramas of the southern Atlantic Coast zone were already participating in SICC, the FSLN insisted upon including them in MISURASATA. There were no Ramas present at the Assembly to give their opinion and the Black Creole members of SICC voiced their disapproval of this non-democratic maneuver. The Black Creoles were denied participation in MISURASATA as Daniel Ortega specifically requested that they not be included. MISURASATA was designated by the FSLN to be the sole representative body of the Atlantic Coast indigenous peoples with representation on the Council of State of Nicaragua. The youth wing won control of MISURASATA and Steadman Fagoth was elected as the Coordinator with Brooklyn Rivera as head of the literacy program.

In the formation of MISURASATA, the FSLN was successful in its plan to create disunity among the Black and Indian ethnic groups of the Atlantic Coast by discriminating against the Black

Creoles and separating them from the Indian peoples. In the Assembly, the FSLN actively promoted the concept that the Indian peoples could realize their aspirations and goals through co-operation with the FSLN. The Miskito Indians present at the Assembly were exhilarated by the ascension of their people to the dominant role on the Atlantic Coast after long years of what they felt had been discrimination, deprivation and denial of oppor-tunities. Unfortunately for the FSLN, however, it had unwittingly stoked the smoldering fires of Miskito ethnocentrism and Indian rights activism, and had rekindled the latent Miskito ambition to return to the former days of the Mosquito Reserve and the King-dom of the Mosquitia, with autonomous rights for the Atlantic Coast, if not outright independence, under the leadership of the Miskito peoples. The FSLN would soon come to regret the outcome of this Indian Assembly as its Marxist-Leninist policies and programs proved to be incompatible with the aspirations, belief systems, culture and traditional ways of life of the Miskitos and Sumos. The initial cooperation turned into confrontation, violence and armed resistance struggle by the Indian peoples, attracted the attention of the world news media, and became a public relations disaster for the FSLN.

In January of 1980, Steadman Fagoth was named the MISURASATA delegate on the Council of State of Nicaragua in representation of the indigenous peoples of the Atlantic Coast. In April of 1980, Brooklyn Rivera became the Coordinator of MISURASATA, replacing Steadman Fagoth who had assumed his new duties on the Council of State. Shortly after the formation of MISURASATA, CEPAD cut off all financial assistance to the SICC movement upon instructions from the FSLN. The SICC members determined that this action was taken because the FSLN, as a policy objective, did not intend to promote the Black Creole people on the Atlantic Coast. In April of 1980, SICC began to coordinate activities with MISURASATA. Steadman Fagoth visited Bluefields and told the SICC members that the Miskitos needed the cooperation and assistance of the Black Creoles as the FSLN did not have good intentions concerning the Black and Indian peoples of the Atlantic Coast. SICC agreed to work with

MISURASATA and began developing a map of the indigenous lands of the southern zone of the Atlantic Coast. Although they were always determined to maintain leadership control of the indigenous movement on the Atlantic Coast, the Miskitos were aware that the Black Creoles had more prepared people and that their participation was essential for the advancement of the interests of the Atlantic Coast and its inhabitants.

By early 1980, through its initial close working relationship with the FSLN and its increasing familiarity with the FSLN philosophies, policies and programs, the Miskito leadership of MISURASATA became aware that there was a fundamental incompatibility between the goals of the FSLN Marxist-Leninist revolutionary national state and the goals of the indigenous peoples. The Indian peoples were deeply concerned over the ownership and control of their ancestral lands and the natural resources that assured the continuity of their traditional ways of life. The Marxist-Leninist FSLN saw the ancestral Indian lands as being the property of the national state and the natural resources therein subject to state control. It was becoming increasingly apparent to the Miskito leadership of MISURASATA that there would be a serious confrontation of interests between the FSLN and the indigenous peoples in the near future and that the indigenous peoples would need the assistance and solidarity of the Black Creoles.

THE CONFRONTATION

The FSLN was highly suspicious and distrustful of the Black Creoles due to what the FSLN termed their "bourgeois" tendencies, their favorable attitude towards North Americans, and their skepticism and distinct lack of enthusiasm for Marxist-Leninist policies and programs. The FSLN was also deeply concerned about the SICC movement. Informants kept State Security abreast of the plans and developments of the movement, including the discussions concerning armed rebellion. The FSLN had difficulty in making inroads into the Black Creole community as Marxist-Leninist ideology attacked the foundations of the Black Creole community, its traditional values and religious beliefs. The Black Creoles were skeptical and cynical about the FSLN intentions and were not attracted to the FSLN programs as were the Miskito Indians initially. The Black Creole young men resented the discriminatory attitude displayed towards them by the western Nicaraguan FSLN cadres. Most of the Black Creoles considered that the national government, and western Nicaraguans in general, had fundamentally racist and discriminatory attitudes towards them and that the present situation was only a continuation of the historical problems between the Atlantic Coast and its Black and Indian peoples and western Nicaragua.

The Black Creoles objected to the influx of FSLN cadres from western Nicaragua and, in particular, to the Cuban advisors and technicians, who assumed control of the former locally-controlled education system and hospital, the fishing industry, and other local enterprises. The Cubans and Soviet-bloc personnel had preference in obtaining food and housing. Rumors and complaints, some apparently justified, circulated throughout Bluefields that the Cuban doctors, who controlled the hospital, were poorly-trained and were performing shoddy surgery that was injuring and killing the patients, with the result that the local people feared entering the hospital for treatment. The FSLN developed and implemented its policies and programs for the region, which dramatically impacted upon all aspects of traditional life, without consultation or dialogue with the local populace. The FSLN prevented the small neighborhood grocery stores from selling goods and passed regulations that all goods had to be purchased from the government food store. Rationing was introduced; the local people could not purchase what they required although it was known that food was piled up and rotting in the government warehouse. Sandinista State Security agents began to monitor the content of church sermons. Several highly regarded and influential Black Creole religious and community leaders were ordered by the FSLN to leave Nicaragua immediately and to go into exile for no discernible reason.

The attempts to set up the CDS *(Comites de la Defensa Sandinista)* block-watch committees created dissension in the neighborhoods. Some of the local fishing boats were confiscated from their owners and Black Creole fishing boat captains were ordered to train Cubans who, it was rumored, were to replace them. The FSLN gave orders that all the fishing boats had to include Cubans as crew members. The Black Creole fishermen were ordered to teach the Cubans, Russians and eastern Europeans how to fish in the area. Parents were upset at radical changes in the approved school curriculum with the introduction of Marxist-Leninist indoctrination. The Cuban advisors and teachers exercised considerable control over the school curriculum and activities. Shortly after the revolutionary triumph, the Atlantic Coast peoples were disarmed when the FSLN sent out squads to every home to confiscate all firearms. Very few weapons escaped this procedure.

As Black Creole dissatisfaction and resentment steadily grew, in 1980 Tomas Borge, the last of the original founders of the FSLN, paid a visit to Bluefields and was angered that the Black Creoles did not come to greet him and show him respect as a hero of the revolution. The only crowd that he could find was at a softball game, where he was mocked and jeered by the Black Creoles when he interrupted the game to make a speech to announce that Fidel Castro was going to honor Bluefields with a visit in the future. Borge, enraged at this negative response, cursed and threatened the Black Creoles, shouting that "they were stupid, ignorant, illiterate monkeys who only lacked tails so that they could be hunted down and shot like animals." This outburst was recorded on tape and played on Radio Zinica of Bluefields until the FSLN seized and destroyed the tape recording. A deep sense of outrage was steadily building within the Black Creole people at the unwelcome presence amongst them. The Black Creoles were a self-sufficient, peaceful, law-abiding people with a profound religious faith, and were deeply offended by the unwanted intrusion of foreigners and a foreign ideology into their community.

The final event that set off the mass demonstration of the Black Creole people was the arrival of an additional group of several hundred Cubans in the latter part of September of 1980. Up to this time, the Black Creoles had been quietly protesting to the local FSLN authorities against the presence of the Cuban advisors and technicians, who were all political and military cadres. The FSLN attitude was that the Cubans were revolutionary brothers and sisters and had more rights than the Black Creoles, who had not taken part in the revolutionary struggle against the former dictatorship. As a result of this latest influx of Cubans, the Black Creole leaders, who were SICC members, gave the Cubans and the FSLN an ultimatum: all the Cubans were to leave Bluefields immediately or else the Black Creoles would stage a massive protest demonstration. The Cubans refused to depart and the protest demonstration began on September 28 with 800 Black Creoles marching from the neighborhood of Beholden to the central park holding aloft signs saying CUBANS AND RUSSIANS GO HOME. At the central park, the crowd of demonstrators swelled to over 10,000 and they then marched to the military Cuartel, where they were joined by thousands more, including members of all the ethnic groups of the local populace. At the Cuartel, the Cubans threw bottles and other articles at the demonstrators from the top floor of an adjacent building and raised a Cuban flag. The Cuban flag was then lowered and burned by the demonstrators and shots were fired into the crowd. The next day the general strike began; people began to stream in from all over the Atlantic Coast to join the demonstration. Brooklyn Rivera, the Coordinator of MISURASATA, who was in Managua at this time, sent word to the MISURASATA members on the Atlantic Coast to avoid becoming involved in the demonstration of the Black Creole people. A squad of special police were flown in from western Nicaragua and the demonstrators dispersed to seek weapons. Obtained were a very small number of old rifles and pistols which had escaped detection and confiscation by the FSLN security police, as well as a barrel of gas, which was used to make Molotov cocktails. Negotiations began between the demonstration leaders, who were SICC members, and the local FSLN authorities.

The demands of the demonstrators were for the removal of the Cubans from Bluefields and the rest of the Atlantic Coast and for the opening of a dialogue with the FSLN concerning its policies and programs on the Atlantic Coast. An agreement was reached with the local FSLN authorities that the Cubans would leave as soon as possible. SICC members then positioned themselves between the demonstrators and the government forces, asking for calm and informing the demonstrators that the FSLN had agreed to remove the Cubans early the next day. The demonstrators then dispersed with plans to regroup the next morning to observe the departure of the Cubans from the community. However, in the early hours of the morning of October 1, the FSLN airlifted a contingent of several hundred elite troops from western Nicaragua to Bluefields with orders to crush the demonstration. The troops and police surrounded the demonstration headquarters and arrested the SICC members found there. Then they went to the Bluefields neighborhoods where the Black Creoles lived and dragged SICC members and other Black Creoles selected at random from their homes. The western Nicaraguan troops and police fired over the heads of the Black Creoles, beat them, clubbed them to the ground with rifle butts, kicked and spat upon them, and hurled vile racial insults. Their protest signs were rolled up and stuffed into their mouths. Rifles and machine guns were fired at their feet and they were ordered to dance the Maypole to the sounds of the bullets. Others were forced to lie down and kiss the ground at the feet of the troops. These sounds were tape-recorded by the FSLN and played over the local radio station with commentary that the enemies of the revolution had been forced to kiss the ground. Approximately 450 demonstrators were arrested, most of them Black Creoles, and 200 of them were transferred by plane to Managua for detention and interrogation. Some of the prisoners were released after several days and others were held for months and subjected to brutal treatment. Several of the prisoners never recovered physically or mentally from the mistreatment inflicted upon them.

As a result of the protest demonstration, FSLN severed the communication links between Bluefields and western Nicaragua and the world. Meetings and gatherings of the people of Bluefields were prohibited. The media coverage of the events at Bluefields was censored and the FSLN later released distorted information. In October of 1980, the FSLN banned the SICC movement in Nicaragua and most of its leaders had to leave the country to avoid imprisonment and further repression. When Fidel Castro visited Bluefields in 1981, Humberto Ortega, the FSLN Minister of Defense, forewarned the Black Creoles that he would order them "shot down like dogs" if they protested or created a disturbance while Castro was there. Fidel Castro was apparently surprised at the numbers of Blacks on the Atlantic Coast and reportedly tried to counsel the FSLN leadership on how it should handle the Black Creoles in the future. Black Cubans were soon sent in increasing numbers to the Atlantic Coast, but this strategy had little, if any, effect upon the resentment and hostility of the Black Creoles towards the FSLN and its policies and programs.

The brutal mistreatment and insulting, racist behavior shown towards them by the western Nicaraguan FSLN troops and police during the crushing of the Bluefields demonstration remain a searing memory that the Black Creoles have not forgotten nor forgiven. These events, and other events that have taken place in the ensuing years, have done nothing to dispel their deeply-held belief that the "Spaniards" of western Nicaragua are irredeemably racist towards them. The Black Creoles feel, in general, that historically it has made little difference whether the national government has been controlled by one political tendency or another, the common denominator has always been racism and discrimination towards the Black Creoles and the Indian peoples, and marginalization of the Atlantic Coast region. There is always present the domination of the white western Nicaraguans over the political process, the local and regional economy, and the national government, and the constant pressure from the western Nicaraguan Hispanic culture to assimilate and destroy the Creole culture and identity. The events that took place in Bluefields in late September of 1980 must be understood in the light of this knowledge, as they illustrate the depth of pent-up anger and hostility of the Black Creole people with respect to FSLN policies and programs being introduced into their communities.

Some of the highly-educated Black Creoles have made a personal accommodation with the FSLN. They have become apologists and spokespersons and have been sent abroad as emissaries and ambassadors to various countries, particularly in Africa. However, most of the intellectuals and professionals have not been willing to cooperate or able to live under the prevailing conditions in Nicaragua and have gone into exile with their families. They are now scattered in various countries throughout the hemisphere and many are pursuing their careers in cities in the United States. The talents and intellectual resources of these Black Creoles are not being utilized for the betterment of the Atlantic Coast or of Nicaragua nor to ensure the continued survival of Creole culture and identity.

The confrontations and problems between the Black Creoles and the present national government are not as well-known internationally as those involving the Miskito Indians, one of the other African ancestry ethnic groups. A large number of Miskitos, approximately 25,000 in total, are refugees in eastern Honduras and have been carrying on a well-publicized guerilla war against the Sandinista government. Our Miskito brothers and sisters are struggling for their indigenous rights, ancestral land claims, cultural identity and traditional way of life. They are joined in this struggle by the Rama Indians, another African-ancestry ethnic group, and by the Sumo Indians. There are also Black Creole groups participating in the armed resistance struggle on the Caribbean coast of Nicaragua.

Our problems with the Sandinista party, which governs Nicaragua, can be summarized briefly as follows:

1) The Sandinista policies and programs are in confrontation with our traditional values, culture and religious beliefs.

2) We resent the suffocating national government control over our lives and we perceive this control as a loss of freedom and as a threat to our cultural identity and traditional way of life.

3) We, as people, feel ourselves to be under siege by the national government which is imposing its conditions upon us without our consent.

4) Due to common heritage and blood ties and shared history, we, as a people, are in solidarity with the aspirations, sufferings and struggle of our Indian brothers and sisters.

Our present problems in Nicaragua are compounded because we are not only a Black minority, but we also have a fundamentally different culture from the western Nicaraguan majority of Hispanic culture, which exercises control of the national government.

Thousands of our Black Creole people have had to leave their homeland due to the prevailing conditions in Nicaragua. They now languish in refugee camps. and as exiles in Costa Rica and in other countries throughout the hemisphere.

We are now in the process of trying to unite our Black Creole refugees and exiles in order to develop our own solutions to the problems confronting us. We do not permit manipulation of our people's struggle by any outside interests. Hopefully, we will be able to work in the future with our people inside Nicaragua to help alleviate their problems and sufferings.

NOTES

1. See Bernard Nietschmann, *Between Land and Water,* Seminar Press, 1973.

AFRO-CUBANS AND THE COMMUNIST REVOLUTION

CARLOS MOORE

AMONG THE most important achievements claimed by Cuba's socialist regime is the elimination of all forms of racial conflict within Cuban society. This presupposes, however, that there was a "racial problem" in Cuba before 1959. On the whole, white Cuban exiles have systematically denied its existence, contending that Fidel Castro "invented"a racial question to divide Cubans. The revolutionary regime has claimed that American imperialism was "at the origin of Cuba's racial problems." So has the ball been kicked around, no one accepting responsibility ....

Practically thirty years after Fidel Castro's coming to power, the state or relations between blacks and whites in the new revolutionary context is glaringly the most neglected aspect of studies on the Cuban Revolution. This void points to the serious analytical limitations of blacks who refuse to challenge the assimilationist code of ethics of Cuban race relations and to the crippling ignorance on the part of whites concerning the subjective world of black Cubans. A profound ignorance of black Cuban society, culture and history, in both pre-revolution and post-revolutionary Cuba, is unquestionably the major factor barring any meaningful reading of Cuba's ongoing racial dilemma.

Since the aborted black insurrection of 1912, a very rigid taboo on the issue of race and politics has been observed by both whites and blacks. This continues to be so today generally for whites, but increasingly less so for blacks. The clash of interests between the two main racial components of Cuban society has been a central issue for centuries. Yet the norm has been to proscribe any open discussion and/or analysis of this long-standing conflict.[1]

PROBLEM OF NUMBERS

The "Majority-Minority" Contention
From the days of slavery, the policy of *blanqueamiento* ("whitening") has been central to race relations in Cuba. For obvious reasons, white rulers during the slave-colonial period systematically claimed to speak on behalf of the racial majority. The census racial breakdowns of that period (1774-1899) are understandably worthless, as Kenneth F. Kiple has demonstrated.[2] The census racial breakdowns of the republican era (1900-1959) are hardly any better than those of the previous period, particularly after the 1912 black uprising and the *Partido Independiente de Color's* insistence on proportional ethno political representation.

The census and population estimates prior to 1959 require the same sort of analytical scrutinizing that Kiple has undertaken for those of the slave-colonial era. However, this has not been the case. Pre-1959 data have been generally accepted as bona fide indicators of the ethno-demographic panorama of republican Cuba, i.e., that the predominant population group consisted of whites.

The picture scarcely changes when examining the revolutionary regime's attitude towards racial statistics since 1959. In a first stage, which lasted until 1981, this attitude consisted of claiming that a racial breakdown of population statistics was "divisive." However, that did not keep the traditional questions regarding race and/or color from figuring in the 1970 census forms?[3] Consequent results though were withheld from the public.

The attitude of the revolutionary regime on race and population figures underwent a significant transformation between 1971 and 1981. That change seems to have been directly related to

Cuba's increasingly heavy military involvement in black Africa. In that ten year period, two censuses were taken and Cuba was declared a "Latin-African" country by Fidel Castro in December 1975. Black Cuban soldiers were explicitly being called upon to fight and die in black Africa to overcome the threat posed by white-minority ruled regimes in Rhodesia and South Africa.

In 1983, the revolutionary regime made a clear break with the policy it had hitherto justified in terms of a new, non-racial consciousness. For the first time census results according to *race* were publicly released. According to *Granma,* the official organ of the Cuban Communist Party, "blacks" made up 12 percent of the population, "mulattoes" 21.9 percent, and "whites" 66 percent.[4] Many Cubanologists, whose estimates of the black population ratio have ranged from a low of 45 percent to a high of 60 percent (Irving Horowitz, Clifford Barnett, Edward Gonzalez, Wayne McGaffey, Hugh Thomas, David Booth, Fernando Ortiz, Roger Bastide, Jean Ziegler, A. Petit, Walterio Carbonell, Boris Goldenberg, Jorge I. Dominquez), in one way or another contested the anthropological validity of such figures.

If the 1981 and 1953 census reports were to be believed, the black race in Cuba had suffered a severe case *of sterility* over the past thirty years. The 1953 census had classified 12.4 percent of the population as "Negro" and 14.5 percent as "mulatto," practically the same as in the 1981 census report. Some specialists blamed the confusing situation on census-taking methodology: i.e. the anthropological criteria of the census-taker. Others evoked problems of "self-image" of Afro-Cubans themselves. Black Cubans did not hesitate to suspect official "manipulation" aimed at blunting calls for "proportional racial representation" in the organs of power (Communist Party Central Committee and Politburo, Government, National Assembly, Council of State, Armed Forces...). Cuban blacks have always maintained that Cuba is predominately populated by people *of African* descent. As their old saying goes: *"El que no tiene de Congo, tiene de Carabali"* ("If your blood is not Congo, it must be Carabali").

Election results and population statistics have always posed serious credibility problems in Cuba. Any analysis of the "facts" relating to racial demography in Cuba–prior to or after the Revolution–must contend with the "majority-minority" syndrome, an issue resting entirely on ethno-political self-interests and absolutely *subjective* criteria in determining who is "black," who is "white," and who is "in between." This alone speaks loudly of the existence of a deeply entrenched *racist* consciousness in the society as a whole.

A purely statistical approach to race relations in Cuba will inevitably clash with the "majority/minority" contention. If a purely statistical yardstick is used, the measurements obtained will vary, even to the point of contradiction. All will depend on what share is apportioned to blacks in the general population to begin with. For example, acceptance of the official version (non-whites constituting 30-35% of the population) has led some specialists to conclude that Afro-Cubans were "over-represented" in the military contingents sent to Angola. The situation is practically reversed, and wholly different conclusions are derived, if one relies on the unofficial estimates which conclude that blacks constitute more than half of Cuba's population. The black share in the military contingents in Angola (an estimated 60 percent) could then appear as "proportionate" to the black share in the general population.

The "Tripartite Racial System" in Cuba
According to the standards of a tripartite racial categorization *imposed by the ruling white segment* since the days of slavery Cubans are either "white," "black" or "mulatto". According to such an "anthropological" criterion, perhaps only one-third of the population of the United States would qualify as "black" in today's Cuba. For example, people who resemble former U.N. Ambassador Andrew Young, General Colin Powell, civil rights leader Jesse Jackson, actor Harry Belafonte, singer Billie Holiday, President Lt. Jerry Rawlings of Ghana, former Prime Minister of Grenada, Maurice Bishop, former heavyweight champion, Joe Louis, are *not* considered "black" in Cuba. In the 1953, 1970 or 1981 censuses they would have been classed, irrespective of their protests to the contrary, as *mulattoes.*

Former Congressman Adam Clayton Powell Jr., Jamaican former Primer Minster Michael Manley, Georgia Congressman Julian Bond, former Senator Edward Brooke, entertainer Lena Horne, or Supreme Court Justice, Thurgood Marshall, would have been unhesitatingly classified as "whites" in any census undertaken in Cuba before or after 1959. According to the racial definition norms upheld in pre- and post-socialist Cuba, it is questionable whether more than five of the current U.S. Congressional Black Caucus members would escape being classified either as "mulattoes" or "whites" in a population count.

In Cuba skin color per se is not the only criterion determining "race." Also considered are facial features and hair texture.[5] Someone who is dark-skinned *but* who has "sharp" features (*nariz perfilada,* as one would say in Cuba), automatically qualifies as a "mulatto."An old saying in Cuba goes: "You can tell a Negro from a white or a mulatto if he is *ugly and black!"* This clearly implies that the 1981 census report (which spoke of "12 percent black," "21.9 percent mulatto" and "66 percent white") *must* be interpreted solely in *Cuban* terms: "black" in the restrictive sense of the anthropologists' "true Negro" or "pure-blooded Negro;" "mulatto" in the sense of people resembling Ethiopians, Somalians or Eritreans of East Africa; "white" in the stunningly elastic sense whereby Fidel Castro, former U.S. presidents John F. Kennedy and Jimmy Carter, former Senator Edward Brooke, Duke Ellington, ex-dictator Fulgencio Batista, Lena Horne and Adam Clayton Powell Jr. could be said to belong to one and the same race.

The criteria for determining race in societies of the "Anglo Nordic" type (Northern Europe, North America, Australia) rest on *ancestry,* not solely on racial features such as hair texture, skin color and facial traits. But in societies of the "Latin-Arab" type (Mediterranean Europe, Arab North Africa, the Middle/Near East, Northern India and so-called 'Latin' America), ancestry is entirely overlooked; facial features *and* skin color remain as the criteria determining race.[6] In societies of this type (Cuba, the Dominican Republic, Brazil and Puerto Rico, for example), "race" is a very elastic and eminently subjective reality. "Race statistics" are therefore a potently emotional, and eminently political issue.

Fernando Ortiz, the Hispanic Cuban anthropologist, is not too far from the truth when estimating that at least *one-third* of those considered "whites" in Cuban censuses are actually light-skinned, "sharp-featured" Afro-Cubans.

Cuba's black population *increased* significantly since 1959 because of three reasons: a) the large *white* exodus that followed Cuba's choice of Communism, b) a veritable boom in the black birth rate, and c) a sharp drop in infant mortality among Cuban Blacks. All three reasons, calculated or not, are related to the Revolution. My own estimate, based as much on what I call "socio-racial common sense" as on the estimates of scholars whose opinions cannot be overlooked, is that presently the *Afro-Cuban*[7] or black population is unlikely to be less than 58 to 60% of the total.

THE "LATIN-ARAB" MODEL OF RACE RELATIONS IN CUBA

The racial question is an eminently *subjective* phenomenon, not necessarily quantifiable. New conceptual yardsticks are necessary to approach an understanding of it, particularly in situations such as Cuba's, or 'Latin' America, where this issue runs up against a veritable brick wall of taboos.

The racial question in Cuba is essentially one of *content* rather than form; i.e., an unquantifiable and extremely complex situation of intertwined *group* perspectives and responses. The latter in turn are the expression of a *subconscious,* day-to-day enactment of an intricate set of role-playing: commanding for whites, obedience for blacks; independent assertiveness for whites, dependent docility for blacks; high racial self-esteem for. whites, low or no racial self-esteem for blacks; sexual fear of blacks by whites, quest for whiteness through sexual proximity to whites and/or "near-whites," on the part of blacks (assimilationism); opposition to, but penetration of, African cultures by whites; shame of, but adherence to and defense of *African* traditions by blacks.

This enumeration could go on indefinitely. It merely emphasizes the fact that no study of race relations in Cuba can ignore either the view Hispanic-Cubans have and project of themselves as *whites*, or the view Afro-Cubans entertain of themselves as *blacks* and of the whites. I designate these two different racial group perspectives as the "white outlook" and the "black outlook" since they are replicated worldwide as the very basis of racism. An understanding of where they converge, where they diverge, how they conciliate or clash, is indispensable to an understanding of the dynamics of race relations *in Cuba,* before and after the Revolution.

Before 1959 the existence of racism was denied by whites, officially and at the popular level, as well as by a large portion of blacks. Since 1959, the existence of racism has been systematically denied by *whites* in government or in exile. What, if anything, has changed on this score because of the Revolution? This question will continue to receive inadequate, if not wholly inappropriate answers as long as a serious analytical study is not carried out to determine *the modus operandi* of race relations in Cuba. This framework, containing and/or reflecting the basic ingredients of racism and its attendant conflicts (consistently masked in Cuba as "economic" or "social" conflicts) is what I have chosen to call the "Latin-Arab model" of race relations.

The Arab-Iberian Legacy

The Arabs who conquered the Iberian peninsula not only introduced black slavery to that part of the world, but also a whole code of ethics on the relationship between blacks and whites. Black slavery was a dominant feature of the social landscape of the Arab world before the advent of Islam. Like all the other Semitic-speaking people of the Near and Middle East, the olive-skinned Arabs are a product of ancient black-white mixtures. Centuries before entering the Iberian peninsula, master-slave and black-white relations were clearly understood by the Arabs and codified into an intricate network of taboos, phobias. and reflexes: Arabs intensely despised so-called "Negroid" features and the Africans who possessed them.

Throughout the various stages of their imperial expansion, Arabs were obliged to defend their monopoly of political and social power over their subject black population. That alone implied continual black resistance (e.g., the black Zenghs' revolution and seizure of power in Baghdad, 870-883 A.D.). The available records show that for centuries Arabs persistently derided their African *Kaffir* subjects; that their harems were full of African concubines; that their domestic service was made up of an inordinate number of *blacks* (eunuchs who also served as homosexual partners); that their armies were largely composed of islamicized blacks.... The forceful literature of Al-Jahiz, the ninth century Negro-Arab writer, extoll the virtues of the blacks and castigating the contempt of them by white Arabs *(Kitab al Sudan wa'l-Bidan)* speaks for itself.

A specifically white Arab racism–elaborated on the basis of the racial domination of Africans–was prevalent throughout the Middle East long before Arab imperialism extended to southern Europe. The black-white code of ethics which Arabs had already elaborated as early as the seventh century A.D., designated clearly delineated social, political and sexual roles for whites and blacks in an environment of manifest inequality. Rulers (Arabs) mono-polized political, religious and social power and "protected" their subject populations. The latter in turn owed obedience to the Arab world-vision (Islam), and allegiance as soldiers and zealots in the imperialistic Islamic expansion.

Black/white 'miscegenation' was a rampant feature of pre- and post-Islamic Arab societies. But it was conceived of as a one-way sexual affair: Arab *males* with their subject *abd* (slave) African women and/or black (eunuch) lovers. Rigid taboos made the *white female* inaccessible to black males. The resultant and increasingly numerous *mulatto* ('mixed-blood') population enjoyed an envied position with respect to the subject black mass from whence it emerged. These 'mulattoes' were accepted into Arab society provided they became fully Arabicized and, of course, Islamicized.[8]

Mulattoization was thus the process leading from slavery to freedom and social recognition in an environment that was decidedly *anti-black*. Religious conversion, the adoption of Arab ways, language and prejudices were the corollaries of mulattoization, or the process whereby blacks became *integrated* into Arab society; no longer as Blacks, however, but as *Arabs*. Integration and one-way mulattoization (Arab male/African female) were inseparables in this process of vertical social mobility for the *abd* population. Hence, the "congenial" veneer of white/black relations in Arab lands.

In the Arab world the 'mulatto' is regarded as the negation of "Africanness," "Negroidness" and "Kaffirness." (Kaffir, by definition, is a non-believer in Islam, but it took on a racially pejorative angle as a global term for African.) 'Mulattoes' thus gained full, or nearly complete acceptance in Arab societies ... as *whites*. White Arabs were themselves the product of ancient white-black admixtures in the Arabian peninsula during the Sabean and post-Sabean periods. The *olive-skinned Arabs* were therefore in no position to draw a strict color line against the 'mulatto' without endangering the stability of their own color/class system. The 'mulatto' was too close in appearance (features) to the "pure white" Arab population for him not to be included as a *bona fide* member of the dominant race.

A system of mulatto "co-optation" into the dominant group therefore evolved over the centuries in Arab societies as a social, political and *racial* necessity. Simply, white Arabs could not draw the color line against the 'mulatto' without drawing it among... *themselves*. That situation is equally observable throughout the Euro-Mediterranean area. In Latin societies of antiquity the conquering white population (Greeks, Romans, etc.) were also forced to co-opt the numerous "mixed-breed" population that had risen from the conquest of southern Europe.

The elaborate system of black-white relations which the Arab world brought into the conquered Iberian peninsula was *the same one which the Spanish and Portuguese colonists introduced into the New World*. A slave system based on "imported" black labor from Africa had functioned in the Arab-dominated Iberian peninsula for centuries and even after the *reconquista*. In fact, indigenous Spanish speaking black slaves were with Columbus on his very first voyage and the first group of black slaves *(caleseros)* brought to Cuba in 1511--1515 came directly from Spain. The

Spanish medieval slave code *(Las Siete Partidas)* was but a mirror of the injunctions on the treatment of slaves in Arab lands introduced by the reforms of prophet Muhammad. The strong clientele-like flavor of *Las Siete Partidas, with* its insistence on "protector/protected" obligations between master and slave, is wholly consistent with the traditional Arab system.

The entire fabric of Arab social taboos, regulations and sexual license concerning relations between black and white was based more on custom than on law. *It was that customary system of race relations which the Spanish and Portuguese inherited* along with Arabized dance and song (flamenco, *fado),* Arabized languages and traditions. An inherited Arab-derived version of relations between races placed on an unequal socioeconomic and political footing is the basis for the so-called "soft" slave system imposed by Spaniards and Portuguese in the New World. Another result of that complex *ideological* framework is the so-called "congenial" system of race relations which is prevalent today throughout Central, South America and the Spanish-speaking Caribbean (Puerto Rico, Cuba, Dominican Republic). A "congeniality," however, that depends strictly on the 'subject race' staying in its "proper place."

"Racial Harmony" vs. "Racial Conflict"
Cuban society has evolved within a pattern of race relations of the "Latin-Arab" as opposed to the "Anglo-Nordic" model. Central to the "Latin-Arab" type is the notion and practice that the race which enjoys the dominant political, economic and psycho-social position has a near-divine *mandate to rule.* Conversely, the races occupying lowly stations in the society ought to agree to *obey* their rulers. In exchange, the latter extends the 'protection' which it considers to be in the polity's best interest. Benevolent *paternalism* is the cement that holds together a psycho-political structure wherein whites monopolize power in the name of the entire society, not only as a ruling class but as *whites.*

The "right to rule and to protect," and the "duty to obey and seek protection," are essential elements of the "Latin-Arab" model. In this context, corporate rights are granted from above and *autonomous* action by the social and racial underdogs is regarded as tantamount to "treason" by the ruling segment The latter considers the processes of power and decision-making as an exclusive racial preserve. Consequently, in situations of the "Latin-Arab" type, "harmony" between the races rather than open conflict is the norm. Conflict only arises when the *modus operandi* of that system is threatened by the autonomous action of the "dominated" segment. Only then may *violence* ensue along specifically racial lines.

Under the "Latin-Arab" system, the point where the subject segment says "No!" is the critical point of rupture where the congenial smile becomes a hateful grimace and the *abrazo* turns into a wrestler's hold. In situations such as prevail in Cuba, *overt* racial conflict is germinated only if and when the dominated segment (Blacks and/or Indians in the New World) refuses to play its assigned role in society, or proposes the adoption of a different set of roles.

One point needs to be kept in mind regarding all dominator/dominated situations: unless the dominated segment has disappeared (what makes it *different* from the dominating group being eliminated), it will always strive, even subconsciously, to perpetuate and in fact heighten those characteristics which made it different in the first place. If no *individual* can permanently live a near-sane existence with a totally negative view of himself, this is even truer for an entire *community* knit together by common values, ancestral traditions and spiritual outlook. Hence, an inferiorized group will, in the long run, seek to turn its "inferior" characteristics into positive values. This will be the case regardless of its efforts to identify with, and in fact be assimilated into, the politically and socially dominant group. Accordingly, *every drive rewards assimilation* on the part of those belonging to an inferiorized and subject community, or the imposition of same by the dominant segment, *will eventually engender a contrary movement.*

White Superiority: The Continued Belief

Anthropologically speaking, no common objective criteria to determine *race* exists in Cuba. But, in social, cultural and psychological terms, race pervades the everyday life of every Cuban, white or black. Cuban society was profoundly *racist* prior to 1959 and remained steadfastly so after. All of the basic racist assumptions which cut across class lines continued to govern the everyday life of blacks and whites, despite the Revolution or on account of it, since under its protective cover most of the old and new racial attitudes and assumptions are perpetuated by Cubans of all walks of life in their daily behavior.

The assumption that whites are naturally superior to all other races is a deeply-ingrained belief in both blacks and whites. Conversely, the conviction of black inferiority is also internalized by both groups. The whole range of complex relations between blacks and whites in Cuba is set between those two poles; not in legal terms but in the more ingrained area of day-to-day, interpersonal, and therefore intimate, social intercourse of the "friendly" type. Politically, this situation translates itself in the *de facto* belief that whites have the right to rule and blacks have the duty to obey. Socially, whites also arrogate the prerogative of assigning blacks "a place" in society: neither separate and equal, nor together and equal. In the economic sphere, blacks have traditionally been concentrated in physical labor, a situation justified in cynical terms: "Negro robustness," "educational retardation," "occupational affinity." It is only on the *cultural* plain that the clash of interests between blacks and whites in Cuba assumes a warring dimension; a silent war with the human psyche as the battlefield. The offensive weapons are: song and dance, proverbs, popular jokes *(chistes)*, religious beliefs and practices, language patterns, culinary preferences, and a sense of *group* historical belonging and destiny. The headquarters on both sides remains the same as in slavery days: a powerful, white-dominated state and church structure on the one hand, the Afro-Cuban brotherhoods and belief systems on the other.

Political

The attitude of whites towards blacks in Cuba *today* can be summed up as follows: "You people had it rough before the Revolution but you're living it up now. So what more do you want?" Countless jokes *(chistes),* conveying that sentiment are repeated with relish (albeit *sotto voce)* by revolutionary whites. Initially, blacks were intimidated but a growing assertiveness emerged from the awareness that *blacks* were the pillars of the new regime. Changing demographics and Cuba's deep involvement in Africa and the Caribbean, starting in the 1970s, has heightened such feelings. In their counter *chistes,* blacks tend to cast themselves as revolutionary heroes and portray the whites as below par when not outright "cowardly."A popular white saying is: *"Si el negro no la caga a la entrada, la caga a la salida, "* ("If the blacks do not *shit* going in, they will surely do so going out"). Blacks have sprung back with a biting counter attack by adding: *"Pa' que los makri resbalen!"* ("Just so the whites may slip"). Thus, *makri,* formerly a prevalent though covert black Cuban pejorative term in *kalo* for a white (to counter the latter's *niche, nichardo* or *negrito:* "Nigger"), has gained currency again.

Social

Since 1959 blacks and whites go to the same places for work, study, recreation, political mobilization and defense. They belong to the same organizations. On the surface, they either participate enthusiastically in, or watch resentfully, the unfolding of a revolutionary process wherein they are protagonists as victims or villains. And yet, the home, the family, still remain inviolable sanctuaries where blacks and whites continue to play out centuries-old battles. For whites, black males still epitomize a sexual threat and black females a sexual prey. Sexual relations between black *males* and white *females* are considered no differently today than they were in the past, i.e., as something detestable and dangerous, if not frankly evil. But *"acostarse con una negra"* ("To get a black woman into bed") continues to be in the eyes of white males a highly titillating experience which enhances their sense of *machismo.* It is also considered a "civilizing" venture as such relations contributes to 'whiten' the Negro population. Black males continue being regarded as endowed with 'barbarous sexual appetites' and 'unusual phallic dimensions.' White Cuban male phantasmagoria is plagued with such ingrained beliefs.

Cultural

The "white norm" is the prototypical esthetic norm in Cuba. Blacks have traditionally sought to become white or to approach it through *sexual* relationships with either 'light' or *white* partners. *Adelantar la raza* ("To improve the race") has been a permanent obsession among blacks, and white males have eagerly responded to it ever since slavery. The basic pattern described by Verena Martinez-Alier in *Marriage, Class and Colour in Nineteenth Century Cuba,* has pretty much resisted the test of time.[9] Far from upsetting that pattern, the attitude of the new revolutionary regime has been to legitimize it. As early as March 1959, responding to a question on intimate inter-racial relations, Fidel Castro had declared:

> *La revolutión no obligará a nadie a bailar con nadie. Pero si todo el mundo tendrá que bailar con la Revolución!* ("The Revolution will not force anyone to dance with anybody. But everybody will have to dance with the Revolution!")

This was in response to a white woman's question to Castro as to whether the drive against racial discrimination implied that white *females* would be 'forced' to dance with black *males.* Since then, the rigorous taboo imposed by the regime on any discussion of the racial issue has merely reinforced the inherited pattern of inequality and racism.

Race and Sex: The Continued Taboo

The quest for "whiteness" among blacks implies "marrying light," if not *white,* for black male and female alike. For white males, it often implies "marrying white" but "sleeping black" For white females, "marrying white" but "fantasizing black," is the norm. In this context the mulatto syndrome has gained reinforced currency *through official sanction.* The assumption is that Cuban society is inevitably evolving towards a racially homogeneous population of near-white and white-skinned people.

The racial eugenics theories expounded in the 1960s by José Elfías Entralgo were officially endorsed with enthusiasm. Cuba's future, said Entralgo, depended on the "de-Africanization" of blacks, the "de-Europeanization" of whites, and the fusion of both into a "mulatto" magma.[10] To the unsuspecting observer this goal might appear as a genuine attempt to arrive at a *non-racist* solution of Cuba's long-standing racial dilemma. On close scrutiny, the official encouragement of "mulattoization" reveals an amazing continuity of the belief that being black is indeed a negative human, cultural and racial condition.

Their avowed attachment to "mulattoization" notwithstanding, ordinary white Cubans continue to fear and resist inter-racial *unions* (though not inter-racial "shacking up" between white *males* and Afro-Cuban females). The fear of *black male* sexuality is very much alive among Hispanic-Cubans as a whole who regard open black-white relationships as something close to 'sexual subversion,' a threat to their dominant position if the white partner is female. Cuba's changing demographics has heightened such fears.

The fear that inter-racial sexuality is but a shortcut to the progressive *ennegrecimiento* ("blackening") of Cuba is more current today than it was yesterday given the greater physical proximity of blacks and whites and the higher visibility and attractiveness of Afro-Cubans in socially approved roles (heroic soldiers, dutiful militiamen, labor heroes, dedicated party or labor-union cadres). There might be much talk about a blissful *Cuba mulata,* but that prospect is rejected by Cuban whites, whether in power or not, both inside Cuba and in exile. Significantly, *Granma's* report on the 1981 census results spoke of the numerical "regression of the white race" in Cuba since 1959. No less significant is the fact that the term *"hemorragia blanca"* is much in use among Hispanic-Cubans to designate the continual exodus of whites since 1959.

Black Inferiority: The Continued Complex
The notion that racial diversity is a temporary phenomenon, doomed to rapidly disappear in a 'melting pot' process ("mulattoization"), is basic to the thinking of the revolutionary regime. The latter has given wide popularity to Jose Marti's rather Pharisaic dictum that *"Cubano es más que blanco, más que negro"* ("Cuban is beyond white, beyond black.") Significantly, that present-day demagogic slogan was equally the motto of the pre-revolutionary liberal and not-so-liberal white establishment and its intellectuals.

The idea of "national integration" relies on the assumption that differences between black and white in Cuba are merely skin deep, no matter how much the reality of ethnic dynamics since the Revolution points in another direction. Greater communication with the rest of the non-white world, particularly Africa and the Caribbean, *has heightened the awareness of race among black Cubans.* Greater racial self-pride and self-assertiveness has brought about shifts in the entire perspective of an entire generation of Afro-Cubans born since Castro's takeover in 1959. The authorities have found this development particularly threatening. The wearing of "natural hairdos" (afros) rather than artificially straightened hair is one such indicator among black women. At first, in the 1960s, "afros" were considered to be "counter-revolutionary." Thanks to Angela Davis' visit to Cuba, to the influence of thousands of African students in Cuba, natural kinky hair, though still frowned upon, is no longer considered as politically "divisive" or "subversive" as a matter of policy.

Despite governmental obstruction, and perhaps to a great extent *because* of it, black Cubans have become more *race conscious* than ever; at least ever since the period of overtly *racial* mobilization by the radical *Partido Independiente de Color* whose ill-prepared insurrectional bid was drowned in blood, with U.S. support, in 1912. But it is equally true that many Afro-Cubans still live in the grips of a near paranoid obsession with "whiteness" and a profound inferiority complex, regarding "blackness."

Overwhelmingly perhaps, black Cubans continue to believe that whites have an almost divine "right" to rule the country and dictate the course of its destiny, even though whites have become a numerical minority. This has led to an infinitely intricate and paradoxical situation. On the one hand, most blacks claim that "Cuban culture" is fundamentally *the Afro-Cuban tradition* and that numerically speaking Cuba is preponderantly *non-white*. On the other hand, they continually strive, in a variety of ways, to attain "white status" in order to escape the psychological stress and sociopolitical disadvantage that *being* black in a white-oriented, Eurocentric environment, continues to represent.

The "black outlook" in Cuba continues to be plagued by a terrible contradiction. An outlook which is essentially joyous, creative and optimistic, is at the same time self-mutilatory and steeped in self-contempt. What becomes of the tension which builds up in such a situation of near-absolute contradiction? The answer can be found in Frantz Fanon's brilliant expose, *The Wretched of the* Earth. A great amount of violence and aggression directed inward builds up among those who live psychologically pent-up as in a corral. In pre-revolutionary days, black-on-black violence and murder had achieved such fantastic proportions that law-enforcement agencies merely took notice of crimes committed by blacks against... whites!

Black-on-black criminality was basically the Afro-Cuban's way of turning their deeply entrenched self-hatred on themselves; it was the answer to the release of tension generated by a contradictory socioeconomic and psychocultural situation that blacks seemed unable to escape from or transform. Has the Revolution significantly upset the pattern of black self-hatred and its consequent black-on-black aggression and violence? Government alarm, openly expressed since the 1970s, at the steady growth of a distinctly *black* "criminality." in socialist Cuba reveals that the answer is negative. To what extent can the new wave of "black criminality" facing the regime be said to be a direct result of the monumental obstacles it places on the way of the free expression by Afro-Cubans of their distinct racial, cultural and historical identity as a people?

Since 1959 the regime has found ways to channel 'black violence' and 'aggression' to its advantage, for its own political purposes: domestic consolidation (state security organs, militia, the Territorial Troops Militia, the block-to-block Committees to Defend the Revolution), or overseas interventionist goals (Special Forces of the Ministry of the Interior, the Revolutionary Armed Forces ...).

Black Cuban troops have slaughtered village populations and "enemy" troops in Black Africa (the Ogaden, the south and east of Angola) engaging in a quite familiar exercise of 'black-on-black violence' and aggression. The canalization of black violence and aggression by the white regime for its domestic and foreign political purposes *has been one of the major racial achievements of the new rulers of Cuba.*

Inasmuch as Cuba's Marxist rulers view any manifestation of "blackness" as divisive and threatening, blacks, are automatically inclined to fall back on old, familiar patterns of black impotent behavior: black docility (toward whites), black violence (toward blacks); black loyalty (to the white regime), black disloyalty (towards blacks). This pattern has been given political legitimacy by the Communist regime: a black who turns in another black to State Security organs is regarded with higher esteem than a white committing a similar act and compensated accordingly.

The continuation, through official encouragement and social rewards, of the old pattern of black self-hatred and racial alienation is perhaps the greatest single indicator of the tenacious persistence of a fundamentally *racist* and white-oriented system of race relations in socialist Cuba. In pre-revolutionary days, 'black docility' was best exemplified in attitudes of "boot-licking" subservience on the part of black *politicos.* Their role was to woo the black vote or to appease the blacks; they never risked confrontation with the white establishment. Since 1959, 'black docility' has continued to run the same course. Blacks' "unswerving loyalty" towards the white leadership and blind obedience to its dictates is best illustrated in Cuba's most popular (black-derived) slogan in time of crisis: *"Comandante en Jefe: Ordene! Para lo que sea! Cuando sea! Cuando sea! Adonde sea!"* ("Commander in Chief: At your command! For anything! Anytime! Anywhere!")

Is it surprising that the black heroes upheld before the eyes of Cuban youth are mostly of the "muscular," "stallion," "matchet wielding," "gun-toting," "skull-bashing" types? The "heroic soldier" is generally a well-scarred veteran of the Angolan war. The "heroic worker" is a stocky, "millionaire" sugarcane-cutter. The "heroic athlete" is a square-jawed mastodon, generally a boxer. These are three of the four traditional, familiar areas where the Cuban system of race relations has allowed—in fact *encouraged*—*black* visibility. The fourth, music and dance, has been relegated to a "folkloric" station by the new regime. There is a *Conjunto Nacional de Danza Folklorica* but no "heroic musician" or "heroic dancer." This is because Cuba's white Marxist rulers abhor Afro-Cuban dance and music, especially drumming, preferring Euro-Slavic ballet and Italian opera instead.

MARXISM, INTEGRATIONISM AND THE MYTH OF A "UNIVERSAL" CULTURE

The *anti-segregationist* measures of the Revolution were avowedly in favor of the "national" and "racial" *integration* of the black population. What the revolutionary regime meant by "racial integration" can be summed up as the elimination of all physical barriers preventing the entry of blacks into public administration, the labor market, educational and cultural centers, the media, security and defense (armed forces, police, etc.). But did the fabric of race relations in Cuba rest on racial *segregation?* Or was the latter in fact but an *aberration* in a system, such as the "Latin-Arab" one, which can only function on an *integrationist-assimilationist* strategy?

'Integration' was a vital catchword of the system of race relations that prevailed in Cuba prior to 1959, wherein Blacks were summoned (ordered!) to become *like whites* socially, biologically and culturally, while waiting to become actually *whites.* Not only in outlook, but in skin color and facial features. Until 1959, however, no government in Cuba had been prepared to confront *segregation* practices head-on and take the integrationist dynamic inherent to the 'Latin-Arab' model to its full and only logical conclusion: *full insertion of blacks in every aspect of public life* in exchange for the total surrender by the latter of their own psychocultural and historical distinctiveness.

Since 1959 Cuba has been experiencing a process aimed at the imposition of a new supposedly 'non-racial' outlook. The major problem is that the revolutionary regime has endeavored to arrive at a common 'non-racial' and 'universal' outlook by attempting to stamp out the *black* one: assaults on the Afro-Cuban religions; abolition of the Afro-Cuban mutual-aid *Sociedades de Color;* persecution of the secret male brotherhood, or *Sociedad Abakuá;* unofficial offensive against Afro-Cuban language patterns ("Afro-Spanish" and the black Cuban creole, known as *kalo);* attempts to discredit the African religious outlook as "primitive," "irrational" and "superstitious;" the banning of the secular, "village" happenings known as *fiestas de solar* (during which *guaguancó* music is spontaneously derived)...

Marxism has been upheld as the 'rational' substitute for the distinctly ethnic Afro-Cuban religions and brotherhoods. And whereas pragmatic political realism led the government to adopt an increasingly conciliatory attitude towards the Catholic Church in Cuba (after a brief period of tension between clergy and government), and to establish good relations with the Vatican, Afro-Cuban religions have enjoyed no such lasting protection. The regime has never made a sincere attempt to establish good relations with the *babalorishas.* Sacred Afro-Cuban religious dances, prayers and songs have been *folklorized,* put on stage and treated as exportable or touristic commodities. Conversely, the *Euro-Slavic* ballet form–under the diva Alicia Alonso–has been promoted as being both authentically "Cuban" and "universal!"

The banning of Afro-Cuban carnivals, and their replacement by Spaniard *corridas,* was envisaged by Castro in 1959. Drumming was severely restricted soon after; at first to certain hours of the day. Later on to certain days of the week. As of 1965, drumming was subjected to government authorization altogether. The defunct Spanish dance, *zapateo,* was encouraged without success. An attempt to revive the *décima guajira* (sad, languid-rhymed Spanish songs formerly produced by the countryside's white peasants, or *guajiros)* also failed. It was to the Italian opera, and European classical music, that the authorities turned in search of 'universal' forms. Afro-Cuban music and dance, the only forms that *all* Cubans do sing and dance, were grudgingly left to run their course in a sort of "house-arrest" situation. Popular musicians, legendary composers, were forced to join subsidized, government-run unions which set the 'revolutionary guidelines' for artistic ... creation.

The 'new' outlook proposed to all Cubans as 'non-racial' and 'universalist' was in fact distinctly *European.* Marxism, imposed as the "national" ideology, was the most accomplished version of the Western rationalist tradition. And the promoted opera and ballet forms, besides being strictly Western and Eastern *European,* had no more "proletarian" qualities than Marxism itself (an ideological whim of the alienated, atheistic intellectual petit-bourgeoisie of the Old Continent). So that the outlook proposed by the revolutionary regime as the only means of achieving national and racial integration amounted to the imposition of *another,* but certainly not 'new,' outlook: recognizably *white,* unmistakably *European* and quite *bourgeois,* in the *nouveau-riche,* left-wing sense. Everything but *national.*

This brings us to one of the major contradictions of the Cuban Revolution: a new order had assumed power in the name of *nationalism* but immediately attempted to uproot and inhibit the production of one of Cuba's two national cultures.[11] In fact, not a single cultural proposal, social reform, or political institution proposed to Cubans since 1959 has had even the remotest filiation to anything home-grown, least of all "proletarian." For the concrete spiritual, social, cultural and linguistic creations traditionally associated with the term "Cuban" emerged essentially from the working class people of Cuba: the *blacks.*

The Myth of a "Syncretic" Culture
Throughout Cuba's history, from slave-colony to the present-day revolutionary Marxist dispensation, the descendants of Africans

(dark and light-skinned alike) have developed a distinct cultural tradition, i.e., a vision of life and the world which is rooted in the collective historical experience, beliefs and traditions of Cuban Blacks. Today there is an unmistakable Afro-Cuban tradition and culture; an oral-literature (tales, fables); a "Black Spanish" language pattern (Afro-Spanish) besides a native-born creole language *(kalo);* a culinary tradition; a particular view of life and death; distinctly African musical patterns in song and dance; definite motifs in the plastic arts; and a distinct spirituality (ancestor cult, spirit-worship) based on a multiplicity of fundamental deities which communicate with mankind through the 'trance.'

The contribution of Hispanic-Cubans to what has become known as "Cuban culture"[12] is negligible. Cuban whites have systematically *co-opted* as theirs what is distinctly the product of the Afro-Cuban contribution. The new regime has therefore done no better than to have given new legitimacy to an unfounded pre-revolutionary proposition according to which "Cuban culture" is an amalgam of Spanish *culture* and African "elements." Pre-1959 and post-1959 Hispanic-Cubans prefer to continue feigning to ignore that Afro-Cuban culture arose during the slave period, not after. A culture of the slave *barracones* and not that of the seigniorial mansions of white, Spanish slave-owners. A culture of the *cabildos* and not that of the white, Spanish Catholic clergy. A culture which emerged from people who boasted a *multi-ethnic* background. People who worked in the fields; cut the cane; made the sugar and took the blows. Not the "culture" of the white, Spanish military hierarchy and/or soldiery. Or the white overseers. Or the late-comer white peasants imported from Spain *(guajiros)* who acted as *ranchadores* (hunters of runaway slaves).

The widely-adhered-to belief in a "syncretic" or "mulatto" culture wherein whites and blacks supposedly contributed "half-and-half" is unfounded. It is symptomatic, however, of the ignorance about what the real Cuba, the popular world of the Blacks, or even that of *urban grassroot whites,* is all about. The Hispanic strain has barely contributed anything to what is called *Cuban culture,* apart, of course, from its *imposed* notions of socioeconomic organization and the Spanish language itself which has already been 'afroized.'

Afro-Cuban culture is an entirely *popular* phenomenon. It permeates the lives and outlook of grassroot whites in ways that even they are hardly aware of themselves. Cubans are spiritually committed to a host of African ancestral spirits and deities (Ifa, *Shango, Eshún)*, permanently invoked as sources of comfort, healing and encouragement. *Cubanness* is inseparable from a cob-web of "extended family" and friendship relations wherein the sense of *community* is paramount. A quasi mystical brotherhood (born in the *barracones)* is expressed in the term *hermano.* There are a host of alternative terms in *kalo* for "brother"–i.e., *asére, bonko, ekobio, monina*–an indication of how emotionally charged and affectionate in intent the term *hermano* actually is. The term "brother/sister" bear such a racially cohesive meaning that the socialist regime regards it as frankly objectionable and has dis-couraged its use in favor of the emotionally neutral term, *compañero* (comrade).

Cubanness is the permanent quest for festive (song and dance) celebrations of life *(fiesta)*; boisterous joking and laughter *(jododera);* an optimistic good mood despite the harshness of ac-tual existence *(alafia* or *no paso* nada); oral transmission *(bolas);* unabashed sensuality; public physical manifestation of affection (the *abrazo).*

In contrast, the psychological world of Hispanic-Cubans is steeped in puritanical mores (virginity), strong sexual phobias and taboos (homosexuality) and is dominated by the idea of sin. A world in which sacrifice is a virtue and solitude a norm. A world bereft of any binding tradition of song and dance. Both the *décimas guajiras* and *zapateo* dance were short-lived. Hispanic-Cubans are in no way responsible for the home-grown *kalo* language which they neither speak or understand. To the contrary, all Cuban regimes from the days of slavery to the present have severely repressed *kalo* as the "parlance" and "patois" of the Afro-Cuban "criminal world" *(hampa).* The burden thus rests on Hispanic-Cubans to demonstrate that Cuba has produced, as they claim, a homogeneous "syncretic" ("mulatto") culture, or even that things are perceived as such by the *majority* of Cubans since the Revolution.

MARXISM VS. NEGRITUDE

Racism continues to be a vivid phenomenon permeating the entire fabric of Cuban society. What makes it such an *unobtrusive* phenomenon is the fact that one is dealing with a *time-tested, commonly adhered-to pattern of psycho-social behavior internalized by both whites and blacks.* In nearly three decades of power, a regime that prides itself on being the embodiment of "racial democracy" and social egalitananism, has steadfastly refused to attack the structure of race relations established layer by layer, over a period of several centuries of black oppression and white supremacy.

Racism in revolutionary Cuba is an integral part of the whites' outlook on Blacks and the Blacks' outlook on...*themselves.* Any attempt to upset that situation is thus perceived *personally* as a serious threat by whites, both in power and at the grassroots level, and even so by certain blacks themselves. The latter's motto is: 'Do not rock the boat!'

The Cuban educational system is "oriented" accordingly in regard to the analysis of the island's history. Blacks and whites continue to be taught a version of Cuban history which legitimizes the old racist assumptions. José Antonio Saco, Carlos Manuél de Céspedes, José de la Luz y Caballero, Francisco Arango y Parreño, and other whites continue to be presented as the "founding fathers of the nation." The fact that these were militantly anti-Negro crusaders (slave-owners or intellectual apologists of the slave system) is minimized, when not justified, or simply denied.

For Cuba's black population, slavery implied a state of permanent insecurity and insurrection; permanent opposition to the slave and colonial system. But enslaved black insurrectionists are not favorably viewed inasmuch as they were *anti-white.* But being anti-white during the long centuries of black enslavement was it not equivalent to being a *revolutionary?* Slave uprisings, their leaders, are *not* subjects to be taught as history, sociology, economics or anthropology under Cuban Communism any more than in pre-revolutionary Cuba.

The approved historians of Marxist Cuba (José Luciano Franco, Julio le Riverend, Oscar Pinos Santos, Salvador Bueno, Juán de la Riva) have generally ignored or minimized black struggles during the slave, colonial and even republican periods. At best, they have portrayed slave uprisings in much the same way as they would a natural calamity: inevitable, unpredictable and negative. More often than not, they have openly condemned them as "racist uprisings" or minimized them in general as "black riots." The black revolutionary uprising of 1912 (about which history books still remain mute) has been invariably denounced as "racist." And the 1812 revolutionary near-uprising *(Conspiración de Aponte)* has been denigraded as "the first attempt to organize a *racist* insurrection in Cuba" by one of the regime's foremost historians?[13]

After almost three *decades* of Revolution, even the anthropological origins of more than half of Cuba's population are treated most trivially by officially-approved anthropologists, like Luciano Franco, who claims that the origin of the blacks is an undecipherable enigma. "From the prehistoric standpoint," he wrote, "we find absolutely no trace of the Negro (in Africa) beyond the neolithic period ...."[14] Such a statement naturally raises the unanswered question: if *even in Africa itself* traces of the blacks are lost beyond a certain period, then from whence came the Negro?

At a time when Cuba had not yet considered involving itself in Africa, Ché Guevara had stated categorically and publicly in 1962: *"African history does not exist....* What Cuban Negroes need to study is Marxism-Leninism, not 'African history.' "[15] The Marxist view of history ("historical materialism"), with its unilinear simplicities of societal changes as an orderly succession of "modes of production," has provided *white* Cubans a most comforting view of Cuba's slave period. Accordingly, black slavery "simply" becomes a socioeconomic category like any other. An entire generation of black and white Cubans have been taught to view slavery as an *inevitable* historical step on the ladder of universal upward mobility towards an ideal Communist societal order. Such a view of sociological and historical realities has had devastating effects on *black* Cubans. Conversely, it has served to reinforce the traditional arrogance of Cuban whites. The Marxist ideology became in that way but an adjunct of Cuba's traditional system of white supremacy.

"The establishment of a slave mode of production in Cuba was not the product of chance," explained Pinos Santos in his *Historia de Cuba.*[16] The transition out of the "primitive" society of the aboriginal Indian population, he asserted, could only have been accomplished through slavery or feudalism since Cuba was not, nor could have been, an exception to the "universal laws" of development. "If we look at things from the historical pers- pective..., history offered only two alternatives for the develop- ment of Cuba: *slavery* or feudalism," he concluded bluntly.

Cuba's African policy has had one notable effect: it has imposed greater public circumspection on the white leadership as regards all issues pertaining to that half of the population which claims origins from that continent. None of Cuba's Marxist leaders would dare say in *public* today what Ché Guerara said in 1962, for example. Yet nothing proves that the white leadership has departed from the position openly stated in 1963 by Juán Otero, then Secretary General of the Cuban Foreign Ministry: "Cuba is not Africa and we *will not allow* any Negro here to pretend he is African. Cuban Negroes are *Cubans;* period! Those who are not happy with being simply Cubans, preferring instead to be Negroes, may pack up and go to Mississippi where they will be treated as such!"[17]

Juan Almeida Bosque (who for years has played the complacent role of the regime's "official Negro") was no less emphatic: "There are neither 'whites' nor 'blacks' in Cuba, only Cubans whose skin is lighter or darker. The Revolution has put an end to all issues of 'race' or 'color'. Those who want to stir up a problem which has already been solved run the risk of finding themselves in front of the firing squad, be they 'black' or 'white'!"[18]

Are Cuban leaders conscious of a possible danger resulting from their deep involvement in Africa and their continued problems with the "black question" in Cuba? The vituperative campaigns against "Negritude" embarked on from time to time by the regime's intellectuals and theoreticians (Roberto Fernández Retamar, Lisandro Otero, Edmundo Desnoes, Nicolas Guillén) would indicate so. Desnoes, writing in *Granma,* stressed the differences between "our Negroes" and those of the U.S. "The American Negro has neither the education nor the proper conditions for a *rational,* intellectual reaction to his plight,"[19] said Desnoes. Contrary to his "Latin" counterpart, he argued, American Negroes exhibit an "emotional" behavior which precludes any sound political analysis of the problems affecting them. Juana Carrasco, also writing in *Granma,* supported that view while underlining that "the idealization of Negritude (by U.S. blacks) has a negative aspect ...."[20]

Writing in *Casa,* the literary review of the regime's intelligentsia, Alberto Pedro openly raised the issue of the danger of Cuban blacks identifying on *racial* or *cultural* grounds with American, Caribbean or African blacks.[21] "To pretend and/or state that 'all blacks are brothers' would be tantamount to accepting the strictly racist premise that 'all blacks are equal,'" he cautioned?[22] "The so-called fraternity among blacks is a trap....It would be interesting to carry out the cruel experiment of shipping off an honest Cuban Negro with bags and all to, say, Haiti or Zaire, for blissful vacations among his 'race brothers' over there, in defiance of class interests and national borders!"[23] The study of Africa, he added, could only be productive in Cuba if limited to "purely *academic* investigations as one would engage in for any other part of the world." He also warned against "the ever-present risks of idealizing (Africa) or falling prey to the fetishistic belief that the world's racial problems can be solved by the mere fact of donning African tribal garments—regardless of their beauty—or by importing a traditional god, like *Shangó,* from Bahia or the Guinea coast...."[24]

Pedro ended on a hysterical note:

> The problem is even more serious since *oppression has practically emptied the Negro's head.* Where there ought to be a clear understanding of the most complex problems of the contemporary world, we are instead faced with *an idiotic, puerile and inconsistent reasoning.* We have noticed with alarm that all too frequently such a narrow reasoning affects not only the mass of blacks, but their leaders and intellectuals as well. It is useless to adopt an ostrich-like attitude when what is at stake is the very dignity of the Negro. Black intellectuals must be cautioned: no one has the right to *replenish the empty brains of the Negro masses with new imbecilities!.*[25]

THE NEW RACIAL-POLITICAL INTOLERANCE

In situations of inequality, *denying the subjected segment the right to express its specific corporate interests is a sure way of generalizing the corporate interest of the dominant and dominating group.* In other words, the integrationist drive of the socialist regime has gone further than any other previous Cuban regime in denying Blacks the right to exist *as blacks,* while legitimizing as never before the role of whites as the beacons of Cuban society. Fidel Castro's assault on the monied classes was not an assault on the 'white outlook', the hegemonic traditions of Hispanic-Cubans, let alone against the "Latin-Arab" model of race relations. If anything, the revolutionary regime's unofficial but effective imposition of a ban on any discussion *by blacks* of matters concerning race, its open and unabashed hostility to anything dealing with self-conscious blackness (from drumming to "afro" hair styles), represents the most formidable assault against black culture in Cuba since the end of the colonial period.

Revolutionary Cuba is a more openly intolerant and inhospitable environment for the expression of black *distinctiveness* than was prerevolutionary Cuba. This has relatively little to do with the absence or presence of racial *discrimination,* or with the nature of the neocolonial white regimes that existed prior to the Revolution. Rather it speaks to the existence of another type of state, *run by whites* which is itself the epitome of intolerance; of another type of ideology; *conceived by whites,* which is the quintessence of 'civilizational' arrogance. And, finally, of another type of party, the one-and-only party, led, organized and geared to the interests of whites who still are the *de facto* rulers of Cuba. Racial intolerance in revolutionary Cuba is masked by and intertwined with a general climate *of political* and *ideological* intolerance, just as in pre-revolutionary days opposition to blacks as such was veiled as a *socioeconomic* issue and *class* snobbery.

The new climate of racial intolerance towards blacks is best exemplified in the regime's insistence that blacks demonstrate their *gratitude* for its having eliminated racial discrimination. An unswerving, blind and total political loyalty and ideological discipline is expected of all blacks. Blacks who are *not* on the side of the Revolution, or who are critical of any of its aspects, are considered "ungrateful" and "double traitors." The only position a black can uphold in socialist Cuba is to support the government. Non-Communist blacks, not to mention counter-revolutionaryb ones, are singled out as targets of avowedly *racist* hatred inasmuch as white revolutionaries consider it "normal" in such cases to openly vent their bigoted feelings, being assured of political impunity.

The severe restrictions that blacks as such have faced to emigrate from Cuba are a case in point. Fidel Castro is reported to have personally issued orders in 1965 to the Foreign Ministry not to grant passports to blacks seeking to leave. Those who have sought to leave Cuba legally report having withstood considerable racial abuse by immigration officials and Ministry of the Interior bureaucrats. As far as the regime is concerned, Cuba is a "paradise for Negroes." Disaffected black Cubans who seek to leave Cuba are therefore viewed as "runaway Negroes;" people to be scorned for *wanting* to leave; severely punished for having attempted to, and despised as "non-Cuban" if they succeed in doing so. Black Cubans are thus hostages of a Communist state to which they "belong," having been 'confiscated' and 'nationalized' along with the oil refineries, sugar factories and land estates that the Revolution took over by decree the early 1960s.

Accommodation to the Regime

Afro-Cuba is a world unto itself, not easily accessible. It was inaccessible before 1959 and is even *more* so today. Many foreigners who have been to Cuba on short visits (mainly West Indians and Africans) report that they *heard* no complaints from blacks about their status. That is absolutely correct. Afro-Cubans regard visitors to Cuba–particularly those who come to attend official festivities—with a great amount of... suspicion. They know that the only visitors allowed to enter Cuba are those whom the regime approves of *politically.* To criticize the regime to an unknown foreigner, presumably a Communist himself or a left-wing sympathizer of the regime, would be an invitation to political suicide. For nearly three decades, blacks in Cuba have learned to cope with their environment. How many would jeopardize their situation in a brief discussion with an unknown visiting outsider?

Black Cubans have learned to accommodate to a Communist regime. They make all of the public demonstrations of unswerving loyalty expected of them. They participate in every mobilization organized by the government and Party. They keep their innermost thoughts for discussion only with whom they feel absolutely safe (white Cubans do the same). Critical topics, such as the prevalence of *racism,* they will discuss only amongst themselves. And because of the omnipresent state security organs and parallel organizations, double care is taken *even among blacks* as to with whom one discusses "forbidden things."

Does black Cuba support the Revolution despite the prevailing and perhaps widening disparity between white power and black aspirations? It is difficult, if not impossible, to determine *the* position of *all* Cuban blacks as a group towards the socialist Revolution and the Communist system of government. Being *Afro-Cuban* does not in any way imply belonging to a monolithic ethnic bloc. After two and-a-half decades of both accommodation and covert resistance to the totalitarianism of the Revolution, only one answer seems to approach the truth: Cuban blacks as a whole, including those who are openly at war against the system, *do not support any of the would-be-alternatives to the present regime.* There is unquestionably a general underground desire for a change *within the same system;* a change that would allow blacks to occupy *the place they feel is theirs in Cuba as blacks.* That feeling is expressed in a variety of ways depending on the position that blacks occupy *individually* in the socialist society.

There continues to be a recognizable "white outlook" in Cuba (basically racist) and, of course, a "black outlook" as well. They coexist in conflict in a "congenial" situation of *abrazos,* with loud protestations of fraternity and reciprocal denials of any sort of tension. They conflict in coexistence in situations of sudden crisis, leading to protestations of"disloyalty," "ungratefulness" and "reverse racism" (whites), or accusations of "racism," "discrimination," "unfairness" and "oppression" (blacks). What all of this implies is that *racism* is altogether alive and well in revolutionary socialist Cuba. It is well-entrenched behind an all-encompassing *ideology religion* which accommodates white supremacy but is intolerant of black distinctiveness.

CHANGE OF TACTICS?

One of the most astounding, even baffling, events of the past decade of Fidel Castro's rule has been his seeming about-face on the "racial question" in Cuba. This change was highlighted by the final resolution on race adopted by the Third Congress of the Cuban Communist Party in February 1986. The policy statement was not unconnected to the alarming migration of some 25,000

black   Cubans to the United States during the massive Mariel
exodus of 1980.

The Mariel "black flight" shocked the authorities and alerted
them to the dangers of continually tightening the screws on black
Cuba. Immediately thereafter, formerly persecuted Afro-Cuban
belief systems *(Lucumí, Mayombe, Abakuá, Arará)* were systematically encouraged to emerge from the underground. Religious
ceremonies began to be allowed to take place freely (without
previous notice to the police). Religious leaders *(Babalawos,
Paleros)* were no longer arrested under the charge of conducting
"unauthorized ceremonies." Even black political prisoners began
to be set free in 1981. And articles began to appear in government
publications stressing, *for the first time since the early 1960s,*
selected racial themes in relation to Cuba. One review even took
to task the critical stance of certain "blacks of Cuban origin" (a
euphemism for exile Afro-Cubans).[26] The latter, the review argued,
were wrong in attacking the Marxist regime as racist. With nearly
one-third of his army bogged down in black Africa, Fidel Castro
may have come to realize that his regime could hardly continue to
pursue its confrontational policy toward black Cuba without
ultimate repercussions.

Outflanking Black Cuba?
The clearest evidence of these changes dates to 1983 when the
regime, for the first time, released census statistics according to
race. Afterwards, visits of non-political African traditional and
religious leaders were encouraged. His Majesty the Asantehene of
Ghana (king of the Ashanti people from whom about fifteen
percent of Afro-Cubans are believed to be descendants) visited
Cuba in early June 1987. He was followed by an even more
symbolically powerful personality: His Majesty Oba Okunade
Sijuwade Olubuse II, the *Ooni* of Ifé (sacred capital of the Yoruba
people, from whom an estimated twenty percent of the Afro-Cuban
population claims descent). The Yoruba religion is the belief
system enjoying the greatest mass following on the island, among
whites and blacks.

The *Ooni's* visit in late June 1987 was preceded by that of Wole Soyinka, the first black to receive a Nobel prize for literature. As could be anticipated, the *Ooni's* presence caused great commotion among black Cubans. As the paramount spiritual authority of the Yoruba people of Nigeria, the *Ooni* could be regarded also as the spiritual leader of all those in the Americas who worship the Yoruba deities *(Shangó, Yemanyá, Eshún)*. The *Ooni* is regarded as the spiritual leader of the *Lucumí* faith, in a sense similar to the way the Pope is to Cuban Catholics.

Olubuse II's visit to Cuba was masterminded by Jose Carneado Rodriguez, the wily Afro-Cuban specialist on African religions whom Castro appointed in 1984 at the head of the Party's Office for Religious Affairs. The *Ooni* and his entourage were personally attended to by the highest authorities: President Fidel Castro, Politburo members Jorge Risquet and Armando Hart. The African dignitary was reported to have urged cooperation with the regime when he received some twenty Cuban *Babalawos* during a private meeting. And at the end of his visit, it was officially announced that Cuba would host the Fourth International Congress on Orisha Tradition and Culture as well as establish a permanent Cultural Mission in Ire.

The *Ooni's* cultural adviser, Dr. Omotoso Eluyemi, an archeologist at the University of Ire and staunch Marxist (Eluyemi spent several years studying in the USSR), was euphoric. *Granma* reported him to have stated at the end of his visit:

> In Cuba the solution of racial problems has surpassed what the so-called industrialized countries have done. *Cuba is the only country I know of up to now where the color of a person's skin has been totally eradicated from the people's mind and this can only be achieved by means of a socialist society.*[27]

The Third Party Congress and Race

Fidel Castro caused surprise at the closing of the Third Congress in February 1986 when he read a terse statement on race (reportedly the product of a three-hour Politburo debate on the racial question *in Cuba*). He acknowledged implicitly that his regime had been practicing *racial discrimination* all the while and promised drastic changes in the area of race relations. The most explicit policy change concerned the adoption of previously rejected *racial affirmative action* schemes. The Congress document stated:

> In order for the Party's leadership to *duly reflect* the ethnic composition of our people, *it must include* those patriots of proven revolutionary merit and talents who in the past have been *discriminated against* because of their *skin color*. The *promotion of all capable members* of our society and *their incorporation into the party* and its *leadership* must not be left to chance?[28]

This cryptic statement said more by omission than Castro himself would have dared admit to his audience: *the massive disaffection of black Cuba from the socialist regime.* The Party's resolution eroded the credibility of those pro-regime stalwarts, in Cuba and abroad, who until then had decried any denunciation of racial conditions in Cuba as being the product of U.S.-inspired propaganda spread by black "agents of the CIA."

The More Things Change ...
Demographically, what is called the "black boom," in contrast to what is designated as the "white hemorrhage," continued on an upward trend during the 1980s. Census authorities spoke in 1983 of the *"decline of the white race in Cuba."* That process could even accelerate in the future. All observers agree: the Cuban population as a whole has been growing *darker* since 1959. Viewed over the next twenty-five years (in which span the present white, male, Marxist leadership will likely have passed away), black demographic preponderance raises the question in everyone's mind of *the inevitability of black majority rule in Cuba.* It bears remembering that the Caribbean is a *black*

ethnogeographic area, and that Cuba *is,* after all, a Caribbean country.[29]

Historically, the prospect of "black rule" has been dreaded by all Hispanic-Cuban sectors and there is no evidence that the reverse is the case today (either in Cuba or among Hispanic-Cubans in exile). Thus, the old phobia known as the *peligro negro* (black menace), may be reactivitated under new mantles the more Afro-Cubans push forcefully for change. On the other hand, if the regime fails to quickly implement its announced policies to promote racial equity, government procrastination could only breed greater black disaffection leading to open opposition in the years to come.

At the time of the Third Party Congress, the situation of Afro-Cubans in decision and policy-making was indeed bleak. Significantly, black officials held only traditionally 'black posts': five out of six ambassadorial posts in the Caribbean were filled by black Cuban diplomats; fifteen out of twenty-one Cuban ambassadors serving in African states were black.... (Only two blacks were reported to have been serving at that period as ambassadors in Asia, Europe or the Middle East.) In 1986, out of a total of thirty-four cabinet ministers, *only five* were reportedly Afro-Cubans. Only an estimated 35 percent of the 481 deputies of the National Assembly of People's Power were reportedly Afro-Cubans. In the armed forces, the situation was even more dramatic: not a single black had been elevated to the rank of division General or Admiral. Cuba's joint chiefs of staff were entirely Hispanic. However, the overwhelming majority (about 60 percent) of the infantry stationed in Angola and Ethiopia in 1986 (between 30,000 and 45,000 men) was reported to be comprised of Afro-Cubans. The overall proportion of Blacks occupying leadership or decision-making positions in the combined structures of power in Cuba in 1986 (Council of Ministers, Council of State, Communist Party Politburo and Central Committee, *Fuerzas Armadas Revolucionarias (FAR),* National Assembly), *did not exceed 9 percent.* And the estimated percentage of rank-and-file black membership in the Communist Party of Cuba was reported to be as low as 34.5 percent.

The Advent of Racial Democracy?

The era of white supremacy (politically, socially, culturally) may be coming to an end in Cuba, irrespective of the political character of the state that is slowly emerging out of the present transitional period marked by the end *of fidelista* rule. The Cuba of the next twenty-five years may be ruled by a regime that will reflect the true racial-cultural composition of the Cuban people. If so, ironically, racial democracy, at least in its embryonic form, will have been achieved *despite*, in fact *against*, the policies of a decidedly Negro-phobic Marxist regime. And yet, these changes will have been the direct result, to a great extent, of the domestic revolutionary transformations and international policies enacted by Fidel Castro's regime over the past twenty-seven years.

The regime's socialization of the economy during the 1960s, which induced the emigration of some 800,000 Hispanic-Cubans, *immediately increased the black share of the general population.* The eradication of diseases that afflicted mainly the poorest sectors of the black population; greater access to free medical care; the confidence inspired in blacks by the Revolution's promises.... These factors contribute to explain the extraordinary Afro-Cuban *demographic* revolution that has been quietly taking place since 1960.

Castro's interventionist African foreign policy, by instilling a new self-pride among blacks while focusing their attention more sharply on matters of *racial* politics, led to the emergence of an Afro-Cuban elite in both the civilian and military sectors. The regime now has to confront the aspiration for power of this black technocratic, military and political elite.

On another front, a black awareness "movement" (termed in the island as *concientización negra)* is growing among Afro-Cuban youth, intellectuals or not. It has its roots in the first protest "movements" of the late 1960s and 1970s. The nearly 20,000 African students in Cuba (most of whom are based on the Isle of

Youth) had their own impact on the sort of clothes Cuban youths wear, the renewed interest in learning African languages, or the wearing of braids by black Cuban women.

In the mid-1980s, black youth began to resort to *Zamisdat*-type activities with underground translation of chapters of books proscribed by the regime (chapters of Marcus Garvey's *Philosophy and Opinions,* articles by Abdias do Nascimento, sections of books by Cheikh Anta Diop, certain speeches of Malcolm X ...). Though it is impossible to evaluate the ultimate impact of this *concientización* "movement" (movement is used loosely here, certainly not in the sense of an organized political opposition group) the regime may have opted already for a strategy of fighting fire with fire: cooptation of the tabooed Afro-Cuban religious brotherhoods (the visits of the Asantehene of the Ashantis and the *Ooni* of the Yorubas might very well fit into such a strategy). Equally startling was the half-page *eulogy Granma* paid Marcus Garvey–the very man the authorities had until then considered a "black fascist"–for having launched a black consciousness movement in the 1920s.

The about-turn on Marcus Garvey (which opens the door to a reassessment of the works of Cheikh Anta Diop, Malcolm X and perhaps even Walterio Carbonell) could be indicative of a novel approach to Cuba's "racial question." Has the Castro leadership finally realized that Cuba is indeed a *bi-cultural* "Afro-Latin nation"? It is more likely that the Cuban leadership has developed some concern over the *growing racial polarization in Cuba,* rather than an awareness that Afro-Cubans are the inheritors of a cultural, historical and psychological legacy of their own.

An even more speculative interpretation of the regime's new orientation on the race issue is that it is preparing the *white* population for changes that are not only inevitable but which are already slowly in the making, so as to avert a 'white backlash.' The racial affirmative action promise made at the Third Party Congress is certainly not a popular issue among Hispanic-Cubans: the white Cuban military-civilian bureaucracy will have to be *drastically reduced in numbers* to make room for its black counterpart. The psychological conviction that power is *white,* anchored in the minds of revolutionary Cuban whites, will also prove hard to overcome since the regime has done very little to reshape minds on matters of race and politics, race and history, race and culture.

In the past, Fidel Castro's regime has made puzzling about-faces. The opening of a dialogue with the Miami exile community and allowing the latter to visit their relatives in Cuba, was one such move. As it turned out, that operation had the effect of irremediably splitting the white exile community for the first time. From then on there would be *dialoguistas* and *anti-dialoguistas.* those in favor of *dialogue* with the Communist regime, and those steadfastly against. It was a risky but masterful stroke that Castro took even in opposition to many Party leaders. Another audacious turn-about, again opposed by many high-ranking Party bosses, was Castro's decision to open up a dialogue with the Catholic Church. So one may not be too surprised at Fidel Castro's turn-about on the race question in Cuba, at a time when black Cubans are being sent to black countries to wage wars against other blacks on increasingly flimsy pretexts.

Mounting pressures from the growing black military-civilian bureaucracy might also be at the root of the regime's new racial initiatives. Cubanologists may continue to ignore the fact that this black elite represents a *new faction* to be contended with in the power struggles that loom in the future. Its claims are not ideological, as those of the largely monolithic white, male bureaucracy that has ruled Cuba since 1959. Cuba's new black elite has the unique characteristic of being able to align its demand for power-sharing with the cultural, religious, psychological, historical demands of the entire black Cuban population. That is a *new* factor in the politics of the Revolution which, in time, could become *decisive.*

Any realistic sociodemographic appraisal of the Cuban situation must acknowledge that the growing black military-civilian elite created by the Marxist regime *will weigh heavily in the process of succession leading to a post-Castro regime.* The Cuban regime of the coming twenty-five years will inevitably be comprised of the offspring of this first generation of black Cubans who rose to positions of political, military and social prominence under Fidel Castro's regime. It very well may be that this Afro-Cuban 'military technocratic-managerial' elite has now come of age and *has discovered its own class interests.* If so, it can regard itself as one of the chief elements of transition towards a post-Castro society.

The road to an authentic *racial democracy in* Cuba presupposes the emergence of new institutional and mental structures, and not just novel socioeconomic arrangements. It presupposes, above all, the opening on the scale of the entire polity, of an honest national debate on every aspect of race, culture and ethnicity in Cuba, from slave-colonial times to the Castro-Marxist period, passing through the neocolonial Republican era. The links between power and pigmentation throughout the centuries will have to be exposed. The interconnection between racial politics and the politics of race will have to be unravelled. The starting point to all this may simply be the sincere recognition by Cuban whites that *they are racists; the* products of many generations of an insidious system of white supremacy premised on an "amiable," paternalistic attachment to multiracialism ... so long as the whites are on top.

On the other hand, the Afro-Cuban people, victimized for centuries under *all* systems and held on a short leash (the massacres and lynchings of 1912 are there to remind us of that fact), must accept that it *has become an accomplice* in the reinforcement of the Cuban system of white supremacy by aping Hispanic-Cuban norms, forms and deformities, and by systematically deriding what is black and African. The quest for whiteness *(mulatismo)* is still alive in the consciousness of black Cubans of all social conditions. Such self-denigration is fundamentally *racist and* Afro-Cubans must regard it as such.

In the next twenty-five years perhaps, the Third Party Congress statement on race and politics under socialism may be regarded retrospectively as the first opening, though unintended, for a profound debate on the most corrosive element in Cuban society: *racism.* One thing is certain: *without a definitive solution* to the racial question in Cuba, no democracy of any sort is possible, and, whatever the political or ideological character of any future state, racial strife will continue to be the breeding ground of future Cuban dictators, regardless of their color.

NOTES

1. Walterio Carbonell's *Como surgió la Cultura Nacional* (La **Habana:** Ediciones Yaka, 1961), published in Cuba and immediately banned, was the first step in that direction by a black Cuban. My own essay, "Cuba: The Untold Story," *Présence Africaine (Paris)* 52:24 (1964), and Rene Depestre's government-sponsored rebuttal, "Carta de Cuba sobre el imperialismo de la mala fe." *Casa de las Americas 34* (February 1966) re-opened Carbonell's debate. Lourdes Casal, a black Cuban émigré scholar, contributed an important study, "Race Relations in Contemporary Cuba," *Minority Rights Group,* Report No. 7, May 1979. With the exception of Jorge I. Dominguez's *Cuba: Order and Revolution,* Cambridge: Harvard University Press, 1978, "Racial and Ethnic Relations in the Cuban Armed Forces: A Non Topic," *Armed Forces and Society* 2:2 (February 1976); and Mariane Masferrer and Carmelo Mesa-Lago's "The Gradual Integration of the Black in Cuba: Under the Colony, the Republic, and the Revolution," in Robert Brent Toplin, eds., *Slavery and Race Relations in Latin America* (Westport, CT, Greenwood Press, 1974), white Cubans in and out of Cuba have avoided dealing with the issue. John Clytus, a black American, provided the first insightful critique by a foreigner, *Black Man in Red Cuba* (Coral Gables: The University of Miami Press, 1970). Hugh Thomas' carefully researched chapter, "Black Cuba" (*Cuba, or the Pursuit of Freedom,* London: Eyre and Spottiswoode, 1971) was followed by a study by another British schoar, David Booth, "Cuba, Color and the Revolution," *Science and Society* 11:2 (Summer 1976). Swiss sociologist, Jean Ziegler, contributed an excellent chapter, "Afro-Cubans and the Revolution," *in Les Rebelles* (Paris: Seuil, 1983).

2. Kenneth F. Kiple, *Blacks in Colonial Cuba: 1774-1899* (Gainsville: University of Florida Press, 1976).

3. In a statement to African reporters in January *1966,* Fidel Castro spoke of the "African blood that flows through the veins of *half* of Cuba's population." See, *Le Monde* (Paris), January 30, 1966, and *Al Akhbar* (Cairo), January 29, 1966).

4. *Granma,* September 4, 1983, p, 1.

5. Reinaldo Barraso, an Afro-Cuban dissident exiled in France, told this author of his battle with immigration officials to change the designation from "*mulatto*" to "*black*" on his emigration form, but the recalcitrant officials maintained that his *nariz perfilada* qualified him as a "mulatto" despite his very dark skin. Interview with the author, Paris, April 20, 1981.

6. Harry Hoetink's *Caribbean Race Relations: The Two Variants* (London: Oxford University Press 1967) provides the most credible explanation regarding

the "Anglo-Nordic" as opposed to the "Latin-Mediterranean" models of race relations.

7. By "Afro-Cuban" is meant here Cubans of *distinctly* African descent, regardless of nuances in terms of pigmentation, hair texture, or facial features.

8. The term "mulatto" most likely originated among Middle Eastern Arabs. *Mwalád,* from which it may be derived, is the standard term to define offspring of Africans with Arabs in Arabicized countries.

9. Verena Martínez-Alier, *Marriage, Class and Colour in Nineteenth-Century Cuba: A Study of Racial Attitudes and Sexual Values in a Slave Society* (London: Cambridge University Press, 1974).

10. José Elías Entralgo, "La mulatización Cubana," *Casa de las Américas,* 36-37 (May-August 1966), pp. 76-80.

11. See, in this regard, Antonio Benítez Rojo, "La cultura Caribeña en Cuba: continuidad versus ruptura," *Cuban Studies/Estudios Cubanos* 14:1 Winter 1984), pp. 1-15.

12. The very concepts of *nation* and *culture,* as concerns most countries of the "New World," requires cautious re-examination nowadays. Most New World societies are *multi-cultural, multi-ethnic* and some may frankly be designated as multi-*national.*

13. Juán de la Riva, "Cuadro sinóptico de la esclavitud en Cuba y de la cultura occidental," *Actas del Folklore* (La Habana) 1:5 (1961), p. 13.

14. José Luciano Franco, "Preséncia de Africa en América," *Tricontinental* 14 (1969), p. 47.

15. Ché Guevara to a group of American students who visited Cuba in the summer of 1963. See More, "Cuba: The Untold Story p. 217.

16. Oscar Pinos Sántos, *Historia de Cuba* (La Habana: Editorial Universitaria, 1963), p. *45.*

17. Juán Otero, secretary general of the Cuban Foreign Ministry, to the author, September 1963, La Habana.

18. Juán Almeida to the author, Santa Clara, August 1961. During our conversion, which took place in Major Almeida's office at the old army headquarters in Santa Clara, the latter pointedly insisted that he was a "mulatto."

19. Edmundo Desnóes, "El movimiento negro en los Estádos Unidos," *Granma Resúmen Semanal,* December 31, 1967, p. 10.

20. Juana Carrasco, "Plus que Jamais, L'unité doit se renforcer," *Granma Résumé Hebdomadaire,* August 24, 1969, p. 9.

21. Alberto Pedro, "Poder Negro," *Casa de las Americas* 53 (April-March 1969).

22. *Ibid.*

23. *Ibid.*

24. *Ibid.*

25. *Ibid.*

26. Pedro Serviat, "La discriminación racial en Cuba, su origen, dessarrollo y terminación definitiva," *Islas,* 66 (May-August 1980), pp. 20-21.

27. *Granma Weekly Review* July 5, 1987, p. 1.

28. *Granma Wleekly Review,* February 16, 1986, p. *15. My italics.*

29. See Carlos Moore, "El Caribe y la Política Exterior de la Revolucíon Cubana, 1959-1983," (CISCLA No. 19, 1986). Universidad Interamericana de Puerto Rico, Recinto de San Germán, pp. 1-8.

THE GARIFUNAS IN HONDURAS*

ROY GUEVARA ARZU

THE GARIFUNAS of Honduras form a group which has its origins in the second Black contingent to arrive in Honduras. The Garifuna people came from the Island of Saint Vincent (Yurumein) in the West Indies. The Garifunas valiantly resisted the colonialist pretensions of the French and English who were interested in dominating the Caribbean Islands. But given the rebelliousness of this ethnic group, the English decided to deport them from the island. The Garifunas arrived in Roatan on the 12th of April 1797. They subsequently spread out along the entire Atlantic coast of Honduras, Belize, Guatemala, and Nicaragua, in addition to having a large number of emigrants to the United States of America, in their search for better living conditions.

It is worth clarifying that the Garifunas constitute the only unenslaved black group in the world, proof of which is that it still conserves its culture, language and traditions intact. Currently, there are about 350,000 Garifunas in the Central American region.

Because of the need for labor on the part of the banana companies (Standard Fruit Company and the United Fruit Company) which had to import laborers from Jamaica, in 1890 there arrived from that country English-speaking Blacks, this being the third and last contingent. This new group, having been under the yoke of the English for more than three centuries, was led to lose its culture, language and peculiarities while inheriting the language of its owners. Currently, members of this group live in the city of La Cuba, Tela, Puerto Cortes and the Bay Islands. It is estimated that there are approximately 20,000 English-speaking Blacks on the Atlantic Coast of Honduras.

The Garifunas have many basic organizations and count among these that of Cristales and Rio Negro which date back to 1896; outstanding is the Black Fraternal Organization of Honduras *(Organizacion Fraternal Negra de Honduras)* founded in 1972 with the purpose of fighting for the socioeconomic, cultural and political development of the Garifunas such that now it internationalizes its struggle and its movement towards development.

To find the means of democratization, taking into account economic and social policies, has been the major concern of Garifuna organizations in spite of the fact that educational limitations and segregation have impeded the obtaining of satisfactory results. This has proven to be sufficient reason to reinforce organizational structures and participation in the modalities of association in accordance with the customs and traditions of this sector of the population.

On the other hand, the organizational initiative to re-order and re-assess the cultural patrimony is notorious, an effort which is congruent with the desire for integrity which should lend itself to balanced development. In this sense, organization for Community and Social Development continues to be the traditional one in the Garifuna dimension; one finds homemaker clubs, youth clubs, councils/foundations, fishing and planting cooperatives, com-ittees, etc.

The Garifunas in Honduras represent *6.5%* of the total popu-lation basically spread out in 5 departments of the country. Unem-ployment and underemployment are latent problems among the Garifuna and contribute to aggravating the deterioration of their living conditions. To this must be added constant strangulation and inflation to which they are subjected by the intermediaries who arrive at their towns to buy their scarce harvest, which is then carried to the principal cities for selling at very low prices, thus assuring that their incomes are not sufficient for dignified living.

HEALTH

In the area of health, the situation is alarming; the greater part of the Garifuna communities do not have basic medical services nor health centers and where they are (in four communities), there are no doctors or medicines; the majority of the population, which has no resources to move to the principal cities in search of medicine, dies of infectious and contagious diseases since it does not receive even basic preventive services such as vaccination.

Housing is insufficient and inadequate for the family group. The majority live in conditions of overcrowding and promiscuity. Dwellings are built with roofs of straw, sticks and bamboo, and generally have one or two divisions or bedrooms, lacking sometimes the minimal acceptable sanitary conditions.

In the majority of Garifuna settlements there are no water, electricity or latrine services. Currently, the means of communication is lacking in the majority of communities, principally in the departments of Gracias a Dios and Colon; transportation is scarce, except by sea, which is dangerous and long; few have the resources to pay for the shipping of their products. The latter makes difficult all types of relationships with the principal activities of the country. In 99% of the Garifuna communities there is no postal service, telegraph or radio and, where available, some of these services are deficient or in private hands which control their operation.

ECONOMY

Agriculture, fishing and commerce are the principal activities of this ethnic group. These activities are carried out at the subsistence level; in some communities the lessening of this activity due to the high level of emigration and the expropriation of lands is notorious. Acceptance and passiveness are occasioned by the resources sent by family members located abroad.

The income of Garifuna families is below the minimum family income, given that their sources of income are through the selling of fish, coconut bread, and cassava; agriculture, washing clothes, selling bananas and plantains, cornstarch, coconut candy, coconut oil; raising and selling pigs, coconut pastries, fried fish, corn tortillos or through very low salaries and day wages.

The majority of the settlements lack title to property except for the communities of Cristales and Rio Negro which have title to communal property of over 7000 hectares, dating back to 1904 when it was ceded by the former president Juan Manuel Bonilla. The best lands are in the hands of Hispanic landholders and the few lands held by Garifunas are the least fertile for developing any type of extensive cultivation. In some cases, the Garifunas are even prevented from profiting from the forests which belong to them by the Honduran Corporation for Forest Development (COHDEFOR). Nevertheless, Honduran companies and private foreign owners are granted permission to exploit these resources without the consent of the towns with common land, thus depriving them of the few resources they possess.

Another important aspect is the lack of effective channeling of financial resources for implementing projects that permit the development of communities. However, the efforts that have been realized by the Black Fraternal Organization of Honduras have allowed many national and foreign institutions to provide some resources for the development of some socioeconomic projects. Currently, into the new National Plan for Development, 1987-90, has been incorporated the area of ethnic groups, through which, for the first time, the State will try to direct actions leading to the integral development of the Garifunas and that of ethnic groups in general.

Resources from the sea are exploited by the Garifunas but at a subsistence level. Various enterprises exist that are dedicated to the exploitation of said resources but do not provide any benefit to the adjoining populations. The situation of natural resources in the

Garifuna populations, basically of the populations in the Departments of Gracias a Dios and Colon, is affected by the presence of refugees, the national army and the United States army, and the counter- revolutionaries of Nicaragua.

Cultivation is carried out with scarce technology; the utilization of mere rudiments influences crop yield which scarcely reaches the amount necessary for consumption and does not provide surpluses that permit reinvestment to increase economic productivity.

EDUCATION

Education covers only the primary level, but this is deficient; buildings, specialized personnel and all types of materials are lacking. The degree of school dropouts is minimal; it has been proven that the children have great difficulty in adapting to the educational structure due to the clash provoked by language and cultural difference. For this reason, the Black Fraternal Organization of Honduras has fought for the implementation of bilingual education in the Garifuna communities. This request has been endorsed by the Ministry of Education, is being programmed, and soon will be put into practice.

This ethnic group, in spite of being in a constant process of acculturation, values resistance to the loss of its cultural riches and values the conservation of its language and customs.

POLITICAL SITUATION

From the time of Independence in 1821, the Garifunas in Honduras had not been considered politically until 1904, when President Manuel Bonilla conceded to them community property title for Cristales and Rio Negro (today expropriated for the installation of the Military Training Center for the conflict between the United States and Nicaragua). From that time, they have been used as a ladder for politicians seeking power; one can establish periods of much repression of the Garifunas, principally in electoral disputes between the two traditional parties of Honduras, the Liberal Party and the National Party. Still fresh in the memories of the people are the three massacres in the Garifuna communities, during the government of Tiburcio Carias Andino, one of the greatest leaders in the history of Honduras (1933-1948); in the village of San Juan, Tela Atlantida, more then 50 men were lined up on the seashore, under the guise of taking their picture, and were cruelly machine-gunned without the people ever knowing the reason for that massacre. Frequently, for every electoral period, many Garifunas died at the hands of fanatics, as much from the Liberal Party as from the National Party. Thus, many preferred to emigrate to safer places, creating settlements along the entire Atlantic coast of Central America.

As a means of self-protection, this group determined to identify itself with both parties; while the woman decided to be a liberal, the man decided to be a nationalist. In this way they protected themselves when the brigades of repression arrived. However, it is prudent to establish the real political and philosophical concept of the Garifunas as an ethnic group. It is one that has characterized itself by conserving the community principle as reflected in the saying, "one for all and all for one."

One can consider the political and ideological tendency of the Garifunas to be that of liberal progressive social Christians. The ideology, in the sense that we understand it here, is not necessarily a formal and structured statement, although it can be so. When ideology is conscious of itself and is formally expressed, we usually speak of ideological elaboration, although for the Garifunas the sense of community is more a sentimental than sociological response to the injustices of reality. This ethnic group has a definition of strategies, which to their understanding implies not only knowledge of their own possibilities, but a concrete vision of their adversaries' possibilities. Therefore, the political arm of the Black Fraternal Organization of Honduras known as the "Vindication Movement of the Black Race in Honduras," is outlining the gradual incorporation of the Garifunas into the national political process in light of the prevailing economic system. The movement to incorporate the Garifuna into the mainstream of Honduran society along with the rest of the ethnic groups of the country is a deliberate attempt to constitute a political force. It was in this sense that the First National Meeting of Ethnic Groups took place in December 1985, with the participation of five other groups, and identifies them as pioneers in the incorporation of the ethnic groups into the political system of Honduras.

One cannot ignore the struggles undertaken by the Garifunas in order to defend their rights since the time of Dr. Alfonzo Lacayo Sanchez, first Garifuna doctor in Honduras, Erasmo Zuñiga Zambula and Gregorio Arzu Martinez, pioneers of the first protest movement by the Garifunas as a social group. It created the conditions for forming a solid base which today is not overlooked, since the Garifuna organization projects itself as much nationally as internationally. Already one can consider as a reality its organized participation in the political commissions of 1990, given the capacity of many young leaders like Ambrosio Sabio Martinez, Salvador Suazo and Cesar Bennedith who have become truly invaluable in the Garifuna struggle in Honduras.

Their consciousness derives from the perception of very concrete injustices, of daily abuse and frustrations suffered by the Black community, as a group, at work, in the street, in the schools, in the welfare offices, in the hospitals; injustices that they have experienced along with their elders, but which the young are not disposed to continue tolerating. Their refusal to accept oppression has made them victims of a more open oppression than that suffered by their elders.

No oppressor ever resolved the problems of the oppressed, nor have the oppressed ever been able to liberate themselves from the yoke of oppression until they assumed the responsibility of forming part of the powerful in order to do so. In this respect, the young Garifunas have taken a significant step. Today, they are found at all levels of the socioeconomic and political system of Honduras.

NOTES

* Translated by Tanya R. Saunders-Hamilton.

BLACK BUSINESS IN
THE FRENCH WEST INDIES*

JEAN CRUSOL

IN THE French West Indies, official statistics do not distinguish between ethnic groups. But whether statistics allow us to prove it or not, one fact is evident to the casual observer: In the islands where the great majority of the population is composed of blacks and mulattoes, a majority of whites still hold a large part of the economic controls. Indeed, very small is the number of blacks that possess assets or businesses of considerable size, whether in agriculture, commerce, industry, or finance. It is true that some do exist; however, they represent a definite minority. For the most part, black businesses are small businesses that have a limited place and play a marginal role in world economic activity.

We surely would not be wrong to affirm that blacks and mulattoes, who comprise more than 80% of the population in the French West Indies, own probably less than 20% of the local capital. Obviously, due to a lack of statistics, we must be satisfied with conjecture. Still, we must point out, as will be seen later in this paper, that during the course of the last 25 years, the position of blacks in this domain have appreciably improved.

How can this situation be explained? What have been the developments throughout history? And what are the possibilities for evolution today? It is to these questions that we would like to

suggest answers. We are not claiming, however, that these answers
are either exhaustive or definitive. It is rather a question of hypothetical explanations because, to our knowledge, there has been no
systematic research either on the history of black businesses or on
their current situation in the French West Indies. Furthermore, the
absence of statistics, already mentioned, makes this task particularly difficult.

After briefly presenting the basic data on the economies of
Guadeloupe and Martinique (section I) and stating precisely the
place and characteristics of black enterprise in the French West
Indies (section II), we will then examine the difficulties of its
historical emergence (section III). Finally, we will attempt to
analyze the current situation and look at future perspectives
(section IV).

I.   BASIC DATA

Martinique and Guadeloupe are two small islands that have surface
areas of 1,080 and 1,800 square kilometers, respectively, and
possess approximately 330,000 inhabitants each. In 1983, the GNP
of Martinique was 1.1 billion US dollars, and the GNP of Guadeloupe was .9 billion, that is to say, an income per capita of $3,900
and $3,200 respectively. These levels are relatively high, compared
to those in effect in other surrounding islands of the Caribbean.
Thus by virtue of comparison, in 1984, the income per capita of
Jamaica was $1,034, that of the Dominican Republic was $1,105,
and that of Grenada $938. On the contrary, during the same time
period, the GNP of Puerto Rico was $5,000, that of Barbados
$4,500, and that of Trinidad and Tobago $6,900. We can consider
the French West Indies, therefore, to be in a somewhat good
position, that is to say, among the territories having the highest per
capita incomes of the region.

The economy of these two islands consists primarily of persons providing services. This sector represents 85% of the global
added value for Martinique, and 82% for Guadeloupe. Employment in services represents between 65% and 70% of total

employment and, included in this, administrative employment represents 30% for each island.

Agriculture—the predominant activity 30 some years ago, since we are dealing with former plantation economies (sugar cane, bananas, pineapples)–represents only 6% to 7% of today's employment. On the other hand, industry, construction work, and artisan productions contribute to about 10% of the GNP and account for around 15% to 20% of the employment. Finally, unemployment, which has been growing during the last 20 years, currently affects 25% to 30% of the working population.

II. PLACE AND CHARACTERISTICS OF BLACK BUSINESSES

It is probably in the agricultural domain that black enterprise is the most important. However, we are dealing with relatively small and very small farms, measuring around 5 hectares, some even less than one hectare. Cultivators owning farms of less than 5 hectares represent 84% of the total number of farms in Martinique for 1980. But this accounts for only 36% of the total land surface under cultivation. In fact, 67.5% of the farmers have less than one hectare, and this represents only 9.6% of the land under cultivation. On the other hand, farms of more than 20 hectares (a total number of 270 of them), appropriated most often by whites, represent 1.4% of the total number of farms, but they occupy 45% of the land under cultivation.

In Guadeloupe, the number and the size of farms owned by blacks and mulattoes are unquestionably more important than in Martinique. We will propose an explanation later in this paper. Still, note that farming areas of less than 5 hectares represent 91% of the total number of farms and that they occupy 50% of the land under cultivation. Farms of more than 20 hectares, appropriated mainly by French companies and whites from Martinique, take up 35% of the land under cultivation, while they represent only 2% of the number of farms.

In the industrial sector, the place of black enterprise is clearly less important. In Martinique, if out of the 4,000 industrial firms counted in 1984, we can say that 3/4 of these are owned by blacks, we must admit that in the case of 2/3 of these we are dealing with firms of sole proprietorship and, for the rest, firms that have less than 9 employees. Businesses that have more than 10 employees (a total number of 161) belong for the most part to whites of foreign birth or to local whites.

In Guadeloupe, the situation is not that dissimilar. The number of industrial firms during the same time period was 4,600. But this number, far from indicating a more important industrial sector, reflects simply the number of very small businesses of sole proprietorship on the island. Indeed, the average number of employees for industrial firms in Guadeloupe is less than 4. Again, it is in this group of small firms that we find the greatest number of black owners. Firms of more than 10 employees are, for the most part, owned by whites from Martinique, France, or the Middle East.

As for the commercial sector, which includes 4,000 to 5,000 firms on each island, we must distinguish three separate groups:

- The first group is composed of a small number of very large import/export companies and a few large supermarkets. This is the shaky sector of the island economy, since it depends mostly on the outside. This sector is almost exclusively owned by a few large local white families and, we might add, more recently (i.e., in the past decade) by a few French companies. Blacks are almost nonexistent in this economic sector. The two or three blacks who work in this area have a minor place and must often thwart more or less regular schemes by the wholesalers who try to exclude them.

- The second group is composed of small and medium-sized distribution companies. It is in this group, which has been in the process of forming during the last 15 years, that we can see the emergence, more clearly in Martinique than in Guadeloupe, of a dynamic class of black entrepreneurs, alongside the stronger, more established whites. They must very often, because of their relatively small size, depend on these latter for imported supplies. Attempts to organize larger groups based on common interests and to form liaisons with the large import/export firms have not yet occurred.

- The third group, very large indeed, is composed of small and very small retail businesses. These go from the grocery stores and small shops to the very tiny stores–what they call in Guadeloupe "lolo," and in Martinique "bri-bri." Small retail businesses are more or less archaic and marginal, and are scat-tered throughout the islands, all the way into the far reaches of the countryside. In many cases, sales volumes do not allow them to be assured of permanent employment. They are owned, of course, in the majority of the cases, by blacks, and they depend completely on wholesalers from large import firms for their supplies.

In short, black businesses in the French West Indies, whatever the sector might be, are usually small, archaic, and dependent on the larger companies held by whites and foreigners, even if certain notable exceptions exist.

How can we explain this state of affairs?

III Difficulties for the Emergence of Black Businesses

In every society, the development of private enterprise and of a community's economic power, or that of a given ethnic group, depends on two types of conditions:

- Objective conditions of the social environment–factors that members of the distinct community would have at their disposal. Namely, their individual freedom to make contracts, and their access to resources and means of production, to financial assets, to training, education, information, and technology.

All of this, furthermore, depends on how the members are treated from the point of view of legal status, property rights, level of income, etc.

- Subjective conditions which are characteristic of the members of the distinct community–namely, their mentality, their collective culture, the image they have of themselves and of their collective and individual roles in society.

These two types of conditions are obviously interdependent. They are transformed throughout history by means of reciprocal interactions and through political and institutional changes. It is thus at the level of history that we must look for explanations for the situation described earlier in this paper.

The societies that we are examining in the French West Indies were originally slave plantation colonial societies. The historical characteristics of this type of society being relatively well known, we will try to be succinct. From a simplified standpoint, these societies are composed of two racial or ethnic groups: whites of European background and blacks of African origin.

- Whites of European background represent less than 10% of the population, but they are the masters. They own the land and capital; they have access to training and information; and they possess the political power as well as the power to repress. They own, of course, the slaves.
- Blacks of African origin, the other racial group, represent more than 90% of the population. They are chiefly slaves, which means that they are devoid of all legal status. They are not free, do not possess individual liberties, cannot make contracts, and have no access to land or means of production. They have access to training, education, information, and technical knowledge only to the extent that it is judged to be profitable for the plantation by the master. They have no salary, but rather upkeep expenses which

include food and clothing. Theo-retically, they
cannot save nor form assets.

From a subjective standpoint, we know the consequences of
the slave system, consequences that often endured after emancipation. We can summarize them in a few words: dependence on
the master, passivity, distaste for work, feelings of inferiority and
incapacity, contempt for oneself and for other members of the
community, lack of the spirit of enterprise, and lack of creativity.

These various characteristics of the slave system have been
studied at length in the United States, so we will not burden you
with them here. It will suffice us to point out an important nuance
between the insular society and what happened on the continent.
In the case of an island, the slave universe is completely closed.
The possibility of escaping to free territories where there would be
opportunities to live in freedom is much more difficult and costly,
because the island territory is very small or one would have to
cross the sea. On the other hand, in the United States, slaves could,
at the price of serious risks I might add, try to escape to the North,
where there were states more hospitable than in the South.

There existed, however, a few rare possibilities for blacks to
emerge from this slave system, that is, to gain the status of liberty,
which is the first condition for the formation of a business:

- Until the beginning of the 18th century, children of a
  master and a female slave were permitted to follow
  the destiny of their father, which created the advent of
  a population of free blacks at the end of the 17th
  century. Since the masters used these free blacks for
  the staffing of slave workshops, they acquired some
  talent in leadership and manage-ment. In fact, their
  power grew to such an extent that they presented a
  menace to the master's power. This right of
  inheritance was abolished at the beginning of the 18th
  century.
- Due to plantation difficulties, especially in Martinique, at the end of the 18th and at the beginning of

the 19th century, planters were obliged to give the slaves access to a small plot of ground in order to feed themselves. Many of them were able to take advan-tage of this by producing for the market. This per-mitted them to save money which could eventually help to buy their freedom.

• Finally, from the beginning of the first half of the 19th century, it should be noted that French authorities, under the influence of the new forces of industrial liberalism, favored emancipation. The creation of salaried workers seemed to be one possible solution for bringing about the disappearance of the old, archaic sugar plantation, and of replacing it with the new technology of centralized refineries, thus opening new markets for their industries.

Due to these various factors, the population of free blacks reached 5,700 in Martinique in 1790, compared to 10,000 whites and 84,000 slaves. For Guadeloupe at the same time, the numbers were: 9,000 free blacks, 13,000 whites, and 92,000 slaves. This movement was to accelerate very sharply during the following decades, because in 1848, on the eve of abolition, there were 38,000 free blacks in Martinique and 31,000 in Guadeloupe, while at the same time white and slave populations had considerably declined. But, in spite of this progress toward liberty under slavery, up until abolition, the development of black enterprise could only be very limited. Indeed, even if there existed a group of mulattoes that was becoming more and more important, land remained the quasi-monopoly of whim planters; free blacks had neither capital, nor sufficient technological and intellectual background to form independent businesses. Furthermore, there existed certain legal barriers preventing blacks and mulattoes from obtaining most of the prestigious positions and professions.

The first important opportunity for the development of black enterprise in the French West Indies came about with the abolition of slavery in 1848. Incidentally, it should be recalled that a first abolition took place in 1794 in Guadeloupe. But this only had a very limited effect on the development of black enterprise for the following reasons. On the one hand, lands abandoned by whites who were expelled or executed during the reign of terror instituted by Victor Hughes, a member of the National Convention, remained the property of the state and were not redistributed among the former slaves, as in the case of the Haitian Revolution of the same period. On the other hand, this period of freedom only lasted a short time, from 1794 to 1802, that is to say, less than 10 years. Finally, the repression that came about after the re-establishment of slavery caused the decapitation of almost the entire elite population of mulattoes in Guadeloupe who were fighting to maintain freedom. However, the weakening of the class of local white property owners in Guadeloupe during those troubled times, facilitated the repurchase of island properties at the time of the sugar crisis (end of the 19th century) by French and Martiniquais interests.

The period from 1848 to the second world war was relatively favorable to the development of black enterprise. In the first place, this is because a certain number of former slaves settled in mountainous regions and devoted themselves to rural agriculture. Others settled in the cities and became artisans, while others devoted themselves to fishing. In the second place, with universal suffrage being established in 1871 with the Third Republic, former free blacks, now the class of mulattoes, strove to reinforce their political power by running for elected office. For this, they relied on the black populations. As soon as they held some power in the local assemblies, general committees, and town councils, they used this influence to establish free education and to create scholarships for blacks who wanted to pursue their secondary education and university training in France. They also took advantage of the liquidation of some plantations during the crisis at the end of the 19th century, by purchasing them with funds from these assemblies and dividing them into smaller lots for the benefit of the black peasantry.

In the third place, during the second half of the 19th century, the most dynamic among the mulattoes created financial institutions, which facilitated access to capital for blacks and mulattoes. This permitted them to reduce the monopoly that the white planters exercised on the financial system, thanks to the creation of the first commercial banks placed entirely under their control. It was at this time, around 1880, after many difficulties, that we saw the birth of the savings banks of Martinique and Guadeloupe, credit unions, and mutual funds. At the same time, we find the "sous-sous," a popular insurance system or tontine, which also helped in the financing of black businesses.

In the fourth place, the crises of 1922 and 1929, and especially the two world wars (1914 and 1939) were favorable to black enterprise. Indeed, during this period, it was not possible to either import or export as in normal times. The population was forced to deal with local producers, peasants, artisans, and fishermen–all blacks or mulattoes–in order to obtain the essential products that they were not able to get any longer from the outside. Their products, substituting for imports, thus became a booming business.

Furthermore, during the wars, if the demand for sugar diminished, that of alcohol, for the needs of war that is, increased. Since the distilling industry required less considerable investments than the sugar refineries (you can produce alcohol with a simple still), many blacks and mulattoes readily took up this business activity. Even if after each of the two world wars, the overproduction crisis ruined a great number of distilleries, some belonging to blacks nevertheless managed to survive.

To a certain extent, these developments were maintained:

- In the agricultural sector, the plots of land were small and the land itself not too fertile. The larger farms managed to keep most of the good land. This situation was a bit better in Guadeloupe than in Martinique. In the first island, the greater availability of land and the weakening of the planter class favored the establishment of a more considerable class of black peasants.
- For the artisans, or tradesmen, the new business leaders had neither the training nor the financial

means to create adequately equipped businesses of sufficient size. Furthermore, since they were working for the local market, which was poor and limited, they were not able to produce large enough profits with which to modernize, expand, and benefit from the economies of scale.

The whole of the insular economy thus continued to depend on the plantation, where the largest part of the island's manpower was employed, the principal revenues were distributed, and the most important of the economic activity was accomplished. The plantation was more and more an almost closed institution, it possessed its own store run under the supervision of the planter, where the workers would get their supplies. Most of the plantations paid their employees with a specific currency, the "caleidon," which could only be used in the plantation store.

In short, if the post-slavery period gave some hope for the expansion of black enterprise, these few possibilities were very narrowly limited by the economic power of the plantation, the planters, and the merchants.

Some new changes were to come about after the last world war. Let us examine how these modified the status of black enterprise.

IV CURRENT TENDENCIES AND PERSPECTIVES

In the 1940s, the situation was as follows: In Martinique, the small and mid-sized farms of less than 10 hectares represented 87% of the number of black-owned establishments, but they compromised only 14% of the land under cultivation. Their average size was less than .5 hectare. Estates of more than 40 hectares, owned by whites, which represented 5% of the number of farms, occupied 80% of the land.

In Guadeloupe, during the same period, the small farms covered only 15% of the land under cultivation and measured on the average less than one hectare. The large farms, on the other hand, occupied 80% of the land. Until 1960, 23% of these belonged to whites from Martinique and 62% to French companies. Each island had about 10 factories, which belonged to local whites and to French companies. However, a good third of the small surviving distilleries in each island belonged to blacks and mulattoes.

The other sectors of the economy assumed little importance. Since most blacks were employed in agriculture, a glance at the level of salaries in this sector gives an idea of their economic situation. The average wage in agriculture was 45 francs per month in 1945, at the time when a liter of salad oil was selling for 30 francs, and a kilogram of codfish for 35 francs.

In the other sectors, salaries were higher, but employment was proportionally lower and concerned few blacks and mulattoes. School teachers, for example, earned around 4,000 old francs per month in 1945, but this group represented scarcely 1% of the working population. Public employees represented on the whole 3% of the working population.

A comparison of these numbers with those cited in section II for the 1980s reveals that important changes have occurred during the course of these last 30 years.

Indeed, the large white farms in 1986 represent only 35 to 40% of the land under cultivation. Blacks and mulattoes employed in public offices represent around 30% of the total employment. The average monthly salary in public offices is around 8,000 francs. The minimum wage is between 3,000 and 4,000 francs per month, and the average salary in construction is even more than that. By means of comparison, a liter of oil costs 7.50 francs and a kilogram of codfish is 25 francs. But the rate of unemployment has reached 25 to 30%, while more than a third of the population has emigrated in these last thirty years.

This evolution is due to many factors: In the first place, the granting of French departmental status to the islands in 1946 transferred a good part of French legislative standards to the islands in social and salary-related matters. In this domain, the struggle of workers in the West Indies permitted some gains in salary levels, social security benefits, schooling, and health standards. These all moved in the direction of the standards in effect in France. Although they have not yet caught up to France, the adaptation of an industrialized country's legislation to these archaic insular economies, along with the rush of government funding that accompanied it, brought about the explosion of economic and social organizations during the course of these last few decades.

Thus, the minimum salary and social security taxes associated with it, while improving the standard of living of black workers, also accelerated the rise of insular production costs. At the same time, competition from continental sugar and low paid tropical producers depressed prices of export products, leading to a crisis in the plantation sector. This crisis, bringing about the liquidation of a growing number of large farming estates and the division of the corresponding properties, helped a large number of new property owners among the black population to gain access to land, while inciting the ruin of numerous small farms. Those who acquired the land were not always farmers, but often people who had liberal occupations–executives or civil servants.

We are consequently facing a paradoxical situation–that is, while we are partitioning the large farming estates, the young farmers are having difficulties obtaining the land that they need. One fact, however, remains established: the monopoly of the land by the large local white families and French companies is tending to become an image of the past.

Schooling and training have progressed rapidly; their contents do not go uncriticized and certain aspects of their efficiency are debatable. But they have permitted new generations of blacks and mulattoes to occupy the large majority of administrative posts (although the management is still often French) and almost all of the liberal professions: doctors, pharmacists, lawyers.

Growth of state expenses and the development of administration have created a substantial demand for housing and consumer goods of all kinds, thus allowing new entrepreneurs, including blacks, to open up new businesses. But these have been limited to more secure sectors such as commerce, construction, transportation, and services, because, unlike businesses involving local production which, due to competition from imported products and the rise in prices, have only been able to stagnate or decline, these sectors, which are naturally protected from or dependent on importations, only slightly feel the effects of competition.

In the second place, the invasion of the new structures of French capitalism have weakened the local monopolies. This is particularly evident in many sectors. In the financial sector, on the one hand, a growing number of banks and French credit institutions, controlled completely or partially by the state, have been locally established. By introducing some competition with respect to the already existing institutions controlled by the local capitalism, they have opened up new financial possibilities for black enterprise. In the sector of lodging and construction, on the other hand, mixed economy companies in charge of building social housing and the large French public works companies have become a very important part of the economy, creating numerous possibilities for black and mulatto entrepreneurs, and a means for new generations of blacks, those who have had higher education, of gaining access to positions involving responsibility (management and executive positions).

Local capitalism, meanwhile, has tried to adapt itself to these developments, and if it has not completely succeeded in holding a monopoly in all sectors, at least it has succeeded in maintaining its hold in the most shaky sector of the economy, that of import/export trade.

For the future and for the long term, two new developments must be examined with particular attention: On the one hand, French interests, having difficulties due to the crisis of industrial countries, are looking with renewed fervor to develop new activities in the peripheries.

On the other hand, the new technological revolution in progress is spreading out over the entire globe. This revolution is accelerating the means of transportation, communication and production, as well as the processing of information. It is also reducing delays. We are measuring time by the 100,000th of a second, and distance by the 10,000th of a centimeter. This revolution has many names: aerospatial engineering, aeronautics, telemetry and telecommunications, automation, biotechnology, genetics, computer science, agriculture, hydroponics, to list just a few of the sectors. We do not yet know all of the consequences of this revolution, but what we can be sure of is that it makes distances shorter to the extent of transforming the world into a village, that it permits us to produce with little manpower and almost no land, and to export on a very large scale immaterial products, such as films, culture, art, scientific knowledge, engineering, various types of tourism, financial products–in short, all kinds of services. This revolution has enlarged the gamut of optimal production sizes, because it permits the miniaturization of all types of equipment. The gigantism of "industrial technology" is no longer a necessary path. It is possible to produce efficiently on a small scale, thanks to the flexibility of "scientific technology." The convergence of these diverse changes has made the human brain and education the principal direct means of production.

The consequences of these new developments for our people are multiple. We will examine two of them. The first is that distance will be considered less and less of a natural protection against cultural, economic, and technological pressures emanating from industrial centers. But, at the same time, the shortening of distances will augment the number and variety of opportunities and expand possibilities for all. The second is that the penetration of outside capital and technology can have two types of contradictory results: on the one hand, it can break up the local monopolies and modernize production methods and business relations, thus opening new avenues for the emergence of new local entrepreneurs. On the other hand, it can hold back the development of black enterprise and make it more dependent.

Here, as always, everything depends on what those mainly concerned, i.e., blacks and mulattoes, do. The only alternative is clear, and Aimé Césaire reminds us of it once again. We can turn our back on these new realities, curl up in our own shells and pretend that we know everything, how to do everything and that we have nothing to learn. In which case, we will only be more dependent and considered more marginal in the long run. On the other hand, we can turn toward the future, toward the learning of new technologies and methods, along with the attitude and discipline that they require. We must examine more profoundly the forces behind the evolution of the world in order to work out the best plan of action.

It is by means of this second alternative that black enterprise has some chance of liberating itself from the chains history has imposed upon it until now. And from this standpoint, the concept of negritude–the idea of cultural identity, as defined by Césaire–must be handled with extreme caution. It is a strong concept, because it is this concept of negritude that can establish the individual and collective will to conquer new domains of knowledge and learn new abilities, to take the economic initiative and the risks attached to it. Negritude can create the solidarity essential to the development of enterprise, and this includes expanding the market. Just think of the market potential that the large urban black populations of Paris, London, Amsterdam, and New York represent for products of their native countries! Emigration, which has so long been discredited, now becomes an advantage. With the shortening of distances and the chancing of destruction and marginalization mentioned above, we must use negritude as a defense to protect our beings, our families, our communities. But the concept of negritude must not be confused with or limited to the emotional and blessed adoration of obsolete knowledge and abilities. It must be capable of absorbing, digesting, adapting, and transforming all available knowledge and abilities. It must also generate new knowledge and abilities, capable of imposing themselves on the universal level. This is so, because in this world that is coming of age with disappearing distances, local norms and standards of quality, efficiency, and competence ought to aim at the universal.

The challenge might seem rough, but it is not insurmountable. In fact, some blacks are already showing us the way. We know some West Indians who have started technologically up-to-date businesses. We know West Indians who are modernizing their small trades, and youths who, instead of looking for the security of a salaried position, are deliberately taking the risk of establishing businesses. They are doing this, not because they want to make a fortune (after all, why would they not have the right to it, since they are also chancing possible bankruptcy), but because they have a thirst for responsibility, dignity, and personal independence. The pioneers then exist, but their number must grow. They must also receive genuine support and understanding from political figures and administrative personnel. Finally, they must have the loyalty and support of the people.

In this respect, the historical responsibility that places decentralization in the hands of local elected officials is very great. In fact, the development of black initiative and responsibility will depend precisely on how efficiently and intelligently these officials use their new powers. Indeed, this will be a question of not only democratizing access to economic and financial resources, of which a considerable part is still monopolized by a local minority and a few French companies, but especially of facing the consequences of the developments to occur on the world scene mentioned above.

The generation of our founding fathers–Aimé Césaire, Léopold Senghor, W.E.B. DuBois, Langston Hughes, and others–in their own time, absorbed and mastered the philosophical, literary, and poetic culture of the West and; using our own culture as a foundation, expressed our humanity–negritude. Why could not new generations do the same with scientific, technological, and administrative culture, which, as far as I know, never belonged exclusively to the West? Perhaps, in so doing, we will have once again contributed to the improvement of universal philosophy.

NOTES

* Translated by Shawna Moore.

PART III

AFRICAN WOMEN IN THE AMERICAS AND THE PROCESS OF CHANGE

TOGETHER

MAYA ANGELOU

THE SALE began. Young girls were there,
defenseless in their wretchedness,
whose stifled sobs and deep despair
revealed their anguish and distress.
And women stood with streaming eyes
and saw their dearest children sold.
Unheeded rose their bitter cries as tyrants bartered
    them for gold.
And men whose sole crime was their hue,
the imprest of their maker's hand,
and small and trembling children, too,
were gathered in that mournful band.
You who have laid your souls that love to rest
and wept above the lifeless clay
know not the anguish of the breast
whose loves are rudely torn away.

FRANCES ELLEN WATKINS HARPER

That is a poem written by Miss Frances Ellen Watkins Harper,
Black lady poet writing in 1852. It is still the same with us. "The
sale began. Young girls were there, defenseless in their wretched-

ness." I don't know Miami, but I do know Washington, D.C. That is true on 14th Street in Washington, D.C. It certainly is true on Central Avenue and Western & Adams in Los Angeles. "The sale began. Young girls were there, defenseless in their wretchedness." It is still the truth on 125th Street in New York City. It is still the truth in Oklahoma and in Tulsa and in Little Rock, Arkansas. "The sale began"—and it is still going on. Sometimes not only with our omission but with our commission. Black women and black men were chased together, hunted together, found and bound together, and sold together on the African continent. We lay spoon-fashion in the filthy hatches of slave ships *together*, the men and women. We leapt into the middle passage *together*. Rather than face the ominous maws of slavery, we preferred to face the ominous jaws of sharks, *together*. We endured also on the slave ship together, lying in our own excrement, awakened from our own nightmares to the real nightmares of hearing the screams and moans and bemoans of our brothers and sisters and lovers and fathers and mothers and friends. We stood together on the auction block, black men and black women, in Barbados, in Cuba, in Jamaica, in New Orleans, in Charlotte, in Richmond, Virginia. We were sold again, together. Together. It is imperative that we see this word as the burden of my song this afternoon. Together. We woke up before sunrise and slept after sunset together. We took the lashes *together*. Sold again, parted again, together. Always, at the same time, despite this caveat that we've heard in the last twenty years that house slaves had it better than field slaves. The truth is "a slave is a slave is a slave."

I think that it is time for us to go back and look at 1492. Not because of what Christopher Columbus supposedly did, but because of a small book written by Machiavelli in 1492. Having been exiled by the powers of the time, Machiavelli, in an attempt to brown nose his way back into the good graces of the powers, wrote that small book, *The Prince*. *The Prince* has become, still is, and forever shall be, as long as we are vulnerable to its dictates, the main diatribe which dictates our lives. Machiavelli suggested that in order to control the people, the masses, the wisest thing that the powerful could do was to separate and rule, divide and conquer. It still works for us. During slavery, interestingly enough, we were together. All of the bad and whatever good we could elicit from that horrible condition, we shared everything together. And then, with the formal end of slavery, the beginning and end of reconstruction, we began to take on the coloration of the ruling powers. We began to entertain differences between ourselves, by class, by color, and by sex. We acknowledged differences; the lucky acknowledged the difference between themselves and the unlucky. The fair-skinned, who were the result, the offspring, of the master's lust, began to acknowledge a difference between themselves and the pure-blood children of Africa. And men began to acknowledge differences between women and themselves. And we have paid, and are paying and shall pay for this foolish lack in our intellectual pursuit.

Black men began to take on the unhealthy chauvinism of white American men and began to look down upon their mothers, their sisters, their lovers, their grandmas, their friends, all those other folks who had endured with them the trauma of slavery, who had stood at their side taking all of it together, and they began to set us aside, set us apart. They exiled themselves to the very enemy who was at their throat and at other parts of their anatomy. To quote Toni Cade Bambara, "What are we pretending we have forgotten?" How did we come so late and lonely to this place? Have we forgotten that in the most hateful time we dared to love each other? We have loved each other. Come on folks. Be real. There is a nineteenth-century shred of a folk song in which a black man spoke of the woman he loved. He said,

The woman I love is fat and chocolate to the bone,
and everytime she shakes,
some skinny woman loses her home.

What is it? What is happening to us? What is it? At some point, the thinker must think. And at a conference so important as this, so thrilling in the classic sense of the word thrilling, it physically moves the body; I mean my body tingles with the importance of a conference like this. And at this conference, we have a time set aside when women may speak. At some point the thinker must think. I mean, I am grateful for this time. Had it not been for this time, my needs and wants and losses and dreams and fears and anticipations might not even be considered. But I wish not to have had it at all. I wish that my concerns were on the table with every other concern of black people everywhere. That is what I feel. But, since we got it, I hope you brought everything you need because I intend to be talking for a while.

Today, we are the focus of anthropologists, sociologists, a group I like to call hysteriologists, who tell the world almost in one voice, "Come! Look at people who don't love themselves. Come! Regard with me people who have no self love!" Even in Mario Puzo's book, *The Godfather*, there is a line in that book that still strips my heart. Here are people who work in the commerce of bodies and lives and drugs and prostitution and graft and greed. And one Mafia don says to another Mafia don, "You don't have to worry about the niggers. They will never come to anything because they don't respect their women." I was completely stripped. I still weep when I read it. I threw the book against the wall. I wish one of them had been standing there so I could throw the book at him. But I threw it anyway; I couldn't stand it.

The truth is there is something we must do, men and women. Something very serious. We are obliged, if we are to continue as a race. We are obliged to remember what we are pretending we forgot. At what point do we reach such a level of sophistication that "mother" becomes a vulgar word? There is a line in Lorraine Hansberry's play, *A Raisin in the Sun*, in which the mother, Mama, asks Walter Lee, "What did I do to you on my knees?" Think about that. The woman was on her knees nightly, praying for him. And when he became angry and told her how bad she was, she asked, "What did I do to you on my knees?"

Now, we are strong. It is true. If we weren't strong, if black women weren't strong, none of us would be here to talk about it. We make the mistake of using words which are pejorative. Aggressive means bad, right? But that is the nature of life. If we had not had some aggression, if black women didn't jump out, standing up and talking back, there would be nobody here to talk about it and this conference would be a dream, a figment in somebody else's imagination. It doesn't mean being rude, but our ideas about what is feminine so often are dictated for us by the size eight or ten young woman, who is one in a million anyway, who is about twenty-two and on the cover of some magazine. And then we decide on those values—the light hair, a waist about that large, and a backbone that would break if it had to face anything. This is not to cast aspersions on black women. It is not to do so. This is not what I've come here to talk about. But rather to see the beauty, the inner strength and the strength in our beauty and remind you, men and women, that we will survive together or we will die together. Black women have spoken to themselves, to each other, and to black men and even to the world at large in poetry and prose and song since 1700s when Lucy Terry began. We have explained what it is like to be black, to be female and black, to be mothers and lovers, lost, lost. We have told you. We've told you what it is like to love black men. Ms. Georgia Douglas Johnson, a 19th century black lady poet, wrote:

> I want to die while you love me.
> while yet you hold me fair,
> while laughter lies upon my lips
> and lights are in my hair. Yes
> I want to die while you love me.
> Who would care to live, to love,
> had nothing more to ask and
> nothing more to give? No.
> I want to die while you love me.
> And there, to that still bed
> your kisses turbulent, unspent
> to warm me while I'm dead.

In all these years, when we have written and wept, when we have pleaded and shouted and fought back and gone to jail and been lynched with you, been left and abandoned, at some point, you must know that our strength is your endurance. Yes! Let me just remind you of how hot we are. Black women, um, I was going to finish with Ms. Mari Evans' poem, "I am a Black Woman."

You know that we are phenomenal. You know that. We are. It is to our glory, the glory of black men and women. For we are your daughters, we are your sisters. We are your lovers. Yes, we're your granddaughters and nieces and friends and playsisters. Yes. We are bad.

Now, we are phenomenal. I know that men are as phenomenal as women are. I know that. Because I know that nature abhors imbalance. I know that nature doesn't indulge or permit imbalance grudgingly; it just does not permit it. Like you, I have been told that 98% of all the species that existed on this little glob of spit and sand are not extinct because they got out of balance. We are *still* here. So obviously, we're in balance. That proves men are as phenomenal as women. Yet, I would say to the men in the audience, you're going to have to write your own poems.

Pretty women wonder where my secret lies.
I'm not cute or built to suit a fashion model's size.
But when I start to tell them,
They think I'm telling lies.
I say,
It's in the reach of my arms.
The span of my hips,
The stride of my step,
The curl of my lips.
I'm a woman
Phenomenally.
Phenomenal woman
That's me.

I walk into a room
Just as cool as you please,
And to a man,
The fellows stand or
Fall down on their knees.
Then they swarm around me,

A hive of honey bees.
I say,
It's the fire in my eyes,
And the flash of my teeth,
The swing in my waist,
And the joy in my feet.
I'm a woman
Phenomenally.

Phenomenal woman,
That's me.
Men themselves have wondered
What they see in me.
They try so much
But they can't touch
My inner mystery.
When I try to show them
They say they still can't see.
I say,
It's in the arch of my back,
The sun of my smile,
The ride of my breasts,
The grace of my style.
I'm a woman,
Phenomenally.
Phenomenal woman,
That's me

Now you understand
Just why my head's not bowed.
I don't shout or jump about
Or have to talk real loud
When you see me passing
It ought to make you proud.
I say,
It's in the click of my heels,
The bend of my hair,

the palm of my hand,
The need for my care.
'Cause I'm a woman
Phenomenonally.
Phenomenal woman.
That's me.[1]

That's my mother and all your mothers and my grandmothers and
all your grandmothers and my great grandmothers and all your
great-grandmothers and my great-great and your great-great and all
you women here and me!

Mari Evans:

I am a black woman
the music of my song
some sweet arpeggio of tears
is written in a minor key
and I
can be heard humming in the night
Can be heard
    humming
    in the night

I say my mate leap screaming to the sea
and I with these hands, cupped the lifebreath
from my issue in the canebreak
I lost Nat's swinging body in a rain of tears
and heard my son scream all the way from Anzio
for Peace he never knew....I
learned Da Nang and Pork Chop Hill
in anguish
Now my nostrils know the gas
and these trigger tired fingers
seek the softness in my warrior's beard
I
am a black woman

tall as a cypress
strong
beyond all definition still
defying place
and time
and circumstance
    assailed
        impervious
            indestructible
Look
    on me and be
renewed.[2]

NOTES

1. "Phenomenal Woman" in *And Still I Rise*. Random House: NY, 1978, pp 8-10.

2. "Marie Evans, "I am a Black Woman" in *I Am A Black Woman.* William Morrow and Company: NY, 1970, pp. 11-12.

THE RELATIONSHIP OF CHILDREARING PRACTICES TO CHAOS AND CHANGE IN THE AFRICAN AMERICAN FAMILY

MARI EVANS

IF THE ultimate goal of childrearing is to engender "wholeness" it might be useful to look at some of the many elements that impact on, and shape, the child's body, mind, and spirit. And if we were to suggest that we can enhance the quality of childrearing in the Black community, we might also need to explore the possibility of entrenched negative patterns in African American childrearing practices, implied patterns that cannot be documented but whose existence, clearly contributory, is suggested by available data.

This paper concurs that racism and oppression are the matrix for the present state of crisis in African American communities. It argues, however, that parental attitudes (which are various responses to racism), in fact, the *condition* of the parent(s) contributes to the chaos and the "changes for the worse" that we decry in the behavior of our young; it maintains that we can, if we are able to acknowledge that we have indeed played a role in the debacle, change that "condition" and begin practicing the some-times difficult parenting options that are available to us.

Even a cursory look at statistics regarding the health and health practices of Black adults by implication say something to us about attitudes, attitudes that may stem from insufficient information, indifference to information, skepticism, or the unavailability of resources and viable support systems. Whatever the reason, there is no denying that our attitudes create the climate in the child's most immediate environment, his home, and seriously shape the childrearing process—often adding our own, unique distortions.

The desperate efforts of entertainer Michael Jackson to re-create himself physically through cosmetic surgery and emotional-ly by fashioning for himself a fantasy world underscore the personality fragmentation that can occur when childrearing con-straints, impositions and demands are out-of-synch with or callously indifferent to the child's deep levels of need.

In the 60's when I tried to say some things about Black writing and Black writers, I used to begin "the writer is the sum of all that is past...." And that, especially in 1987, defines the child who is, of course, also the sum of all that has gone before: He is the continent, the ancestors, slavery, colonization, oppression, the stress and distortion of being mired at the bottom, the pressure of waiting to move on up, and the rage that comes with frustration. The Black child in North America is the result both of how our ancestors coped with achievement and with adversity and the result, whether we are able to admit it or not, of our own coping skills or our lack of them.

The rebellion, the callousness, the utter abandon of a large portion of our young today, I suggest, are merely outward manifes-tations of their deep need for some sense of order, an order they already understand is missing from the chaos of their lives. Be-cause they are human they must have it, their souls require it, and *will* have it even if the introduction of that order is through a struc-ture as harsh as incarceration.

I suggest, therefore, that it may be the *absence* of order, funda-mental and discernible, that characterizes childrearing in today's society and that this missing element, the empirically logical harmonious relationship of one thing to another, is vital to human development and productivity. I believe that the *absence* of this order, given the levels of stress inherent in the underbelly of a colonized community, is easily apparent in the childrearing practices in many contemporary African American homes. Some Black homes have managed to pare childrearing down to consistent, logical, nurturing basics. To concepts; many have not.

The purpose of this paper is to identify some of the missing basics, to examine the havoc their absence has created, and to suggest that for an oppressed people there are imperatives, there are mandates.

Is there an African American over 40 who has not at some point in his or her early life faced a challenger defiantly with "I don't have to do but two things: 'Stay Black and die.'" We do have a given: Color is irrevocable. It remains an absolute, even when change can be simulated. Since society assigns value or non-value (and according to Fanon, the "native" represents "not only the absence of values, but also the negation of values" and is, in fact, "the enemy of values"), does it become an exercise in futility for the individual who is designated as being "of little value" to dream of existence as *valued* when his assignment, his designation, his category, is, "of little value?" And is this merely a rhetorical consideration? Not at all; it is that axis around which our life experiences find shape and form. It is the crux of the dialogue about our very existence that we and our young carry on with society. It is the adrenaline which throbs through our interpersonal relationships, determining which of us live, which of us die, and in what manner. It is this very basic issue, then, of how one survives and prevails over the environment that has shaped African childrearing patterns from the very beginning.

In the beginning, there was no confusion: African societies were rarely deluded about the relationship of the individual to the group. The individual survived to the extent that the security and well-being of the group was preserved. Therefore, both group and individual were responsive to and responsible for the other. In such a milieu, the community, with nature's cooperation, could prosper. Childrearing, as manifest in the African age-sets model (Chancellor Williams, 1974), became merely one of the orderly, systemic processes of African high civilization as it existed prior to the introduction of the Western slave trade. With that holocaust there came an interruption in African practices, an interruption in *structure*.

During the trauma of overt slavery, Black women, who owned neither their bodies nor those of their children, were victims—they *and* their children—of childrearing practices that were externally imposed. Infants and toddlers, if cared for at all, were loosely overseen by a slave too old, too young, or unable for any number of other reasons, to work in the fields. Or, failing that, they were taken by their mothers to the fields, deposited nearby, and left to fend for themselves. The stories of infants overwhelmed by snakes, hunger, or dehydration are by now part of the chronicles of the brutality imposed on both the captured Africans and their enslaved descendants:

> Blackshear had them take their babies with them to the field and it was two or three miles from the house to the field. He didn't want them to lose time walking backward and forward nursing. They built a long trough like a great long old cradle and put all these babies in it every morning when the mother came out to the field. It was set at the end of the rows under a big cottonwood tree. When they were at the end of the row, all at once a cloud no bigger than a small spot came up and it grew fast, and it thundered and lightened as if the world were coming to an end, and the rain just came down in great sheets. And when it got so they could go to the other end of the field, that trough was filled with water and every baby in it was floating round in the water drowned. They never got nary a lick of labor and nary a red penny for any of them babies. (Ida Hutchinson, Library of Congress)

The slave experience was not monolithic. Obviously, contradictions and paradoxes abound. Nevertheless, certain constants were endemic: repression, containment, and exploitation for the owner's interests. Accordingly, in those states known as "breeder states," infants had greater value than did infants and toddlers in southwestern and lower states, where it was often more in the owner's interests to allow the child's death or sale than to provide for it until it could begin to earn its keep:

> ...Just before the steamboat put off the lower country, two Negro women were offered for sale, each of them having a young child at the breast. The traders bought them, took their arms, and offered them to the highest bidder: and they were sold for one dollar a piece, whilst the stricken parents were on their way to the New Orleans market. You are aware that a young babe decreased the value of a field hand in the lower country; whilst it increases her value in the "breeding state."
>
> 120 Negroes for Sale—The subscriber has just arrived from Petersburg, Virginia, with one hundred and twenty likely young Negroes both sexes and every description, which he offers for sale on the most reasonable terms.
>
> The lot now at hand consists of plough boys, several likely and well-qualified house servants of both sexes, several women with children, small boys without their mothers. Planters and traders are earnestly requested to give the subscriber a call previously to making purchases elsewhere, as he is enabled and will sell as cheap, or cheaper, than can be sold by any other person in the trade. (*American Slavery: As It Is*, 1839)

Whatever the traumatic details, clearly the *will* of the mothers did not during those stages play a central role in establishing the loose childrearing patterns that existed in the average slave community. Nevertheless, that community, morally and spiritually attuned, established and maintained its own values and survival systems and these included the group's overseeing of, and active participation in, the nurturing and direction of its young. Childrearing was not so much an individual as a group process, with both blood parent and child seen as part of the whole and, therefore, responsible to the group. Terms such as auntie, uncle, brother and sister, cousin, big mama, lil sis, etcetera, were loosely applied throughout the community and the respect due such familial relationships maintained.

Childrearing patterns then, as now, were shaped by the extended community's approval or disapproval and were based, at that time, on adherence to certain fundamental concepts endemic to survival in a hostile environment: Lies were told, alibis constructed, hiding places protected, wounds attended, and food, however meager, shared with the aged and with runaways; dogs and, occasionally, masters were poisoned or fed broken glass—all in an ad hoc effort to protect the group and the individuals who, by reason of ancestry alone, were a part of it. There were other imperatives if one was to survive the "institution of slavery." Preservation of an inherent moral conviction, respect for the group and its structure, and a belief in powers outside one's self but responsive to one's well-being—therefore, certainly beyond white control. Every attempt was made to resist the violent disruption caused by brutal whites, to comfort one another after the callous imposition of white will and, insofar as possible, to shield the members of the embattled group from further assault. That sense of family, of national group as family, inculcated into the young at birth and reinforced by the group through practices assumed to be natural, held, regardless of where, through no choice of his own, the slave found him or herself. Support was always at hand.

In 1987, that sense of family no longer holds. Feelings of isolation and alienation from the larger population, common to Black students who have the white campus experience, cause a significant minority to gravitate toward Black student organizations, where they exist. However, the larger segment of the Black student population often ignores such organizations and quite pointedly demonstrates a disdain for establishing any meaningful bond with others like themselves. Not having experienced the emotional support and the political protection of "family," they ignore their racial reality despite the fact that such an identity alone is sufficient to evoke not only subtle, but overt and even murderous racist responses. We have raised several generations of young people who, by and large, are very little if at all bonded to "strange" Black people. That is, they relate very little, if at all, to other Black people on the basis, alone, of shared ancestry, since they do *not* see themselves as part of an oppressed *Nation.* What is most chilling is that they see this distance from other Blacks as natural, rather than unnatural, and that they certainly do not understand themselves as oppressed. They view racism, by and large, as merely individualistic acts, sporadic and capricious.

It is the loss of security that resulted from understanding the community as haven and as caring and oneself as valued and protected that has impacted so severely on those of us, adults and children, who presently comprise the Black communities across the country. Our rootedness dissolved when the Black community responded to America's changed economic and political realities by re-fashioning its own values and re-shaping its previously clear vision of itself as oppressed, thus embarking on a strange journey down strange and tortured paths. A journey unforced, in the main, and reactive. We *chose* to believe false signals; we *wanted* to believe.

We reacted to notions that the wars had been won and only the bodies remained to be counted, to notions that corporation-land was indeed Canaan and the family could be reclaimed after the manna had been gathered; to notions that traditional Black values were no longer germane thus no longer desirable in this society where the individual took precedence over the group. Parents became acquaintances and caretakers: "friends;" and media and the street became "parents."

The problems faced by African Americans in North America at this point in the 80's are multifaceted. This paper will touch on three of those facets: (1) we have an oppressed relationship to the dominant society; one that will yield only to serious economic restructuring at a time when the Federal government, with its cutbacks in education, health care and related social services, is moving in a totally opposite direction; (2) despite easily accessible information, we have what is largely an inadequately informed Black adult populace, whether upwardly mobile, middle, or underclass, so shaped by the stress of its struggle for economic survival that it is less able to provide quality emotional and psychological support for its young than it is to provide materially for them; and (3) our young, who after nearly three decades of non-intentional neglect, are difficult. Interacting with them is often abrasive, disconcerting and painful. The bottom line, of course, is that we are a colonized people, operating within a racist structure. Only in part, however, does that account for the ways we rear our children. Regardless of how abraded, how stressed, how worn out and frustrated we are, the truth is—there are things we can change—if we will.

The African American community is not monolithic—there is no *single* method to which most parents subscribe, no consensus on how children should be raised. There is, however (and this is central to any conclusions we may be able to draw), a consensus on what the result should be: upstanding or, depending on parental drive, outstanding individuals. The nuances provided by lifestyles determine the fine definitions. Thus, any attempt to generalize about childrearing patterns in the Black community should rightly be open to challenge.

In our search for possible patterns, we might look first at the methods we have employed over the past several decades and what our efforts have or have not accomplished. What is not open to challenge are the recent studies which contain up-to-date information on employment, health, incarceration, education, mental health, and an assortment of additional concerns. Obviously any examination of childrearing practices in the African American community is a high risk endeavor that walks a fine line between what could be seen as blaming the victim and what must be seen as having the courage to be introspective about what is true. And I argue that what is true is that the African American family is in trouble.

I would like to quote the protagonist in Ellison's classic, *The Invisible Man,* who, on regaining consciousness in the hospital, said "When I know who I am then I shall be free." What we find in 1987 is that very few of our young have an accurate sense of who they are and this, most inappropriately, as we near the end of what has been almost a century and a quarter of incredible Black achievement.

What is intended, in this paper, therefore, is not a rebuttal of Black family strengths, but an exploration, if that is possible, of behavioral tendencies within the family structure as they apply to raising children.

Parenthetically, as someone intrigued with words, I find it significant that two phrases are operative: most Black people tend to speak of "raising children" while professionals concerned with the condition of children speak of "childrearing." If nuances are central to getting at the truth, then possibly two separate processes are involved. And I suspect that our concern should be that during the last three decades we have done more "raising" than "rearing."

During the 122 years which separate us from legal slavery, we have moved from one kind of physical bondage to another, from one kind of psychological bondage to another, from control that was overt and thus clearly understood as control and in the main, therefore, determinedly resisted—to control that is sophisticated, frequently "benevolent," that cleverly understands the value of appearing to delegate or relinquish power; control that in its various forms is often misunderstood and, therefore, all too often, accommodated.

It has been within these climates that we have raised our young. As the society has changed, so have our perceptions of ourselves and of our relationship to the society. And, as a result, so have our childrearing patterns. As long as oppression could be clearly identified, African Americans coalesced around the maintenance of values that insured the rearing of what was known then as "race men and women." When, in response to struggle and pressure, the forms of racism changed from overt to covert, the perceptions held by African Americans changed; somewhere along the way we lost our clear view of racist forms and started "hoping more than knowing."

John A. Williams, in *The Man Who Cried I Am,* allows the protagonist, Max, to reflect on the psychopathology of his fiancee's death. "They," Max muses about the society, "gave Lillian the photograph, the image of the American family group. But when she looked closely, she wasn't in it: she wasn't even the blanked out one...but they let her teach about America the beautiful....She knew it was not, but hoped it was, and my darling Lillian—you got to hoping more than knowing....Baby—didn't you understand?" Like Lillian, most African American parents, lacking clear vision, continue to hold to The Dream. A dream, defined all too often—and unfortunately for all of us, in the narrow terms of material acquisition. An oppressed people whose dreams are dependent upon the illusions they harbor and protect have to contradict themselves and the values which mold their behavior and shape their lives if they are to teach their young that freedom is also concrete, liberation possible, and struggle imperative. Childrearing should be the primary concern of an oppressed people and although the rearing of "race men and women" is obviously a stressful, complex and tedious process, it should be entered into at birth.

We have allowed generations of what should have been psychologically sound, spiritually buttressed, physically healthy, politically committed young Black men and women to be sacrificed on the altar of parental indifference, self-interest, and/or lack of sufficient information and effective coping skills. The sad reality is that our children are street smart; across the board they see us and, regardless of age, they are rarely deluded by our claims versus our reality; they understand us far better than we understand ourselves. They must—for they experience themselves at our hands. They accommodate our capricious and frequently abusive behavior out of some deep-rooted love; they cling to us because the level of their dependency is very real to them, and they express their rage in aberrant behavior because of their hopelessness and their overwhelming sense of being otherwise powerless.

I am confused, therefore, when I read the work of Black social scientists, many of whom I know, and love, and whose scholarship I respect. It is almost as if there is a tacit understanding that very little that is critical will be said about the Black family. For example, when we decided to examine Black teen pregnancy our approach, while multi-faceted in programming for pregnant teens and new mothers, was singularly lacking in preventive programming for preteen males and females and their parents—precisely the point where childrearing practices need to be reevaluated and strengthened.

Possibly the most baffling circumstance I encountered as I began the research for this paper was what translated as almost a consensus by Black social scientists that *despite* certain problems such as those listed by Marian Wright Edelman, "the Black family is alive and well." Edelman offers the following statistics (*Ebony,* August 1986):

Compared to white children, Black children are twice as likely to:

- be born prematurely
- die during the first year of life
- suffer low birthweight
- have mothers who received late or no prenatal care
- be born to a teenage or unmarried parent
- see a parent die
- live in substandard housing
- be suspended from school or suffer corporal punishment
- be unemployed as teenagers
- be unemployed parents
- live in institutions

three times as likely to:

- be poor
- have their mothers die in childbirth
- live with a parent who has separated from the other parent
- live in a female-headed family
- be placed in an educable mentally retarded class
- be murdered between five and nine years of age
- be in foster care
- die of known child abuse

four times as likely to:

- live with neither parent and be supervised by a child welfare agency
- be murdered before one year of age or as a teenager
- be incarcerated between 15 and 19 years of age

five times as likely to:

- be dependent on welfare; and

eleven times as likely to:

- live with a parent who never married

When fear is rampant in the Black community and when it is not as much fear of adults as it is fear of our *children*, it is fear *caused* by our lack of communion with our young who, overnight, are no longer petulant pre-teens and adolescents, but teens and young adults who now prey on their own community: on Black females of all ages, on their elders and, in fact, on each other.

We can only continue to maintain with straight faces that the Black family is alive and well if we do what we have been doing for some time, that is, close our eyes to the fact that these young men and women are members of *somebody's* family and they are the result of Black childrearing patterns or the lack of them.

Moreover, rebellion and estrangement are not the singular province of the underclass, the poor. Black middle-class and professional families are similarly affected and somewhere within the larger structure of these families are estranged young men and women whose relationships with their parents are troubled if not severed and whose rebellion often takes the form of putting as much distance between themselves and the primary home as possible.

A decade and a half of discussions and observations suggest that despite anything the parent thought he or she had done, had tried to do, or had provided, real communication had either been lost or had never to any great degree existed. Therefore, the *real business* of the home—that of psychological support and nurturing, had, in fact, been inadequate for the child in question. As a result, the child was left with the unshakable conviction that he or she was not loved.

In the absence of communication, the parents had been unaware of the *child's* perception of the relationship or the parents had been unwilling to face either the truth, or the source, of those perceptions; or, finally, the parents had been unable to internalize the importance of the relationship to the child's mental stability and emotional well-being and, therefore, the importance of reevaluating, reshaping, and redirecting the relationship.

Parents are often unaware that real communication has ceased since it is less stressful and less threatening to dismiss the silence, the surliness, the recalcitrance as simply "typical," negative teenage behavior. And many parents, rather than face their inadequacies, cling to the delusion that adults are omnipotent. And for many there appears to be an entrenched need to protest that their child is "all right." To feel otherwise would be to make tacit admission that they might, somehow, be at fault. Therefore, the child's indications of distress and increased disassociation are dismissed as his/her evidence of irresponsibility, hardheadedness, or an inherent determination to be difficult. These same parents convincingly express their belief that the child in question will "make it." But many of our children are not all right, a lot of them do not make it, a lot of them will not make it: they are tied into emotional and psychological knots.

America is a pressure cooker; our children experience the heat and the pressure just as we and, in great part, *because* they are trying to second-guess parents, friends, schools, and a society in which their color is the referent for their oppression.

And we, having lost our clear vision, are unable to share with them the fact that in North America they are an in-place nation/state; unable to share with them the fact that their oppression is structured, not merely capricious; nor can we seriously suggest the dynamics on which struggle is based, by which wars are won. For those are the very facts that we, in our efforts to distance ourselves from the many facets of our "negritude," are determined to resist. So we cannot, and do not, teach them what they should be taught nor love them as they must be loved.

Although certain mandates for "raising" children have changed very little in the past 122 years—Black parents continue to be inordinately concerned that their children be fed, clothed, warmly housed, and "properly" educated—there are major differences and those differences have had a catastrophic effect.

What has changed is the sense of security the child traditionally felt: the sense of being in the center of a circle of caring adults who were serious about keeping their society orderly. A child knew that limits were in place—he had them, and he or she knew what they were; knew what was allowed and what was not.

For all Americans, however, the structure of the family has changed drastically over the course of the last three decades. In 1955, 60% of American families consisted of father, housewife, and two or more children. By 1980, this construct represented only 11% of all families and by 1985, only 7%. One-fourth of American households presently consist of people living alone and 50% of American marriages now end in divorce.

The statistics for African Americans, however, are much more shocking and indicate quite clearly that we will either stop "raising" children and start *rearing* them, or we will not survive. The latest prognosis, based on statistics advanced in a University of Chicago study, is that in the next 13 years, 70% of all Black children will be born into homes where there are no males and that 70% of all Black males will be unemployed.

If the Black child is viewed as a legitimate part of the Black family, the Black family must be seriously reevaluated. We have only to look at some of the available statistics. They leap at us from every possible source and even if we dismiss the researchers, if white, as racist, or if Black, as uninformed and non-political, there are the children themselves: prima facie evidence.

Studies done by The Task Force on the New York State Dropout Problem (1985) indicate that low self-esteem, caused by a broad range of concerns, is at the root of the dropout problem and that the dropout factor is central to the escalation of many other socioeconomic ills. What is significant and encouraging is that low self-esteem lends itself to treatment. It can be reversed by any concerned parent, parent substitute or determined community effort.

The New York State Task Force found that dropouts leave for three major reasons, all guaranteed to induce debilitating levels of low self-esteem: 1) in-school experiences, 2) *family conditions,* 3) work and economic factors:

> Boredom, alienation and the hostility of the school environment are frequently identified by at-risk students and dropouts as reasons for school-leaving. Additionally, five in-school experiences have been identified as major factors in dropping out: (1) personal, cultural and linguistic dehumanization, (2) academic humiliation, (3) institutionalized discharge, (4) discriminatory high school admission policies and practices, and (5) lack of appropriate instruction for language minority students.

Further, it is estimated that "58% of this country's young have used cocaine or marijuana" (and that figure escalates significantly when alcohol and other substance abuse is factored in). The Select Committee on Narcotics Abuse and Control recently reported evidence of a positive correlation between drug abuse and dropping out of school:

> Drugs and a feeling of being lost in a crowded impersonal environment lead many students to drop out. Dropouts appear to use drugs more frequently and to require treatment more often than their school-attending peers.

The Select Committee Report cites studies demonstrating an association among "low-esteem, drug abuse, boredom, peer pressure, truancy and dropping out." (*Drugs and Dropouts,* Washington, D.C. Government Printing Office, 1986).

In addition, all too often educational deficits are caused by "insufficient parental guidance and by the lack of encouragement to achieve." Inasmuch as the thrust of this paper is to challenge us to view childrearing as a process designed to engender "wholeness" in our African American young, we need to program into the process all the ingredients necessary for a successful transition from harmful modes of "childraising" to "childrearing". The critical component, the second only to parental attitudes in impacting behavior and the one most often neglected or ignored when we explore long range solutions to the serious concerns of the community, is that of preventive health education and care.

The Steckler Report (1985) indicates that African Americans experience a lower use of preventive health services for pregnancy and that Black infant mortality is double that of whites. Blacks also use dental services less frequently, e.g., 44% use for Black children ages 4-16 to 68% use for white children; and Black children have pronouncedly different vaccination utilization patterns. These are merely random statistics, of course. But they are relevant because they suggest that drastically altering childrearing patterns in Black communities can significantly impact not only the life expectancy of our young, and make dramatic inroads on their susceptibility to certain diseases, but it is possible to speculate that when corrective health measures are indicated and provided, behavior itself can be altered in direct relationship to the child's new sense of self-worth and of being valued. Obviously the relationship of heath to behavior is an area that needs more focused research. When that is done, it is probable that significant study results will be found among the poor.

Poor nutrition, a major concern, must be reversed. Just as American scientific, governmental and private sectors coalesce to offer at the international level critical treatment and care for malnutrition, we must require of them and of us a responsiveness in ways that are equally intense and comprehensive to the admittedly less dramatic but equally devastating hunger that afflicts America's poor and destitute. Debilitating conditions accrue from insufficient food and inadequate nutrition and impact most severely on infants and children in that segment of African Americans who exist below the poverty level and who comprise approximately one-third of the national Black population.

Insufficient food and inadequate nutrition affect nearly every aspect of the present and future well-being of our young, contributing to diabetes, hypertension, low birth weight and a multitude of other ills. The early symptoms, easily identified, are often listlessness, disinterest, lack of energy, and diminished application. It is no accident that the figure for Black life expectancy is only 69.6 years, a figure attained by whites 36 years ago.

Central to reversing health patterns in the Black community, then, is *access* to nutrition-high foods, a willingness to change present eating habits, and this may entail preparing more food at home and consuming fewer fast foods; it presupposes an awareness of new research findings and an open approach to creative food preparation. The really critical problem, however, remains that *of securing* nutritional food, a problem which the impoverished may find nearly impossible to solve. Moreover, many parents need help in deciding how to spend for food and how to prepare available food in ways that enhance the nutritional value. Significant changes in our approach to the preparation and consumption of food are possible, they must occur, and they will, provided serious educational campaigns are waged. I argue that the Black community is neither indifferent nor insensitive to the welfare of its children; it is, however, involved in ways that only scratch the surface of childrearing and it is seriously underinformed about the active roles we as parents and extended family play in the ways our young develop and the choices they ultimately make.

The rationale for presenting what appear to be "random statistics" such as those that follow is to emphasize the network of concerns that must engage us if we are to influence and enrich the quality of childrearing practices in the Black community. The Steckler Report is full of alarming information, e.g.: for Black women, heart disease and strokes assume the same importance as do homicide and unintentional injuries for the young Black male. Hypertension, cirrhosis and diabetes are all significant to the excess death rate of both Black males and Black females.

Blacks under 45 years of age have a relative risk of death
from all causes nearly twice that of whites; the death rate
for lung cancer is 45% higher among Black males than
non-minority males, (smoking is highly contributive, scientists insist) and non-minority women showed a 20%
decrease in cervical cancer deaths 1973-81, while Black
women experienced a 27% *increase* during the same
period.

The usual prerequisite for access to medical care is the ability
to pay for services and this, of course, has a direct relationship to
income and insurance. Since Black median income is substantially
lower, less disposable income is available for the purchase of
health care. Access and availability become problems for the
parent and the community. What can and must occur, to expedite
solutions, is sufficiently leveraging Black pressure—maintained at
levels that encourage cooperation from both public and private
sectors.

The Steckler Report repeatedly attributes the significant dis-
parities discovered in their studies to "social or environmental
factors rather than inherent genetic or biologic differences." While
this should not be news to Black folk, it reemphasizes how little
we are doing to re-create ourselves by establishing new *patterns*
for our children. Obviously, educating toward preventive Black
health practices, toward greater access to and utilization of health
services, and an escalated drive toward good nutrition is mandated
if we are to implement the drastic changes in Black childrearing
patterns that are necessary to improve the overall level of African
American wholeness.

What is needed is the long view; change is possible, but it must
begin with child *rearing*. I remember hearing a Black probation
officer comment that "many if not most Blacks have never had
enough of anything but trouble" and I suggest that this may be the
powerful reason many things have an escalated importance in the
Black community, an importance that far outweighs their tangible
or intangible value.

Athletics, still considered by too many Black families as *the* most viable way out of "the ghetto," have a significance we cannot overlook as we explore childrearing patterns in the African American community. Athletics offer positive use of leisure time and, not at all incidentally, provide valuable channels for the release of pent-up energy, deep levels of anger, and frustration. Fanon speaks of the settler's "keep[ing] alive in the native an anger which he deprives of outlet," arguing that the settler can only achieve a "pseudo petrification, [for] the native's muscular tension finds outlet regularly in bloodthirsty explosions in tribal warfare, in feuds" or, we might well add—at the highest level—in athletics. Sports can be character-building and can result in long-lasting attention to the care and maintenance of the body and to good health practices.

The concern of this paper, therefore, is not to "attack sports," but to argue that we have not sufficiently explored the concept of "play," with all ins ongoing ramifications. We introduce Black children *to contact* sports at an age when many are too young to conceptualize the *nuances* of violence and, often having experienced it first-hand, are reluctant to participate in the organized expression of it. Coerced, however, they can and do internalize the premise we insist on teaching: that manhood and violence are synonymous. This premise supports and nurtures what I term a "pathology of disregard and indifference" which directly contradicts notions of appropriate "male" behavior society will require of them later. In America, "play" is political; it is openly viewed as a transmitter of certain cultural notions, and contact play as a device for the inculcation of the ruthless, aggressive attitudes and values endemic to Western manifestations of masculine success and power. Toward these ends, "play" becomes the provider of periods of intense conditioning; it affords early indoctrination into *method* by demonstrating the need for structure if aggression is to succeed, and often contributes heavily to establishing and nurturing a pathology of disregard for the welfare of other human beings, especially those weaker, those less able than oneself. Even very young children are taught to disregard the possibility of doing serious physical injury to another human being while ostensibly engaged in "play"—the "get-that-man-at-any-cost" syndrome. Hostility, anger, distorted values, and the aggrandizement of one's most selfish and trivial aims are not only vicariously *learned*, but systematically taught or modeled under the rubric of "play." The proliferation, in the world of professional sports, of personal assaults that have resulted in maiming or crippling injuries attests to the seriousness of the indoctrination that occurs early in life. Obviously, African Americans, regardless of gender, must begin to convene around the significance of the concept of play itself.

Clearly an oppressed people needs to be confrontational; needs to be aggressive. Structured aggression and violence in their various forms are endemic to the efforts of any oppressed group to free itself. In fact, they are imperative if the group is to emphasize the earnestness of its demands. The statistics for Black on Black homicide, however, and the level of violence among our young men and women indicate that we have sent mixed signals to our young about the relationship of manhood (or personhood) to violence and aggression. We have not been clear about options and nuances. We teach English and mathematics but "raising" contains no ongoing unit on the many faces of violence; no continuing dialogue to explore with our young the dimensions of interpersonal, structured, nor finally, political violence. We seem to expect them to "know" what is correct and, for some unknown reason, to value human life and limb despite the contradictory messages we have sent.

I would argue that we ourselves have not fought through those very necessary distinctions and that while we respond to the odiousness of violence our response is not action-oriented, nor does it at all include "play" as a primary communicator of values and a sense of personhood.

Our childrearing patterns have included very little acknowledgements of Fanon's insight that: "The native is a being hemmed in...his last resort is to defend his personality vis-à-vis his brother" (Fanon, 1961). If Fanon is correct, and our experiences suggest that he is, and if contact play provides an early indoctrination into the "pathology of disregard," then we must re-examine and redirect our notions of what play delivers that is residual, that is shaping, and that molds psyches which are in the process of becoming adult mindsets. We must seriously consider whether through certain forms of "play" we are creating the psychological backdrop for tomorrow's confrontations: confrontations that regardless of their locale—global or more immediately within our own communities—are predicated on our disregard for the weak, the "losers," those who "can't cut the mustard," who don't have "the right stuff," who "blink," or are different. In fact, former President Reagan, demonstrating his continuing callous disregard for the lives and well-being of millions of human beings, reduced U.S. foreign policy to the level of an American game with his political version of "chicken," or his classic "we didn't blink" remark, merely one example of the disastrous potential when deadly concepts internalized during "play" become residual and inform behavior even during moments of international confrontation and crisis.

Although the development of positive character traits is essential to manhood and womanhood, once we move past the topic of acquiring an education, there appears to be very little ongoing dialogue between Black adults and our young regarding the development of character. It may be a word we are no longer able to define, just as our notion of manhood seems confused, with many, across gender lines, subscribing to the notion that "manhood" can be equated with "success" in the workplace, or the level to which Black males can acquire or provide material or status items. And, whether stereotyped or not, sexual prowess is still seen by many males, professional as well as non-professional, as an indication of "manhood."

Character is rarely mentioned as a necessary or useful quality. "Get whomever you can and get them before they get you; just get over,'" appears to have replaced credos such as "Up you mighty race," "Each one teach one," and "Lifting as we climb." All clichéd and hoary, nevertheless, they are all responsible, in part, for what movement we have had. One cannot but note the difference in focus: from concern for the welfare of the group, as manifest in the past, to the selfish individualism of the present. Is that part of the "progress" we are told we have made?

Adolescence, it seems, is a season of trauma and travail, a period involuntarily devoted to questioning, to self-doubting, to anxiety, rebellion and challenge. Years of extremes—moodiness, depression, unbridled celebration—all pushed to the wire. No one knows for sure what will play in Hoboken tonight. For the Black young, add the nuance of being Black and unequally received in a society where inherent racism is largely undiminished and where, even in many Black adolescent circles, the word "Black" is still downright pejorative and used as such. Can we assume that the panoply of adolescent behaviors is largely theater acted out for the sake of an audience or for instant, if partial, catharsis; that the noise, the belligerence, the audacity, the violence are escape hatches for troubled, malfunctioning human mechanisms?

When Black teens are violent, it is often toward each other, it is usually sporadic, and it is usually because they lack a sense of appropriate options or because that sense, not finely developed, breaks down. The ability to analyze a situation and to *employ* options is a skill that must be taught as such during the child-rearing process.

Impulsive aggression based on misplaced value systems and a thoughtless disregard for options is reflected in current statistics. Regarding excess Black deaths, the Steckler Report (1985) indicates that one Black woman out of 104 has a lifetime chance of becoming a homicide victim; the figure for white women is 1 in 369. The imbalance was greater for Black males where the figure is 1 in 21 opposed to white males whose lifetime chances of becoming a homicide victim are 1 in 131. Current figures suggest that 94% of all Black homicides are committed by Black perpetrators.

I would argue that many Black homicides are directly related to distorted notions of what "manhood" means. Teens appear to define "manhood" loosely, as the imperative not to "punk out" physically when challenged or in any way confronted. They "take each other to school," reprimanding and threatening those who prefer not to settle issues with physical violence. At this point in time weapons seem a necessary adjunct, not only permissible but in most instances more desirable than unarmed combat with one's peers. This willingness to do mindless battle rather than "lose face" is directly and largely responsible for the preponderance of Black youth homicides. Where Black childrearing patterns have contributed to feelings of inadequacy and to an overwhelming sense of low self-esteem, "loss of face" becomes more serious a matter than it would in a community where self-esteem is bolstered by love, possessions and by a sense of success as inevitable.

There are statistics regarding the incarceration of Black Americans and these speak of another terrifying level of Black/white imbalance, for example: in Wisconsin, where Blacks constitute approximately 3.4% of the population, they are roughly 39% of the prison population: in Maryland, Blacks are approximately 22.7% of the state's population and 71% of the prison population; and in Illinois, where Blacks are approximately 14.7% of the total population, they comprise 60.7% of those behind bars. (American Correctional Association Directory, 1984 Ed., p.xv., and the U.S. Statistical Abstract, 1982-83)

In addition, there are approximately 1,500 individuals on Death Row nationally; 42% or roughly 630 are Black. This is a blatantly racial imbalance that criminal justice authorities almost concur can be attributed to racially motivated sentencing patterns. Other statistics indicate that 43% of all homicide victims in 1983 were Black and of that number 94% were murdered by Black assailants.

The youngest person on death row in the United States at this writing is a young Black female presently incarcerated in the Indiana State Women's Prison at Indianapolis. Brutalized and buffeted by life, herself, this Black teenager was only fifteen when in an act of particular brutality and senselessness, she, with several female companions, murdered a white Sunday School teacher who had befriended them. Now 18, and in many ways typical of young women that age in our own families, she is bright, attractive, strong-willed, courageous. She may also be prototypical of all those other young men and women we see and hear, as they walk toward us: young men and women, hair groomed in the latest innovation, preceded by 90 decibels of either a male soprano anguishing over love or some triple-tempo rap pouring from a "ghetto blaster" so heavy it depresses one shoulder a full six inches and influences the direction in which they stumble, still cool.

Far too many of our young are indeed as "disassociated" as social scientists and psychologists allege. The disassociated child is defined as unattached, as a child without conscience, a child filled with rage built of this helplessness, hopelessness and anger; a rage that seethes beneath the surface of his adolescence and renders him extraordinarily dangerous. He or she can be identified by a number of criteria, among them " a lack of attachment, cruelty to animals, and severe control problems." The more we must interact with these young people, the more we are confronted by them in their roles as students, neighbors, family members—the less we may like them.

The more we dislike them, the more we are unwilling to give them our serious time. Over half of all violent crimes are committed by unattached children, and judges, of course, are not trained to treat aberrations, only to sentence. The result is overcrowded detention centers and child-warehousing facilities.

The strength of the Black family is that we do love. The weakness of the Black family is that we are so stressed that we often fail to demonstrate that love in ways that *translate* into love, *in the child's language.* In today's family, it is not uncommon for love and concern to be announced by an ongoing stream of invectives, angry accusations, dire predictions and the most sophisticated forms of psychological abuse. Children are expected to identify this as "caring" parental behavior. Conversely, the child is rarely if ever deliberately engaged in a one-on-one conversation about any issue at all that does not directly concern his shortcomings. Even more rarely is he or she engaged in conversations rooted in Black political awareness; conversation central to establishing a base of moral, ethical and political concerns and values that the child will, hopefully, come to understand and adopt. Our children return violence for violence; they will be able to demonstrate love only if they have received it; and they will view political activism on behalf of the group as a natural responsibility only if they have been guided in that direction and to the extent that they can see it and respect it when it is modeled.

Obviously, there is a connection between self-esteem and the ongoing security of not only *being* loved, but of being touched in love, which becomes even more important. "Have you hugged your child today," is a reminder of enormous significance.

Many, if not most, of our young men and women are seldom touched in love, or in what substitutes for tenderness and love, except in the transient and fleeting sexual relationships they, to meet a plethora of needs, establish with each other. The label "love" may or may not be placed on these relationships, and it would appear, from conversations shared or overheard, that more often than not, no such label is necessary. In 1986, 40,000 adolescent females dropped out of school as a result of pregnancy and presently one-half million children are parenting other children. Given the critical relationship of the first 16 months of a child's care to his/her emotional development; the fact that infants and toddlers in public or inadequate foster care experience a break in the critical bonding process; and the neglectful, improper, often abusive care that is inevitable when youngsters give birth and are forced to parent, we must expect an escalation in the number of unattached children in the Black community within the next ten years. Effective parenting is difficult even under the best circumstances, and the teen parent, only partly schooled in most instances and educated very slightly, if at all, is generally unemployable in any but the lowest paying or in minimal wage positions. In many if not most instances, emotionally immature and stressed, he or she is hardly in a position to model effective parenting.

While Black and white teens are discussing "safe sex," and given today's imperatives these are necessary discussions, we have seen Asian teens of the same age, time, and space, talking of their priorities, and sex seems not to be one of them. Preparing for a productive, rewarding life is advanced as their "group" goal; therefore, as individuals, they are part of their own mainstream, not concerned with imitating people whose priorities and needs are different from their own.

We cannot turn back the clock, but it should not be impossible to rear children who are so loved, so filled with self-esteem that they do not need to search for love through procreation, nor to view sexual activity as a way of deriving self-esteem. What is quite clear is that the disassociated child (and our communities are filled to overflowing with them) will only succeed in ways that are not negative to the extent that his or her parents, or parent substitutes, communicate love in ways that are markedly different from those they have previously employed.

No one can function well or function long unloved or, more importantly, without *feeling* loved. To do so is to experience disconnection so severe that alienation can become an entrenched condition, and man and womankind can, with pronounced hostility, be viewed as "other" and ultimately as appropriate prey.

If the parent/child support system is markedly less than satisfying and if positive substitute systems are not in place, each will bond with others of its kind: the child with other disassociated children, the parent with other adults who see the young as the enigmatic enemy. Nevertheless, reconciliation, while difficult, is certainly not impossible, for each still contains a basic willingness, however slight, *to be* loved. Use of the phrase "parent/child support system" is deliberate, since that may be part of the problem. Parents seem to expect some return from children; happily, they will receive it. But I suspect that prior to its emotional maturity no return from any child is a given, and any return, from any child, is a bonus.

Love deliberately and consciously expressed, pumps huge measures of self-esteem into a child and without that input no personality adjustment is possible. Self-esteem is bone marrow, blood and oxygen. Without high levels of it, our young cannot survive a hostile environment; certainly they cannot live positive, productive lives. With it, "ain't no mountain high enough" to impede their forward movement.

California recently decided that self-esteem was so important to human development that it established a "self-esteem task force" to research and implement ways and means of inculcating self-esteem in "marginal" individuals, and the state funded it to the tune of one-quarter million dollars a year for the next three years. Conversely, in the Black community, even "the color [hue] of a child can affect the quality of parental love and the child's position in the family" (Ross and Wyden, 1973), and accordingly his or her self-esteem.

When we lose our sense of "communion" with our children, it may be that we are threatened by their apparent determination to resist our control. This willfulness of theirs, which might be interpreted as a need for independence expressed in ways that are negative, may well stem from an unwillingness to accept the flawed, capricious and often dishonest pronouncements of their parents as any more acceptable than their own flawed, experimental probings. Conventional logic carries little weight behind this speculation.

Since many of our young seem to have no sense of mission that transcends secular levels of reasoning, no "holy grail," as it were, for which they strive, our encounters with them, our confrontations, often have such deep-structured levels of resentment that we are frightened, not so much *of* them—but almost always for them: we wonder what their end will be.

This would cease to be the problem that it is if we were to structure solid moral and spiritual components into our approach to childrearing. To use the word "moral" is not to advocate a set of taboos toward a morality that is restricting and limiting. I would suggest a morality that empowers. Nor does the word "spiritual" refer to organized religion with its sects and doctrines, but rather to a spirituality that transcends dogma and the secular imposition of denominations.

Further, I would argue against the clichéd "throwing the baby out with the bathwater." The church, the Black church in the Black neighborhood, is the last bastion of the structured Black extended family. It is the only institution left where Black parents, Black children and the Black community can come together across professional, political, and socioeconomic lines to experience themselves as part of a vital, harmonious whole. The Black church remains the only sure facility left where we can gather to experience our Nationhood. It is a political hotspot, and if it is not, we should make it so. It is the last unmined diamond and it should be utilized for this potential.

We tend not to teach our young methods of ascertaining options, we rarely talk to them in terms of concepts, especially not the *concepts* involved in their behavior, possibly because most of us do not shape our own lives nor choose our directions with any thought of concepts in mind, or with an informed and objective sense of our own options.

I maintain, therefore, that when our young, our restless, our dissident act out their rebelliousness and alienation, act out their need to bring order, however quixotic, to their private chaos—what we are watching is, in part, their longing to be loved and to be held—but this cannot be documented. Our lack of communion with our young can be reversed, however, when we spend as much time rearing as we presently do "raising." Challenged to distinguish between the two, I would say that raising is "providing for," while rearing is "responding to." Raising can be satisfied by providing the essentials: food, shelter, clothing and reasonable care. "Rearing" is a carefully thought out process. Rearing begins with a goal and is supported by a clear view of what are facts and what is truth (and the two are not necessarily synonymous). Rearing is complex and requires sacrifice and dedication. It is an ongoing process of "preparation." Joe Kennedy reared presidents; the British royal family rears heirs to the English throne; and when a young African doctor, born on the continent and presently in self-exile in a neighboring country because of her ANC (African National Congress) commitment, was interviewed on the news recently and was asked if she was not afraid for her four-year-old son, given her political activism, said, "He has a duty to lay down his life for his people. He is my son, but he is also the son of an oppressed people," she announced the rearing of a "race man."

Obviously, something *different*, some carefully thought out *process*, some long-range *political* view is present when one has a clear sense of one's reality and, therefore, intends to rear presidents, rulers, or *free men* and *women*.

For the past 20 years, I have maintained that the literature of an oppressed people should be a political literature, a literature designed to call the people to view the nature of their oppression, to identify the oppressor, and to suggest the dynamics of destroying that oppressor, and to suggest the dynamics of destroying that oppression—of prevailing. If that is true of our *literature*, is it any *less* true that the childrearing practices of an oppressed people must, if we are to prevail, at least have as sound a political base as our literature?

For students, I define colonization as "suppression and exploitation designed to keep a people powerless, dependent, subordinate, and mystified." If there is any validity to that definition, the addition of an overt political posture to our childrearing is mandated, significantly, when, after sharing that definition, I ask students in classes of 30 to 40 persons whether or not they "know of" people who are colonized, four or five hands will be raised. *They* know about South Africa and, while they understand colonization in terms of their cousins there—they resist the notion that they, too, may precisely fit the definition of colonization just advanced.

I argue that by and large African Americans live in a world of dreams and eternal hope, rather than one of vision, commitment, and the clarity necessary if the final solution to our oppression is to be that called for so movingly by Margaret Walker:

> Let a new earth rise. Let another world be born. Let a bloody peace be written in the sky. Let a second generation full of courage issue forth: let a people loving freedom come to growth. Let a beauty full of healing and a strength of final clenching be the pulsing in our spirits and our blood. Let the martial songs be written, let the dirges disappear. Let a race of men rise and take control (For My People, 1941).

We are fond of quoting Rev. Martin Luther King's famous phrase, "I have a dream" and indeed this *is* a world conceived by visionaries, but it is also a world born in struggle and confrontation; a world moved into place by hard work. This is not a dream world but one where clarity must be a way of life for an oppressed people, if they are to prevail.

How strangely slow we are not to connect the disassociated behavior of our young with our own misplaced values and our own willingness to adopt white parenting models. It is all too apparent that we are quite clear about some things. We are clear about how we would like our young to look, and to sound, and to be: the character of Denise while on the Cosby show may well be an example. Over and over, we are told we have made progress and we have rushed to affirm this delusion. We are so eager to believe, we need so badly to believe, that we have closed our eyes and closed our minds to the difference between *progress* and *movement.* Our childrearing patterns reflect this blind belief in illusion.

Many of us program our children for success as if our *desire* could make their encounter with the society "work." I am inclined to question whether our young professionals need the designer drugs, the designer clothes, the designer accoutrements because on a subliminal level they're scared to death. No one has told them, but do they somehow understand that the shakiest thing out there—is success, as *allowed* them by white America?

If our young, "programmed for success," think only of themselves, is it because we have not taught them how to extend love and concern past the immediate family, if even there. If they have a certain bravado, as if they were set for life, when in fact they are virtually powerless, owning little—is it because we did not teach them the truth of their relationship to the society; and is that because in 1987 far too few of us understand that relationship sufficiently ourselves? If we do not access information, how can we put it in words? In what ways do we share political concepts with a two-year-old, a four-year-old, a fourteen-year-old?

"Clarity," Kgositsile said, "is more than a concept, it is a way of life." Or it should be.

Admittedly stress, disaffection, insufficient information, and/or insufficient coping skills are basic to negative childrearing practices, but it may be that offending parents do become aware of the compulsive and negative nature of some of their responses for it appears that many introduce a "pleasant principle" to offset the stress of the climate they have created. Thus, movies, extensive or unlimited TV viewing, mall trips and "wish shopping," the purchase of popular items the family cannot afford, trips in the family car or fast food treats are provided as compensatory acts in an effort to "square" things. As a matter of fact, this compensation, pleasure in return for pain inflicted, only serves to reinforce the child's confusion, his sense of fundamental disorder, and his or her frustration.

Further, childrearing practices are affected by even "incidental" drug and alcohol abuse. Despite any intent we have to be good, caring sensitive parents, when substance use is involved, whether it is merely grass or whether it is cocaine or crack, whether it is a six-pack, wine, or a fifth of Vodka a day—the behavior of the substance user changes. It changes toward his family, toward his children, toward what he sees as his responsibilities. The parent becomes quixotic, capricious, erratic, and his children can never second guess whether he or she will be benevolent and permissive or suddenly surface as the rigid, cruel and overbearing taskmaster. One 14-year-old in my neighborhood walked around with a cast on his forearm a good part of one summer. It was common knowledge that his father broke the arm. One loving father, while drinking on a winter outing, insisted that his terrified sons, four and eight, accompany him on a walk on the ice over a broad, partially frozen creek. Another anxious parent with his or her eyes on a child's upward mobility grounds a 13-year-old for a month. No evening television, no afternoon play, no visiting, no visitors. "You will stay with that math and those projects 'til you bring your grades up." The adults and siblings go about life as usual, and the problem, multifaceted, which should be solved on several levels by already stressed parents who normally address very few, if any of these levels, is left with an already confused and ill-prepared 13-year-old.

The African American parent who is interested in upgrading his or her approach to childrearing should, at this point, be asking a thousand questions and so should we: Who is the child's math teacher; how often has the parent visited the teacher and impressed on the teacher his concern with his child's progress; how effective is the parent in the teacher-parent relationship; does his own lack of academic skills render him submissive to hostility? Is he aggressive? Assertive and firm? Should the child's ability to correct his own inadequacies be assumed; does the home offer the climate, the patience, the skills for tutoring? Is the child being loved and supported or merely pressured and punished? And how is he or she handling anxiety—by aggressively rejecting the entire situation; by withdrawing and projecting a defensive indifference, or by accommodating the consensus that things really are too difficult and that he or she simply cannot learn. Now, add to the complex of emotions that pulse our child-raising efforts the fairly common phenomenon of alienated parents who love but do not like one or more of their children. We can only speculate about the long and short-range effect of those relationships. We haven't the time, but we must *take* the time, to get to the bottom of all this.

Many of the concerns advanced in this paper could be reversed by dramatically altering the extent to which we as Black adults are willing to be involved with Black children. The real challenge, however, is whether we can be at all receptive to the charge that our childrearing efforts, efforts which exhaust us and which appear sincerely motivated, leave a lot to be desired. Our children must be taught ways to achieve inner serenity, how to enjoy being alone with themselves, the art of analysis in order to identify options and alternate ways of problem solving, consideration for others, integrity, if possible, and if there is time, grace. There is, of course, no way the parent can teach these values if his or her life contradicts their very essence. We can only reverse the intractability of our young when we revive the practice of teaching values from birth. It is not only a lost art, but one that will be difficult to retrieve since parents, themselves, often find it difficult to apologize, to express appreciation, to be truthful, to behave with honesty, with integrity, and to convincingly model self-discipline.

Enrichment programs, available in most communities, fill in some of the gaps left by the inadequacies of the public education available to most Black children—but nothing fills the gaps left by parents and parental substitutes who do not understand or are indifferent to the need for certain ways of communicating love and a sense of self-worth to our young who so badly need to be listened to, conversed with, held. Our eyes, our faces, our body language, our tones of voice—all these are intangible but forceful and mean-ing-filled ways of saying to our young Black men and women either that we care and they are loved or that we are exasperated, at our wits end, and that we know our life would be easier without them. Our voices tell them that we wish we did not have to be bothered with them, regardless of what words we are using; our eyes tell them we resent them and see them as our "problem" even as we discuss our plans for them and as we in-differently or angrily brush aside the issues they raise with us. We could not more clearly say how they really rate with us on a scale of one to ten. We do not fool our children with the clothes, the food, and the lodging we provide. Nor with the money some of us are able to hand out. When it comes to love, and holding, and eyes that share their griefs and attempt to understand their loneliness—we all too often miss the boat because *we* have not been sensitized to isolate the important nuances nor to be able to respond to them. Our own analytic skills are, it appears, at an all time low because our self-interest is so high. Much like the present school system, we really just want children who will be quiet and do as they are told, not human beings who require our sensitive attention. We sidestep the mandate a chaotic society imposes: that is, if the child is to survive an oppressive and racist environment, love must be communicated in ways that are positive and, except for the expenditure of time and concern, cost nothing.

We are a society *programmed to disbelieve what we experi-ence.* Most of us believe that the Black family is still strong. I would argue that it is not: that it is at its weakest, that it is in fact, in crisis. But I also argue that we must believe in its potential to re-form itself; we must trust its good intentions, its resilience: we can begin our rebuilding with those.

If we are to survive the 20th century and move with purpose and commitment into the 21st, our childrearing patterns must change drastically. We must commit ourselves to *rearing* children, as opposed to "raising" children. Rearing a child is a project—a deliberate plan: it is conscious, it is tedious, it is the group's only sure survival technique.

It begins with a political mandate; it must be supported by a spiritual component; empowered by academic and skills requirements; nourished by a moral imperative; and from beginning to end, pulsed by love—love that is communicated in the child's language, not merely implied.

What is imperative, if our reevaluated approach to Black child-rearing is to succeed, is that its initial political mandate be one that is structured around the concept that what is *normal* is Black control of issues that affect Black people and what is *abnormal* is white control of issues that affect Black people, and that our goal is normality. That while power can be shared, real power must be acquired. Power changes hands only as the result of an offensive, and in this society, in 1987, the offensive must be multifaceted.

As long as we are unwilling to acknowledge how high the stakes, how catastrophic the prognosis, our ultimate fate will be decided by our unwillingness to do the nuts and bolts work, in short, our abdication, or by our willingness to turn ourselves around in midstream, for we are fast approaching whitewater and the boat is near to capsizing.

Author's Note: In the more than three-year period between the preparation of this article and publishing of it, much has changed. The toll of dead and destroyed from drug related activities has skyrocketed. Death, violence and diseases tride an already embattled Black community like grotesque leviathans, viciously in control. In Miami, Florida, police report that 70% of all crime in that city is directly or indirectly related to crack cocaine, and whole families are being torn apart as they become both users and dealers. A Drug and Crime report to the Governor of Florida, in February, 1989, mentions that career criminals are typically 18-24 years old, drug users, unmarried and sporadically unemployed, "who began to commit serious crimes well before they were sixteen...."

The thrust of this article remains the same, but the need to reconsider and initiate a *process* for rearing Black children that will engender "wholeness" becomes even more critical, more urgent, more obligatory.

THE BLACK WOMAN
IN BRAZIL

Lelia Gonzalez

To INTRODUCE my subject I will quote from a recent work according to which,

> The first half of the decade was the peak of the Brazilian miracle....The women's labor force doubled from 1970 to 1976. Even more interesting: in 1969, there were 100,000 women in universities compared to 200,000 men. By 1975, this number had risen to about 500,000 women compared to 508,000 men, thus changing the ratio from 1:2 to 1:1, in 1975. In five years, the number of women in universities had increased five times. This demonstrates how economic factors act to reinforce behavioral factors and vice-versa. This may partly explain the fact that in the first five years of this decade—even without having an organized movement—there has been an acute interest in women's problems. It was in this five-year period that the greatest transformation in history in the condition of women took place in our county. (Muraro, 1983:14)

Of course, the above quote has nothing to do with black women even though it refers to *women*. Another book only reinforces what I have just said: "Women definitely not only tend to attain better distribution in the occupational structure, but also abandon those sectors of activity that absorb the less qualified and less remunerated work force, while increasingly seeking place in industry and modern services" (Hasenbalg and Valle Silva, 1984:40). Both references refer to white women.

As regards to black women, their inclusion in the labor force is, as for black men (92.4%), mostly concentrated in manual labor (83%). This means that more than 4/5 of the black labor force have occupations which are characterized by low levels of remuneration and schooling. Black women are placed in rural manual occupations (from farming to vegetal extraction industry) and in services. They are hired hands or are autonomous and non-remunerated. In contrast, the proportion of white women who do manual labor is much less (61.5%).

In non-manual occupations (white collar occupations) black workers are represented in smaller proportions: 16.8% as against 38.5% for whites. These occupations are divided into two levels of activity—middle and upper—whose analysis shows interesting aspects regarding the difficulties of rising social mobility for the black woman. At the middle level (office personnel, elementary school teachers, nurses, receptionists, etc.), the concentration of women is higher than that of men. But, if we then include the racial dimension among the first, we find that the proportion of black women (14.4%) is also much less than that of white women (29.7%). It so happens that because many of the activities at the middle level require direct contact with the public, black women encounter obvious difficulties in being hired in this sector, as witness the classified ads for such jobs which mention that a "good appearance" is required of the candidates. In practice, "good appearance" means that the candidate belongs to the dominant racial group.

The presence of black women is even more limited when we deal with the upper level (professionals, administrators and businesswomen): the ratio is 8.8% white for 2.5% black.

As regards the difference in average income, the 1980 Census yields the following data: up to one minimum monthly salary (about 50 US dollars), 23.4% white men, 43% white women, 44.4% black men and 68.5% black women. From 1 to 3 minimum monthly salaries: 14.6% white men, 9.5% white women, 8% black men and 3.1% black women. Among those who earn over 10 minimum monthly salaries, the proportion was: 8.5% white men, 2.4% white women, 1.4% black men and 0.3% black women (Hasenbalg and Valle Silva).

From the foregoing one may conclude that race and sex discrimination make black women the most exploited and oppressed segment of Brazilian society, limiting their levels of aspiration. In terms of education, for example, it is important to emphasize that a depreciative vision of blacks is transmitted in school texts and perpetuated in a racist aesthetic that is constantly transmitted by the mass media. If we add to that sexism and the valorization of class privileges, the picture is then complete.

Starting with these ideological articulations adopted by schools, our children are induced to believe that to be a man, white and bourgeois constitute the great ideal to be attained. In contrast, they are also induced to consider that to be a woman, black and poor is one of the worst evils. One should think about the effects of rejection, shame of one's self, loss of identity to which our children are subjected, especially our black female children. One of the factors which contributes to the high rate of truancy is exactly this kind of ideology advertised in schools (of each 1,000 children who enter elementary school, only 60 reach the third year). The other factor is economic and relates to the work of minors. Our children join the work force very early due to the conditions of poverty and misery in which the great majority of black people live. Their work, starting at the age of 8-9, contributes to improving their family's low income.

In comparison to poor white families, the situation of black families, living in slums and peripheral zones of the cities, is not one of equality. According to the PNAD-1976, the following was the situation in terms of family income up to three minimum monthly salaries: some 50% of white families compared to 75% of black families. The differences also continue to be marked when one deals with the rate activity: that of black families is higher than that of white families. This means that a much greater proportion of black family members are in the work force than those of white families in order to obtain the same family income.

In recent research carried out with low-income black women (1983), few of the interviewed started working as adults. The great majority started working generally around 8-9 years of age "at the homes of families" (i.e., as domestic workers), especially in the case of those who were the oldest of the family children. And this meant leaving school. One of the women I interviewed, Maria, related the difficulties of a poor black girl, of unknown father, confronted with a unidimensional teaching system, (i.e., Euro-centric) which dealt with values not her own. When speaking of her difficulties in learning, Maria also criticized the attitude of teachers (authoritarian and colonialist) who, from the start, despised poverty and blackness in favor of the practices and methods of "knowledge par excellence": that of the dominant class, race and sex.

Despite her situation of extreme inferiorization, the black woman at the family structure level has played an important role in uniting the black community in resisting the effects of capitalism and the values of a bourgeois western culture. As a mother (real or symbolic), she has been the great generator in perpetuating Afro-Brazilian cultural values and transmitting them to the new generation (Gonzalez, 1981, 1982).

BLACK WOMEN'S PARTICIPATION IN THE SOCIOPOLITICAL STRUGGLE

The development and expansion of social movements in the second half of the 1970s made possible the mobilization and participation of large sectors of the Brazilian population, not only in terms of the revindication of their rights but in a more direct intervention in politics, especially in the Black Movement and in the Favelas (slums) Movement.

The Black Movement has played (and continues to play) an extremely relevant role in the anti-racist fight in our country, even sensitizing the non-black sectors which seek to mobilize the

different sectors of the Afro-Brazilian community for a discussion
of racism and its practices.

> Suffice it to say that the major actors in the current black
> political movements are the children of the first blacks
> who entered, definitively, in the working and middle
> classes, the heros of internal migration; they are among the
> first black students to enter university, young workers and
> black laborers and *soul-dancers*—the modern symbol of
> the black youth struggle against white domination and the
> shortsightedness of liberals in relation to racism and their
> false national consciousness (Cardoso, 1983-1984:46).

The centers from which the struggle grew are the cities of Sao
Paulo and Rio de Janeiro, large urban centers of the Southeast
where the contradictions of the "Brazilian miracle" became
instantly evident. Among the political black movements, it is worth
citing the Unified Black Movement *(Movimento Negro Unifi-
cado*—MNU) which, in its first two years of existence (1978-
1980), not only reached other states in the Southeast, the South and
the Northeast, but also developed a series of activities which greatly contributed to the advancement of the democratic consciousness
(anti-racist and anti-colonialist) in our country. The black woman's
presence, not only in its creation but also in its direction, cannot be
forgotten (Gonzalez, 1982).

While the Black Movement originated in sectors of the black
middle class, the Favelas Movement was created by the urban sub-
proletariat, living in the slums and peripheral areas, in residents'
associations. We have seen earlier that the slum population,
especially in the great urban centers of the Southeast (Rio and Sao
Paulo), has been multiplied several times and today constitutes a
highly representative number of their urban populations. Their
revindications refer to better conditions in transportation, housing,
education, health, etc., and to the title to ownership of the urban
land they now occupy. Needless to say, the presence of black women in the Favelas Movement has been highly significant.

Given its innovative character, in terms of Brazilian society, the Favelas Movement (like the Black Movement, which started the process of germinating an anti-racial national consciousness) also influenced the white middle-class sectors towards organizing what came to be known as the Community Neighborhood Movement (Movimento de Bairros). Thus, in terms of Rio de Janeiro, for example, we have two kinds of organizations which correspond to both movements: FAFERJ (Favelas Movement) and FAMERJ (Community Neighborhood Movement).

I now come to the question of black women's participation as such. The first organized groups of black women appeared within the Black Movement itself. This can be explained first by the fact that the non-manual sectors of the black population that compete on the job market are those which are the most exposed to discriminating practices (Oliveira, Porcaro and Araujo Costa, 1980). Thus, in the Black Movement, there is a growing political awareness of racism, its manifestation and its relationship to class exploitation. Secondly, the Women's Movement, originating in the more advanced sectors of the white middle-class, generally "forgets" the racial question.

Sexual exploitation of women is also another factor of major importance in understanding the relationship of oppression and domination in our society. The women who participated in the rebirth of the Black Movement in Rio de Janeiro, for instance, used to meet separately to discuss their specific problems before presenting them to the whole group, with a view of developing non-sexist practices. It should be noted that this reorganization process of the Black Movement in the 1970s (1973) was due to the initiative of several black women under the leadership of historian Beatriz Nascimento.

In 1975, when the feminists were meeting at the Brazilian Press Association to commemorate Woman's International Year, black women were there to denounce the super-exploitation and oppression of the black woman (Gonzalez, 1982). However, given the many different tendencies within the Black Movement, this pioneer group broke up and its members continued to be active in various organizations which appeared thereafter, but only as activists of the Black Movement.

The years following saw the creation of other black women's groups (Aqualtune, 1979; Luiza Mahin, 1980; Black Women's Group of Rio de Janeiro, 1982) which, despite the efforts of their members, ended, like the earlier group, in being absorbed by the Black Movement as a whole. In other words, all the women went back to the condition of black activists who, within the various organizations (such as Research Institute for Black Cultures - IPCN, Unified Black Movement - MNU, Andre Reboucas Working Group, Society for Exchange: Brazil/Africa - SINBA, etc.), attempted to denounce the macho practices of our brothers who many times tried to leave us out of the decision making process by giving us more "feminine" tasks.

Involvement in the women's liberation movement brought about contradictory reactions. At white feminist meetings and congresses, black women were often considered "aggressive" or "non-feminist" because of their insistence that racism had to be part of the feminist struggle since, like sexism, racism was equally a structural form of oppression and exploitation. Nor was the issue of the exploitation of the black majority domestic workers by their employers a welcome point on the agenda of Women's Lib; it was argued that by being remunerated, they would be "liberated" to be engaged in the "women's" struggle. And if police violence against black men was denounced, the reply was that the violence of repression against leftist political organizations was far more important. In the long run, only certain sectors of the movement became supportive of black women's revindications. In any case, as one author has noted, the Brazilian Women's movement, while coming out of Western Women's Lib, still reproduces its "cultural imperialism" (Bourne, 1983).

THE BRAZILIAN *MULATA*: IN A CATEGORY ALL HER OWN

Carnival. Rio de Janeiro. As always, the leitmotif is liquor, women and samba. It's a magical, fairylike show, according to radio and television commentators. There are feathers, sequins, much extra-vagance and luxury, emperors, pioneers and explorers, African and Indian gods, animals, gay people, kings and queens, maharajahs, slaves, soldiers, "bahianas," gypsies, Hawaiians—everyone following the command of the drum beats and the hip-sashaying of the mulatas who, according to many, are "out of this world."

"Look at them in the fancy car—there."

"What thighs, man!"

"Look at that 'passista' who's swinging. What a backside! Watch the way she moves her belly. She would be great in bed! She's driving me crazy!"

And there they go, the swinging and smiling queens throwing kisses, as if they were blessings, to their hungry subjects, all throughout that magic, fairylike show. Just like a fairy tale.

The myth described here is that of racial democracy, for it is precisely at the moment of the Carnival ritual that the myth takes on its full symbolic impact. It is at this moment that the Afro-Brazilian woman is transformed into a sovereign, into that "mulata, my samba goddess" who, as the song says,

> ...passes by so gracefully,
> teasing, swaying,
> feigning innocence
> and driving us out of our minds.

It is during the Samba School parades that the mulata, in her finest splendor, loses her anonymity and is transformed into Cinderella: adored, desired and devoured by those who have come just to ogle her. Knowing that tomorrow her photograph will be on the pages of every national and international magazine, praised and admired all over the world, there she magically goes, lit up brighter and brighter in that luminous spectacle (Gonzalez, 1983).

As happens with all myths, the one of racial democracy conceals more than it reveals, especially when it comes to the symbolic violence against the Afro-Brazilian woman. According to Sahlins, it is due to a connection with the symbolic system that the place of the black woman in our society, as one of inferiority and poverty, is codified into a racial and ethnical perspective (1979: 196). That same symbolic logic determines the inclusion of the mulata in the category of *sexual object.*

Thus, it is not by chance that Ilma Fatima de Jesus and O. Oluwafemi Ogunbiyi tell us that, historically, "The sexual act between white man and black woman was not seen as normal lovemaking; that's the reason for the word 'trepar' (copulation, get laid), which qualifies coitus as an *animal act.* We suppose that the term 'mulata' has its origin in that grotesque vision of the dominant society system" (1984:4, Emphasis mine). After, we know that the work "mulata" comes from *mule—hybrid animal,* product of the mating of a male or female donkey with a horse or mare.

When analyzing the mulata's presence in Brazilian literature and folksong, it is her physical appearance, her erotic and exotic qualities that have been exalted. That is why she is never a *muse,* which is a category of culture. At most—as someone has already said—she may be *a fruit to be eaten,* but in any case, is a permanent prisoner of nature. The definite establishment of capitalism in Brazilian society had its effects on the mulata: she became a professional. Even now, she is not recognized as a human being and no move has been made to restore her dignity as a woman. She has been clearly transformed into merchandise for domestic and international consumption. Nowadays, mulatas are being trained to appear in nightclub shows. That's the market demand.

The following excerpts are extremely clear in reference to the logic of that domination/exploitation imposed on black women. They are taken from an article published by a newspaper in Rio de Janeiro, *O GLOBO,* on July 10, 1986 (Emphasis mine):

> For Maria Luzacir, age 22, *domestic maid* from the Northeast, no stammering or tripping up on the stage could jeopardize the brilliance of the evening. It was Tuesday and very cold outside, but she was perspiring and bursting with pride....*Starting from that evening she would be*

transformed into a mulata That is to say, a professional mulata.

It took 90 hours of training for Luzacir and 41 other Brazilian girls, aged 16 to 30, neither all white nor all black, to fit into that *national category of skin for exportation*: mulata. But to become a finished product, it was not enough to be born with the *color blessed by God, Europeans and Americans;* to become Rio's *agencies of mulata distribution,* 'OBA OBA' was transformed into a school for their initial professional training.

Institutional authorization for the OBA OBA to operate was given by SENAC (National Service for Commercial Apprenticeship), which coordinated the initiative, and by RIOTUR (Rio's official touring agency) which gave the program the necessary support. After all, *the mulata enterprise is a very lucrative business.*

During the two-hour show, the performers exhibited their finest shape and abilities. In tiny bikinis and bras trimmed with sequins, or in elaborate and exquisite fancy costumes, and inevitably wearing extremely high heels, the mulatas, as highlight performer of Samba Schools, danced, *contorting their bodies like Oshum's daughters and stretching themselves as in a single gymnastic class, like girls from Impanema.*

It was quite delirious for cameraman Hermann Engle who made a video clip for the *German Television ZDF. He was quite sure that the clip would lead his countrymen to madness....*

Despite the absence of her waiter boyfriend, who refused to watch the show, Rosemary stated enthusiastically:

"Ah! When we reach the stage our *blood boils....* There's no way out! I want nothing more than to shake. It's so fantastically delicious! Sometimes one doesn't know what to do but get lost among the other girls, but we always ad lib something."

If the *chief-mulata* heard that she would not approve of it. The show's producer and teacher of modelling from SENAC, Ilan Amaral, was almost hysterical each time her students got confused on the stage. Aged 34, *living in Paris* for four years now, where she works *as a model for Paco Rabane*, Miss Amaral confesses she only came to Brazil to help put on the show. During the presentation she kept controlling the mulatas' entrance and exit and helping them to sing with the microphone.

At the end of the show, when each girl had to say "good night" in different languages, Nazareth Claudina was frightened to face the audience and the microphone. She almost cried when the public demanded that she join the mulatas dressed in Japanese, African or Spanish costumes. Pity that it had to happen to Nazareth who wanted to perform so well in order to get a contract with OBA OBA. For who knows? *She could have shared a better life with her mother* in a home on Governor's Island. She had been one of the best candidates in her group and had learned many things, including a special way to walk....

Marcia Andreia, 18, and Leonora Vidal, 20, hardly noticed what Nazareth was doing. *They are tall and pretty.* According to Miss Amaral, they would be wonderful candidates for opportunities in Italy and Japan. But Marcia doesn't want to become a professional mulata. Her greatest dream is to be a model....

Gloria Cristal, a typical example of a successful mulata to the new graduates (she has two excellent jobs: at OBA OBA and Globo TV), says: "To be a mulata is *the best profession in the world*, because one has the opportunity of becoming a lady. Everybody treats you with tender loving care. *Sometimes I think I am a porcelain doll and I like it very much.*"

It happens that porcelain dolls make very little money when starting in their careers. Such is the case of mulatas who are finishing their apprenticeship. Rio's night clubs pay the monthly minimum salary to beginners. The entrepreneur, Elias Abifadel, owner of OBA OBA, confirms that every start is difficult. However, in the case of Maria Luzacir, for example, her salary is twice as much as what she is now making as a domestic maid in Copacabana, i.e., less than forty U.S. dollars a month.

Just to give an idea of the demand in a market that suffers from a shortage of trained mulatas, 200 candidates have presented themselves for proper training. According to Marcia Andreia, the candidates were thoroughly examined *"as if they were horses."* It's absolutely necessary that they be physically perfect....

Last but not least, there is *the most important prerequisite* otherwise the group would be reduced to three students. *A mulata must have delicate white features if she is to expect guaranteed success* which it must be said, is not so easy to find, observes Ilan Amaral. In her opinion, even if the mulata doesn't have a narrow nose and well shaped lips, she may be outstanding on the stage and invincible in her profession if *"she learns how to be a woman."* This, says Miss Amaral, can also be taught. How? *"In social etiquette classes,"* she says.

This most eloquent article needs no comment. It aptly expresses what being a mulata in the "racial paradise" called Brazil means.

THE BLACK WOMAN AS OBJECT IN BRAZIL: IDEOLOGICAL CONTEXT

Two ideological trends define black identity in Brazilian society: on the one hand, the notion of *racial democracy* and, on the other, the ideology of *whitening (branqueamento)*, resulting in a kind of *double bind*. According to Marlena Chaui (1984:207),

the double bind consists in affirming and denying, prohibiting and allowing something at the same time (the logicians affirm that double bind leads to impossibility of making decisions; the psychiatrists consider it the major cause for schizophrenia, and the anti-psychiatrists consider the double bind the typical practice of family science).

The notion of racial democracy, developed by Gilberto Freyre in the 1930s, has constituted the public and official view of this identity. Accordingly, blacks are citizens like any other citizen and, as such, are not subject either to prejudice or discrimination. The Brazilian images of carnival and soccer are widely used (especially abroad) as "concrete proof" of Brazilian "racial harmony." What does predominate in Brazil's "racial democracy" is *the prejudice of not being prejudiced.*

Previous to the notion of racial democracy, the ideology of whitening served as a justification for a policy developed by Brazilian governments to whiten the population of the country by encouraging massive European immigration, especially during the period 1890-1930. This was directly due to the result of Brazil's first census of 1872 (and confirmed by a later one in 1890) that the major of the population was black.

It should be noted that the historical period mentioned above (which corresponds to what is called the "great immigration") was a time when the ideologists of whitening were elaborating their theses on the superiority of the white race, calling attention above all to the dangers that threatened Brazil for not becoming a civilized country because of its blacks, Indians and mestizos. Colonized heirs to European racist theories, these ideologists were often of African descent themselves.

The changes which took place in Brazilian society during the 1930's resulted in certain political and ideological rearrangements and, among them, the elaboration of the *racial democracy myth.* However, despite the fact that the policy of whitening did not materialize in demographic terms (although it did result in the genocide of a large portion of the black population), ideologically, it has remained effective on other levels: the projecting of Brazil as a country that is racially white and culturally European. Promoted along with the myth of racial democracy and thus making a double bind, it is still today defining the identity of blacks in the Brazilian social context.

While the myth of racial democracy works at public and official levels, the ideology of whitening defines the black at the private level, in two dimensions. In the conscious dimension, it reproduces what white people among themselves say about blacks, which constitutes a whole repertoire of popular inferiority: "a black standing around is a suspect and when he is running he is a thief;" "if a black doesn't do something wrong when entering the place, you can be sure he'll do it when departing;" "a white woman to marry, a mulatto woman to make love to and a black woman to work."

Secondly, there is the subconscious level which corresponds to the stereotyping of the roles and places attributed to the black man (or woman). He (or she) is represented as a non-qualified worker or else as someone who has risen socially, *but always within the channels of social mobility which are considered appropriate for him (or her)*. In this regard the most positive images are those in which the black person represents the social roles attributed by the system: singer and/or composer of popular music, soccer player and "mulata." In all of these images, there is a common element: the black is seen as an object of pleasure. This cultural typification of the black, from non-qualified worker to "entertainer" also points to another common element which can be condensed in *corporal attributes:* strength/physical resistance, rhythm/sexuality. Needless to say, the black man or woman who does not fit these categories is rejected (Gonzalez, 19779-b; Hasenbalg, 1982).

In this context, the experiences of black women are quite significant: it is not rare that a black middle-class housewife, when answering the door, is surprised by a door-to-door salesman who insists on speaking to her employer. Or the fact, more common still, that the porters in the bourgeois or higher middle-class buildings prohibit black women from using the front entrance, insisting that they use the service door. In both examples, the stereotype establishes the relation: black woman = domestic worker. The saying, "White woman to marry, mulatto woman to make love to and black woman to work," is exactly how the black woman is seen in Brazilian society: as a body that works and is over-exploited economically; she is the washer, cleaner and cook, the "work mule" for her white employers; she is the body that generates pleasure and is over-exploited sexually; she is the "mulata" of the carnival whose sensuality falls within the category of the "erotic-exotic." "In a society which has separated spirit from body, making the former something superior to the latter, valuing reason over passion, intelligence over sensitivity, the praising of the rhythmic sensuality of the blacks and the mulatas is the finished and perfect form of the double bind: praising the same that society regards as inferior and condemns" (Chaui, 1984:228).

In contrast to what generally occurs in the United States, blacks and whites *do* live together in Brazil. So, at first sight, one may have the impression that this is a country where racial relations are harmonious. But, as a Brazilian comedian once said: "There is no racism in Brazil because the black knows *where his place is"* (emphasis mine). The logic that rules our social classification system, inherited from Portugal, is such that it determines "a place for each thing, each thing in its place." Or, as Da Marra remarked: "The *white man* is always united and on the top, while the *black man* and *Indian* form the two legs of our society, being always below and being systematically covered (or framed) by the white man" 1981:82. Emphasis mine).

BIBLIOGRAPHY

Araujo Costa, Tereza C., Garcia de Oliveira, Lucia E. and Gonzalez, Lelia (1983). *Mulher negra: uma proposta de artuculacoa entre raca, classe e sexo* ("Black Woman: a proposal for the articulation of race, class and sex"). Rio de Janeiro, Ford Foundation.

Bourne, Jenny (1983). "Towards an anti-racist feminism" in *Race & Class,* Vol. XXV, no. 1, Summer 1983.

Cardoso, Hamilton (1983-1984). "Movimentos negros e preciso" (We need black movements) or Aspectos economicos da opressao racial (Economic Aspects of racial oppression) in *Afrodiaspora*, Year 2, no. 3, Oct./Jan.

Chaui, Marilena (1984), *Repressao Sexual, Essa Nossa (Des) Conbecida* (Sexual Repression, This (Un)Known), Sao Paulo, Brasiliense.

Da Marra, Roberto (1981). *Relativizando: Uma Introducao a Antropologia Social* (An Introduction to Social Anthropology). Petropolis, Vozes.

Farias, aira Ary (1983). *Domesticidade: "cativeiro" feminino?* (Domesticity: feminine "prison"? Rio de Janeiro, Achiame/CMB.

Gonzalez, Lelia (1979). *Cultural, Tenicidade, Trabalho* (Culture, Ethnicity, Work). Pittsburgh, LASA.

—— (1979). *Racism and its Effects in Brazilian Society.* Venice, World Council of Churches Document.

—— (1982). "O Papel da Mulher Negra na Sociedade Brasileira" (The Black Woman's Role in Brazilian Society), in *Lugar da Mulher*. Rio do Janeiro, Graal.

—— and Hasenbalg, C.A. (1982). *Lugar de Negro* (The Place of the Black). Rio de Janeiro, Marco ero.

—— (1983). Racismo e Sexismo na Cultura Brasileira (Racism and Sexism in Brazilian Culture), in *Movimentos Sociais Urbanos, Minorias Etnicas e Outros Estudos* (Urban Social Movements, Ethnic Minorities and Other Studies). Brasilia, ANPOCS.

—— (1984). *The Black Woman's Place in Brazilian Society.* Baltimore, mimeo.

Hasenbalg, Carlos A. (1979). *Discriminacao e Desigualdades Raciais no Brasil* (Racial Discrimination and Inequalities in Brazil) Rio de Janeiro, Graal.

—— and Valle Silva, Nelson (1984). *Industrializacao, Emprego e Estratificacao Social no Brasil* (Industrialization, Employment and Social Stratification in Brazil), Rio de Janeiro, IUPERJ - Series, Studies No. 23.

Muraro, Rose Marie (1983). *Sexualidade da Mulher Brasileira* (The Sexuality of the Brazilian Woman). Petropolis, Vozes.

Oliveira, Porcaro and Araujo Costa (1980). *O Lugar do Negro na Forca de Trabalho* (The place of the black in the work force). Rio de Janeiro, IBGE.

Ogunbiyi, O. O. and Jesus, W. (1984). *A Mulata e a Tal?* (Is the Mulatto Woman the Best?). Sao Paulo, mimeo.

Sahlins, Marshall (1979). *Cultura e Razao Pratica* (Culture and Practical Reason). Rio de Janeiro, ahar.

THE CONTINUING SAGA OF BLACK WOMEN IN AMERICA

Bettye J. Parker Smith

THE BLACK American woman, her varied demographic components notwithstanding, can hardly tolerate another inquisition into her already belabored and controversial condition: her attenuate political, economic and social margins. Without a doubt, the Black woman in America has been the subject of frequent intrigue by astute analysts and dauntless orators, alike. She continues to be spread-eagled on page after page of popular studies which graphically expose her defeats and vulnerabilities to the world.

Needless to say, this flow of attention is not some new phenomenon. Rather, the long trail of inquiry coincides with her fall from grace: from "being a respectable and honorable member of African society to a sinister and repugnant creature..." and, from being the "universal symbol of womanhood and purity [which] was originally considered by many early Christians to be a Black Woman" (Clarke, Feb. 1975, 20). so, while the controversy around America's not-so-favorite daughter is overwrought and certainly overwhelming, it does not appear—by any stretch of the imagination—to be nearing an amicable solution. Therefore, this effort to review the Black woman in relationship to herself and to her significant other (the Black man) is obviously not a new juncture, does not suggest a new crisis, nor does it propose a new strategy. Instead, it acknowledges an already constituted debate and elects to use literary criticism as a model for scrutiny. In this regard, the writer subscribes to Dr. Hortense Spillers' theory relative to the use of literary criticism.

In a long and involved discourse on "The Politics of Intimacy," Dr. Spillers suggests that literary criticism is an appropriate instrument to use in assessing Black womanhood, because it "gives us a clue to the text of our own experience..." (Bell, Parker, Sheftall, 1979, 88). Additionally, and in defense of the use of fiction as a medium to attempt some solution to the problems that plague Black women, she asserts:

> The grammar of fictional situations is the easiest one to manipulate because the characters are beyond change or corruption. They are free. They are still. They contain a contradiction more readily than we do because their lips are not their own, but these unchanging characters may ultimately yield up some bright secret about our own dynamic experiences. (Bell, Parker, Sheftall, 1979, 88)

Further, in reference to the power and use of fiction as a means of touching upon reality, Richard Wright once acknowledged that:

> ...an imaginative novel represents the merging of two extremes; it is an intensely intimate expression on the part of a consciousness couched in terms of the most objective and commonly known events. It is at once something private and public by its very nature and texture. Confounding the author who is trying to lay his cards on the table is the dogging knowledge that his imagination is a kind of community medium of exchange: what he has read, felt, thought, seen and remembered is translated into extensions as impersonal as a worn dollar bill. (Wright, 1940, vii)

The growing body of literature by and about Black women writers provides a wide lens for viewing the Black woman's situation, not because these writers have obtained some specific claim to the genre of fiction, but because of their demonstrated perspicuity on the complexities of Black womanhood. Because Black women are the primary bearers of African culture in the new world, as creative writers, they are natural historical and cultural linkages. Therefore, by constantly energizing the rhythm and pain of their lives, their literature becomes indicative of both their lifestyles and artistic pursuits. So, by being in touch with their own sensibilities and by fostering the desire to right the wrongs historically heaped upon Black womanhood, Black women writers maintain a familiarity with the boundaries of fiction and their own reality.

To address the wrongs is to first understand the dilemma which sociologist Joyce Ladner argued several years ago. Dr. Ladner asserted:

> Because there has been much controversy and concern over the Black woman, and since there are a great number of misconceptions and myths about who she is, what her functions are and what her relationship to the Black man in fact is, it is necessary that one understands some of the historical background that has shaped her into the entity she has become. It is important to realize that most of the analyses concerned with Black women...are historical. (Ladner, 1971, 4)

Since Black women writers create out of a sense of their own exaggerated history, they provide a composite of fictive characters large enough to possibly afford some understanding of the larger, more intimate and controversial problem that plagues us: their role in the gender quarrel. Hence, specific fictional works by Black women writers who wrestle with the pressures of pain, disappointment, emptiness and grief are fertile plots for careful probing into the Black female/male drama. Obviously, literary characters, due to their fixity, are imperfect analogies to the unfeigned, everyday problems that face Black women. Dr. Spillers has accorded some thought to this detail:

> Indeed, we could go so far as to say that a certain quality of mental and imaginative life is inconceivable without the dreaming, mystic mind, but reality intrudes on myth and seeks to plunder it. The burden of consciousness appears to be the negotiation between myth and reality. (Bell, Parker, Sheftall, 1979, 89)

Alice Walker, southern born, novelist, poet, short story writer, essayist, Pulitzer Prize winner and the eighth child of share-cropping parents, has designed a menagerie of female characters. In fact, this writer has observed in another source that Alice Walker utilized her literary license to "call together a meeting of Black women." This observation shares some interesting details:

> ...They are plain women. They grow petunias. They struggle endlessly and are harmless because they know no wrong; mostly just ordinary church-going or church-been women who sometimes in their confused state, amalgamate VooDoo with Christianity....Different though they may sometimes seem, they all push against the same barb-wire wall of racism, sexism, age, ignorance and despair. (Evans, 1983, 479)

Alice Walker's preoccupation with this group of women surfaced, at least fictionally, in her first novel, *The Third Life of Grange Copeland.* In this work, she was searching, looking for answers to unarticulated questions. Though she recognized some sameness, "oppression, the insanities, the loyalties and triumphs of Black women" (Evans, 1983, 479), she nonetheless set out on a mission of inquiry into the behind-the-scene props which allow for these conditions. This struggle for clarity reached its apex in her last and prize-winning novel, *The Color Purple.* Here, in this book which runs a close second, in some places, to the Bible, the Black woman has come full circle. She advanced from being knocked around and abused to a level of self-love and respect: She reclaims her royal position.

The publication of *Third Life* landed like a bombshell. It came on the trail of the Civil Rights Movement and, therefore, impinged on the celebration of some political achievements for Black people in America. To air in public quarrels among the sexes was viewed as untimely and ungodly, especially among the Black male population. Black men may well have accepted these still characters had they not been viewed by them as replicas of out-of-fiction situations. Indeed, they felt that dirty linen ought not be hung in public. The women in this work all ended with the same fate: they were destroyed both physically and psychologically. Their demise was caused by the men in their lives. On the printed page, these women were brutalized and stomped into the red clay dirt of the South, the same soil which oozed the blood of Harriet Tubman.

In a worn-out argument with her husband, Mem, one of the major female characters in *Third Life*, babbles her defeat and vulnerability:

> I have worked hard all my life, first trying to be something and then just trying to be. It's over for me now; but if you think I won't work harder than ever before to support these children you ain't only mean and evil and lazy as the devil, but you are a fool. (Walker, 1970, 87)

To which her husband, Brownfield, retorts:

> Who the hell you think'd hire a snaggletoothed plow mule like you? (Walker, 1970, 87-88)

This argument (if it can be called such since the word argument presumes equality of power) if carefully examined, has many levels. Mem, who abandons her career as a school teacher, married Brownfield. She was quiet and timid and a victim of her own naivete. The bleak world in which she lived as an unwanted extended family member was unfulfilling and lonely. She had been privileged to attend school and had met the meager qualifications of her time to teach. Brownfield, despite his rustic mannerisms, brought some energy to her form. He asked her questions, made her laugh and sought her help in eliminating his literacy. Upon request, Mem taught him to write his name. After she married him and he began to abuse her, she had absolutely no place to turn. So, on the one hand, the argument above both acknowledges and laments her loss of self. Secondly, despite Mem's fear of Brownfield, she moves past reality and clutched fantasy, taking a hard and energetic stance about the children. She makes clear her commitment to take care of them. Thirdly, she uses the opportunity to acquaint Brownfield with the kind of man he has become, in her opinion. Of course, he responds in kind.

Had Mem lived in an early African society, she could have exercised a different set of options. According to the noted historian and scholar, John Henrik Clarke, this kind of negation of her personhood would have never occurred because Mem would have been in a socially acknowledged position of power. Dr. Clarke draws upon Cheikh Anta Diop's study, *The Cultural Unity of Negro Africa*, to reach an interesting set of conclusions about rights and privileges in the early African family. Dr. Clarke observes the following from Professor Diop's work:

> The woman does not leave her family group and can turn out her husband...if he fails to provide enough food for the common provender. Whatever may be the reason for any separation, the children remain entirely in the mother's gens. This proves, if proof is needed, that the women in these old societies had respected rights. (Clarke, 1975, 14)

Mem's position in society is far removed from that about which Dr. Diop wrote. Diseased relationships such as that which existed between Mem and Brownfield are related with creative genius by Alice Walker. However, such stories are based on actual situations which occurred outside the realm of fiction. Mary Helen Washington, an Alice Walker critic, shares the following:

One vital link to those "historical and psychological threads" of her ancestors' lives is the stories passed on to her by her mother....Once, when questioned about the violence and pain in the lives of so many of her women, she recounted an incident from her childhood which was the basis for the story of Mem. (Bell, Parker, Sheftall, 1979, 136)

Perhaps it is appropriate at this juncture to raise questions: What factors contributed to such an abusive and degenerative relationship as that experienced by Mem and Brownfield? They entered a relationship with a socially approved formula: Boy meets girl, boy falls for girl, boy marries girl, and they go forth to live happily ever after. What is the distance between her being romanced as "someone to be loved and spoken to softly" and becoming a "snaggletoothed plow mule?" What caused Brownfield to beat her and question contemptuously: "Why don't you talk like the rest of us poor niggers? Why do you have to be so damn proper?" (Walker, 1970, 55,56). Perhaps it was an issue of saving face when his sharecropping deal turned sour at the end of the year.

In western society, family support is viewed as a solely male responsibility, directly related to the issue of maleness. In a male-oriented society, such as exists in America, male dominance is also the norm. So, is the question one of power, because maleness is equated with power? Are not social position and male economic viability integral parts of the concept of power? Black men and women have been socialized by a system and have entered into the prefabricated personal arrangements of that system where the rules are designed and pre-assigned by the dominant male population. Therefore, the notion of male control filters into personal relationships and the same edicts apply. For the Black male figure in America who must accept the reality that he possesses no economic, political or social control in the first place, some substitution for this power-void is demanded. In Alice Walker's fiction, this loss of manhood or the threat thereof yields a flow of violent male lava. Black women become the depositories of these frustrations brought on by the absence of power, which is predicated upon a false sense of manhood. In her decision of power, Dr. Spillers argues:

> ...the partners either share power or engage in hierarchy of motives, but relationships whether they end or not, have an outcome—thus, the motive of power. (Bell, Parker, Sheftall, 1979, 88)

So, what about Mem? Does her very presence, her femaleness, make her open prey to Brownfield's violence? Do the rules require her to suffer endlessly for a cancer which she did not create? Does she not have a parental responsibility to work at whatever job is available to her, in order to feed the children; the fact that Brownfield is unable to fulfill his prescribed role, notwithstanding? Is Mem damned if she does and damned if she doesn't? Could the tragic end have been avoided: Mem coming home worn and weary from her job where she worked as a domestic; Brownfield lurking in the doorway with senses dulled by constant drunken binges; Mem terribly involved with the shifting pain in her back; Brownfield pointing a loaded shotgun in her direction, as aiming was beyond his grasp; Mem's body now rising and falling swiftly from the shot's impact. Might Mem's presence in the world have been more timely?

These female vessels as repositories of male violence are not taken lightly by Ms. Walker. And, the relationships in which her women find themselves are not easily sluffed off as an every-now-and-then occurrence. As a group, these women's pain and confusion saturate both her long and short fiction. They accept the violence. In their defense, Ms. Walker explains:

> They were suspended in a time where the options for Black women were severely limited....And they either kill themselves or they are used up by the man, or by the children, by...whatever the pressure against them. And they cannot go anywhere. I mean, you can't, you just can't move, until there is room for you to move into. And that's the way I see many of the women I have created in fiction.

They are closer to my mother's generation than to mine. They had few choices. (Bell, Parker, Sheftall, 1979, 138,139)

By contrast, and relative to the role and position of the early African woman, Dr. Clarke advises:

... The African man (is) the father of mankind and the African woman the mother of mankind. In the first African societies, the woman played a major role without demeaning the man or making his role less important. (Clarke, 1975, 15)

As a point of clarity, he elaborates:

Dr. Diop writes that during the entire history of the Egypt of Pharaohs, African women enjoyed complete freedom, as opposed to the condition of the segregated Indo-European woman of the classical periods... "no evidence can be found either in literature or in historical records—Egyptian or otherwise—relating to the systematic ill-treatment of Egyptian women by their men." (Clark, 1975, 15)

Without a doubt, the women who Alice Walker creates are systematically mistreated by their men. She has assured us that this situation on which she reports is not imagined. Mem's counterpart was the mother of one of Ms. Walker's childhood friends who was murdered by her husband. Ms. Walker was thirteen at the time but had a vivid memory of this incident. On a slab in the funeral home:

...there she was, hard working, large, overweight, Black, somebody's cook, lying on the slab with half her head shot off, and on her feet were shoes that I described—hole in bottom, and she had stuffed paper in them....We used to have, every week, just such a murder as these (in my home town), and it was almost always the wife and sometimes the children. (Bell, Parker, Sheftall, 1979, 136)

Before reaching their ultimate level of demise, the women in Ms. Walker's fiction go through a lengthy suffering process. They first lose their dignity, an attribute that historically was the African woman's armor. In *Third Life,* Margaret was Brownfield's mother. She named her son Brownfield because, when he was born and she looked out the window, she could only see brown fields spread out in front of her. Margaret was meek and quiet and enveloped in loneliness. Her husband, Grange, ignored her and treated her like a piece of the furniture. He cleaned himself up each weekend, drove into town and entertained Margaret's old rival, Fat Josie. At first Margaret subsisted on her fantasies: She "washed and straightened her hair. She dressed up and sat, all shining and pretty, in the open door, hoping anxiously for visitors who never came" (Walker, 1970, 12). This aloneness and loneliness eventually drove her to an action that was foreign to her character. She also began going into town, first looking for her husband and later accepting any male companionship. Her entire character changed and she describes her behavior graphically:

> Your daddy and me had another fight,...oh, we had us a rip-rowing, knock-down, drag-out fight with that yellow bitch of his throwing the punches....You'd think he'd be satisfied, me feeding him and her fucking him. (Walker, 1970, 16)

Margaret later committed suicide. Brownfield found her "curled up in a lonely sort of way...as if she had spent the last moments on her knees." (Walker, 1970, 21) In Margaret's case, as in that of countless other women in this fiction, the tragedy was not in her death but in her life which was wrought with tremendous mental and physical anguish. Margaret, like Mem, had absolutely nowhere to turn, no family, no shelter for battered and abused women, and no sisterhood or other support group with which she could identify.

Whatever it was that she expected from a marital relationship was non-existent. There was no fullness to her life.

Grange, like his son Brownfield, had no emotional stability and was unable to cultivate a relationship built on love and respect. They lacked the inner force necessary to bring order to their own being. The only power of which they boasted hung, like heavy lead, from their groin. An example is found in a dialogue which Brownfield engaged with his friends. He advises on methods of keeping women in their place:

> Give this old blacksnake to her...rubbing himself indecently, exposing his secret life to the streets, and then I beats her ass. Only way to treat a nigger woman. (Walker, 1970, 56)

The need to resort to violence, to "beat her ass," is an historical and an abusive use of Brownfield's superior physical strength. The male sexual organ, in these characters at least, takes on a special personality of its own. It moves about among its female population taming and whipping them into shape, punishing them and promoting the barefoot-and-pregnant syndrome. The women accept their fate.

In *Meridian*, Alice Walker's second novel, she continues the search for clarity on this ill-fated group of women. In this book, the question of choice is perhaps more heavily noted than in *Third Life*. While the major female characters do not live on the edge of abject poverty, as did Mem and Margaret, and do not have barren environments, they do suffer from the same pain of a locked-in social position. Early in the book, Meridian Hill, the character around which the plot evolves, is stricken by the languid stance her mother takes on life:

> Her [Meridian's] mother was sacrifice. A blind, enduring, stumbling—though with dignity (as much as was possible under the circumstances)—through life. She did not appear to understand much beyond what happened in her own family, in the neighborhood and in the church...she

complained only about her husband, whose faults, she felt, more than made up for the ignorance of whatever faults might exist elsewhere. (Walker, 1976, 72)

Meridian's mother was a school teacher. During her young years, she enjoyed the freedom that accompanied being single, professional and financially comfortable. To enhance her social status, she married the man who became Meridian's father. He was also a school teacher and "walked over the earth unhurriedly....He cried as he broke into her body, as she was to cry later when their children broke out of it" (Walker, 1976, 40). Mrs. Hill was not prepared to accept the responsibilities of marriage and motherhood, even though she handled them both quietly and with dignity, only allowing the pain to scream inside her own soul:

...Her frail independence gave way to the pressures of motherhood and she learned—much to her horror and amazement—that she was not even allowed to be resentful that she was "caught." (Walker, 1976, 40)

Mrs. Hill represents her generation well. While she profiles the other side of the coin from Margaret and Mem—both in terms of status and time—she is nonetheless option poor. While trying to be responsive to both her biological needs and to her marriage vows, she "got caught." Pregnancy followed by children extracted the beauty out of life for her. As a result, her sense of discomfort and failure was transmitted to her children. Meridian was confused by her mother's pain and grew up feeling guilty about something she could not articulate. When she asked her mother to help identify the source of her guilt her mother's response was, "Have you stolen something?" Meridian understood that the thing she had stolen was her mother's "serenity," "shatter[ed] her emerging self...she was unable to understand how this could be her fault" (Walker, 1976, 41). But because of the definitions assigned to male and female roles in western society, and the manner in which responsibilities are divided up, more often than not, the impact is negative upon self-image. This was especially the case for

Meridian's mother's generation—women who were some two or three generations removed from modern birth control methods. She gave up herself by having children she never wanted, a supreme sacrifice. When the children came, resuming her career as a teacher was no longer an option available to her:

> In the ironing of her children's clothes she expended all the energy she might have put into openly loving them. Her children were spotless wherever they went. In their stiff, almost inflexible garments, they were enclosed in the starch of her anger....(Walker, 1976, 73)

When the children grew up and demanded less of her time, she made efforts to return to her teaching post. She was greeted with new rules regarding qualifying examinations. Now, instead of teaching, Mrs. Hill could only be a teacher's wife, learning to make paper flowers and prayer pillows. Knowing someone was responsible for the disorder in her life, she was not sure where the blame should be placed. Madness came in small internalized stages and the war she waged was against unknown forces. In the meantime, her husband's life was virtually unaltered by the addition of a family. Mr. Hill continued to teach and perform his role as provider while Mrs. Hill was but an extension of his life. He was a kind man. Mrs. Hill did not suffer the burdens of physical and psychological abuse, which had her sisters of lesser fortune, Margaret and Mem. But, for the sake of convenience, she ultimately blamed Mr. Hill for her level of discontent. The constraints of religion and social expectations bound her to the relationship. These were lives lived out, and tragically so, in God's name.

Meridian Hill was a 1960s woman whose search for fulfillment led her over many unpleasant hurdles. Her mother's and grandmother's level of endurance was unyielding; a legacy which she was not especially interested in inheriting. An early pregnancy, a divorce and adoption of her child taught her the painstaking trials of youth, ignorance and innocence. Meridian disliked the consequence of sex. Her early pregnancy made her "suspicious of pleasure. She might approach it, might gaze on it, but retreat was inevitable." (Walker, 1976, 61)

As a late entry college student during the Civil Rights Movement, she set about trying to fashion a life for herself as a student. Competition for men on her campus involved the white exchange female students from the North. She broke off the relationship with Truman—someone she had chosen to love—after discovering his relationship with Lynne Rabinowitz, who had been impregnated by Truman. Growing wiser, she accepted the fact that sexual pleasure, for women, may have consequences far beyond the moment. Certainly, a woman's search for happiness embodies a number of unseen risks. Meridian's male counterparts, on the other hand, walked away from their sexual engagements with their personal freedom unimpaired. After the abortion, and after the lecture from her doctor on morality, she was again approached by Truman:

> You know...I don't know what was wrong with me. You're obviously a stone fox. I don't see why we had to break up....Have my beautiful black babies. (Walker, 1976, 112-113)

Meridian lived during an era in which she was able to exercise a set of options different from those of her mother. Whether to have beautiful Black babies was finally a choice she could make, The future and security of Meridian's children were not matters of concern to Truman. Nonetheless, Meridian did respond to Truman's request:

> ...she drew back her green book bag and began to hit him...she hit him across the ear and a spiral from a tablet cut his cheek...when she noticed the blood she turned and left him to the curiosity of the other students crowding there. (Walker, 1976, 113)

Alice Walker is particularly conscious of placing her characters against the proper historical backdrop. Dr. Mary Helen Washington has noted this tendency:

What particularly distinguished Alice Walker in her role as apologist and chronicler for black women is her evolutionary treatment...that is, she sees the experience of black women as a series of movements from women totally victimized by society and by the men in their lives to the growing, developing women whose consciousness allows them to have control over their lives. (Bell, parker, Sheftall, 1979, 137)

Third Life is Ms. Walker's inquiry into the danger zone where these pitiable women lived. These women are suspended in time as defined by Walker. Their lives are not their own because they are destined to sacrifice themselves for others. They are the sacrificers of the race and mules of the world: women baptized in pain. *Meridian* on the other hand, is a visitation into the lives of women who, by chance rather than by design, have a slight edge on the first group. They have some social and economic possibilities and, therefore, can engage in relationships which may be less threatening. Like the women in *Third Life*, this group's progress toward affirmation of self is thwarted by gender-based inequality. *The Color Purple*, Ms. Walker's latest and most controversial novel, finally brings all the pieces together. This group of women break through the steel clamps of encrusted and convoluted sexism. Equally as important, they break through their own world of possibilities. To their utter surprise, they find that they can co-exist in healthy relationships if they first take care and control of their own lives; they accept Hortense Spillers' revelation: "Men are, in fact, men, and what they decide unto themselves is beyond the ken of women-reason." They moved away from their stagnant behavior of allowing their energy to be "man-compelled" or "man obsessed" (Bell, Parker, Sheftall, 1979, 99).

In *The Color Purple*, Celie's letters are her healing properties, allowing a mirrored vision of herself. Here, too, John Henrik Clarke shares the opinion of other historians of African life and culture who detail the exalted place of African women. Celie's life is antithetical to this historical fact. In the world in which she lives, the old ways have long been replaced by a hierarchical system which seizes women's minds and bodies. Celie is negotiated into marriage by her stepfather and a neighboring widower who has been left, by the death of his wife, with four children. Barely more than a child herself, Celie has already given birth to two children, both of whom have been taken away by her stepfather and sold. In one of her letters to God, she informs Him of her first day's activities as a bride:

> ...I spend my wedding day running from the oldest boy. He twelve....He pick up a rock and laid my head open. The blood run all down tween my breats....The girls hair ain't been comb since their mammy died....So after I bandage my head best I can and cook dinner—they have a spring, not a well, and wood stove look like a truck—I start trying to untangle hair....But I don't cry. I lay there thinking bout Nettie while he on top of me....And then I think about Shug Avery. I know what he doing to me he done to Shug Avery and maybe she like it. I put my arm around him. (Walker, 1982, 13)

While Celie does not seem to place this log of activities in the category of complaints, she may have, just for the sake of information, posed some questions to God while she had his attention. For her own record, she might have questioned: "By what set of guidelines have you judged my sins?" Without waiting for an answer, she might have continued: "Am I being visited by the sins of my mothers?" Instead, she spared God the depth of her agony, finalized her duties for the day, and put her "arm around him."

Celie, her real life parallels notwithstanding, is a character of fiction and, thereby, carries out her role consistent with her design. It is understood that her life is not her own: she can only be maneuvered in and out of situations. But, the fact that she even exists in fiction, that Ms. Walker has used her literary license to give birth to her, is demonstrative of a disease which, if not abated, like racism, will destroy all in its path.

In this condition, can Celie adequately take on parental responsibilities and raise four children to become responsible adults? Should she? Celie is not attuned to her own sensibilities and spends her time looking over her shoulder for the hand that will strike her (both big and small). Choices are non-existent. In the first place, her responsibilities are mammoth. She attends to the children and assumes all the household chores, including bringing in the water and wood. Secondly, she must protect her own life from the dangers which lurk around her. Thirdly, she is obligated, by vow of marriage, to perform sexually at her husband's request. She brings to bear a renaming of, if not in fact, a new Alice Walker category: the chattel wife. Walker's literary license does, as has already been established, afford her the privilege of exaggeration; the right to take the balloon to the point of bursting. However, the relationship between Celie's allegorical behavior and Black women's comportment outside of fiction, borders closely on similitude.

This fact of Black women's lives is widely supported by devastating demographic studies. Accordingly, during the decade 1970-1980, there was a 41% increase in the number of Black children growing up in fatherless families. Specifically, the growth of the mother-headed household is detailed: In 1979, 35% of all Black families in America were headed by women. In that same year 61% of those Black families lived below the poverty line and were headed by women. 1983, 42% of Black families were headed by women as compared to 12% for whites. An especially frightening reality is that young Black women are facing a shrinking pool of marriageable (economically stable) men. Further, studies reveal that paranoid psychosis is the most common form of mental illness among Black women and that elderly Black women are amongst the poorest in the world (Report of Secretaries Task Force, 1985). A large percentage of Black women under the age of forty-five are victims of homicide. Between the ages of forty-five and sixty-four, hypertension is a major cause of death among Black women. This statistic is 85% higher than that of white women. Black women are more likely to be raped, 2.7 times greater than white women (*Focus*, pp. 8-10). The reality of the

Black woman's situation out of fiction is as overwhelming as her literature-bound counterpart.

Living so close to the edge, being victimized by so many "isms," as Celie was, was almost like not living at all. When one hangs limply between life and death, one either slips on over to the other side or makes a turn for the better. In some rare situations, however, one remains suspended for an unusual period of time. For Celie, life took a remarkable turn for the better. With the help of another woman, she was introduced to herself for the first time. She shook hands with her emotions and realized that, by virtue of birth, she had the right and responsibility to protect herself from harm. Celie was a fast learner and grew to understand that hers was the only behavior which she could control. Joining with other women in love can generate power and power allows both the identification and exercise of options. In *Purple*, Alice Walker uses the African Olinka community to comment on the ways in which sisterhood develops in some African societies. In one of the letters which Celie's sister, Nettie, wrote to her, she reveals:

> It is in work that the women get to know and care about each other. It was through work that Catherine became friends with her husband's other wives...the women share a husband but the husband does not share their friendship...the women are friends and will do anything for each other...they giggle and gossip and nurse each other's children.... (Walker, 1982, 13)

Therefore, to celebrate her new selfhood, Celie began to tread her water. Shug was her teacher; in Shug she found a deep and re-warding relationship. Like the Olinka women who empowered and affirmed each other's identity, Shug and Celie's identities were reinforced by their friendship. For the first time, her femaleness surfaced. In a conversation about sex, Celie confided her negative views on the subject to Shug.

> Why Miss Celie...you still a virgin. Listen...right down there in your pussy is a little button that girls gits real hot

when you do you know what with somebody. It git hottor
and hottor and then it melt...That the good part....Here take
this mirror and go look at yourself down there. I bet you
never seen it, have you?

I lie back on the bed and haul up my dress, Yank down
my bloomers. Stick the looking glass tween my legs. Ugh.
All that hair...lips be black...inside look like a wet rose.
(Walker, 1982, 69)

The situation supports the notion that once self-realization is
actualized, whether having been detained by ignorance or
servitude, or both, as in the case of Celie, a call for perfect order
can be initiated. Reluctantly, she pushed her way inside herself and
surveyed her chaotic condition. Then with rusty edges, she located
God's existence within herself. Shug's analysis made sense: "God
ain't a he or she, but a it." And, like the Olinka women, she began
sharing in the process of quilting a sisterhood (Walker, 1982, 167).
First she settled her score with the man who had bought her, body
and soul, under the legality of marriage. Then, she announced that
she was leaving him. He required of her an explanation. To the
great shock of the community of people gathered at the table, Celie
responded:

You a low down dirty dog is what's wrong. It's time for
me to leave you and enter creation. (Walker, 1982, 170)

In Memphis, where she settled, she opened her own pants company
and hired a group of women to assist her. She was on her way to
recovery; a necessity before she could engage in another
relationship with a man. Celie had elevated herself to the level of
royalty; a position that commands respect.

In *The Color Purple*, Alice Walker poses a serious challenge
to Black women; a challenge which, if measured correctly, can
make the difference between living and existing. Hierarchical
personal relationships are antiquated and self-defeating. This claim
is effectively detailed through the fictive characters in Ms.
Walker's novels. The women in her works have cried out across

the pages for fair and equitable treatment and their cries have gone unheard until the publication of *Purple*. Now, Black women are ready to go to the negotiating table.

The male characters in her fiction are blessed with the ability to change; they do so in the late stages of their lives. For men, Ms. Walker's redemptive quality is consistent and honorable. Grange Copeland changes for the better in the end before his violent death; Truman takes on an acceptable level of responsibility at the conclusion of *Meridian*; and in *Purple*, Albert was challenged to accept himself contrary to his father's low opinion of his own worth. Therefore, despite the tension and the rough times, the possibilities for positive female/male relationships in Ms. Walker's fiction, and thus, in the world of reality, remain viable. Dr. Spillers speaks to the position of women in this regard:

> Women must seek to become their own historical subject in pursuit of its proper object, its proper and specific expression in time...male absence or mutability in intimate relationships is not the leading proposition of a woman's life, but a single aspect of an interlocking arrangement of life issues. (Bell, Parker, Sheftall, 1979, 105)

Until the complexities necessary for change, in and out of fiction, are realized, the story of Black women in America will continue to be confused by the maddening echo of their double-edge sword: Damned if you do, and damned if you don't.

BIBLIOGRAPHY

Bell, Roseann, Parker, Bettye and Sheftall, Beverly. *Sturdy Black Bridges: Visions of Black Women in Literature.* New York: Doubleday and Company, 1979.

"Black and Minority Health," *Report of Secretaries's Task Force on Black and Minority Health,* U.S. Department of Health and Human Services, 1985.

Clarke, John H. "The Black Woman: A Figure in World History," *Essence Magazine,* May, 1971, p. 28.

Evans, Mari. *Black Women Writers: 1950-1980.* New York: Doubleday and Company, 1984.

Ladner, Joyce. *Tomorrow's Tomorrow.* New York: Doubleday and Company, 1971.

"Poverty and Family Structure," *Focus,* 8 Summer, 1985.

Walker, Alice. *The Color Purple.* New York: Harcourt Brace Jovanovich, 1982.

———. *Meridian.* New York: Harcourt Brace and World, 1976.

———. *The Third Life of Grange Copeland.* New York: 1970.

Wright, Richard. "How Bigger Was Born," *Native Son.* New York: Harper and Row, 1940.

A HISTORY OF BLACK
WOMEN IN CANADA*

ADRIENNE SHADD

Blacks in Canada have a long and rich history which, although still largely unacknowledged in mainstream history texts and school curricula has come to light in a number of historical writings and sociological studies over the past twenty years. By 1980, historian James Walker could claim that over 300 books, articles, theses and published collections existed on the topic, and that the study of Blacks in Canada was in "a very healthy condition" (Walker, 1980:4).

Yet, it is still the case that only a minority of Canadians are aware of Blacks' 350 year history, believing that their presence is a result of more recent immigration from the Caribbean. Outside the country, one of the biggest misconceptions about Canada is that it is a country inhabited by Caucasians only (with the exception of a few aboriginal peoples).

Part of the problem is that official census statistics have always severely under-represented the numbers of Blacks in this country. For example, the 1981 census indicated that there were approximately 240,000 Blacks—representing about 1 percent of the population—in several categories: 31,000 Haitians, 160,000 of other Caribbean origins, and 48,000 African and Canadian-born Blacks. Estimates, however, claim at least twice that number.[1]

Within the context of the apparent lack of awareness of the historical presence of Blacks and their contributions to Canadian society, even less attention has been focused on the Black woman, her specific struggles and achievements. With the exception of Jim Bearden and Linda Jean Butler's (1977) biography of Mary Ann Shadd Cary, and Carrie Best's (1977) autobiography published in the same year, there have been no major works written about Black women in Canada. Two main resource materials on the subject are Enid D'Oyley and Rella Braithwaite's *Women of Our Times* (1973) and Rella Braithwaite's updated of the same, *The Black Woman in Canada* (1977). These works provide short biographical accounts of a number of women, past and present, who have made notable contributions. Unfortunately, while they represent important sources of information about specific women, they contain little general information on such themes as Black family life, or employment patterns for Black women, or many other aspects of the study and analysis of the Black female.

The present article will attempt to fill this gap. Although information is sparse and derives almost exclusively from secondary sources, the history of Black Canadian women will be outlined from the earliest times to the present.

The story of Black Canadian women deserves to be told. Women have had a vital role to play in the escape to freedom, the establishment of early Black communities, the struggle for equality and dignity, as community leaders and activists, and in the contemporary women's movement. Oppressed as Black people and discriminated against as women, Black women hold a pivotal position in the history of oppressed peoples in the Americas. Hopefully, the following article will shed light on this hitherto unexplored topic of Black Canadian history.

SLAVERY AND THE EARLY BLACK SETTLEMENTS OF THE MARITIMES: 1700-1815

Black history in Canada dates back to the early settlements of 17th century New France, when slaves, both Black and native, were used to alleviate a chronic shortage of unskilled labor. The first known Black Canadian was a young boy from Madagascar, baptized Olivier Le Jeune. He was brought to New France as a slave in 1628 and sold to a Quebec resident. By the time of the British Conquest in 1759, there were more than a thousand slaves, about half living in and around Montreal. Most were employed as domestic servants, and few households possessed more than two or three slaves.

Many Black women slaves were being traded, sold or bequeathed along with property. The Quebec Gazette in 1783 published the following announcement:

TO BE SOLD

A Negro Wench about 18 years of age....She has had the Small Pox. The Wench has a good character and is exposed to sale only from the owner having no use for her at present. Likewise to be disposed of a handsome Bay Mare (Walker, 1980:20).

Such advertisements were common in this period, as were notices offering rewards for the return of runaway slaves.

Resistance to slavery occurred in a variety of ways and Black women, when caught, were punished as severely as men. A case which occurred in the spring of 1734 in Montreal illustrates the point. Upon learning that she was to be sold, a female slave named Mari-Joseph Angelique set fire to her master's home and destroyed part of the city of Montreal. Angelique was captured and sentenced to make restitution dressed only in a shift, a rope around her neck, holding in her hands a flaming torch two pounds in weight before the main doors of the Parish Church of Montreal; to be taken to this spot by the Executioner in a cart used for collecting refuse; to have a notice reading "Incendiary" hung in front and behind her, and bareheaded and kneeling to declare that, with ill will, she lit the fire and caused the conflagration to which she confesses and for which she begs forgiveness of God, the King and Justice. After this, she is to have her fist severed on a stake placed before the church then to be led by the Executioner in the same cart to the public square and to be tied to a stake with an iron chain and burned alive, her ashes to be thrown to the wind.

This brutal sentence was modified. Her fist was not severed, and she was hanged before being burned (from M. Trudel, 1960, as cited in Case, 1977:10).

After 1759, under British rule, slavery was given greater impetus for a time and became associated strictly with members of the African race. The single greatest reason for this had to do with the American Revolution and the influx of thousands of United Empire Loyalists into Nova Scotia (which then included New Brunswick) and the Canadas. In attempting to re-establish themselves and their families, these "loyalists" to British custom and institutions brought their most prized possessions. This included their slaves. Thus, while the 1767 census showed 104 slaves throughout Nova Scotia, 54 living in the city of Halifax, the arrival of Loyalists to the province after 1781 brought an estimated 1,232 more, often designated "servants" or "servants for life" (Walker, 1976:40)

An indication that slavery would never gain the foothold that it did in the United States became clear from the very beginning. For example, one Loyalist sent 19 slaves to his cousin's plantation in Dutch Guiana because he could not use them. In a note to the latter's agent he wrote: "They are all American born and well seasoned....The Women are stout and able, and promise to increase their numbers" (ibid:5).[2]

Ironically, the same movement which increased the numbers of slaves also brought its first major wave of freed Blacks into the province. The "Black Loyalists" comprised a group of approximately 3,500 men, women and children who were promised their freedom, land and full equality under British law for fleeing their masters and escaping behind British lines. While tens of thousands of escaped slaves joined the British forces, the majority were later sold back into slavery in Canada or the British and French West Indies (ibid:3-8). Nevertheless, at least 10 percent of all Loyalists were Black, a little-known fact that was ignored by historians until recently.

Black Loyalists had auspicious beginnings. One-third or more of the men served the Revolutionary War effort, as intelligence agents and guides through slave territory, as soldiers, sailors, pilots on coastal waters and officers of all-Black regiments. Many were skilled craftsmen such as carpenters, blacksmiths and sawyers (ibid:5-6, 47). Women did the cooking, washing and sewing.

The presence of large numbers of free Blacks made it difficult for white slaveowners to convince their slaves that they deserved to be in servitude, and it was relatively easy for slaves to escape into free Black communities and remain safely hidden. Nevertheless, Nova Scotia was a "slave society," with all that implied, and severe limitations were placed on Blacks' freedom and opportunities. They were viewed as a source of cheap, exploitable labor, and women and children, too, were the victims of much cruelty and injustice in their efforts to eke out an existence (ibid:41-42). The following case of Black Loyalist Lydia Jackson is illustrative:

> Lydia was living in great distress in Manchester when Henry Hedley invited her to work for him. After several days, he demanded payment for her board, or, as an alternative, her indenture to him for seven years. Though Lydia refused the seven-year term she was eventually persuaded to place her mark on an agreement for a one-year term. Hedley, however, took advantage of her illiteracy to substitute a term of 39 years in the articles of indenture. She was then sold for 20 pounds to a Dr. Bulman, of Lunenberg who, with his wife, beat her with fire tongs and kicked her in the stomach, though Lydia was then eight months pregnant. A court case on her behalf, brought by a Lunenberg attorney, was dismissed by the magistrates. After three years with Bulman, Lydia learned of his intention to sell her as a slave in the West Indies. To avoid this fate was worth the risk of capture and punishment as an escapee, so she left Bulman's farm and fled to Halifax. John Clarkson, the passionate Abolitionist who interviewed Lydia Jackson, said he met "many other of a

similar nature," and cited five by name (ibid:50).

Court records also document the threat of being returned to slavery, as in the case of Mary Postell who, along with her children, was claimed by one Jesse Gray. Although Mary possessed a certificate of freedom, the court granted the alleged master one year to prove his ownership (ibid:51).

Once again, when Blacks were brought before the court for breaking the law, Black women were punished equally severely to Black men for the same crimes for which whites received fines. Between 1784 and 1789, Shelburne court records expose the inhumanity of the times with regard to women of color. Dianna, convicted on two counts of petty larceny, suffered the incredible sentence of:

> Two hundred lashes at the Cart's Tail next Saturday, at 12 o'clock, at noon, for the first offense, and one hundred and fifty lashes on the following Saturday at the Cart's Tail for the second offense.

Another woman, Alicia Wiggins, "received 39 lashes in April 1792 for theft," but was sentenced to hang in July for stealing 3s. 11d. worth of used clothing.

> Alicia pleaded a stay of execution on the grounds of pregnancy but "twelve Matrons or discreet women," on examining her, found that she was "not four months gone with child," so she was executed as ordered.

In Guysborough county between 11 October 1785 and 8 February 1791 no white suffered corporal punishment:

> Theft, slander, assault, "keeping a house of ill fame," even riot, were punished by fines. But when a Black Loyalist woman, Sarah Ringwood stole some butter, she was "ordered for Punishment to receive Thirty nine stripes on her naked back at the Public Whipping Post in Man-

chester." Another [Black woman, Eleanor Bourke, received the same punishment plus a week's imprisonment "for being a Vagrant, Idle, Disorderly Person." This was during the famine of 1789. In one year, four [Black men were whipped for stealing food, and another [Black woman "for abusive, Lewd and Indecent behavior." (ibid:56)

What becomes clear from these cases is that Black women resisted their bondage, whether it was in the form of legal slavery or a more informal servitude, in the only ways they knew how: by fleeing, by taking their cases to court, through criminal action, and so forth. What is also interesting, particularly in the latter two court cases involving women, is that a certain image of the Black woman is suggested—that she was indecent, immoral, or otherwise lacking in white womanly virtues. This myth, widely held in antebellum America, justified a system of sexual exploitation of Black women on southern plantations (Gray White, 1985:29). Although we do not know much about the sexual conduct of Black women vis-à-vis white men in Loyalist Canada, this "Jezebel" stereotype in all likelihood found its way to the British colonies north of the Republic, and can only have added to the degradation which many were forced to endure.

Despite the suffering and hardships which they faced, free Black women nevertheless went about the business of raising families and helping to establish communities. For the most part, Blacks were settled together on small parcels of land in their own segregated settlements and, with the support of philanthropic organizations, began to build their own schools and churches.

However, women of the late 18th century held few positions of leadership in these nascent communities. On the odd occasion when a Black woman was hired to teach in the school, it was at half the salary offered men (Hill, 1981:159). And while women were as influenced by the spread of the gospel, it was men who ministered to the congregations and otherwise ran community affairs.

Officials commented on the strength of family ties among the Black Loyalists and observed that 'family' went beyond the British definition to include god-children or simply Black people from the same community. Common-law marriages were frequent and the children of such unions were baptized and treated the same as those of legally-sanctioned unions (Walker, 1976:85). Whether these customs emerged from slavery or, as in the case of the extended family, can be traced to West African pre-slave origins, the Black Loyalists had begun to develop communities with their own institutions and social mores; and women played a vital, if subordinate, role in this development.

Many Black Loyalists were unhappy in Nova Scotia. They had been promised not only their freedom, but also land and the full rights of British subjects under the law. These expectations went unmet, given a situation in which white Loyalists, officers and soldiers were accorded priority in the granting of land and other assistance. After much effort to make their grievances known, approximately one-third emigrated to Sierra Leone in 1792. To this day, descendants of the Loyalists still refer to themselves as the "Nova Scotians" (ibid.).

A third group of about 2,000, known as the "Refugees" (Winks, 1971), quickly replenished the numbers of Blacks in the province. Escaped slaves primarily from the upper slave states of Virginia and Maryland, they landed in 1815 after being granted freedom for deserting their masters and joining the British during the War of 1812. Thus, Black Refugees and the remaining Loyalists established the oldest settlements of free Blacks in Canada.

THE FUGITIVE SLAVE ERA AND THE EMERGENCE OF BLACK FEMALE LEADERSHIP: 1815-1870

The 19th century ushered in a new period in which Black women stood shoulder to shoulder in many cases with their men in the struggle for freedom and equality. With the fugitive slave era (1815-1861), an estimated, 40,000 Blacks, slave and free alike, made their way to Upper Canada, now Ontario, where it was known that Blacks were welcome as free citizens. In 1834, slavery was abolished throughout the British Empire by an Act of Parliament, although it had been severely curtailed in Upper Canada by a bill passed in 1793 prohibiting the importation of slaves into the province, and allowing the gradual emancipation of existing slaves (Winks, 1971:96-99, 111; Walker, 1980:25; Hill, 1981:91).[3]

In this period Black women escaping from slavery to freedom were active on the Underground Railroad network, were newspaper editors, businesswomen, teachers who opened their own schools, spokespersons for their communities, and organizers of women's cultural and benevolent societies. The Black experience was viewed as a test of Blacks' ability to succeed as free citizens and the talent and skills of both sexes were necessary to prove the point.

Although Harriet Tubman, famous liberator on the Underground Railroad and Mary Ann Shadd Cary, teacher, author, newspaper editor and lawyer, stand out as the best-known examples of female leadership in Canada West,[4] they were by no means the only influential women.

A leading spokesperson for Hamilton's Black community was Paola Brown. In 1837, she led a protest against the arrest and imprisonment of a fugitive from Kentucky, Jesse Happy, who was accused of stealing his master's horse to escape North. a petition was sent to Lieutenant-Governor Sir Francis Bond Head to ask for Happy's release and, in October of the same year, Happy was set free "on the ground that to send him back to Kentucky would automatically return him to slavery, a condition that British law considered illegal" (Hill, 1981: 95).

In the 1840s, when Black children were refused admittance to the common schools in Hamilton, Paola Brown and 'the Coloured People of Hamilton', officially protested such discrimination to the Governor General Lord Elgin:

> ...we have tried every lawful and civil means to get our children into the common schools, and as yet have failed in the attempt....We are called nigger when we go out in

the street and sometimes brick bats is sent after us as we pass in the street (ibid:150).

Although by 1851, Black children were attending Hamilton schools, Paola was asked by over 200 Blacks to speak out against the poor quality of education the children were receiving:

It is lamentable that many of our children go to school from four until they are eight or ten and sometimes fifteen years of age, and leave school knowing but a little more about the grammar of their language, than a horse does about handling a musket; and to answer a person correctly general questions in Geography, and to hear them read would only be to disgust a man who has a taste for reading...(ibid:154).

In the case of Miss Julia Turner, however, it was clear that Black society was not completely comfortable with the idea of women in leadership roles. Miss Turner began teaching in the Amherstburg for Black children[5] in 1854 only to resign in December 1856 "after some of her pupils' parents, opposed to a woman teacher, drew up a petition asking for the appointment of a man." (ibid)

Clearly the fugitives had wanted to pattern their family structures after the patriarchal model of their white counterparts. For many "legalized marital status placed the Black male in a position of authority and responsibility which had been denied to him in slavery." And to make the picture of patriarchal order and virtue complete, as Dorothy Shadd Shreve observes, "When he acquired a plot of land on which he constructed a log cabin, he achieved distinction as a property owner." (Shadd Shreve, 1983:121-2)

Thus, when Mary Ann Shadd Cary, widely acknowledged as the first Black woman editor of a newspaper in North America, took over the editorship of *The Provincial Freeman* in 1854 in Toronto, she initially thought it wise to conceal the fact that the editor was a woman by using only her initials as a byline

(MacDonald, 1987:37). According to some researchers, the well-educated Mary Bib is probably more responsible for the style and content of *The Voice of The Fugitive* than her husband Henry Bibb, who is credited with having founded and edited the Sandwich, Ontario antislavery newspaper in 1851 (Ripley, 1986:108).

However, in an editorial of the following year, as if to underscore the fact that Black women could not realistically be held back, Shadd Cary wrote:

> To colored Women we have a word—we have broken the "Editorial Ice" whether willingly or not for your class in America, so go to editing as many of you who are willing and able and as soon as you may, if you think you are ready.[6]

In terms of employment opportunities, the booming towns and cities of early Ontario acted as a "pull" to the masses of fugitives who were pouring into the province. In Chatham, Ontario, considered a "mecca" for Blacks in the mid-19th century, 30 percent of Black females worked outside the home in the 1861 census. Twenty-three percent were unemployed, many being unmarried young women living at home, and 47 percent were housewives. Of those employed, 51 percent held skilled or semi-skilled jobs. For example, two-thirds (or 35) of Chatham women were seamstresses, 7 were cooks, and there were two each of teachers, nurses, milliners, stewardesses and mid-wives. There was 1 editor, 1 weaver, 1 shoebinder, and 1 missionary. Many of these jobs were performed in the home. Women listed as independents comprised 2 grocers, 1 tavernkeeper, and 1 innkeeper. In all of the latter cases, women worked alongside their husbands who were the proprietors of the business.[7] Women who worked in skilled/semi-skilled and independent occupations were usually married to men in these same categories or they were the widows of such men (Walton, 1979:129, 290-91, Tables 4.5, 4.6).

Forty-four percent were employed in unskilled occupations such as servants, washerwomen or laborers. These women were likewise married to or were the widows of men in unskilled occupations (ibid.).

By contrast, an 1847 census for Philadelphia revealed that:

> close to half the female Black population consisted of washer-women and domestic servants. About 10 percent were needle-women, and 5 percent involved in trades like hairdressing and dressmaking (Giddings, 1985:48).

According to Paula Giddings, the white female labor force was comprised primarily of single women, whereas Black women, both married and single, were forced to work (ibid.).

Clearly, although Blacks faced prejudice and racial hostility in Ontario, their position in terms of employment opportunities was far superior to that of Blacks in major northern United States cities at the time.[8] This is why so many Black women could afford the luxury of staying home, even after the depression of 1857, which forced many more out into the workforce to supplement their husbands' earnings. (In the 1851 census, only 5% of Black women worked.) It is also why Blacks attained a certain "stability" in their family lives. The overwhelming majority of Chatham's Blacks married and the typical family was a two parent household with at least two children (Walton, 1979:65).

The above statistics provide a glimpse of Black life and the employment picture of women in an urban setting. While most Blacks ended up in urban areas because they could not afford to buy farmland, some families did settle in rural areas and establish farms. In the Elgin or Buxton Settlement,[9] most women listed their occupation as "housewife," which means that they were not wage-earners but rather worked within the context of family farming. The typical household contained two parents, three or four children and an adult relative (Walton, 1979:224). A very small number of women did list their occupation as "farmer." Perhaps these latter women saw their contribution on the farm as important as their husbands', or perhaps some were widows who now held the responsibility of running the family farm (ibid: Table 4.18, 304-5; Table 5.31, 353).

Probably the most influential category of employment for Black women of the time was in schoolteaching. When Mary Ann Shadd Cary first immigrated to Windsor, Canada West in 1851 with her father and brother, members of a free Black family from Delaware,[10] she opened a school for the town's Blacks. Shadd Cary taught 10 classes, including geography, history, arithmetic, grammar, reading and botany. She was considered an exceptional teacher and received the praise of the community (Hill, 1981:155). Unfortunately, a dispute with Henry Bibb, editor of the *Voice of the Fugitive*, over what Cary considered his abuse of power led to her dismissal from the teaching position. The dismissal eventually led to the founding of *The Provincial Freeman*, a second antislavery newspaper which would be independent of Bibb's influence.

Mary Bibb, wife of Henry, opened a classroom in her home in Sandwich, Ontario in January 1851. Within a month, the school moved to a larger room, although it was ill-ventilated, with a shortage of equipment, and Mrs. Bibb had to carry firewood quite a distance to heat the schoolroom. Her salary was $10 for a whole eight-month term! (ibid:156)

In 1854, two Black student teachers from Dominica were brought by Reverend Martin Dillon, who had been asked to come and set up a Mission and school for Blacks in London, Ontario. Sarah and Mary Ann Titre were the first Black women to teach in fully integrated classes in the province (ibid:153). Emaline Shadd, younger sister of Mary Ann, graduated first in her class at Toronto Normal School in 1855, winning an award of 5 pounds 10 shillings. She later taught in Peel and Kent Counties before moving to Washington, DC to teach at Howard University (ibid:205).

In 1856, a young woman, Amelia Freeman, who had taught at Avery College in Pittsburgh, began a "select school for children." Her school offered instruction in painting, drawing, music (voice and piano) and writing. It catered to Chatham's skilled class and was intended as a training center in social refinement. By June 1857, the curriculum had broadened to include standard subjects such as reading, writing, and arithmetic, geography and so forth, and the more "cultural" offerings became electives for which she charged a separate fee above the regular one. Those unable to pay could attend gratis (Walton, 1979:77).

These Black schools, which sprang up in almost every community where Blacks settled, owed their existence to the fact that Black children were denied access to the common school and to the importance which fugitives placed on education. Although access to an education was often spotty or inadequate, the separate school, unlike the churches, did provide an avenue for Black female leadership and role models.

Black women's activism in mid-19th century Ontario was also evident in the proliferation of ladies' literary, intelligence, temperance and moral improvement societies. According to Paula Giddings, these societies came into being in the United States because of the pressure on free Blacks to prove they could be acculturated into American society. "For Black women, *acculturation* was translated as their ability to be 'ladies'—a burden of proof that carried an inherent class-consciousness" (Giddings, 1985:49).

This was no less an issue in the Canadas. Mary Bibb presided over a Mutual Improvement Society organized by "...the Colored Ladies of Windsor." This group met to hear speeches and "improve their minds" (Hill, 1981:179). However, despite their titles, these organizations did more than pursue cultural activities. There were numerous organizations set up by women in Toronto to assist refugees who flooded into Canada West in the 1840s and 50s. Among these were the Ladies Colored Fugitive Association, the Ladies Freedman's Aid Society, the Queen Victoria Benevolent Society led by Mrs. Ellen Abbott, and the Ladies Association for the Relief of Destitute Colored Fugitives. The report for this latter organization for the period 1853-55 stated:

> During the past inclement winter, much suffering was alleviated, and many cases of extreme hardship prevented. Throughout the year, the committee continued to observe the practice of appointing weekly visitors to examine into the truth of every statement made by applicants for aid. In this way between two and three hundred cases have been

attended to, each receiving more or less, according to their circumstances (ibid.).

In January 1854, Black wives in Chatham, led by a Mrs. Charlotte Hunter, formed the Victoria Reform Benevolent Society, whose function was to provide money or "social relief" to its members who were in need. In order to join, one had to pay a monthly fee (which meant that the organization was not for the poor), and members could not be alcoholics, prostitutes, already ill, or practicing polyandry. The fact that these rules were stipulated in the constitution implies that such cases must have existed among Chatham's Black women at this time (Walton, 1979:71).

While most of the early Black settlements in Canada were located in the Maritimes or Ontario, Free Blacks from California also migrated to British Columbia when increasingly restrictive legislation was enacted against members of their race in that state. A group of six to eight hundred set sail for Vancouver Island and landed in Victoria in 1858. The Prairies also became a place of settlement when 200 Oklahoma Blacks settled in Saskatchewan in 1909 and another 300 settled in Amber Valley near Edmonton, Alberta in 1910. Most established farms and supplemented their incomes during the winter months in nearby towns and cities (Walker, 1980:56-7, 68-9).

Out West, as in Eastern Canada, Black women homesteaded alongside the men, taking an active role in settling the land and developing communities. Likewise, among the leaders of these settlements were women. A prominent member of the California migration was Sylvia Stark who, along with her husband Louis Stark, arrived on Saltspring Island British Columbia with 15 cows and bought 100 acres of land. A former slave, Mrs. Stark died there in 1944 at the age of 106 (Winks, 1971:277-78). One of the leaders of Maidstone, Saskatchewan where Blacks first took up land in the 1900s was Mattie Hayes. "A slim and determined woman of sixty who had been born a slave in Georgia, (s)he and her husband Joseph brought their ten sons and three daughters, and their grandchildren from Tulsa and Muskogee, together with ten other families...[Until her death in 1953 'Mammy' Hayes was the matriarch of Maidstone." (ibid:303)

After the Civil War, it is estimated that three-quarters of the "fugitives" returned to the U.S. following the outbreak of hostilities.[11] Slavery had ended in the United States, removing the need for Canada as a haven for escaped slaves, and many returned to reunite with family and friends or to lend their skills during Reconstruction. Some of the returnees attained high political office in the South. An Arkansas judge, a U.S. senator from Alabama, and a number Representatives and local officials all migrated from the British colonies north of the border (Walker, 1980:62). Mary Ann Shadd Cary became a recruiter for the Union Army during the Civil War and remained there after the war. She taught in Washington, DC and later became a lawyer and women's rights activist. Blacks who remained in Canada were keenly interested in the welfare of their newly freed brothers and sisters south of the border. For example, the Committee of Colored Ladies of the British Colony of Victoria, V.I. (Vancouver Island) raised funds from bazaars, Sabbath-school exhibitions and other events to assist the freedmen and Afro-American institutions (Ripley, 1986:510-11).

In essence, the experiment with freedom had largely been successful and Black women had played a very important part in carving out a niche for Blacks in the frontier societies of Canada West, British Columbia and the Prairies. While Blacks had wanted to emulate white patriarchal family structure, the fact that women were leaders, established schools, operated businesses, homesteaded, formed clubs and self-help organizations, and actively participated in the betterment of their communities demonstrated an influence and freedom which white women in all likelihood did not share. Thus, Black women actively earned their right to equality with men and demonstrated an early feminism which must be understood precisely in these terms.

Conflicting Images and Separate Realities: Domestic Service and Black Women's Activism, 1870-1960

The position of Blacks declined in Canada after 1870.[12] With the abolition of slavery, many sympathetic whites lost interest in the plight of African people in Canada, and with the steady increase of white immigrants of varying skills and talents, Black labor became expendable. The pattern in most of the areas of Black settlement was that after an initial period in which there was little overt resistance from whites, the "Color line" crystallized in these communities and a pattern of de facto segregation emerged in Canada. The color line was evident in residence patterns, public accommodation, restrictive Canadian immigration policy, and the existence of separate schools, churches, and social clubs. Moreover, Blacks tended to be relegated to the most servile, low status occupations.

Racial stereotypes were the order of the day. Black women were invariably portrayed as either oversexed temptresses or oversized "Mammies." Winks notes that "[i]n Vancouver in 1903, there were said to be one hundred and thirty-eight 'dusky houchie kouchie girls' from the 'jungles of Africa' who did 'business by the gleams of a red torch' upon black skin" (Wink, 1971:293). And Uncle Tom and Uncle Remus, and "the faithful mammies, Lize and Chloe, were part of the mythology that was the heritage of smalltown Canada as well as of rural midwestern America." (ibid: 295).

In 1891, 12 percent of the total female population in Canada worked and the majority (41%) were employed in domestic service. Schoolteachers were the second largest group with 7 percent. In the early decades of the 20th century, domestic service and teaching remained the two major employers of women, who also worked in dressmaking, millinery, in canning factories, and textile mills, as telephone and office clerks, in department stores, and as professional nurses. Even into the '30s, teachers and civil service women were required by law to resign upon marriage, and in other occupations, social pressure was placed on women to become full-time wives and mothers once they were married (L'Esperance, 1982:25, 53).

If occupational choices for Canadian women as a whole were limited, they were even more so for Black women. In 1930, Ida Greaves observed that the majority of men in the cities were employed as sleeping car porters and most women were domestics. In addition, she states:

> A few who are light in color find employment as waitresses, but unless they have no marked negroid features coloured girls cannot obtain work in offices or stores. A few are also teachers in Negro schools, but the field here is too limited and unremunerative to attract the really capable (Greaves, 1930:56).

In 1941, 80 percent of employed Black women in Montreal were domestics (Potter, 1964:142) and in many Maritime communities, it is still the only employment available for Black females (Walker, 1980:132).

Not only were indigenous Black Canadian women associated with domestic service but women from the Caribbean were being allowed into Canada to work as domestics. Eventually, as white Canadian and European immigrant women moved out of this area of employment, and the remaining numbers were not enough to satisfy the demand, the Canadian government introduced the West Indian "Domestic Scheme" in 1955. It stipulated that Black "girls" would be allowed into Canada if they would work as household servants for at least one year. Between 1955 and 1960 this scheme resulted in a few hundred female immigrants each year (Walker, 1980:70).

Black women also went into public schoolteaching like their white counterparts, as teaching at the lower levels became synonymous with women's work. However, few were admitted into training schools and often had to wait until positions became available in the predominantly Black schools of southwestern Ontario, such as in North Buxton (Roach-Brown, 1987:18-20) or Nova Scotia.

While it is clear that the vast majority were relegated to stereo-typed occupations, as were their male counterparts, Black women did distinguish themselve in other areas. Two women, Christina Jenkins and Carrie Best, were newspaper publishers/editors. *The Dawn of Tomorrow* first began publication in 1923 by James Jenkins who was succeeded by his wife Christina after his death in 1931. The London Ontario newspaper was the voice of the Black southwestern Ontario community and, at its peak in the '50s, boasted a wide circulation. Carrie Best published *The Clarion* (later renamed *The Negro Citizen*) between 1946 and 1956. She wrote about racial discrimination in Nova Scotia and championed the cause of Black rights (Winks, 1971:402, 407-8).[13]

What is interesting about these women is that they were both staunch community activists whose influence went far beyond their work as newspaperwomen. Best in particular was doubly honored in 1975 by being awarded the Order of Canada and an honorary Doctorate of Laws from Saint Francois Xavier University for her long involvement in community affairs and civil rights (Braithwaite, 1977).

Hence, given the limited opportunities available at this time, it is not surprising that D'Oyley and Braithwaite should comment that "...the Canadian [B]lack woman, until recently, made her greatest contributions through humanitarian pursuits" by being active in community work, service clubs and other such organizations that worked toward the betterment of the race, or the larger society" (D'Oyley and Braithwaite, 1973:2).

Women played important support roles in Black organizations. When Marcus Garvey's Universal Negro Improvement Association founded chapters in cities like Montreal, Halifax and Toronto in the early '20s, women were integrally involved. For example, the Italian invasion of Ethiopia in 1936 prompted women in the Toronto chapter to spearhead a fundraising effort in aid of their African brothers (Richmond, 1987:17). Likewise, when the Brotherhood of Sleeping Car Porters were organized in 1942 by CPR porters, a Ladies' Auxiliary was formed to bring the families of porters together at social events and organize fundraisers to send delegates to the Sleeping Car Porter Conventions in the United States.

However, for the most part, the scope of Black Canadian women's activism remained very much within the confines of the local community. There was no equivalent of the Black women's club movement in the United States, which by the 1920s represented 50,000 women in 28 federations and over 1,000 clubs (Giddings, 1985:95). In discussing women's organizations in Montreal, D'Oyley and Braithwaite (ibid) describe typical associations run by women:

> In the 1920s a Little Mother's League was formed in Montreal to make "Negro girls proficient...in household duties." The Phyllis Wheatley Art Club, formed in 1922 by Mrs. Lillian Rutherford offered cultural stimulation and later developed in the 1930s into the Negro Theatre Guild of Montreal. [The Women's Club formed in 1902, and later the] Woman's Charitable Benevolent Association, founded 1919...worked tirelessly to look after the poor and sick, to run soup kitchens, roll bandages for the Red Cross, and to provide temporary homes for returning soldiers.

One other organization, The Canadian Negro Women's Association of Toronto, played an historic role in the development of Black women's organizing. Established in 1951, it boasts a long tradition of humanitarian and social service work in that city. It was particularly well-known for providing scholarships and aid to promising students. In 1973, however, it became the sponsoring organization for the Congress of Black Women of Canada, currently the only national organization of Black people in this country.

COMING TO THE FORE: BREAKING DOWN THE BARRIERS AND
THE CHALLENGE TO THE WHITE FEMINIST MOVEMENT, 1960-
1980S

With the liberalization of Canadian society in the '60s, a process
which had begun earlier with the enactment of the Canada Fair
Employment Practices Act of 1953, many of the more blatant
employment barriers began to break down. Black employees
became more common in hospitals, department stores, restaurants
and offices. In 1962, and more extensively in 1966, Canadian immigration policy was reformed so that families of landed immigrants could be admitted and Canadians could also "sponsor" those
who might not otherwise meet the requirements (Walker, 1980:71).
This produced a massive increase in the number of immigrants
from the Caribbean, and to a lesser extent Africa, many of whom
are skilled and educated. These new Canadians have shattered
traditional employment patterns, and it has meant that more and
more Black women have been able to move into the business or
professional spheres. Of course, these changes did not occur by
chance and were very much tied to what was happening outside the
country in terms of the African liberation movements and the end
of formal colonial rule, the American Civil Rights and Black
Power movements.

Nevertheless, despite these improvements, traditional employment patterns have been resistant to change. First, data from the
1971 census reveal what the Black community has always known:
that Black women have worked outside the home in greater
numbers than other groups of women. Forty-nine percent of Black
Canadian-born and 68 percent of Black immigrant women were
active in the employed labor force in 1971. Forty-three percent of
all other Canadian-born and 42 percent of all other immigrant
women were employed.[14] Unemployment rates of 6.2 percent for
Canadian-born and 7.3 percent for immigrant Black women
compared with only 3.9 percent for all other women combined
indicate that discrimination in hiring affects Black women far more
than other groups of women. In 1971, Black women were 1½ to 2
times more likely to be unemployed than other women.

Domestic service continues to be a key area of employment in the Maritimes, where economic opportunities for minorities are far worse than in other parts of Canada because of the depressed nature of the region. In Ontario, Quebec, British Columbia and other provinces, indigenous Black Canadian women have largely moved out of "service" occupations. However, Caribbean and other immigrant women continue to be brought in to fill the demand. Unfortunately, unlike the Domestic Scheme first instituted in 1955, temporary employment visas are being issued to these workers, which means that they are not automatically entitled to landed immigrant status. It is far more difficult for such women to move into more rewarding fields or to upgrade their skills. The long hours, low wages, and the difficulty of monitoring the working conditions in individual homes makes the "live-in" domestic the most invisible and exploited of Canadian workers (Silvera, 1983). The domestic worker, plus the disproportionate numbers of Black and Third World women who work as laborers in factories, in food and other personal services such as nursing assistants and attendants, hotel cleaners and maids, etc., in some ways define what is considered to be "Black women's work" (Brand, 1987:35).

Ironically, Black women have broken down the barriers to achievement in practically every career field. Teaching and nursing, which "defined" middle-class occupations for Black women a generation ago, have been overshadowed in some respects by positions which have far more inherent or potential power. Politics, law, accounting, the technical fields, writing, and so forth, are all careers which contemporary Black women pursue. For the record, it should be pointed out that Black women attain their goals in spite of, not because of, employment equity policies, the latter of which have benefitted primarily white women.

The Black woman's historical involvement in organizing for equal rights for Blacks and her traditionally greater involvement in the labor force have placed her ahead of white women in terms of understanding that feminist issues are very much her issues. However, focus on Black liberation struggles, and the fact that white women have been slow to broaden the base of the movement to include women of color and different classes of women, kept Black women from fully embracing feminist politics in the beginning. But there were exceptions.

One of the exceptions, Rosemary Brown, came to her feminism early. Originally from Jamaica, Ms. Brown was first elected to the British Columbia legislature in 1972 and was returned to office three more times before retiring from provincial politics in 1986. She gained national prominence when she ran for the national leadership of the New Democratic Party in 1975 and came in second. Describing how it "clicked" one day in the late '60s as she drove home from her job as a councilor at Simon Fraser University "feeling tired, depressed, unloved and unlovely," Rosemary listened to a CBC broadcast of the briefs being presented to the Royal Commission on the Status of Women. She explains:

> Feminism soon became for me the coordinating force, the link which held all of my other strivings together. As a member of a social democratic movement, my struggle to end racism, my commitment to preserve peace, my respect for the environment, my belief in the intrinsic worth of all persons all came together in my development of a feminist socialist (Brown, 1987:19).

Yet the reality is that white women have only recently begun to confront their race and class privilege and their domination of the women's movement as its spokespersons and theorists. Particularly in Canada, white feminists have barely noticed the existence of working class women, let alone those who belong to racial minorities. A theory which speaks to the situations of women in varied racial and class circumstances has been lacking. A case in point is *The Basset Report: Career Success and Canadian Women* (1985).

Motivated by the increased participation of women in the workforce, and the effect which the women's movement has had on middle-class women's occupational mobility, Isabel Bassett reports the findings of a Canada-wide survey of 400 career women conducted in the spring of 1984. Attitudes on all aspects of their careers were surveyed, including how they arrived in their current positions, how they integrated their home lives and their careers, why there are so few women in the upper echelons of corporate management, and so forth. Although 33 percent were of ethnic origins other than "English," "French," "Scottish," "German" or "Irish," there were no women other than those of European origin who were identified as such in the report.

When asked whether she had interviewed any racial minorities, the author responded that indeed she had, including two Black and several Native women. However, Bassett deliberately left out the issue of race so as not to "confound" the findings on gender discrimination with the question of racial discrimination. In fact, the author claims that the women themselves did not know whether the discrimination they had experienced was due to their sex or their race.

The decision to exclude the issue of race is a problematic one, for two main reasons. First, the question of "double" and "triple minority status," or the cumulative disadvantages which minority women face because they have two or three negative statuses— female status, minority racial status, and working class status— could have been explored. It could have added a level of awareness and sophistication to the discussion, precisely because it is more reflective of the greater complexity of today's multiracial Canada. For Black women, these are relevant issues which deserve attention. Of course, given the premise of the study and its obvious middle-class bias, the whole discussion of working class status is moot in any case.

Second, whether wittingly or unwittingly, Bassett's approach perpetuates an image of Canada which is devastating—that of a country inhabited strictly by white people. Once again, the so-called "visible minorities" remain invisible on the mainstream agenda.

Perhaps one of the first major attempts to forge a more broad-based feminist movement occurred when the organizers of the 1986 International Women's Day (IWD), whose slogan read "Women Say No! to Racism From Toronto to South Africa," invited a host of women's groups from Toronto's Black, Native, Chinese, Japanese, South African, Southeast Asian, Philippine, and Central American communities to be a part of the organizing effort. Speakers representing these groups comprised the rally at Convocation Hall on March 8 and a series of workshops at Ryerson Polytechnic Institute addressed their concerns. The (white) feminist movement "caught hell" that day from each and every speaker on the podium. Despite reports of tension and hostility behind the scenes, there was a sense that the women's movement had embarked on an unalterable path toward representation of all women. Certainly, white feminists have become more aware of the need to address issues of race and class and to include all segments of women in its ranks and theoretical writings (Valverde, 1987:21-22).

Where racism is concerned, however, change is slow in coming. For their part, Black women continue to strive for a voice, for greater political clout, for economic equality and social justice. On a political level, organizations run the gamut from the middle-class-oriented Congress of Black Women of Canada with chapters across Canada to the racial feminist Black Women's Collective of Toronto, one of the key groups behind IWD, 1986.

Women are at the forefront of what can only be described as a Black "cultural renaissance" in Nova Scotia. The women's a capella singing group, Four the Moment, is receiving wide acclaim across Canada and the African tradition of weaving has been turned into an artform by such individuals as Edith Clayton and Daurene Lewis, the latter having also gained prominence after being elected the first Black woman mayor of Canada in 1984, in her home town of Annapolis Royal. Writer and broadcaster Sylvia Hamilton has written a screenplay about Black Nova Scotian women and Maxine Tynes' poetry looks as much to mother Africa as it does to Dartmouth in defining herself as a Black woman (Fraser, 1987:16).

In the rest of the country, according to Juno award-winning Lillian Allen in an article appearing in *This Magazine* (Dec. 1987/Jan. 1988:20), dub poets "have created a national Black cultural presence in Canada, and set the standard for political art unparalleled in this country." A leading proponent of dub poetry and performance,[15] Allen credits the massive support of the women's movement for first having catapulted her to national prominence. Her poetry raises issues not only of racism in this country, but also of women's oppression and patriarchy (ibid:19). One of the foremost Black writers in Canada today, Dionne Brand, has published a number of books of poetry and political writings. Currently pursuing a women's studies program at the graduate level, the Trinidadian-born author is developing a feminist theory which is informed by Black women's lives, particularly here in Canada.

Two magazines recently launched out of Toronto have caught the attention of a wide audience: *Excellence*, which patterns itself after the American publication *Essence*, and *Tiger Lily*, a literary, cultural, feminist periodical which features writers from the "black diaspora, Latin America, Native North America, South and East Asia." Jamaican-born writer and publisher Ann Wallace is "committed to publishing a magazine that fully acknowledges our contributions and strengthens the bonds of sisterhood" (Wallace, 1986:1).[16]

These women and many many others are a creative and social force with which to be reckoned. In many respects, the latter half of the 1980s is an exciting time as the powers that be are increasingly obliged to acknowledge our presence and take heed of our demands. The rediscovery of our history and culture as Black women is integral to this process of empowerment because it reminds us that our history is one of strength and, yes, feminism. The very nature of the struggles which we have had to face as Black people and as women have demanded it. The resistance to slavery inherent in such acts as arson or the escape to freedom, homesteading and the establishment of communities, the formation of clubs and organizations whose mandate went far beyond social and cultural pursuits, speaking out when it was not popular to do so, becoming wage earners and striving for a better life for our children, agitation for social change on all levels—these activities are all part and parcel of a true feminist history and they are the very essence of the history of Black women. But history is only important if it can clarify the present and shape a vision of the future. For Black women, it has been a long journey, and there is still a long way to go, but at least we know we are up to the challenge.

NOTES

* The author is indebted to Professor Frederick Case for providing the opportunity to prepare this paper, and for offering critical feedback and suggestions on an earlier draft. The author also thanks Ayanna Black for her valuable comments and suggestions.

1. Since there was no question on the census asking racial origin, large numbers of Canadian-born Blacks were omitted if they did not write the word "Black" under the appropriate questions on ethnicity. This under representation in the census has been a problem related to Blacks from the earliest times. For an excellent discussion of the problem see Robin Winks, *The Blacks in Canada* (Montreal, McGill-Queen's Press, 1971, pp. 484-496). The 1986 census added the category "Black" under a question about ethnic origin, but at the completion of this article, the figures were not yet available.

2. The absence of a plantation-type economy militated against the evolution of slavery as an important institution in British North America. Slave property was expensive to feed and clothe in a northern climate and indentured servants could more efficiently perform the services needed in a frontier society. The depreciation of slave values, the fact that escape into the frontier was very easy, and the legal uncertainty involved in defending slave property—all these factors contributed to its gradual abolition.

3. As a compromise to existing slave owners, the bill stated that slaves already living in Upper Canada were to remain slaves for life. The children of slaves who were born after 1793 were to become free when they reached the age of 25 and if they, in turn, had children, those children were to be immediately free.

4. Ontario was originally called Upper Canada (1791-1841), then Canada West (1841-1867), and finally received its present name when Canada became a confederation in 1867.

5. A Section of the Common School Act of 1850 stated that a group of five or more Black families could voluntarily establish a separate school if they so desired. This clause was used by whites to force the latter into segregated institutions. Similar legislation was passed in Nova Scotia. Robin Winks, *The Blacks in Canada* (op. cit., pp. 368-376); James Walker, *A History of Blacks in Canada* (Hull, Minister of State for Multiculturalism, p. 110). For a less innocent interpretation of the Common School Act see Frederick I. Case, *Racism and National Consciousness* (Toronto, Plowshare Press, 1977, p. 13). According to Case, it was no coincidence that the legislation came into effect the same year as the Fugitive Slave Act in the United States and that, judging from correspondence and several court cases, it was not the aim of school administrators to offer Blacks freedom of choice in the schooling of their children.

6. From *The Provincial Freeman*, June 30, 1855, as quoted in Daniel Hill, *The Freedom-Seekers* (Agincourt, The Book Society of Canada Ltd., p. 187).

7. Hill (ibid:163-177) provides many examples of women in 19th century Ontario who operated businesses independently of their husbands. Such establishments included dressmaking and hat shops, restaurants, and one beauty parlor and wig shop. They were located in cities like Toronto, Hamilton, Owen Sound, Collingwood and Stratford, Ontario. There was even a successful herb doctor who ran a "practice" in Collingwood.

8. For example, Walton reports that in the 1851 census of Chatham, 51% of Black males were engaged in skilled or semiskilled work, and 41% were unskilled. In Hamilton, 45% were skilled craftsmen or professionals, and 47% semi-or unskilled. Hill states that the Toronto of 1846-47 shows 81 Black men listed. Of these, 31 were laborers, 34 trademen, 6 proprietor-businessmen, 1 minister, a cabman, 1 sailor, and 1 teamster. Although Detroit showed 52% as skilled or semiskilled in 1850, New York, Washington, Pittsburgh and Cincinnati had ranges of only 17-20% in this category. See Jonathan Walton, "Blacks in Buxton and Chatham, Ontario, 1830-1890: Did the 49th Parallel Make a Difference?" (Ph.D. thesis, Princeton University, 1979); Michael B. Katz, *The People of Hamilton, Canada West: Family and Class in a Mid-Nineteenth Century City* (Cambridge, Harvard University Press, 1975, p. 68); Daniel G. Hill, "Negroes in Toronto, 1773-1865," *Ontario History* (Vol. LV:73-91).

9. The Elgin or Buxton Settlement was one of several Black "colonies" set up for fugitive Blacks between 1830 and 1851. They allowed fugitives to settle on lands set aside for them at special terms and to develop their own industries and institutions. Of four such colonies, the Elgin Settlement was the most successful. The others were plagued by poor management and leadership, and ended in failure. The Black farming community of North Buxton, near Chatham, Ontario is an enduring remnant of the Elgin Settlement. See especially William and Jane Pease, *Black Utopia: Negro Communal Experiments in America* (Madison, The State Historical Society of Wisconsin, 1963).

10. A significant segment of the Black population which emigrated to Canada were not runaway slaves from the southern states but free Blacks from the North and upper slave states who were fleeing anti-Negro legislation. In particular, the Fugitive Slave Act of 1850 allowed a citizen to arrest and detain any person of African descent suspected of being a runaway slave. Alleged runaways did not have the benefit of jury trials.

11. This massive outmigration does not apply to those Blacks who entered the Maritime provinces between 1783-1815. This group arrived 1-2 generations earlier and had, by this time, lost all contact with friends and relatives in the United States.

12. For information on Chatham see Walton, "Blacks in Buxton and Chatham, Ontario, 1830-1890" (pp. 195-220). Between 1871 and 1882 the percentage of employed adult males in skilled/semiskilled occupations in Chatham had decreased from 40% to 31% (p. 204). By this time, Walton argues that opportunities were no less available in the developing urban North and Midwest United States. For Canada as a whole, see Ida Greaves, "The Negro in Canada" (M.A. thesis, McGill University, 1930), and Robin Winks, *The Blacks in Canada*, (op. cit).

13. Amazingly, at the completion of this article, Carrie Best was still active in her 85th year.

14. This information derives from a special tabulation run by Statistics Canada. The very high employment figures of Black immigrant women is partly explained by the nature of the immigrant population, which tends to be highly skilled and educated. The continuing migration of Caribbean women who work as domestics is another reason for the high figure.

15. Dub poetry is a distinct poetic form originated from Jamaica and relying on the spoken word as its primary mode of communication. It developed out of the popularity of reggae music. Lillian Allen, "De Dub Poets, Renegades in a One Poem Town," *This Magazine* (Vol. 21, #7, December 1987/January 1988).

16. In fact, Wallace, co-owner and manager of Williams-Wallace Publishers, Inc., has been at the forefront as a publisher of multicultural books, promoting women writers such as Brand and a host of others since the '70s.

BIBLIOGRAPHY

Allen, Lillian, "De Dub Poets, Renegades in a One Poem Town," *This Magazine*, Vol. 21 #7, December 1987/January 1988: 14-21.

Bassett, Isabel, *The Bassett Report: Career Success and Canadian Women,* Toronto, Collins, 1985.

Bearden, Jim and Linda Jean Butler, *Shadd, The Life and Times of Mary Shadd Cary,* Toronto, N.C. Press, 1977.

Best, Carrie. *That Lonesome Road: The Autobiography of Carrie M. Best*, New Glasgow, The Clarion Publishing Co Ltd., 1977.

Braithwaite, Rella, *The Black Woman in Canada*, West Hill, 1977.

Brand, Dionne, "Black Women and Work: The Impact of Racially Constructed Gender Roles on the Sexual Division of Labour," Part One, *Fireweed,* Issue 25, Fall 1987: 28-37.

Brown, Rosemary, "Women of Conviction: Ten Dynamic Women Share Their Views," *Herizons*, Vol. 5 No. 2, March 1987:10.

Case, Frederick Ivor, *Racism and National Consciousness,* Toronto Plowshare Press, 1977.

D'Oyley, Enid and Rella Braithwaite (eds), *Women of Our Times,* Toronto, The Canadian Negro Women's Association, Inc. (printed by Sheppard & Sears), 1973.

Fraser, Sharon, "Taking the Measure of Maxine," *Atlantic Insight,* Vol. 9 No. 9, September 1987: 16-18.

Giddings, Paula, *When and Where I Enter, The Impact of Black Women on Race and Sex in America*, New York, Bantam Books, Inc., 1985.

Gray White, Deborah, *Ar'nt I a Woman? Female Slaves in the Plantation South*, New York, W.W. Norton & Co., 1987.

Greaves, Ida, "The Negro in Canada," M.A. thesis, McGill University, 1930.

Hill, Daniel G., "Negroes in Toronto, 1773-1865," *Ontario History,* Vol. LV, 1963: 73-91.

———, *The Freedom-Seekers: Blacks in Early Canada,* Agincourt, The Book Society of Canada Ltd., 1981.

Katz, Michael B., *The People of Hamilton, Canada West: Family and Class in a Mid-Nineteenth Century City,* Cambridge, Harvard University Press, 1975.

L'Esperance, Jeanne, *The Widening Sphere: Women in Canada, 1870-1941,* Ottawa, Public Archives Canada and National Library of Canada, 1982.

MacDonald, Cheryl, "Mightier than the Sword," *Woman's World,* Vol. VIII, No. 15:36-7.

Pease, William and Jane Pease, *Black Utopia: Negro Communal Experiments in America,* Madison, The State Historical Society of Wisconsin, 1963.

Potter, Harold H., "Negroes in Canada" in *Social Problems,* Richard Laskin (ed.), New York, McGraw Hill, 1964: 139-47.

Richmond, Norman "Otis," "A History of Toronto's Anti-Apartheid Movement, 1921-1986," Part One, *Fuse,* Vol. X No. 5, April 1987: 14-21.

Ripley, C. Peter (ed.), *The Black Abolitionist Papers, Volume II, Canada 1830-1865,* Chapel Hill and London, The University of North Carolina Press, 1986.

Roach-Brown, Maureen, "Making the Grade," *Excellence,* Vol. 1 No. 6, May 1987.

Shadd Shreve, Dorothy, *The AfriCanadian Church: A Stabilizer,* Jordan Station, Paideia Press, 1983.

Silvera, Makeda, *Silenced,* Toronto, Williams-Wallace Publishers, Inc., 1983.

Valverde, Mariana, "Women of Conviction: Ten Dynamic Women Share Their Views," *Herizons,* Vol. 5 No. 2, march 1987: 21-22.

Walker, James W. St. G., *The Black Loyalists: The Search for a Promised Land in Nova Scotia and Sierra Leone 1783-1870,* New York, Africana Publishing Co. and Dalhousie University Press, 1976.

——, *A History of Blacks in Canada,* Hull, Minister of State for Multiculturalism, 1980.

Wallace, Ann, "On the Origins of Tiger Lily," *Tiger Lily,* November-December 1986:1.

Walton, Jonathan W., "Blacks in Buxton and Chatham, Ontario, 1830-1890: Did the 49th Parallel Make a Difference?" Ph.D. thesis, Princeton University (Ann Arbor: University Microfilms International), 1979.

Winks, Robin, *The Blacks in Canada: A History,* Montreal, McGill-Queen's University Press, 1971.

PART IV

THE AFRICAN WORLD
AND THE CHALLENGES
OF THE 21ST CENTURY

THE CONTINUING CRISIS OF IDENTITY IN THE AMERICAS

VAL T. MCCOMIE

THE SEARCH for self is a powerful drive in both individual and social life. It involves the knowledge and understanding of one's innate characteristics as shaped by history, geography, education and environmental influences.

Ethnic identity is a matter of shared self-perception, the communication of that perception to others and, perhaps most crucially, the response it elicits from others in the form of social interaction. Like all aspects of social identity, it is manifest both in terms of what is subjectively claimed and what is socially accorded. Knowledge of self is, therefore, the essential first step in the process of exploring one's identity. To quote an old African saying, "to know who you are is the beginning of wisdom."

The search for identity in the Americas has been both agonizing and confusing. In the case of African peoples who were brought forcibly to this hemisphere as slaves, they constituted only one of many migrant groups that came mainly from the Old World.

The interaction of peoples and cultures in the Americas has been plagued by more than its fair share of psychological pollutants. Legends, myths, romantic notions and other distortions created the schizophrenic environment that makes the search for identity difficult. It is not possible to determine the cultural identity of any one particular group without taking into account the impact of all these elements on the environment as a whole.

The confusion began when Christopher Columbus intruded into the Caribbean in his search for a new route to the legendary Cathay in the belief that he had discovered the Indies. The decision to portray Columbus' feat as a European discovery had far-reaching consequences in dictating the dynamics of geographical and cultural identity in the hemisphere. Starting from that event, the modern history of the hemisphere has been largely shaped by the European outlook on the world and its concept of its civilizing mission. By giving the connotation of discovery to what was in fact the chance meeting of two segments of humanity separated by mutual ignorance and inadequate technology, Europe asserted its own alleged supremacy. The assumed European superiority conferred on the conquerors the prerogative of defining the conquered and imposing their own cultural values on the indigenous culture, even to the extent of destroying it.

There were some other important distortions associated with the arrival of the European on our shores. As a result of later exploration by Cortez, Balboa, Cabot and others, it became evident that Columbus had neither discovered India nor a westward passage to India. So a cartographer named Martin Waldseemuller, realizing that two voyages made by his friend Amerigo Vespucci had revealed the new lands to be a continent, proposed that it be named America after its discoverer "since both Europa and Asia bear names of feminine form." So, not even his contemporaries gave Columbus his due. The aboriginal inhabitants were mistakenly given a new racial identity. Since Columbus happened to land in this hemisphere in his search for India, it was logical for him to conclude that they were Indians. For many years it was even argued that the Indian, unlike the European, had no soul. It is also intriguing that no serious effort has been made by hemispheric scholars to find out what was the name the native people of this hemisphere gave to their land when the Europeans invaded, nor has there been any serious movement to correct the record with respect to the misnomer imposed on the indigenous inhabitants.

The use of the name America, itself, has generated other complications with respect to national identity. The most powerful European-based nation in the hemisphere, the United States of America, has appropriated or expropriated the name America to define its national boundaries and therefore its citizenry. As a result of this historical misuse of the term, all of us who have been born in other parts of America have been precluded from characterizing ourselves as American. A sense of embarrassment and insecurity has stemmed from this denial, since we have not been able to affirm who we are, even from a geographical view point. This deprivation is not assuaged by the stratagem of pluralizing the name.

The identification of America with the United States has also given rise to another counter-balancing distortion of nomenclature by the descendants of the Spanish conquistadors. In an attempt to reject United States domination and assert their cultural identity, they searched for a term which would embrace the Spanish, French and Portuguese elements and came up with Latin-America. When challenged as to the place of the indigenous peoples in such a classification, the reply given is that the Indians are the American element in terminology, since in the United States they are often referred to as native Americans.

But perhaps the most sweeping of all distortions, not exclusive to our hemisphere but having important connotations in America, is the grouping of people as black and white on the basis of skin color.

In the first place, it is anthropologically unsound unless this science has now capitulated to the realpolitik of skin pigmentation. I prefer to accept the commonality of "homo sapiens" as defined by Professor Wilton Krogman of the University of Pennsylvania in these terms:

The basic homogeneity of homo sapiens is exemplified by the statement that there are approximately 44,000 pairs of genes for human beings; of these, 90 percent or 39,600 are shared in common, leaving 4,000 as racial; of these, 50 percent or 2,200 are allowed for variation; hence only 2,200 pairs of genes may, in varying combinations, enter into hereditary differences of form and function in the peoples of the world.

In the second place, it does not reflect the identity of the people known as Black. If they had chosen to be named black to designate racial or ethnic origin, it would in that sense reflect their identity. But the term has been imposed on them in order to rob them of their true identity. The African people in South Africa, for instance, have been labeled black rather than African, because if it were admitted that being African was one of their primary characteristics, they would then be on the same human level with the ruling white minority who want to project themselves as African.

Thirdly, it reflects a certain form of imperialism practiced by Afro-Americans who make a fetish of blackness. Twenty-five years ago, when I had the privilege of teaching in Ghana for a year, I do not remember Africans referring to themselves as black. Europeans were identified by nationality and not by skin color, and Africans spoke of each other either in terms of tribal or national origins. Today, the power of the United States has become so pervasive that every African leader who visits this country has to proclaim his blackness if he is to expect solidarity with his cause. In the United States, the concept of blackness has been used to classify people who are non-white, independently of their racial or ethnic origin. This has posed a special problem for Latin America, since Latin Americans are usually classified as non-white, but as a people they tend to perceive themselves as non-black. Latin Americans in the United States are lumped together as "minorities" with all other non-white groups, and this factor often is the basis for racial or ethnic discrimination against them.

Finally, the classification of human beings into black and white promotes the ultimate triumph of the heresy of apartheid. The fact that people of African descent would have been willing accessories to this heresy does not make it less tragic. It is now so much easier to internalize feelings of racial superiority and devise subtle forms of segregation within an accepted psychological framework of separate but equal.

The transfer to America of the European way of life resulted in a drive to convert the indigenous population to European beliefs and to impose European social structures. That zeal for spreading European values in America originated missionary work that was not limited to the religious and ethical field, but included the transplanting of institutions and cultural traits alien to the native people. The social scheme built in colonial times persisted after independence, and is still today superimposed on the Amerindian, African and other ethnic cultures of our peoples. The dichotomy between innate culture and transplanted institutions flows from the initial distortion of the encounter of two worlds, and it is an additional factor compounding the difficulty in establishing an identity for the groups who are not of European descent.

Just as their ancestors confronted the powerful impact of European culture, the people of the Caribbean and Latin America face today the erosive penetration of the dominant culture of the United States. The initial confrontation of cultures has sown the seeds of a distinctive people and civilization, particularly in the Caribbean. The current encounter may result in a blending of forces that will in the end strengthen the autochthonous character of Latin American and Caribbean culture. However, the struggle against the alien influences of the groups that wield power has been and continues to be a formidable challenge to the survival of the ancestral civilization in America.

There are two ethnic groups who have suffered most severely the assault on their identity by the dominant groups throughout the modern history of this hemisphere: the indigenous people and the people of African descent. The Europeans were able, not only to keep their cultural traits alive in America but also, as I have indicated, to try to impose them on other people in the hemisphere. Other groups, mostly of Asian or Indian extraction, who originally came as indentured laborers, were also allowed, to a large extent, to maintain their own culture, although it was always regarded as having a somewhat lesser status than that of the European.

The aboriginal people have survived in relatively small numbers the clash with the European conquerors. Insofar as they have managed to survive, the few remaining native groups had two important advantages that were denied the African: the ability to conserve their languages and to keep their cultural identity intact by living in so-called "Indian" reservations, with all the limitations imposed by what has in fact been a form of segregation. In several Latin American countries, the original inhabitants of the land have left a strong mark on most of the population, as well as some remnants of their culture. However, except for a few cases, there has been conscious effort in the region to try to disclaim the indigenous ancestral legacy and to assimilate the dominant European culture. What has survived of the vernacular, mostly in Latin America, but also to some extent in the United States and to a lesser degree in the Caribbean, is to be found in music and dance, in some forms of religious expression, and especially in the handicraft arts.

African people were initially brought to America to work for the European ruling classes as slaves, and thus stripped of human dignity and freedom. A conscious effort was made to deprive the African migrants of their own cultural identity. The Africans originally brought to America were of different tribal origins and spoke diverse languages, most of them mutually unintelligible. They were intentionally dispersed so that they could not easily communicate with each other, and their first effort had to be to find a means of verbal communication with other Africans in their new environment. As time went by, the original African languages were forgotten and "pidgin" languages became "creole," which is still today an important form of social communication, mainly in some Caribbean islands.

The development of a new language by the African people in America was one powerful example of the resilience of the human spirit and the inner strength of culture in the midst of apparently insurmountable odds. Other instances of African roots in American culture can be found in religion, which adapted ancestral ways for relating to the European God, as can be observed in many places of the hemisphere, among them Brazil, Haiti, and the Commonwealth Caribbean. While most plastic arts are not an African discipline, wood carving, which was important cultural expression of the African people, has also been cultivated among their descendants. Vernacular architecture, facing today the threat of being overcome by modern technology and imitation of foreign mores, is another important manifestation of the evolving culture. Music and dance are probably the best known artistic symbols of Afro culture in America. They have been an important instrument of cultural cross-fertilization in the hemisphere and even have been influential at the world level. Music and dance of Afro-American extraction have also been the cultural expression best able to permeate the dominant groups of society.

It would be a mistake to think of Afro cultures in America as being just a manifestation of African culture in a new environment. There is no such thing as an African culture transplanted intact to America. The diversity of cultural manifestations of groups of African origin in several countries and regions of America reflect indeed some African traits, but they are also inspired by indigenous feelings and concerns related to politics, religion and social interaction.

One common feature of the evolution of African culture in the hemisphere is that it has been characterized by repression and marginalization. In its formative stages, it became an underground way of life that was made to appear somewhat inferior to the culture of the rulers even in the eyes of the people giving birth to it. For Afro culture in America to affirm itself, it has yet to overcome the sense of scorn to which it has been subjected to for centuries.

The terrible burden imposed on people by slavery is easily understood and generally recognized, as are the brutality it represented and the cruelty it embodied. It is not commonly realized, however, that emancipation exacted its own toll. The emancipated people in all nations of America had to adapt to a set of social institutions completely alien to their experience and their way of life, a society based in many cases upon the plantation system and the predominance of mercantilism.

Segregation was the response imposed by the system, a concept that denied the principle at the root of emancipation since it institutionalized the notion that people are not equal, but different on the basis of their color. Segregation was in many ways a continuation of slavery without forced labor.

Like slavery and apartheid, segregation has sprung from the division of people into black and white, through which ruling groups have sought to maintain their power. Even after segregation was formally abolished in the United States, the notion governing relationships between different ethnic groups can be characterized as psychological apartheid. By referring to all non-whites as black, the challenge to relate to one another as human beings has been shirked. This attitude, prevalent in United States society, makes it difficult for some people in that country to address the problem of apartheid in South Africa as a question of human rights. They see it in terms of solidarity with kith and kin.

People of African ancestry in the United States are a minority, both numerically and in terms of the power they wield. They have made great progress in establishing their rights as equal members of society, however, the road ahead is still a long one. Their accomplishment has on occasion been made more difficult by some attitudes of Afro groups attempting to use the same distinctions and instruments of separation the whites have used, only in reverse way. People of African descent are an important part of the population in a few Latin American countries. Their relative power is also weak, probably weaker than in the United States. Only in the Commonwealth Caribbean, and in Haiti, are people of African lineage the ones who wield political power. It is in this region that I think the affirmation of a strong ethnic identity will first be achieved.

There are several unique features of the Caribbean experience which support the belief that the identity question will be best resolved there.

There is, however, no such thing as an African culture in the Caribbean. No other region of the hemisphere was a recipient of so many varied ethnic and cultural influences as the Caribbean, and in no other place was the interaction as intense. They have all left their imprint on the emerging Caribbean culture. The initial superposition of European culture on the original inhabitants of the islands was so pervasive as to almost extinguish aboriginal culture, of which some few traces still remain. Different European powers engaged in a fight for hegemony in the Caribbean, and they all left their legacy in the region. After emancipation, indentured laborers mainly of Asian and Hindu extraction were brought to the region in conditions different from that of the African slaves. This confluence of peoples and cultures has given birth to a vibrant Caribbean cultural identity. I foresee in the not too distant future the emergence of a people who will be ethnically identifiable as Caribbean, the result of many centuries of blending people of different lineages within a society that has overcome the artificial barriers of racial taboos. A people who will be able to fulfill their destiny as human beings, beyond the limiting categorization of black and white. A distinctive Caribbean people endowed with their own cultural baggage and their unique social arrangements. Their language and their institutions will be predominantly European. Their ethnic identity, culture and sociological attitudes will reflect a definite African legacy. Their national identity will be their own, hopefully strengthened by a movement toward true integration, the end result of all that has shaped the history of the region.

As the Caribbean people consolidate their own identity and project their image to the rest of the nations of the hemisphere, they will be in a position to make a strong contribution to the betterment of America. The affirmation of Caribbean identity will, among many other things, be a firm support for other Afro cultures in the hemisphere to foster their own search for identity. The day will hopefully come when we shall all be Americans, bound together by our mutual respect as human beings, and finally free from the trammels of race and ethnicity that have kept us apart for much longer than the progress of mankind can afford.

CONCEPTUALIZING THE AFRICAN DIASPORA

RUTH SIMMS HAMILTON

USING THE larger world systems as the frame of reference this paper explores conceptual ideas which may inform investigations into the nature of "peoplehood" and the processes by which a people are developed and transformed over time and space. The macrocosm or global context within which the experiences and perceptions of peoples of the diaspora emerge and develop is the central focus of analysis.

Some of the issues relate to the following queries: Are there broad sets of experiences which link the *diverse* communities of the African diaspora, temporally and spatially? How do the experiences of a people relate to larger world system forces and relations? Given the contradictions internal and external to a people, and given the political nature of all action, to what extent can people of African descent be conceptualized as a group acting "for itself"?

CENTRAL DEFINING CHARACTERISTICS OF THE AFRICAN DIASPORA AS A GLOBAL SOCIAL FORMATION

It is argued that the African diaspora represents a type of social grouping characterized by a historical patterning of particular social relationships and experiences. As a social formation it is conceptualized as global aggregate of actors and subpopulations differentiated in social and geographical space, yet exhibiting a commonality based on *shared historical experiences* conditioned by and within the world ordering system. Three historical characteristics my possibly distinguish the diaspora as a global formation from other socially differentiated groups:

A. *Geo-social Displacement: The Circularity of a People*
   Historical dialectic between geographical mobility and the establishment of "roots"

B. *Social Oppression: Relations of Domination and Subordination* Conflict, discrimination and inequality based primarily, although not exclusively, on race, color and class

C. *Endurement, Resistance and Struggle: Cultural and Political Action* Creative actions of people as subjects of their history; psychocultural and ideological transformations; social networks and institutional dynamics.

GEO-SOCIAL DISPLACEMENT: THE CIRCULARITY OF A PEOPLE

The emergence and endurement of the Black diaspora in the modern world is a direct result of forced displacement from Africa. Since this profound dispersal, the geographical mobility of persons of African descent has been worldwide. In general, the global movements of peoples of African descent are conceptualized as flows conditioned by two interrelated levels of phenomena. At one level are structural forces generated by the larger system (exogenous); and at another level are individual or group-generated strategies (indigenous) for survival and the quest for decency.

The forceful movements of Africans as the principle commodity of exchange, labor, during the early European expansionist period across the Atlantic and Indian Oceans and the Arabian Sea have been justly accorded a great deal of significance as a prime reason for the dispersal of people of African descent throughout the world. Yet the scope analysis and interpretation of the diaspora must exceed the narrow view of slavery and its aftermath. From the later 18th century onward profound changes in technology and in the organization of monetary and business transactions would set into motion the industrial revolution, a process that would be global in scope although the level and scale of industrial development would remain uneven throughout the world. The flow of goods, natural resources and people from Africa, the Caribbean and Asia would be especially vital to the industrialization process in Europe and North America.

Industrialization, urbanization, and attendant processes have been directly related to the migratory flows of people of African descent. For example, how is Black geo-social mobility related to the following: a capitalist and later a competing socialist system on a world scale; periodic world economic crises such as the depression in the early decades of this century; transnational economic policies such as the Marshall plan and the reconstruction process in Europe following World War II, major world wars; the emergence of transnational organizations such as the Caribbean Common Market (Caricom) and the European Economic Community (EEC), and the implications of associated tariffs and trade agreements; and the United States unilateral Caribbean Basin Initiative?

One of the more obvious forms of displacement is labor procurement whether under conditions of slavery, indenture or temporary work programs; or whether under circumstances of force, coercion, self-direction or friendly persuasion. Moreover, Black labor mobility and recruitment within and between subsectors of the world political economy require analysis of public and private policy *de facto* and *de jure*, as related to particular work schemes, labor legislation and immigration laws.[1]

Over centuries other forms of displacement relate to colonization schemes and liberation movements, military conscription and political refuge. These may range from back-to-Africa movements to the predominantly Black cultist followers of Jim Jones of Guyana; or to the flight of Ibos (Nigeria), Ethiopians and Haitian "boat people" to metropolitan centers. Viewed within the aggregate context but at a more individualistic level have been an impressive cross section of persons in pursuit of adventure and self-actualization, cultural identification and political ideology (e.g. pan-Africanists); religious freedom and alternative life styles; education, professional and intellectual development (e.g. artists, entertainers, athletes).

CIRCULATORINESS AND THE DIALECTICS OF DISPLACEMENT

Since initial dispersal from Africa the geographical transitoriness of persons of African descent has been a worldwide process including significant returns to the original center of departure. Circulatoriness engenders shifts in centers of population concentration as well as centers of displacement. Significant alterations may occur in age and sex distributions; the differential circularity of women and men, young and old, has direct implications for the reproductive capacity and work capacity of the diaspora as a whole. Another example of the implications of the circularity process is the nature of intra-group relations among diverse subpopulations of the diaspora as affected by numerical ratios, immigrant status or socio-economic attributes; e.g. cooperative, competitive or conflictive relations between Africans and West Indians in France and in Great Britain; between Black "strangers" and Black "indigenes" in the United States and Canada; or between "down islanders" and "indigenes" in the Virgin Islands.

The point is that the circularity of a population, over time and space, occurs within a complex web of relationships involving people, objects and ideas, conditioned within and standing in relationship to the larger world system. Thus the three types of flows are interrelated and require analysis as such.

The geographical displacement of people is a complex *social* process not just a physical movement. The movements of population must be conceptualized as contributing to the definition of what people were, what they are, and what they may become. The relevance of such a view to the African diaspora rests on two basic assumptions. First, the emergence or genesis of global diasporas is directly related to a first order, forced, displacement from a territorial ancestral-based "homeland." Second, the further development and reproduction of diaspora peoples may be attributed to multiple orders of historically conditioned displacement mechanisms and processes. The dynamics resulting from first-order and subsequent orders of displacement mechanisms impact the geo-social movement of a people in a manner that appears dual and contradictory in character. That is, the mobility of a population is both a source/cause of diaspora formation and a consequence/effect of diaspora formation.

The genesis of a people cannot be divorced from their material existence, the political and economic context within which they come into being and within which they have endured for over five centuries. It follows that continuing dispersion must be viewed as directly related to the material realities, the conditioning factors, and to the strategies for coping with constraints and contradictions over time and space.

It is imperative to move beyond contemporary social science which conceptualized the movements of peoples of African descent and other groups largely within the scope of a paradigm which variously translates these movements into "pull-push" factors. Thus the flow of trained minds and skills of peoples of African descent to European countries is attributed to the attractions of these center nations (pull) and their absence in the dependent peripheral nations (push). Such explanations are not only simplistic but devoid of the capacity to discern and analyze the historical and changing nature of multiple forms and processes of periodic displacement.

In summary, geographical transitoriness, whether induced or voluntary, must be viewed within the historical context of the larger group experiences and at a global level. The so-called "brain

drain," labor migration, legal or illegal migration, political re-
ugees and their specific explanations at best deal with *forms of
flows*. Yet it is the essence of the flow, the historical conditioning,
that underlies the configuration of events and circumstances which
constitute the experiences that must be fully understood and
analyzed. The challenge, therefore, is to capture the *essence and
significance of the historical flows* and movements of a people as
conditioned by various social forces and in relationship to the
forms, patterns and directions of the flows.[2] It is the latter that will
move our knowledge base to a deeper level of understanding
regarding diaspora formation as a socially defined entity.

SOCIAL OPPRESSION: RELATIONS OF DOMINATION AND SUBORDINATION

The international system may be viewed as a particular type of
social order, reflecting degrees of harmony and disharmony of
interests, and is based on differential distributions of power and
privilege with some groups being dominant and oppressive while
others are subordinate and oppressed, e.g. the global distribution
of people along various poles, "have and have-nots," rich and poor,
metropoles and satellites.[3] Such structural inequalities are his-
orically conditioned—a dynamic process by which certain segments of a social order achieve dominance by various mechanisms
of control and exploitation, forcing and constraining other groups
in the lower levels of the social system.[4]

It is within the foregoing context that the most pernicious and
persistent experience of the African diaspora must be examined:
Black people have existed and survived in hostile, socially
oppressive, environments. *Two structures of inequality, race and
class, are particularly critical in assessing this preponderant and
summational experience*. Analytically, they reflect different
properties of social selection; in the instance of race, selection is
determined by location and group relations in a social hierarchy
based on somatic and biological differences; in the instance of
class, selection occurs by location and relations in a largely

material production and distribution process. Both are associated with attributes of power which means they have a determinative effect on the accessibility of opportunity structures, e.g. jobs, education, income, life style, mobility, quality of life, and life chances in general.

RACE

In the modern world the attributes of power are associated with European peoples and nations stretching from the United States and Canada on one side of the Atlantic Ocean to the Soviet Union on the other. Accordingly, a globally racialized social order has emerged dominated by whites and characterized by racist principles of selection prevalent throughout all areas and levels of social life on a world scale. It is necessary to more carefully consider the classic observation of W.E.B. DuBois that "The problem of the twentieth century is the problem of the color line."[5]

Race and the formation of a people. While racial distinctions are biologically based, the meaning of the racial factor is socially relevant because of the psychological, cultural and political significance attributed to it. Primarily from the 15th century onward European expansionary forces conquered and colonized people of color, migrated to and settled in the "hinterlands" to form and control forces of production as "grand blancs," e.g. planters, merchants and mineowners. In the process, they institutionalized a racial division of labor throughout the mines and plantations of the Americas, Asia and Africa. Indeed this was the beginning of the modern world system.

Therefore, as the contours of the modern world system crystallized, a particular significance was placed on race. The very struggle of creating a new world order imposed upon race enormous meaning and prominence in distinguishing fundamental characteristics of people arranged in an order of ascending and descending human qualities. The issue of race would become particularly important as a powerful rationalizing ideology based upon quasi-scientific validation and as a mechanism of social selection.

The dislocation of millions of Africans, their uprooting and transportation to various parts of the world, would significantly change their identity and the sense of peoplehood that had been theirs in various African societies. From this early displacement to the present, *race* would become a central defining factor. For this reason the primary experience of being defined as an inferior race and in racial terms is pertinent to the people formation process. Racial definitions have constituted a fundamental reality imposed upon the African diaspora, and informed their fate within a racially divisive system. Racist principles of selection have been overriding determinants in maintaining and compounding subordinate social position.

In response to such a system and in terms of their own efforts to survive and develop as a group, it is virtually impossible for peoples of the Black diaspora to avoid being conscious of race. It is justifiable to propose, therefore, that race would be examined and considered as a prime factor in the group's own social formation and in the development of their sense of peoplehood. From a sociological perspective, therefore, populations such as the Black diaspora that are of a given racial heritage can become, under particular historically conditioned circumstances, a distinctive people.

Given the total history of Black people and their broader relational experiences on a world scale, several assumptions about the racial factor should inform any serious work on the subject:

1. Race, in its structural and ideological dimensions, has operated as a central persistent element at all levels of modern society with varying form and content over time and space.

2. Race prejudice and racial ideologies permeate all levels of the human/social interpersonal experience to the extent that they constitute a primary feature of the world cosmology and ideology.

3. Racial inequality, manifested in diverse socioracial structures, operates within and across societies with direct implications for the Black diaspora as a social formation, and for the form and content of "peoplehood."

In general, race as a contributing factor to the people forming process must be understood in its concrete manifestations in specific situations, and as a central and persistent element in the global dominance system.[6]

CLASS

The manner in which the lives of a people are organized to interact with nature and by which their lives are materially sustained must also be considered as part of the historical process by which human beings become somewhat distinctive people. When an institutional structure is created which can significantly divide individuals and groups, particularly in terms of political and economic organization, there is set into motion at least the possibility of creating different peoples. It is argued that the general position of the Black diaspora in the global system of production and distribution, the international division of labor, should be considered a significant factor in their formative process. The empirical questions revolve around the extent to which the general class position of Black people, on a world-scale, results in a fundamentally different way of life such that they are viewed discernibly; and the extent to which a basis is provided for the development of group consciousess or recognition of common identity.[7]

THE DOUBLE BOND: COVARIANCE OF RACE AND CLASS[8]

Race and class have been particularly powerful contributing forces in shaping the experiences and consciousness of the diaspora. While it is possible to separate race and class for analytical purposes, in reality the division is more difficult. The challenge, therefore, is to *discern the particular properties and the patterns of each,* to investigate the ways in which they interjoin and the extent to which properties of each structure are shared or remain exclusively within one sphere or the other.

It can be argued that the relationship is overlapping, forming a covalent bond of inequality with race and class pulling across one another, conflicting with one another, and contradicting one another.

Their separate yet intercoupled relationship heightens our understanding of the nature of conflicts and contradictions within and between them without resorting to reductionist interpretations.[9] It is additionally assumed that *the ways in which they covary and the properties they share change under historically conditioned situations.*

More concretely, under what circumstances is race or class likely to constitute the primary contradiction for people of African descent? To what extent do changes in the socioeconomic structures have a measurable impact on the character of racial inequality and conflict and vice versa? If increased opportunities and social mobility open up the class structure for Blacks (e.g. United States, England) in a profound way, what are the specific implications for internal relationships among Blacks and external relations with non-Blacks? E. Franklin Frazier argued that the Black bourgeoisie was Black in skin but white in mentality, aping the white middle class. This was perceived to be detrimental to the social development of the Black bourgeoisie as well as to any obligations they owe to Black people as a whole.[10]

Other intriguing concerns relate to understanding how different socioracial structures combine with different socioeconomic structures within particular modes of production, e.g. combination of a two-tier socioracial structure within a feudal or capitalist or socialist mode of production. When one structure combines with another structure, what kinds of changes occur? What is the essence of the forces that hold the race-class bond together.

The covalent bond has direct implications for other structures of inequality produced by the larger system, especially gender inequality. The latter is not reducible to race or class but some of its dimensions are particularly meaningful within the context of these relationships. In the West Indies, for example, the economic conditions have direct implications for a changing sexual division of labor in many of the countries, vis-a-vis female agricultural laborers. Relatedly, West Indian women who migrate to metro-politan centers, especially Canada and Great Britain, have been in large part, relegated to low level service jobs.[11] A broader and systematic explanation of gender relations may provide opportunities for conceptualizing a more complex arrangement of bonding structures.

In summary, the position has been advanced that Black people have historically existed in hostile, socially oppressive environments. Race and class have been particularly powerful contributing forces in shaping the experiences and consciousness of the Black diaspora. The latter contention requires extensive empirical study to which end a number of queries have been advanced.

ENDUREMENT, RESISTANCE AND STRUGGLE: CULTURAL AND POLITICAL ACTION

While there is little doubt that people of African descent have been objects of oppressive social, political and economic structures, the complete picture requires an understanding of this population as *subjects of their history*. To paraphrase Ralph Ellison,[12] life for Black people is a discipline just as any human life which has endured so long is a discipline teaching its own insights into the human condition, its own strategies for survival. Thus Black people are not mere products of their economic and sociopolitical conditions, but products of the interaction between these conditions and experiences and efforts to develop their own sense of what they are and what they want to be, to deal with life in particular ways and to live life as they transform life.

Accordingly, a people are not simply reactors but creators, devising their own mechanisms of survival, their own ideological tools and social networks, their own vehicles of struggle over time and space. This is the cultural process, a dynamic creative expression of the totality of relationships which characterize their physical and historical reality. Culture is the dynamic synthesis of a peoples' experimental knowledge, beliefs, values and norms which *express* and *derive* from the conflicts at each stage of their development in the search for survival and progress.[13] Thus culture is the fruit of a peoples' history and a determinant of history, not infixed in the past but an ongoing interaction between the past and the present.

It is proposed that the dispersed people of African descent, separate and interrelated, be conceptualized as "communities of consciousness" engaged in an ongoing quest for human dignity and collective self-actualization. This notion encompasses the *cumulative* and *shared* endeavors to make themselves the kind of people they would imagine themselves capable of being; to make their own development; to realize their humanity in their own terms; and to deny their status as simply social objects, e.g. objects of labor in some other peoples' development as non-wage or wage laborers. Consequently, to struggle for human dignity and social decency, and to maintain some dynamic conception of human freedom, is a particular kind of *formative* experience that shapes the cognitive landscape and social infrastructure of a people. The challenge is to discern how these shared experiences and consciousness are crystallized and transformed into various forms and relations within a geo-social and institutional framework at different points in time.

DIASPORA AS A "FIELD OF ACTION"

Historian Robert Hill, in an attempt to capture some of the dynamics and relationships among people of African descent, refers to the diaspora as a "field of action."[14] In analytical terms, this notion may be further interpreted to mean that in sociospatial terms the diaspora is an "active site" of cultural and political action and struggle. This embodies various elements of Black cultural and social development including symbol and meaning construction processes; active social and physical planes of creativity; and a range of political activities and solutions engendered to resolve conflicts which characterize each phase of diaspora history. This "field of action" may become crystallized in a number of ways with varying implications; three instances are illustrative.

Aspects of the symbol and meaning construction process may be gleaned from an understanding of the *geister* cultural views of the world which characterize every generation; that is, the content of thought, components of the cognitive landscape. It is a question of how people view their everyday world of reality, their basic cosmology as reflected in their belief systems, values, attitudes, and their views of existence and being. What, for example, are the definitions of success and failure in everyday life, the meanings of life and death? World views manifest themselves in a number of forms reflecting the obvious complexities of individual and social differentiation but may include popular culture, life styles, linguistic and symbolic behavior, literary movements (e.g. Negritude, Negrismo, Authenticity, The Harlem Renaissance)[15] or the substance of the knowledge base endemic to childrearing. For example, are there particular values and nuances that Black adults transmit to their children that condition the outlook of the young and prepare them for coping with the contradictions of social life they may encounter? How do these factors of childbearing and socialization translate as perceptions of the world, as behavioral boundaries, as expectations of the future?

The diaspora as a "field of action" may be concretized as an infrastructure of linkage networks and relationships by which ideas, information and knowledge are transmitted and circulated within, between and across communities of the diaspora. This entails further reflection on the people who carry information and knowledge such as students, military personnel, intellectuals, laborers of every description, diplomats and so on. Additionally, it is a question of the forms, content, long and short-range consequences of the transmission process, and the nature of mutual aid and assistance within and between various substratum of the diaspora. In the spirit of pan-Africanism[16] there are a range of advocacy and lobbying groups which support a number of causes in the Black world and which also perform as transmission belts of knowledge and human material resources, e.g. TransAfrica.

Perhaps the most pervasive manifestation of the diaspora as an "active site" relates to the forms of political expression and struggle as reflected in the various strategies of liberation, resistance and rebellion. This would range from slave rebellions and the ebbs and flows of worker militancy to urban insurrections of more recent years; from the Haitian revolution of the late 18th century to the ongoing revolution in Grenada of the late 20th century; from flight or marronage and the formation of maroon communities (*palenques, quilombos, cumbes*)[17] to the planned settlements of emigration and back to Africa movements[18] as well as the formation of Black utopias.[19] There have been clearly orchestrated Pan-African movements such as the Pan-African Congresses in 1919, Paris; 1921, London; 1923, London and Lisbon; 1927, New York; 1945, Manchester and the All-African People's Conference in Accra in 1958.[20]

The exciting empirical undertaking is to look broadly across time and within the various geo-social contexts to discern the similarities and differences in the organization, components, and the directions of struggle; to determine the nature of the ideological and structural linkages, and the possible interchanges of symbolism and interactive relations (e.g. the impact of the Haitian revolution on other slave rebellions; the impact of the Civil Rights movement and the spread of "Black power" as an ideology and as a movement throughout the diaspora; the cross-fertilization of Black labor and union movements in the early decades of this century). Relatedly, Hill suggests analysis of the "shifting centers of historical gravity"[21] within the diaspora, meaning the places, people and events that seem to represent or embody the most "active sites" of conflict and change at particular points in time.

These examples are merely suggestive of the scope of mobilized and directed action to escape and to dismantle the forms of domination. Comprehensive and systematic study and analysis of these various political actions permit better understanding of the diaspora as a dynamic cultural entity "in itself." Moreover, to the extent that these diverse "fields of action" are interrelated and may represent acts of deliberate cross-fertilization and interpenetration, it may be possible to assess the degree to which diaspora peoples represent a "conscious force" acting "for itself."[22] In any case, the more important concern is to recognize that the nature of struggle must be understood within the context of the specific structural and institutional contexts as well as within the historical imperatives of the global system.

CONTRADICTIONS OF CULTURE[23]

The search for the shared and cumulative aspects of the cultural process points to the direction of debunking the essence of those experiences which undergird the development of the African diaspora as a particular type of formation. To recognize the existence of common and particular features does not imply cultural unity or the existence of only one culture of the Black diaspora. The circumstances into which individuals and substratum are locked affects the extent to which they can embody various elements of their culture and history. The degree to which a group moves toward a common recognition of itself as a distinctive people is in part directly related to the degree that certain ideas and values are cognitively internalized. The issue is one *identity*, which in the framework of the cultural process means "... at once the affirmation and denial of certain attributes defining individuals or sub-populations in relation to others at any point during their development."[24]

The work of Frantz Fanon, *Black Skin, White Masks*, illuminates the problem of how a subordinated people may be culturally and psychologically penetrated by their dominators.[25] Using language as an example he contends that:

> Every colonized people...finds itself face to face with the language of the civilizing nation; that is, with the culture of the mother country. The colonized is elevated above his jungle status in proportion to his adoption of the mother country's cultural standards. He becomes whiter as he renounces his blackness, his jungle.[26]

Such an observation points to the need to further elaborate and uncover many of the contradictions and conflicts within the diaspora revolving around competing forms of identification to which individuals relate, e.g. class, color, nation, religion, Africa as a concept of heritage and roots.

The ongoing struggle of Black people for human dignity and liberation is a creative process. It embodies contradictory cross-currents and conflicts such as the dialectical relationship between creativity and action, travail and reaction. It is essential to recognize that culture is an expanding and developing phenomenon. No culture is ever a complete, perfect, finished whole. The elements of culture are comprised of strengths and weaknesses, of positives and negatives, of factors of stagnation, regression and progress. Moreover, among peoples of the diaspora, the quantitative and qualitative levels of cultural action and practice vary significantly.

Finally, it should be emphasized that to learn about the persistency, endurement, and struggles of the African diaspora is to be conscious of their value as a people in the context of *universal civilization*. It means to compare their historical experinces and realities with that of other people. This is not a view of deciding superiority or inferiority. Rather, it is to determine in the general framework of human progress what contributions of people of African descent have made and can make, and what kinds of support they can and should receive. Relatedly, to understand people as subjects of their history is to help retrieve, preserve, and provide a more objective and meaningful interpretation of that history within the universal context.

NOTES

1. For an example of this relationship see Ruth Hamilton and Reber Dunkel. *A Microcosm of Dependent Underdevelopment in Two Peripheral Caribbean Social Formations: The African Diaspora in the British Virgin Islands and in the Virgin Islands of the United States*. Working Paper Series, No.2, African Diaspora Studies Project, Department of Racial and Ethnic Studies and College of Urban Development, Michigan State University, June 1980.

2. For a good introduction to the conceptual and empirical problems consult Alejandro Portes and John Walton. *Labor, Class, and the International System*. New York: Academic Press, 1981. pp. 21-65.

3. See Johan Galtung's "A Structural Theory of Imperialism," *Journal of Peace Research*, No.2, 1971, pp. 81-117. In addition to the seminal work of Galtung, several important works provide an orientation to the subject of international inequality: Susanne Bodenheimer, *The Ideology of Developmentalism: The American Paradigm-Surrogate for Latin American Studies.* Beverly Hills, California: Sage Publications, 1971; Theotonio dos Santos, "The Structure of Dependence," *American Economic Review*, LX (May 1970) pp. 231-236; Andre Gunder Frank, *Capitalism and Underdevelopment in Latin America.* New York: Monthly Review Press, 1969. Perhaps the most provocative work is Samir Amin, *Unequal Development: An Essay on the Social Formations of Peripheral Capitalism.* New York: Monthly Review Press, 1976.

4. Robert Blauner. *Racial Oppression in America.* New York: Harper and Row Publishers, 1972, pp. 21-22.

5. W.E. Burghardt DuBois. "Of the Dawn of Freedom," in *The Souls of Black Folk.* Greenwich, Connecticut: Fawcett Publications, Inc., 1961, p.23.

6. Selected works on the global dimensions of race: Ralph Bunche. *A World Review of Race.* New York: Kinnikat Press, 1968; George W. Shepherd, Jr. and Tilden J. LeMelle, (eds.) *Race Among Nations.* Lexington, Massachusetts: Heath Lexington, 1970; Tilden J. LeMelle and George W. Shepherd, Jr., "Race in the Future of International Relations," *Journal of International Affairs*, XXV, 2(1971) 302-314. Works of E. Franklin Frazier are particularly important: *Race and Culture Contacts in the Modern World.* New York: Alfred A. Knopf, 1957; "Racial Problems in World Society," in G. Franklin Edwards (eds), *E. Franklin Frazier on Race Relations.* Chicago: University of Chicago Press, 1968, pp. 103-116.

7. E.P. Thompson. *The Making of the English Working Class.* London: V. Gollancz, 1980. Thompson observed that the English working class of the 19th century was so different in way of life that they were viewed as a people not just as a source of labor. Similarly Karl Marx contends that a Klasse un sich by its consciousness can become a Klasse fur sich; the point: A group by its own common identity.

8. Idea of covalent bond of inequality is borrowed from chemistry and the principles of molecular structure as related to the nature of the chemical bond. In essence there is a similarity between the investigations of the chemical composition of substances and their reactions, and the nature and substance of particular social relations and their interactions and reactions. Special thanks to Dr. James B. Hamilton, professor of chemistry, Michigan State University, for sharing and discussing the ideas with me and for exposing me to the work of Linus Pauling. *The Nature of the Chemical Bond.* Ithaca, New York: Cornell University Press, 1960.

9. This criticism is generally directed to so-called Marxists who tend to reduce all explanations of racial conflict to class conflict. The reverse is also true when race becomes the only explanatory variable without considering class relations.

10. E. Franklin Frazier. *Black Bourgeoisie: The Rise of a New Middle Class in the United States.* New York: Collier Books, 1962, pp. 162-175.

11. Frances Henry. "The West Indian Domestic Scheme in Canada." *Social and Economic Studies* XVII, 1 (March 1968) 83-91; Jane Sawyer Turrittin. "Networks and Mobility: the case of West Indian domestics from Montserrat," *Canadian Review of Sociology and Anthropology* XIII, 3 (1976) 305-320.

12. Ralph Ellison. *Shadow and Act.* New York: Signet Books, 1966, pp. 119-121.

13. Amilcar Cabral. "National Liberation and Culture," in *Return to the Source: Selected Speeches of Amilcar Cabral* (edited by African Information Service). New York: Modern Reader, 1973, pp.41-42.

14. Based on a lecture by Professor Robert Hill, "The Changing Balance of Forces within the African Diaspora from the Haitian Revolution to the Present," presented at Michigan State University, November 18, 1976. (Professor Hill is at the Center for Afro-American Studies, University of California, Los Angeles.)

15. O.R. Dathorne (ed.) *Caribbean Narrative: An Anthology of West Indian Writing.* London: Heinemann, 1966; and *Dark Ancestor: The Literature of the Black Man in the Caribbean.* Baton Rouge: Louisiana State University Press, 1981.

16. George Shepperson, "Pan-Africanism and 'Pan-Africanism': Some Historical Notes," *Phylon* XXIII, 4 (Winter 1962) pp. 346-358.

It may be found helpful, both in tracing the origins of "pan-Africanism" and in employing the term accurately in studies of contemporary African politics, to use, on some occasions, a capital "P" and, on others a small one...

"Pan-Africanism" with a capital letter is a clearly recognizable movement: the five Pan-African Congresses....

On the other hand, "pan-Africanism" with a smaller letter is not a clearly recognizable movement.... It is rather a group of movements, many very ephemeral....

17. Richard Price (ed.) *Maroon Societies: Rebel Slave Communities in the Americas.* 2nd edition. Baltimore: The John Hopkins University Press, 1979.

18. Howard H. Bell. "The Negro Emigration Movement, 1849-1854: A Phase of Negro Nationalism," *Phylon* IX (Summer 1959) 132-142; and "Negro Nationalism: A Factor in Emigration Projects, 1858-1861," *Journal of Negro History*, XLVII (January 1962) 42-53. There are two papers on planned emigration to Haiti in the 19th century by James Theodore Holly and J. Dennis Harris in Howard H. Bell (ed.) *Black Separatism and the Caribbean, 1860.* Ann Arbor: The University of Michigan Press, 1970; Martin Robinson Delany. *The Condition, Elevation, Emigration, and Destiny of the Colored People of the United States.* Philadelphia: privately printed, 1852; Martin Robinson Delany and Robert Campbell. *Search for a Place: Black Separatism and Africa, 1860.* Ann Arbor: University of Michigan Press, 1969, reprint; Floyd J. Miller. *The Search for a Black Nationality: Black Emigration and Colonization, 1787-1863.* Urbana: University of Illinois Press, 1975.

19. William H. Pease and Jane Pease. *Black Utopia: Negro Communal Experiments in America.* Madison, Wisconsin: The State Historical Society of Wisconsin, 1963.

20. Shepperson. *Op. Cit.* p. 346.

21. Hill. *Op. Cit.*

22. *Ibid.*

23. This discussion draws heavily upon Amilcar Cabral. *Op. Cit.* pp. 39-56.

24. Hussein Abdilahi Bulhan. "Black Psyches in Captivity and Crises," *Race and Class* XX, 3(1979), p. 246.

25. Frantz Fanon. *Black Skin, White Masks.* New York: Grove Press, Inc., 1967.

26. *Ibid.* pp. 18-19.

THE ROLE OF BLACK INTELLECTUALS IN FORGING BLACK UNITY*

Manuel Zapata Olivella

After 500 plus years since the arrival of Columbus' ships in America, there still remain to be explained the contributions of millions of human beings who from that moment changed the unilateral course of history for the peoples of the world. In the light shed by studies of ethnohistory and cultural anthropology, the transcendent meaning of the 12th of October 1492 was *not* the discovery of this continent but the collision of three millennial cultures of America, Africa and Europe.

For the 50 million indigenous Americans who were violently conquered, decimated and shackled to colonial society[1] and for the descendants of the 100 million Africans constrained by the slave trade, only one-half of whom arrived to this continent, the history of the conquest and colonization of America poses for us urgent tasks which may contribute to demythify the ethnocide, never before or since eclipsed, perpetrated by the barbarism of the European conquerors.[2] Perhaps the epilogue of this drama, which still continues for the black people of South Africa and for millions of indigenous Americans, may be the nuclear disaster with which we are threatened by the direct descendants of those who carried out the infamy of slavery.

From this macabre perspective of the future we find ourselves obliged to remember the past. It is especially an unpostponable obligation for black peoples—and we use this term in its broadest cultural connotation—because their descendants in Africa, America, Asia, Oceania and Europe, after five centuries of oppression and violent exile, still suffer from the burning shackles of neocolonialism. There is the added aggravation that the modern methods of massive repression surpass the deadly power of the sword, the horse and *flare guns*. We, its victims, continue naked before the antiriot tanks which in seconds eliminate the defenseless neighborhoods of Soweto; bombers, missiles and nuclear warheads permanently threaten Angola, Mozambique, Zimbabwe and Namibia; bacterial, chemical and psychological poisonings destroy agriculture, animals and humans in Colombia, Brazil, Bolivia and Central America; dogs specialized in pursuing, discovering and rending blacks apart are used in the European capitals against the descendants of former colonial subjects. However, such methods pale before the threat of nuclear war, a procedure already tested in Hiroshima and Nagasaki for the extermination of "inferior" races. The same procedure of massive reprisals is used by the afrikaners of South Africa to achieve total white supremacy.

THE SOCIAL SCIENCES: AN OVERWHELMING WEAPON

Although we terrifyingly speak of the highly technological weapons of the colonizers, we, their victims, know that we have at our disposal a portentous strategic defense: sociology, cultural anthropology, economics and, above all, the social creativity of our peoples.

This affirmation could be considered so ingenuous that you would think we are still in the age of magic when our forbears fought against bullets with bows and arrows. Don't be mistaken, many of us have university experience and have learned that the sciences of human knowledge are the only effective means for withstanding the insanity of the destroyers of humanity. Besides helping us to build defensive arms with the same technology as that of the oppressor, they permit us to spiritually and morally equip our peoples; to unify our forces regardless of the language actually spoken; to spread the message of ethnic and cultural unity which ties us to the same historical destiny; to disassemble the psychological mechanisms of mental slavery;[3] to develop alphabets which immortalize the knowledge and combative experience of our forbears and remote ancestors; to delve deeply into the religiousness of the *muntu*[4] with their concepts which make all things brothers of one family: the dead, the living, nature, animals, plants, stones, stars and tools; in a word, the most profound ecological consciousness now forgotten by the corrupters and polluters of life.

At this time, we have already learned from cultural anthropology the place we occupy as *homo sapiens*, whatever the race, in the human evolutionary chain. Let us not be confused by the sophism which divides people into supertechnical or barbaric; we know the role played by economics in social development; we have penetrated the mystery surplus value: the genius and the effort of the worker create the riches of society. The phantoms of televisions, movies and radio no longer frighten us or deceive us with their false histories of superman in which only whites control the destiny of oppressed peoples. We are familiar with the fable of the Tarzans, Rambos and Bionic women and we know that never again will the material creativity of people be overcome by the fabulous monsters of racist cinematography.

THE DIASPORA REVISITED

More and more, the social sciences reveal to us how devastating were the desolations of slavery and colonization to the conciousness of peoples uprooted from their native continent and dispersed throughout the world without the remotest possibility of return. Although today we feel ourselves to be owners of a new culture, proud citizens of the countries where we were born, and firm combatants in the search for our own destiny, the scars of cultural colonialism still continue to unconsciously determine some of our acts of recovery.

We refer to the trauma left by centuries of systematic ethnocide and genocide against millions and millions of free men in an attempt to change them, without success, into simple units of barter,[5] into blind laborers, into labor zombies.

Nevertheless, to achieve total colonialist disalignment, it is necessary to rescue from forgetfulness many of the tactics used by our ancestors, purifying them of alienating mechanisms which prevent us from assuming a unifying attitude in the face of modern oppressors. It is a complex process of assimilating, recreating and eliminating the positive and negative factors of sociocultural crossbreeding which have been unfolding in the most diverse circumstances and whose psychological content still remains hidden in our voluntary and subconscious acts: the negation of life and liberty; the hunting of humans perpetuated over 350 years; slave ships where the stackings, punishments, tortures, executions and throwing into the sea of rebels and the sick made death more bearable than the terror; the crushing mines of bones; the plantations where the sun and the whips sowed fire and wounds on human backs; the impossibility of satisfying sexual needs due to the violent monopoly of Black and Indian women by slavers; the destruction of filial feelings by the sale and separation of parents from their children; the prohibition against the speaking of African languages, the proscription against protective gods; the punishments for laughing, singing, playing music and dancing; the nakedness under the sun, the rains, the winter and the plagues; the torment of hunger and chronic malnutrition; the repudiation of moral precepts received from the millennial African cultures and finally, the elimination of habits which spring from human society: social, civil and political rights.

We ask ourselves, as once did Marcus Garvey: where are the black historians, sociologists, anthropologists, economists, philosophers, religious men, artists, musicians, painters, scientists and warriors who will reveal to us the secrets of the ancestors and bequeath to us, who are in the most subhuman conditions, the African spiritual and material legacy present in the contemporary culture of humanity.

BLACKS IN THE 20TH CENTURY

In all fairness, we are aware that even if much remains to be clarified about the strategy used by our forebears, we do already know enough about the tactics employed in their fights as maroons, the uprisings, the linguistic creativity, the religious and cultural syncretisms. And today, our brothers in South Africa have taken the decision to unhesitatingly make the daily offering of martyrs necessary to achieve triumph.

But in the modern battles that we face, it is not enough to know how grandfathers did it. Rather, one must search for the profoundest essence of their action, the fire which inspired their battles and their inextinguishable faith in victory. What was the all powerful armor that permitted them to undermine the scaffolding of slavery and repression with only the use of the chained fist, the amputated tongue and the agonized soul?

We suspect that there is an imperishable flame, common to all African peoples, an undying flame capable of spreading, like the leaves of a tree or the sparks of a fire, a flame found wherever the strong wind of the diaspora scattered their bodies.

In light of the most recent anthropological studies, we can affirm that every human being is the product of an ethnicity and a history. Even when taken from his ancestral context (however naked he finds himself, with his hands shackled or his mind bound by iron masks), as long as life persists, there is a cell to recreate the basic genetic elements of his culture in the most adverse of social environments. Collectively or individually, each of our forefathers did precisely that under slave-colonial regimes of America.

Resplendent is the light which illuminates the night of the African enchained in America. How from his memory, aptitudes, and attitudes did he succeed in recreating nature in a society where he was imprisoned?

It is in this personal African experience that we should find our current power: the unity of black peoples from Africa, America and Southeast Asia. We are not speaking of romantic unity, of the perhaps unachievable recovery of lost origins, but of another communion which arises from the attitude and the action which yesterday united our grandparents against slavery and which today should bind us together in different parts of the planet against the same oppressors. In other words, we are calling for the return from the diaspora to the primary fountain of blood and spirit. Saying it in the poetic imagery of the great ones: ""Te manatee returns to the source where it was nurtured in its infancy."[6]

Students of American Africanity—the Nina Rodriguez', the Arthur Ramos', the Jose Antonio Saco's, the Fernando Ortiz', the Roger Bastide's, and others—have detected for us the many cultures taken from Africa and dispersed in America—Carabali, Wolof, Arara, Mandingo, Congo, Ashanti, Angola, Brang, Lucumi, Nganga, etc.[7] All these authors agree that chains unified the members of these different communities less than did the invisible but indestructible cord of a common African culture.

The manipulative word of the colonizer made the African into a thing, a simple object of barter. How revealingly significant when today we know that the bag of skin once measured by centimeters, kilograms, teeth, sex and fingers actually contained the rich inheritance of African ancestral technologies: agriculture, shepherding, metallurgy, navigation, medicine, astronomy, mathematics, society, religion, philosophy and, above all, that vital and inexhaustible creativity which allowed them to arm the system of a new culture wherever they were able to plant a son and a family.

The powerful body, the inexhaustible physical energy, the zombie is reborn from myth and legend with its real human dimension. Although much of the road has been retraced, still there are many hidden footprints of the black man in the documents written by brother Cain.

BLOOD AND THE SCIENCES

No contemporary people has spilled as much blood for its freedom as has the African. However, we are not going to declare that blood is the best testimony of the African's passage through history. On the contrary, we want to plumb the depths of his cultural past in order to give an unbloody direction to our future.

We begin by learning the lesson: we will be part of a bloodless history. The hour of sacrifice has arrived for us the living to contribute our daily quota of concrete, real, unrenounceable work. Although we may proceed to clarify our history, we cannot leave for tomorrow the construction of the present. The sciences, as already said, are our modern arsenal of arms for combat.

THE STRENGTH OF THE DEAD IN THE FISTS OF THE LIVING

The correct application of the social sciences in the analysis of the philosophy of the peoples of Africa, America and Oceania means recovering the philosophical content of its mythologies, religions and epic legends. That which was considered lies, superstitions and paganisms of primitive minds constitutes the richest observations of empiric magical thought concerning nature, society and liberation struggles. To the extent that their abstract conception of reality is understood, one can appreciate their mythic cultural values as forming part of the secular world, projected onto life itself, and not as mere metaphysical speculations. Experiences or empiricism reveals to us the most profound fundamentals of popular wisdom.[8]

The religious and scientific prejudices of the colonizers, exalting the great power of their conquering hypotheses and gods, encounter insurmountable contradictions when they try to confront empiric thought with academic analysis; magic with religion, the experience of the living with the inheritance from the dead; when they make gods of their generals, emperors and saints and reduce to the category of fetishes the orishas and legendary heroes of our peoples' oral tradition; when they do not recognize the identity between the physical laws which rule the universe and the African deities which order life, nature and society.[9]

Therefore, upon scientifically analyzing the religions of our ancestors, we should enlighten ourselves with the unalienating lights that allow us the correct interpretation of our ethnicity and culture. We must separate ourselves from pseudo-suns, those which illuminate only the face of science while insisting on disavowing the accumulated truths of empiric wisdom.

Our truth must be new, unalienating and creative. Diagnoses, hypotheses, and their proofs will be insufficient for us to forge the family of the *muntu*, where the dead and the living, nature and mankind can live together. There will be no Atlantic, Pacific or Indian oceans, nations or neocolonial empires which in the name of pseudo-democracies or technical development will divert us from the new shore. We were voyagers of history long before the Europeans overwhelmed the civilizations of Africa, Asia, and America. And our course, already conceived during the unfortunate night of colonialist oppression, shall not be diverted from the ecumenical and fraternal destiny laid out by our ancestors.

THE SUN DOES NOT MOVE BACKWARD IN ITS DAILY PASSAGE

A look at the contemporary actions of black peoples against modern forms of oppression—"apartheid" in South Africa, denial of the right of self-determination in Namibia, aggressions in Angola and Mozambique; persistence in racial, political and social discrimination in the United States, Brazil, Colombia, Haiti, Panama, etc.—reveals that the combative spirit of our forebears has neither died nor gone backward in its persistent fight for liberty of the *muntu* and cultural emancipation.

This combative legacy has gone beyond the mere social, political and economic aspect to the rescue and defense of cultural values. Vigorous indications of this black renaissance, resonant of Harlem and Negritude, are the Pan African Festivals of Black Arts, the Congresses on the Orisha tradition; the programs of Afro-American Studies in the universities of the United States; the institutes and centers of study of the Black presence in the cultures of Brazil, Peru, Ecuador, Colombia, Panama, etc; the massive increase in Afro-American religions (Candomble, Voodoo, Macumba, Santeria, etc.); the contemporary and popular musical movements (jazz, rock, reggae, samba, salsa, cumbia, marinera, etc.); the modern dance and folkloric groups; the literary, pictorial and theatrical currents of the black spirit with its most recent Nobel Prize Winner, Wole Soyinka.

We would not be consistent with the ethnohistory if we forgot that the current manifestations of the black spirit are the flourishing of the African seed scattered in Asia, Oceania, and America by the prehistoric African migrations and the later dispersion in our continent of the hundreds of millions of Africans during the past four centuries.

The origin of the African presence in America goes back to the first transpacific migrations of black peoples of Polynesia and Melanesia, whose antiquity is calculated at 30 to 40 thousand years by the French scholar Paul Rivet.[10] In the Easter Islands are the megalithic and sleepless "mays" with their open eyes looking at the steps of the *muntu* in America; the great pyramids and sculptures of Peru; or in the Mount of Idols (Colombia) where the stone faces of African ancestors take the forms of jaguar priests, serpent women and eagle men. And dispersed from South to North, we again find in Central America (El Salvador) and in the Gulf of Mexico the gigantic Olmec heads, precursors to the art and civilizations of the Mayas and Aztecs of Mexico. The millennial sun of the black peoples of the world continues to illuminate the spirit of humanity whose light the legionnaires of night cannot put out.

The Fixed View

There are brothers (*ekobios*) with a myopic view of our future who become discouraged or mute in the struggle without seeing the potential contained in the creativity of our ethnicity. It is certain that hundreds of brothers are sacrificed in South Africa; millions die of hunger and misery in the slums of the Americas and many brothers in Oceania, trapped by empiric magic, still throw a fish-hook into ocean depths to fish out the shipwrecked moon.

This is true, but is only half of the truth. *There also exists a growing consciousness among black peoples of the world that they possess a common unique identity.* More and more they know that the blood of the oppressed and assassinated of all races flows to the same river which, overflowing, will drown the last vestiges of modern slavery. Sometimes one sees only the leader who has fallen and not his fearful and silent troops; one does not notice that in many countries in the Americas where it was not known that the descendants of Africans existed, those descendants are raising their voices and proudly claiming their place in the cultural identity of the country.

Also certain and painful are the confrontations between brothers of the same ethnicity, looking at each other with the eyes of the colonizer who gave them names in Spanish, English, French and Portuguese, confronting these names with their true African surnames. But at the same time, the congresses, festivals, seminars, expositions, concerts, books and struggles of black peoples proclaim their identity with beating drums wherever they may be on a continent, an island, or a European city. In the most unexpected places there is a response, sounding the alarm with the same language of ethnicity and culture.

THE BLACK INTELLECTUAL

It is in the gathering of highsounding, subversive and alienated voices that one should begin the objective and analytical work of our social sciences. We cannot expect the old tribal weapons that opposed the slave trader to be efficient against the modern means of oppression developed in the universities, factories and arsenals of the neocolonialists. It is up to the so-called black intellectuals (artists, musicians, writers, actors, cinematographers, economists, sociologists, psychologists, thinkers, religious leaders, and politicians) to take to their respective foxholes.

It is not a matter of shirking the common responsibility of fighting against the oppression of all peoples, but of being able to aptly distinguish between the right to be black or white and the right to be free. Justice can be obtained by all ethnicities. We should be lucid revolutionaries, capable of assimilating the lesson of Frantz Fanon when he put us on guard against becoming alienated carriers of the colonizing mentality and thereby making that mentality part of our liberating goals.

We cannot presume or aspire to be taken for "pure" intellectuals dedicated to a single creative action for the simple reason that the colonizing system can scarcely guarantee specialization to its select and capable. *Whatever place the black intellectual may occupy in a class society, he has to be aware that his strength and his ideal should be measured by the degree of misery, hunger and need of his ethnic brothers.*

The first responsibility of the revolutionary intellectual, and of course we are addressing ourselves to our race brothers, is to add his knowledge and talent to the historical current of our peoples; and, as a more specific commitment, to make his greatest efforts and sacrifice to those battlefronts lacking in combatants and consciousness.

Frequently one hears voices which dichotomize the general battlefront, voices in favor of the least dangerous foxhole so as to convert it into a high-walled castle that has no bridges to link it with the rest of the battle action. In defense of their eagle's nest, they argue lack of talent, professional incompatibilities, urban or rural marginalization. Tergiversation abounds. Is this the kind of doing in response to an objective comprehension of social reality or does it reflect a colonizing alienation? We will not answer here what each must answer for himself in his own time and space. Our most intimate conviction, however, is that the more the black intellectual is committed to the battlefield, the closer he will be to the tradition of our ancestors and to his oppressed brothers.

IDENTITY AND THE POLITICAL STRUGGLE

The political dimension of ethnicity and culture has been systematically underestimated by those who want to reduce the complex action of oppressed peoples solely to the dynamic of economic infrastructure. Again, it is important to remember Fanon when he warns us against the intrusion of colonialist thought. There are two ways to interpret *factual* events: a man as *object* or as *subject* of his own history. With respect to the problem of the presence and culture of black peoples in the Americas, there are researchers who assume the posture of feigned asepsis, subjectively observing black peoples as if they were laboratory mice, objects appropriate for dissection, comparison and speculation with other ethnicities. Thus they allege in the name of all mighty science that rigorous historical analysis should be founded on documents, dates, fossils, tools of torture and other weapons that reveal like a fingerprint the identity of the victim.

Of course there are chronicles written by doctors, captains and religious men that describe the illnesses of the captives and the terrible conditions of stacking in the holds of the slave ships. In the notary offices and sacristies throughout the entire continent there abound the registers of notaries and priests who give testimony to the number of amputated toes, broken bones, empty eye-sockets and scars of the Africans upon being sold or baptized.

With pathetic cynicism, the high percentage of the dead that had to be discarded during the Atlantic crossing was calculated in the ledger; fraudulent statistics abound concerning the number of transported prisoners; the recording of deaths by emaciation and chronic malnutrition on the plantations and mines; the quantities of cocoa, tobacco, sugar, molasses or indigo shipped from the colonies to the centers of the European empires.

This type of history has served to write allegations, denunciations and even paternalistic litanies on slavery. They are indeed very important documents for understanding the origin of accumulated wealth in Europe, of how monopolistic capitalism developed and why there exist today highly technically developed peoples and underdeveloped peoples, but they offer little clarity concerning our history.

Contrary to the "classic" researchers, we adhere to the scientific criteria which conceives of people as forgers of their own history even when they act under regimes that deny them their creative liberty. We attribute more importance to the man who creates with his tools of labor than to he who whips him. We consider anonymous workers who forge the social structure more decisive humanity than the emperors and generals who take possession of it. For us, the historic discourse is not a cumulation of heroes, but the masses who make possible the enrichment of mankind.

Consequently, in historical analysis, we will not act passively like guinea pigs. When they split our skin with a scalpel we react with live flesh and not like a simple stain of melanin. When one speaks of us as "slaves", our blood comes alive with the sentiment that our grandparents never accepted this epithet due to their conviction of having been born free. Faced with mathematical calculations to determine the number of Africans brought to the Americas—14? 25? 50 millions?—we lose the reasoning of quantifying numbers to the degree of indignation boiling in our blood.

We praise the concept of ethnic and cultural identity as a political act. As long as we limit ourselves to anthropological examination, we will be following in the footsteps and conclusions of the oppressing analysts. As long as we do not think of ourselves as lucid and independent consciousnesses opposed to the colonizer, the color of our skin, the sense of our actions, the philosophy of our struggles will continue to revolve around the eternal return of slavery.

RACISM AND CREATIVE CAPACITY

When the first philosophers of racism—Aristotle and Hegel—divided human nature into two categories, the masters and the slaves, they were not creating metaphysical realities. They referred to white, black and yellow peoples who inhabited the then known world. The ideology of power in the hands of those elected by God to govern the barbarians was described in detail by Hegel who alluded concretely to blacks, affirming that, like dogs, they lacked a soul and understanding.[11] At no time did they put forth human creativity as a universal condition of all peoples. It was precisely from this ontological sophism that the racist ideology of nazism, apartheid and colonialism which divides men into masters and slaves, and peoples into developed and underdeveloped was born and perpetuated.

Starting from the scientific criteria of the new social concepts, we frankly reject the racist ideas and practices of the neo-colonialists. We recognize the common identity of all blacks, wherever we may have been hurled by the ancient migrations of our African ancestors and the more recent compulsory dispersion by the slavers of the Christian age.

UNITY AND DIVISION OF BLACK PEOPLES

The creativity of black people under slavery was not always directed toward the forging of its own destiny. This is a very important aspect in our fight for cultural disalienation. Not a few are the racist concepts and attitudes inherited from colonial society which still persist among the descendants of former masters and, what is worse, in the minds of blacks themselves. We do not have the necessary space here to examine these prejudices. We will limit ourselves, then, to pointing out some alienating factors of slavery which prevent us from strengthening the alliance of black peoples for the achievement of their total liberation.

FACTORS DERIVED FROM AFRICAN ETHNICITIES AND CULTURES

Quantity and diversity of African peoples; different expressions of philosophical knowledge, religions and technologies; ancestral rivalries, many of which persist and still are emphasized in America; age, sex and physical strength; the temperaments and attitudes in the face of slavery (belligerent, resistant, suicidal, etc.); regional illnesses; the variety of the American ecology where African peoples were settled, etc.

FACTORS DERIVED FROM EUROPEAN ETHNICITIES AND CULTURES

Spanish, English, Portuguese, French and Dutch colonizers and their different levels of technological development; diversity of Christian religious creeds (catholicism and protestant sects); attitudes towards race mixing; various types of economic exploitation (plantations, mines, ranches, domestic professions, etc.); the social and psychological mechanisms used to destroy and alienate African cultures, religions, languages, destruction of the family, separation of married couples, sale of children, racial segregation, etc.; ethnic confrontations supporting ancestral rivalries already in force in Africa; racial marginalization and segregation; different systems of payment (gold roll and silver roll); distinct social status (half-breeds; mulattoes; half Indian/half black zambos; baptized; stupid, cunning, rights, etc.; systems of identification (mutilations, castrations, dress, uniforms, cards, etc.).

If we consider that such practices occurred for centuries, generation after generation, there is no reason for us to wonder about the traditional confrontations among the different black communities of the world due to political issues, concepts of identity, workers' organizations, religious cults, literary, music and folkloric movements. The history of the black peoples' fights for emancipation is full of rivalries, frustrations and treasons resulting from a lack of ethnic and cultural consciousness and from the ignorance of our own history. We would win much, therefore, if we assumed responsibility for advancing the tasks of disalienation from the psychological and social behaviors inherited from cultural colonialism and which, encrusted in our minds, prevent us today from achieving unity of action among black peoples.

And finally, we, the descendants of Africans, reject being accused of racism solely because we proclaim, affirm and defend the unity of the black peoples of the world.

NOTES

* Translated by Tanya Saunders Hamilton.
    1. Angel Rosenblat, *Nuestra lengua en Ambos Mundos*, (Navarra: Alianza Editorial, 1971).
    2. Darcy Ribero, *The Americas and Civilization*, (New York: E.P. Dutton, 1971).
    3. Frantz Fanon, *Los condendos de la tierra*, (Mexico: Fondo de Cultura Economica, 1963).
    4. A muntu is a human being (congolese). Black, mulatto, zambo (Indian/Black), and mestizo scientists, consistent with their history, are in a position to achieve unity of thought and action among the oppressed, whatever their race, nation or continent. Nothing will prevent the return of unity to the African peoples dispersed throughout the diaspora by the colonizers.
    5. A "pieza de india" was a unit of measure for the productive power of a slave; therefore, the work of a woman slave plus one child might be considered equivalent to the productive power of one able-bodied male slave at the height of his physical prowess, i.e., one medium of exchange.
    6. Léopold Sédar Senghor, *Libertad, Negritud y Humanismo*, (Madrid: Tecnos, 1970).
    7. Gonzalo Aguirre Beltrán, *La Poblacion Negra de Mexico*, (Mexico: Fondo de Cultura Economica, 1972); Nina Rodriguez, *Os Africanos no Brasil*, 2nda edicion, (Sao Paulo: 1935); Arthur Ramos, *As Culturas Negras No Novo Mundo* (Sao Paulo: 1946); Jose Antonio Saco, *Historia de la Escalvitud de la Raza Africana en el Nuevo Mundo* 4 volumes (Habana: Nueva Edicion, 1938); Fernando Ortiz, *Los Negros Brujos* (Madrid: 1971); and Roger Bastide, *Las Americas Negras* (Madrid: Alianza Editorial, 1969).
    8. Claude Lévi-Strauss, *Arte, Lenguaje, Etnologia* (Mexico: Siglo XXI Editores, S.A., 1969).
    9. Placide Tempels, *Bantu Philosophy* (Paris: Presencia Africana, 1969); James G. Frazer, *The Golden Bough. A Study In Magic and Religion* (London: Macmillan and Co. Ltd., 1925).
    10. Paul Rivet, *Los Origenes del Hombre Americano* (Mexico: Fondo de Cultura Economica, 1969).
    11. G.W.F. Hegel, *Worlesungen Uber die Geschichte de Philosophie* (Berlin: 1843).

THE EVOLUTION OF RACISM INTO THE 21ST CENTURY

Iva E. Carruthers

D URING THE past sixteen years, a basic and applied high bio-technological research movement has given birth to a new eugenics approach that continues to establish the parameters within which the notion and manifestation of racism will affect the world in both the last quarter of the 20th century and into the 21st century.

This new eugenics approach is embodied in sociobiology; that is not to suggest that all sociobiology is targeted at or motivated by racism. It does say, however, that the umbrella of sociobiology is but another refuge for racism.[1]

For the purposes of this essay, racism is thusly defined: Any set of beliefs *empowered* by a system of institutional and individual relationships which propagates or reinforces an ideology of su-premacy based on socio and bio-scientific definitions and distinctions of race.

Few would argue with the statement that "the unchecked expansion of the West led to an unprecedented development of science and technology in the 19th century. This material progress [is] now manifesting itself with renewed force: *white supremacy*. The development of the 19th century social sciences bore the imprint of this white supremacist arrogance ... to legitimize *in a scientific manner* the hegemony of the West and the supremacy of the "white man" (Moore, 1972, 11-12). Therefore, in a functional sense and for all practical purposes over the last 200 years, racism is further defined as the successfully imposed hegemony, by design or effect, of white culture, color or ethnicity over the world's populations and the world's order, i.e., white supremacy.

That a Black scholar would examine racism in a biotechnological context often elicits several predictable responses: (1) the scholar is a reverse racist, or (2) racism, in the context of eugenics as an issue or dialogue, is better left alone because it fosters racial conflict, not racial harmony. The risks notwithstanding, anytime one admits that the race question is an essential question, then one must inevitably look at the biological prescriptions which make valid those *social distinctions* in the context of changing times and space.

Understandably, Black people, and Black scholars in particular, during the last two centuries, have spent inordinate energy rejecting and refuting theories and polemics relative to biological determinism. Most Blacks are firmly wedded to the monogenetic theory of the origin of humankind and the environmental determinism of race behavior. Thus, for Blacks to even broach this subject is scorned; to reexamine the issue from an Afrocentric view raises questions concerning theories of polygenesis and genetic determination of racial differences and behavior. Yet, one thing is clear: The whites in the Euro-Western world view their existence and that of Blacks world over in a matter-of-fact manner. Neither Blacks in the Americas nor continental Africans can afford to ignore the Western approach to survival, or the scientific basis upon which that approach is rationalized despite its incompatibility with our moral and ethical worldview.

Our history teaches us that our moral and ethical position puts us at a severe disadvantage in dealing with the world as it is presently organized under European hegemony. While I am not suggesting that we abandon our moral and ethical view, I do believe that we must unveil the myth of universality—while we are the only ones believing it—and move forward to understanding the

Euro-Western worldview, to which Western science and technology is essential because it is becoming increasingly evident that the future of the Black race is threatened by the emergent theories and practices of eugenics or population genetics. Thus, we cannot afford, at this juncture of our history, to ignore biological prescriptions of humankind, race, ethnicity and culture, based on biochemical differences, including the depigmentation or melanin-based theories. Therefore, this essay, *heuristic in nature*, intends to bring additional clarity to the nuances and vicissitudes of racism in a global technocracy. It is presented in three major parts:

(1) Methodological considerations
(2) A review of the neo-eugenics era, and
(3) A call for a changing paradigm from racism to "usism."

METHODOLOGICAL CONSIDERATIONS

Engagement in any so-called "intellectual, scientific or research exercise" first requires methodological considerations which include *a priori* assumptions. The extent to which *a priori* assumptions are operative, yet unspoken, is the extent to which social theory construction becomes developmental and institutional. The extent to which these assumptions have cultural validation, in any given time and space, is the extent to which science and art reflect the reality of society.

An Afrocentric understanding of racism in Western society—more specifically the Americas—requires that we first reject the *primacy* of Western scientific methodology upon which knowing, proving, and explaining are predicated (i.e. Western epistemology). If one examines the history of Western science, one sees that inherent in it is a belief system with *a priori* assumptions which: 1) mandate that the highest ambition of scientific inquiry and progressive humankind, and thus social and physical organization, is to control nature and natural mankind; and that, 2) African people and culture, the African race and color, are at their lowest ebb and are the epitome of natural as opposed to "progressive" humankind. Attendant to this Western belief system is the perennial quest for "better life," "immortality," "a truce between religion and science" and "a reconciliation between the European view of humanism and the universality of man."

To distinguish between *using* Western scientific method and *being used by* Western scientific method is one challenge Black scholars, collectively, confront. And to step outside Western paradigms and raise different questions with different meanings, using different tests of validation and reliability, is essential to creating Afrocentric social theory and order. In short, the Afrocentric test of validation of correctness (epistemological sense) and rightness (moral sense) of our ideas, intellectual and artistic pursuits, and actions must be based upon the experiential history of the masses of African peoples and judged by the overall criteria of "race redemption," both individual and collective. It should be pointed out that such an approach to our validation is not inimical to the moral and religious belief systems of the world, in that all Western religion has its roots in African belief systems.

Among the most seminal and significant restatements on a functional definition of racism was put forth by Neeley Fuller and Frances Cress Welsing. One of their assumptions is that racism *is* white supremacy because three-quarters of the world's population is non-white and subjected to domination by a minority of the world's people who classify themselves as white.

> ... racism is not merely a pattern of individual and/or institutional practice but is indeed a universally operating system of white supremacy rule and domination in which the effective majority of the world's white people participate...[and] that various economic systems such as capitalism, communism and socialism have been devised, used and refined in the effort to achieve the primary goal of white domination. (Welsing, 1970, 4)

A functional definition of racism is "the behavioral syndrome of the individual and collective color inferiority and numerical inadequacy which includes patterns of thought, speech and action as seen in numbers of the white organization [race]." (Welsing, 1970, 12)

There is overwhelming evidence to support this functional definition of racism as "white supremacy" in both historical and contemporary theory and practice. Implicit in this definition are two other important assumptions: (1) institutions are systemic and have a life and culture of their own which perpetuate the values upon which they are built, and (2) structural and institutional systems and relationships exists only within the context of power: power to control ideas and power to control the behavior of others.

COLOR/RACE—PHENOTYPIC VS. COLOR/RACE—GENOTYPIC

Dubois was correct when he prophesied that the question of the 20th century would be on the color line. And in that space and time race(ism) was a function of color and the necessary cultural and social reinforcements which accompany institutionalization of any "ism." Racism and the processes of social and cultural reinforcements may have varied, given specific colonial, slave and ethnic experiences, but the commonality of purpose is revealed by the impact that racism or white supremacy has had upon us.

What Dubois may not have anticipated and predicted, yet what we have to confront, is not that the question is still with us, but that the new racism is not merely a function of color in a physical/phenotypic sense (how we look correlated with white supremacist ideology) but racism in a biological/genetic sense (how we are, i.e., physical, spiritual substance correlated with white supremacist ideology).

Though Welsing's notion of melanic deficiency as a construct to understand collective white behavior and systems of white supremacy was and is seminal, I would dare say that many, if not most, Black intellectuals the world over reject this construct, particularly as a casual explanation for individual or collective Euro-Western behavior. Fifteen years since the publication of her theory, there may not be a consensus on Cress-Welsing's psycho-analytic approach to explaining Euro-Western behavior, but one cannot deny that her work was prophetic, since the operational-ization of racism, in the form of a new eugenics agenda, is being ushered in by the expansion of molecular biology and is clothed by the threads of sociobiology. Thus, a 21st century prospective examination of racism must move beyond the phenotypic/color paradigm and address the genotypic/race paradigm.

REVIEW OF THE NEO-EUGENICS ERA

Since the late 1960s, revolutionary transformation of bio-technology and information transfer has been quietly taking place on a global scale. This move towards a Euro-Western technocracy has made even the significance of race in sociopolitical terms more complex. Moreover, it has created even greater challenges for those committed to the struggle against racism. The biotechnology industry to which I am referring is now approximately a 15 to 20 billion dollar industry.

In 1975, Edward Wilson, Harvard University zoologist, published *Sociobiology: The New Synthesis* in which explanations of human behavior are explored by and in the context of genetic determinism. This "new science" of the Western world attempts to bring all of the various European disciplines together in order to explain reality. Indeed, African science has always assumed the unification between the natural and social sciences and so this so-called new science is but another theft by the Europeans of basic African wisdom and the resultant European distortion of that truth. Wilson says:

> We are likely to see some of most exalted feelings explained in terms of traits which evolved... Sociobiology is being used to explain racism. Ethnic pride as well as racism can be viewed as an irrational generalization of the biological tendency to distrust strangers and prefer the company of individuals who look like ourselves. (*Time*, 1977, 57).

Implicit in this acknowledgement of the European self, the new sociobiologists acknowledge important differences between people and emphasize a genetic explanation of cause. If we carry this inquiry a bit further, we can see why the Euro-Western sciences have been plagued, since Plato, with eugenics as a part of their survival strategy. We can also see why the Euro-Western scientific defense against the portending and ominous threats of AIDS and the African killer bees has serious sociopolitical implications for the future of Africans—for many in control of the global technocracy and the Neo-Eugenics movement (including the media) have labeled Africans as the "purveyors of pestilence."

The proceedings of a 1970 conference held in Johannesburg by the South Africa Institute of International Affairs reflected the following concerns:

> European populations represented 17.5% of the world population in 1920 and is projected to drop to 8.6% by 2000. The populations of Western Europe are old. The birth rate has fallen by about 10% and it has not yet been proved that this is due to any marked behavior change... the use of the pill is not enough to explain the drop. We must ask ourselves will birth rate and fertility go on falling and [what] will be the political repercussions? ... We have not dealt here with population genetics... but biological discoveries may well pose completely new problems. (Barrat, 1972, 4)

In attendance at the conference were representatives from Israel, Japan, Australia, France, Britain, Germany and the Netherlands and such individuals as Spengler from Duke University, Organski of the University of Michigan and Enke from General Electric Company. Organizational sponsorship included Ford and General Motor Companies, Goodyear, Volkswagen, Holiday Inn and IBM.

Barrat comments that European population growth is at a critical level due not just to birth declines but because the crude death rate continues to decline despite decreased mortality (Barrat,

1972, 4). This increase in numbers of deaths is caused by apparent increased vulnerability of Europeans to influences of the aging process. Thus, we see the evidence of Western bio-technology focused on epidemiology, including aging, and eugenics.

When one further examines the kinds of research being undertaken by various disciplines within the natural and social sciences, it is logical to speculate that the "biological discoveries" to which the South African Institute of International Affairs Conference refer may have to do with the negative effects of melanic deficiency or depigmentation or mutation of the European populations to which Welsing refers. Before reviewing such research, it is important that we put the questions of population genetics in a global context.

In addressing the issue of world stratification, Escott Reid, former Director of the World Bank, made the following observation:

> Of the 920 million people who live in rich countries... more than six (6) out of seven (7) live in white countries in the northern hemisphere... the only rich white country with a large colored population is the United States. There are 2,450 million people in the poor and very poor countries with about 2,100 million poor colored representing almost 60% of the population of the world and three (3) times the number of the rich northern whites... these 2,100 million poor colored people in low-income southern countries are separated not just by color and poverty—but also by hunger, illiteracy, ignorance, disease, social inequality, culture, tradition, religion and ways of life. The greatest gulf which divides mankind is not between east and west or between communism and capitalism; it is between the rich northern whites and colored southern poor. (Reid, 1973, 30)

Whether we agree with this observation or not, racism, color and ethnicity have taken on a direction in Euro-Western science and thought worthy of examination as a neo-eugenics movement. And so we turn to a review of research literature in the sciences which are forging this new scientific synthesis and being conducted by European scientists worldwide.

As we abstract and summarize the kinds of research being undertaken in this area, we should keep in mind several points: (1) Definitions of race are socially construed and partly defined by politics, culture and biology. As long as "race" has social meaning, then "racism" has societal and structural outlets which are subject to observation and, hopefully, to change. (2) Social stratification, distinctions and outcomes, as a result of class, sex, ethnicity and religion, are operative and correlated to race. Yet, as long as world order is organized as it is now, race cannot be dismissed as a mere by-product, a dependent and unuseful research construct, as some would argue. (3) Africans in diaspora are probably the most heterogenous group, certainly by gene pool, color and acculturation, if not ethnicity. (4) Despite notions of scientific empiricism and objectivity, the application of biological determinism to racial distinctions today is as much prescribed by sociopolitical exigencies and "intellectual" speculation as it was a century ago. (5) Isolation and expression of causal factors of any behavior in a genetic frame of reference is exceedingly difficult because there is no real holistic understanding of genetic (biology) vs. cultural (environmental) convergence and divergence; and (6) Africans in diaspora, African Americans in particular, live in the heart of and are most exposed to Western information transfer and high technology.

When we speak of races in the biological sense, we are referring to those major groupings of man which differ from each other by certain hereditary traits which are both phenotypically distinguishable, i.e. visible (e.g. color, hair texture, facial and body features) and/or genotypically discernable, i.e. subject to biochemical discovery (e.g. lactase tolerance, cold tolerance, dyskinesia, blood type, vitamin D regulation). Historically, European sciences have thus identified three major races, ending in *oid*, meaning *like*: Mongoloid, Caucasoid and Negroid, with varying classification schemes describing sub-races. Ironically, however, with the greater sophistication of Euro-scientific technology and what appears to be the acknowledgement of and concern for Western evidences for biological racial vulnerabilities and in the face of the "non-white population explosion," race and racial typologies in a social science sense are being rhetorically deemphasized (even by Black intellectuals as, for example, in Wilson's *Declining Significance of Race*).

Delving further, we find that what may appear "human"—such as aging; as innocuous and innocent as the interest in bio-rhythms, popularly viewed as an extension of the astrology chart; or artificial lighting variation, seen as mere commercial options to getting desired effects for different settings, has its roots in the melanic status of whites. Likewise, differential development of motor coordination, neurological functioning, cold and milk tolerance, all as a function of race, are evidenced in the literature.

Dr. Edlestein, in Massachusetts, has been at the forefront of American gerontology in examining the correlation between melanin and the aging process. He asserts that:

> Melanin may be well serving a very important function in its ability to absorb harmful energy during the aging process and thus impede the aging process... It is conceivable that the individuals with high melanin content—Blacks for the most part—might have a natural resource for longevity. (*Ebony*, 1977, 126)

He points out that in the United States there is a group of Caucasians in the population whose organs get smaller as they age. But as these organs get smaller they accumulate tremendous amounts of melanin. This disease is called "brown atrophy." His research reveals, however, that despite the reduction in size of these organs, the heart, for example, which may be reduced by one-third or one-half the size of the normal heart, functions as well or better than the normal heart.

> We feel that is because of the melanin... Because of the potential function of melanin, individuals who have increased amounts of it within their cells have the

potential to function more efficiently. It's conceivable that this may be, in part, one explanation for the remarkable physical ability of many Blacks. (*Ebony*, 1970, 126)

The inability of white persons to absorb the sun's energy, the result of melanin deficiency, is being addressed by Western scientists in identifying ways in which the natural environment can be manipulated to their needs as determined by their evolutionary dictates. Western scientists at Massachusetts Institute of Technology now suspect that changes in light intensity, whether resulting from solar seasonal changes and the sun's pattern of giving off rays and heat for the body's energy, or whether resulting from man-made light, affect the "dial rhythm" in the rate at which normal human subjects excrete melatonin; thus, the term biorhythm. Without sufficient melatonin synthesis, which is regulated by light, there is a concomitant effect on the maturation and cyclic activity of the sex glands. This effect is known to induce sleep, inhibit ovulation and modify secretion of other hormones in experimental animals (Wurtman, 1975 and Quevedo et al, 1975). Obviously, there may be implications here for declining births for Europeans.

Natural sunlight acts directly on the cells of the skin and the inability to respond to these ultra violet rays results in pathologies. A most familiar pathology is sunburn in which the effect of the rays on blood vessels or from the release of toxic compounds from the epidermis cells damage the capillaries and cause reddening, heat, swelling and pain. A more serious pathology for whites is skin cancer, for which white incidence is significantly higher than for Blacks (Williams, R., 1975, 67) (Wurtman 1975) (Blum 1961). The result of this research is that whites are now experimenting with 1) dietary measures which can increase melanin synthesis and 2) light manipulation which likewise will ensure greater protective responses to disease for the melanic deficient populations. In the Soviet Union, coal miners are now being exposed to doses of ultraviolet light every day on the theory that increased melanin function can protect them from Black lung disease (Wurtman 1975).

Research in several countries in Europe, as well as on a "normal white" population in St. Louis, Missouri, reveals that due to melanic levels, too much sunlight can produce vitamin D toxicity (Poute 1976) leading to kidney disease and elevated levels of calcium and too little light can lead to such diseases as rickets (Poute 1976) (Loomis 1967). And thus, Wurtman concludes that "properly designed indoor lighting environments—phototherapy—could serve as an important health measure to prevent the undermineralization of bones among the elderly and others." Further:

> ... the physiological superiority of melanization as a means of protection against ultraviolet was demonstrated by the ability of the... slaves to outwork the American Indians... Africans living near the equator and exposing almost all their body surface to the ultraviolet of the tropical sun do not suffer from kidney stones and other evidences of hypervitaminosis... Melanization is a defense against the oversynthesis of Vitamin D from solar ultraviolet. (Loomis, 1967, 503, 505)

To further illustrate this new science of control and social policy, let's turn to the debates over the Super Sonic Transport (SST) and its effects on the ozone layer. In 1973, the National Academy of Sciences released a study showing that a 5% reduction in the ozone layer over the United States would mean a 26% increase in harmful radiation (which) would cause roughly 8,000 cases of skin cancer among Caucasians. It would produce symptoms of aging... [and] might increase human mutation (Poute 1976, 25). After presenting a hypothetical plot in which Colonel Muammar Al-Gaddafi, representative of the "proletariate of colored peoples, threatens Soviet and American scientists with thinning of the ozone layer unless food and political concessions are granted," Poute, an arms control specialist for the Pentagon, concluded:

... the increases in ultra violet radiation and thinning of the ozone layer can directly do far more damage to Caucasians than to people with protective skin pigmentation. Thus, an attack on the ozone layer can be a race-specific weapon of war, and might seem an ideal tool to a racist fanatic—an apt answer to triage policies he sees as genocide. (Poute, 1976, 127)

Obviously, European science has identified some benefits of pigmentation as a necessary source of life. Therefore, the other side of the eugenics war is to study those persons with melanin, specifically Blacks. It stands to reason that sickle cell anemia research provides a crucial link to the biological imperative because it provides an opportunity to research the genetic formation and reformation of blood cells, that is, molecular transformation, which may be desired or needed for white survival. Experiments with cyanate in this regard view this substance as "the first member of a new class of drugs: substances that modify an abnormal gene" (Cerami, 1975, 50).

Black intolerance to milk has been identified by military research as "a poison to which Caucasoids are largely adapted" (Larson, 1970, 9). In Europeans, intolerance to lactose or milk sugar rarely occurs. Research on lactose deficiency and its implications for the theory of evolution and natural selection (McCracken 1971) (Kretchmer 1972) has given rise to race specific weapons and genetotrophics, the study of dietary needs in relationship to genetic determinism.

In human and animal experiments, melanocytes are more susceptible to cold injury. Extensive research on World War I Senegalese troops, World War II U.S. troops and Ethiopian troops in the Korean War was undertaken as a part of this inquiry. Additionally, when vials containing clones of B16 melanoa cells were frozen, maintained and reconstituted, the highly pigmented cells proved to be the least viable so that subsequent generations tended to be less melanotic (Post et. al., 1975). Clearly this research unveils issues of war specific weaponry, the practical issue of why Blacks are cold when whites appear comfortable, besides having implications for the origins question.

Research in the area of perceptual and motor skills proclivity in the context of child development (Rich 1973) and sports (*Time* 1977) are also being scrutinized by this new eugenics movement. If anyone doubts the thoroughness of this research direction, then perhaps Pawson and Petrakis' research on "Comparison of Breast Pigmentation Among Women of Different Racial Groups" will jog the non-believer into the reality of the unremitting subjection of the race question to "scientific methods" towards "scientific ends."

The sociobiology/eugenics movement demands the immediate attention of African scholars if the race is to survive and liberate itself. Cloning and experiments with artificial replication of "human life" is a reality; the identification of criminal chromosomes, XYY, wherein a disproportionate number of the incarcerated population is Black is a reality; at least 46 states have a genetic screening program, most of them mandatory, where hospitals automatically test newborns for genetic defects. All of the foregoing are in the control of a people and civilization which have consistently proven to have alien and detrimental designs for African life.

In conclusion, this literature review clearly reveals that he theories and policies of the past centuries of scientific racism will be considered benign in comparison to the potential devastation of African people and lands by this subtle and calculating new race science. Unless African people develop a counterstrategy for race defense, this science has potential to either fully control or exterminate African people.

We can say that race and racial typologies and racism have been propelled into more sophisticated contexts for scientific examination both bio-chemical and bio-sociological. It should be noted that there are European and Euro-American scholars who have examined the new eugenics/bio-technological movement with alarm and have called for greater caution and control of this Western scientific explosion, noting that: 1) it has potential to destroy democracy and freedom for all humanity; 2) it predisposes humankind to and makes viable a "race bomb" which could be forged in a number of ways by a few technocrats committed to racial politics; and, 3) it is retrogressive and turns away from the "understandings" and "manifestos" of the post World War II notions of human equality.

Eighteen years after the South African Institute meeting and ⋅ fifteen years since Escott Reid's observation, Western demographers are assessing and impacting public policy by examining issues of racial/cultural changes and trends which have economic and geo-political implications. A major issue which has emerged from this research is the concern for the consequences of the "birth dearth." A specific response to the changing reality is the European Economic Community's confederation into the "United States of Europe," to be effected in 1992.

Ben Wattenberg, an internationally recognized demographer, has advanced serious concerns and possible solutions to avoiding certain racial/cultural/geo-political consequences in this global bio-technological era. Specifically, he concludes that the Western industrialized nations, in general, and the United States in particular (which coincidentally happens to be, more than not, rich and white), are experiencing a critical birth dearth. This fact is in contrast to the third world or poor Americans (who coincidentally happen to be, more often than not, colored and non-Western) who are experiencing a too slow retardation of high fertility rates. According to Wattenberg, in 1950, the Western communities represented 22%-25% of the world's population; by 2010, they are projected to be at 13% and, 100 years from now, they will represent approximately 5% of the world's population (Wattenberg, B., 1987, p.81). He points out that:

> Less than 20% of legal immigrants to America today are of white European stock... and today 80% of the current total U.S. population is of Western European stock... and demographers have projected that one century from now the Western European share of the U.S. population will be down to 60% and still shrinking. (pp. 112-113)

Wattenberg argues that:

what happens in an America, with birth dearth conditions, under... current immigration rates, or higher ones... will yield some unnecessary social turbulence. And it won't be the fault of the immigrants, Hispanics, Blacks, Asian or Moslem Americans... what's coming down the road at us demographically is asking for some extra trouble and it is self-inflicted. (p. 114)

He concludes by stating:

Pride and fear... should be present in our own demographic equation.... Our central problem is in the realm of spirit.... Suppose we could re-enspirit this generation to understand and take pride in the fact that they are a part of a remarkable, potent, productive, humane, beneficent culture. Suppose our young people in America and the other Western nations came to know in the marrow of their bones that the West is the last best hope of mankind... that only they can preserve it and there is something real to fear if they don't.... After all, it's not such a big deal: all it involves is having another baby. (168-69)[2]

Wattenberg recommends consideration of many pro-family public policy options, e.g., the United States to convene an international meeting of free Western nations facing birth dearth situations; foundation/corporate/educational leaders publicly call for reduced fertility rates in the non-white world and increased fertility rates in the West out of self-interest and without fear of being called racist or colonial; incentives for changing individual women's decisions to abort with appropriate incentives for others to adopt; college grads could have loans upon birth of children; establishment of a progressive child allowance system, rewarding those with the most children; establishment of a trust/bonus of $2000/year for each new baby. (Note that one female reporter's response is that Wattenberg wants white women to carry the burdens of the world.)

In fact, African people have moved beyond the culture of poverty and the IQ debate and are questioning the guises of "equality of opportunity" and "development" schemes for continental and other African societies world over. It should be noted that there is significant, *though clearly insufficient*, effort by Black scholars to undertake basic research in sociobiology. Special attention seems to be focused on the role of melanin in DNA formation and its relationship to neuro-psychological functioning. Additionally, there is probably even more such involvement in research related to ethnic disease etiology. The research collaboration of these scholars must significantly contribute to the development of an Afrocentric, proactive and distinct approach to racism and race theory.

When one looks at Western race theory and policy (racism) historically, one cannot but conclude that the results are always injurious to the interest of African people the world over. Perhaps this is true because we have not developed a race theory of our own, but have, primarily, reacted to racism and European theories of race. And so the greatest challenge for African peoples at this time is to articulate such a theory and implement a proactive plan of action. I assert that the most immediate need is for Blacks to look beyond racism and examine "usism," because in many cases our own worst enemy is ourselves. Professor Rex Nettleford cautions us that "herein lies the greatest danger of attempts at finding an identity in terms of race. For a people who do not believe in themselves cannot hope to have others believing in them" (Nettleford, 1972, 33).

We can further refer to Frantz Fanon's notion of the collective unconscious as a result of the imposition of culture, i.e. Euro-Western culture:

In other words, the Black man should no longer be confronted by the dilemma, *turn white or disappear*; but he should be able to take cognizance of a possibility of existence. In still other words, if society makes difficulties for him because of his color, if in his dreams I establish the expression of an unconscious desire to change color, my objective will not be that of dissuading him from it by advising him to "keep his place"; on the contrary, my objective, once his motivations have been brought into consciousness, will be to put him in a position to *choose* action (or passivity) with respect to the real source of the conflict—that is, toward the social structures. (Fanon, 1967, 100)

We are in a war of competing paradigms, concepts, ideas and worldviews from which ultimately all policies and institutions flow, i.e., the social structures to which Fanon refers. These are the *a priori* assumptions which go unquestioned as we move from day to day and answer the more universal questions of our collective and individual development and reality. We no longer need European intellectuals and elites to articulate agendas for racism, for we now have our own who 1) take the elitist capitalist position and "empirically" prove the declining significance and or irrelevancy of race and argue that socioeconomic gaps between Blacks and whites are mostly a figment of our imagination and, in point of fact, are a function of classism not racism; and 2) who espouse the primacy of patriarchy and monopoly capitalism as the casual factors of African American oppression.

I am certainly not saying that classism or sexism are illegitimate issues for our collective agenda; indeed, they must be addressed and understood within the context of racism, not to the exclusion of racism. And as we turn to the implications of this heuristic discussion for building a theory of race, there are some beginning points around which further debate, synthesis and consensus can occur from an Afrocentric perspective.

Sizemore's view of the role of scientists is instructive:

In spite of arguments to the contrary, most scientists are motivated by certain cause-belief ideas stated as assumptions which determine what phenomena they will study, what hypotheses they will test, and what method-ologies they will use. In this sense, every scientist is a victim or benefactor of his/her own values, norms, standards, rules, regulations and laws. The culture, defined as the sum total of artifacts generated by the person's (or group's) struggle for survival, which means the socio-economic-political ability to preserve one's body (mental, physical, and spiritual health), to reproduce that body, and to take care of the progeny, confines the investigator or scientist. (Sizemore, 1985, 269)

Chancellor Williams refutes the notion that race redemption can occur outside the definition of race; thus, individual Africans must submit to the goal of collective liberation or perish as fools.

As one continues to move on down through the centuries, countless events and situations may continue to make supporting additions to what has already been established as an unassailable fact. Yet that truth may be so repugnant, so utterly void of any rational or intelligent reason for its existence, that hardly any historian would wish to state it in his work....Yet I did just that when I wrote that the whites are the implacable foe, the traditional and everlasting enemy of the Blacks....The necessary re-education of Blacks and a possible solution of racial crisis can begin, strangely enough, only when Blacks fully realize this central fact in their lives; *The White man is their Bitter Enemy.* For this is not the ranting of wild-eyed militancy, but the calm and unmistakable verdict of several thousand years of documented history... for the Black people of the world have come at last to destiny's crossroads...[Blacks] must make some fundamental deci-sions as a *single people* [and] realize that they are one people with a common destiny and that no matter how scattered over the world, the treatment suffered by one Black group is suffered by all. (Williams, 1974, 329, 334)

Cheikh Anta Diop's research concluded:

We know that mankind originated in Africa and that this mankind was deeply pigmented or black-skinned. No serious scientist would contest that today. It would seem that among those Upper Paleolithic Black populations which had ventured far north towards the Baltic Sea during the warm period, definite biological changes took place leading to the appearance of Alpine and Nordic white types. At any rate, as far as science knows today, before 20,000 B.C. there were no whites in existence. Yellows appeared even later around 10,000-15,000 B.C. Today, science can rely on irrefutable material evidence to illustrate these facts...There is absolutely no doubt that the white race which appeared was the product of a process of depigmentation. (Diop, 1976, 32-33)

Diop's research raises the question as to what extent do these assertions of biological and social history of the European's origin vs. the African's origin affect the present biological and social reality of the European and African worlds today? Diop asserts that there is insufficient evidence to account for the historical behavioral differences and traits of European and Africans as biologically induced. Thus, his two cradle theory identifies European social consciousness and racism as resulting from culturally and/or environmentally induced and reinforced traits which are bound by the concept of European cultural xenophobia (fear of strangers). This cultural xenophobia is distinguishable from the basic precepts of African social consciousness and cultural xenophilia (love of strangers). Diop thus presumes an evolutionary-monogenetic theory of the white man's development vis-à-vis that of the Black man.

Now we can categorically affirm that white Europeans originated in Europe itself and that their origin can be found nowhere else than in Black populations which migrated from Africa into Europe tens of thousands of years ago. As to exactly how a white race developed out of these Black European populations is still scientifically obscure, but there is no doubt that such was the case. (Diop, 1976, 3)

The authors of *Voodoo and IQ* assert the biological priority of the African from the archeological evidences and the biological impossibility of producing offspring of color from whites. The relationship of melanin to the functioning of the central nervous system is addressed as essential to the understanding of African psychology. "Melanin refines the central nervous system and, in so doing, produces a highly sensitized sensory motor network... we are convinced that the absence of melanin is directly associated with the malfunctioning of the central nervous system" (Clark, et al. 1976, 8). The authors point out that Parkinson's disease and PKU disease, most unique to whites, are physiological results of dysfunction associated with melanin. Further, melanin is associated with emotional arousal and thus

...we believe, in short, that non-whites are indeed "more emotional" than whites, and not only is this positive... it is directly related to that phenomena we call intelligence....Sensitivity and consciousness underscores the fact that African Psychology adopts a different philosophical base than Euro-American Psychology. (Clark, 1976, 10)

The research of Archie Hearne, Richard King and Marsella Stewart examines melanin and the bodily functions or dysfunctions which are associated with it. Hearne calls for the

creation or discovery of methods by which we can better assay the imperative conditions for Black people in this rapidly changing and highly technological society.... Dr. Wasserman, a white South African, is hotly on the trail of investigation and dictating research methodology related to skin pigmentation, behavior and Black people.... [I]t is now most important that we research the subject instead of our white counterparts (Hearne, 1978).

He further asserts that melanin must have predated DNA and served as a protection from radiation. All of these researchers underscore the point that melaninization as a physiological process is manifested both in biological and social behaviors.

Bobby Wright provides an additional construct around which to examine our own responses to racism. Wright asserts:

> ... that in their relationships with Blacks, whites exhibit the behavior of psychopaths and their behavior reflects an underlying biologically transmitted proclivity that is deep rooted in their evolutionary history. Menticide is the ultimate goal of that behavior... the deliberate and systematic destruction of a person's or group's mind... In order to fully understand the menticidal process, it is essential than an analysis be done of the personality of its creators and purveyors, namely the white race. (Wright, 1978, 5)

In affirming and identifying both the roots and transcendent nature of Euro-supremist notions in theories of western capitalism, socialism and communism, Carlos Moore concludes by posing a significant question which too often has divided our collective interests.

> Can an ideology that incorporates subtle philosophical-racist principles serve as a tool or weapon against racism? Marx's and Engels' political judgments, theoretical conclusions and philosophical analyses on the most wide-ranging questions were naturally conditioned by their being Westerners, not Africans or Asians; whites, not Blacks or Yellows; free men of the 19th Century, not chattel slaves or colonial subjects. It is thus clear that their political, ideological, cultural and historical evaluation of non-European mankind must be categorically challenged. We must also challenge the "universalist" pretensions of certain "general laws" emerging from a strictly Aryan socioeconomic and cultural mold. (Moore, 1972, 42)

Wade Nobles provides some insight into the nature of an African worldview which must be holistic as validated by African culture and tradition:

> Culture is in fact the basis of consciousness... and culture becomes the necessary and sufficient condition for understanding the natural human processes of a people.... Cultural substance is the essence or essential nature or ingredient of the culture....By substance we mean the material base or essential character of culture...the essential ingredient would be *melanin*. When melanin converts via the essential melanic system (EMS) into consciousness (mind), one is able to identify the unique way in which Africans respond to their reality...science and scientific techniques, as tools for struggle, must by definition be reconstructions of the African cultural substance (melanin), culture, and common sense. To fall short of this is to substitute or adopt another manifestation of oppression (another paradigm or theory) and perceive it as liberation. Science will only become a tool for struggle when it serves as the sustaining psychological offense allowing ones to control the nature and definition of the process of history (i.e., secure our capacity to act or react in relation to our material and spiritual conditions). (Nobles, 1977, 27)

The relationship between color and consciousness as viewed by Africans and those of African descent raise other important questions of intra-racial analyses. Shawna Maglangbayan asks:

> Does this mean that the only traitors in the Black race are those with light skins? Far from it. The traitors from within the race are of all skin colors. The difference between the dark skinned and light skinned traitor, is that, in general, the latter uses his lighter pigmentation to assert himself in a racist fashion as "superior" to all those of darker complexion. (Maglangbayan, 1972, 34)

Chancellor Williams instructs us to seek explication of this issue of Africanity as specifically related to our mothers who were so often raped. "We should begin by drawing a vast African circle of honor around all those millions of Africans of mixed blood... who have stood steadfast and loyally identified with the race of their originally Black mothers" (Williams, 1974, 355).

Today, therefore, the realization of our Africanity, and the mulatto question is no longer a significant question of African color, but one of African consciousness. We must create an African worldview, principles of organizing the world around our tradition and interests, from which will emanate all our social and institutional development.

Political and diplomatic expediencies aside, at this very moment, the African world must sense the humanism of the South African spirit in the face of Aryan domination and supremacy (as reflected by the masses, in the living dead, and in the words and deeds of the Mandelas, Tutus and other leaders). And so the reconciliation of the contradiction and/or salvation of African humanity for humankind is yet another question which we must answer, and I suspect, answer as we live it. As John H. Clarke suggests "we have always just invited our future conquerors to dinner."

> I'm saying we people really need to take a good look at ourselves and we need to begin to exercise the essential selfishness of survival. I'm saying that our first *allegiance*is going to have to be our Blackness or *our Africanity*. We will have to ask questions and make alliances that are based on our self-interest. If it is not to our self-interest, to hell with it, no matter how good it sounds....We have to stop talking about multi-racialism. People in power do not talk about multi-racialism. They talk about their laws, and either you obey them or you get out....Because we're so non-racial, because we're so tolerant, because we're so kind, we do not produce the kind of safeguards to protect ourselves....I'm saying that *only* out of your nationalism and your Africanity can this happen. (Clarke, 1970, 30-31)

At this point one must reiterate the research entrapments posed in the first part of the paper by recognizing the process by which validation of reality occurs. Language itself becomes an issue as we are tempted to organize our ideas around Euro-centric conceptualizations of evolution, race, culture, monogenesis, poly-genesis, environmental determinism, genetic determinism, etc. Consistent with this methodology are presumptions of compart-mentalization, scientific finality and mutual exclusivity. Secondly, one must recognize that social theory is a mere expression of the consciousness and reality which emerges from a people and can be no more or no less independent of human socio-political expression than can humankind itself, i.e. social theory substan-tiates and perpetuates our being, and good social theory is what we need to that end.

Thus, Africans at the crossroad must address these issues from the vantage of race redemption. These beginnings, of course, raise other questions around which much deliberation must be given. Is "pre-man," "pre-history" or culture-without-civilization possible? Do the origins and primacy questions have to be wedded to evolution and mono-genesis? Does the concept of mutation deserve greater examination as a process of polymorphism and subsequent mutated groups who died out and the relationship to polygenesis? Given certain alternative explanations, what is the developmental life cycle of racial men? How much melanin is sufficient to validate the social definition of race for our purposes and what other traits are likewise relevant?

These times require that we acknowledge the fact that one of the greatest problems we face ourselves; and that we face up to our inability to embrace what we already know and to build upon what we already have and to incorporate in our lives that which gener-ations before us have passed on. The truth of the matter is that too many of us still believe deep down in the myth that we have made it on our own; that we owe no one anything, and that our only problem is "white folks" and "white institutions." Well, it is time to see the difference between those factors which cause racism and those factors which help to sustain it, for in some cases, it is "usism."

John Henrik Clark challenges us

from this (point) Black people must go to another stage, much higher and more meaningful for mankind. After reclaiming our own humanity, I think we will make a contribution toward the reclamation of the humanity of man. First, we will have to realize that in the kind of world we live in, being Black and beautiful means very little unless we are also Black and powerful. There is no way to succeed in the struggle against racism without power. That is a part of our new reality and our mission. (Clarke, 1970, 10)

The empowerment and protection of any interest group is the direct result of its active participation in the process of theory ideology development and policy formulation, resulting in planned change. The immediate demands of the 1980s and the long term requisites of the 21st century require proactive initiatives through the development of thinktanks and advocacy groups and activists. Such groups must take responsibility for concretizing theory and knowledge into viable, relevant and measurable goals and objectives for our communities/countries and to plan and direct change in concert with all sectors of our community/country both of which are labeled as less developed countries by the European white world; least developed countries of Africa and the Caribbean or least developed cities or communities of Black America. The day is gone for the lone scholar, activist, theorist, community organizer, businessperson and political leader. What we need is the coming together of interdisciplinary teams of trained professionals and lobbyists, capital formation through syndication, and leaders who will take the ball from the charismatic leaders and develop institutions which serve the interest of our people, based on our history, tradition and needs. We need community development plans which are proactive and initiated through our self-defined interests and which are based on information and knowledge (e.g. elevator repairers, computer analyzers, genetic engineers, oceanographers, gerontologists, pregnancy and nutrition experts, and food cooperatives). Our criteria for evaluation should include how it serves our collective and shared interests.

And this brings me to my final point: To effect Black unity and empowerment in the 21st century, we must strengthen existing institutions and create new ones which truly meet the needs of our people. I am afraid that these institutions will require of us a new leadership and a new leadership agenda, the foundation of which is a new value system which fosters unity without uniformity and a mind set from which planned strategies and action emerge. What we need is mutual respect, trust and reciprocity—quite basic. Our leadership must emerge and be solidified from the bottom up, not from the top down. The real measure of institutional leadership and strength is the ability of a system to function and put forth its values and mission, independent of personalities. To be sure, charismatic leadership may be necessary, but it is hardly sufficient. The charismatic leader without a partnership with real institutional development has reduced chances for serving interest if for no other reason than the nature of the global, high-technological society in which we live, where there is increased competition for resources.

Dare to do the near impossible—envision a world without racism and ask whether, how and when life would change for people of African ancestry.

This is a perfect ending for beginning a more situational examination of our internal issues of classism, ethnicity, color and sexism, from the varied perspectives of Africans worldwide. For ultimately, only by maximizing our internal strengths and redressing our internal contradictions will we achieve full participation on the global stage of humanity during the next millennium.

NOTES

1. Some would argue that sociobiology is but a developmental phase, or natural extension of Western cultural orientation or worldview.

2. *From Racism to "Usism" A Changing Paradigm for a Black Theory of Race.*

BIBLIOGRAPHY

Barrat, John and Michael Louw, *International Aspects of Overpopulation*, New York: St. Martin, 1972.

Blum, Harold, "Does the Melanin of Human Skin Have Adaptive Value?" *Quarterly Review of Biology*, V. 35, 1961.

Cerami, Anthony and Charles Peterson, "Cyanate and Sickle Cell Disease," *Scientific America*, April, 1975.

Clark, Cedric, Phillip Mcgee, Wade Nobles, Na'im Akbar, "Voodoo or IQ: Introduction to African Psychology," *Black Pages*, Institute of Positive Education, 1976.

Clarke, John H., "Black-White Alliances," *Afrocentric World Review*, V. 1, #2, Spring, 1974.

Clarke, John H., "The Growth of Racism in the West," *Black World*, October, 1970.

Diop, Cheikh A., "An Interview," *Black Books Bulletin*, V. 4, #4, 1976.

Ebony Magazine, "Can Blackness Prolong Life" Chicago: Johnson Publishing, June, 1977.

Fanon, Fantz, *Black Skins, White Masks*, New York: Grove Press, 1967.

Hearne, Archie, "Dyskinesia-Schizophrenia-Melanin Triad," 1978.

King, Richard, *Melanin Selected Annotated References*, Los Angeles: Fanon Research and Development Center, 1979.

King, Richard D., "The Self and Creativity: The Synthesis of Opposites," December, 1977.

Kretchmer, Norman, "Lactase or Lactose," *Scientific America*, October, 1972.

Larson, Carl A., "Ethnic Weapons," *Military Journal*, November, 1970.

Loomis, W. Farnsworth, "Skin-Pigment Regulation of Vitamin D Biosynthesis in Man," *Science*, V. 157, August, 1967.

McCracken, Robert, "Lactase Deficiency: An Example of Dietary Evolution," *Current Anthropology*, October-December, 1971.

Magangbayan, Shawna, *Garvey, Lumumba and Malcolm: Black Nationalist Separatists*, Chicago: Third World Press, 1972.

Moore, Carlos, *Were Marx and Engels White Racists? The Prolet-Aryan Outlook of Marx and Engels*, Chicago: Institute of Positive Education, 1972.

Nettleford, Rex, *Identity, Race and Protest in Jamaica*, New York: William Morrow and Co., 1972.

Nobles, Wade, "African Consciousness and Liberation Struggles: Implications for the Development and Construction of Scientific Paradigms," Institute for the Advanced Study of Black Family Life and Culture, Oakland, California: 1977.

Pawson, I.G. and N.L. Petrakis, "Comparisons of Breast Pigmentation Among Women of Different Racial Groups." *Human Biology*, December, 1975.

Ponte, Lowell, *Cooling Off*, New Jersey: Prentice Hall, 1976.

Post, Peter, Farrington Daniels, Robert Binford, "Cold Injury and the Evolution of White Skin," Human Biology, February, 1975.

Quevedo, W.C., T.B. Fitzpatrick, M.A. Pathak, K. Jimbow, "Role of Light in Human Skin Color Variation," *American Journal of Physical Anthropology*, V. 43, November, 1975.

Reid, Escott, *Strengthening the World Bank*, Chicago: Adlai Stevenson Institute, 1973.

Rich, Cynthia Jo, "Difference at Birth," *Race Relations Reporter*, September, 1973.

Sizemore, Barbara, "Pitfalls and Promises of Effective Schools Research," *Journal of Negro Education*, V. 54, #3, 1985.

Steward, Marsella, *Melanin and Sensori-Motor Development in the Afrikan Child: An Alternative View of the Developmental Style of the Afrikan Infant*, Nashville: Vanderbilt University, Department of Psychology (Major Area Paper), 1981.

Time Magazine, "Black Dominance," V. 109, May, 1977.

Wattenberg, Ben J., *The Birth Dearth*, New York: Pharos Books, 1987.

Welsing, Frances Cress, "The Cress Theory of Color Confrontation," Washington, D.C., 1970.

Williams, Chancellor, *Destruction of Black Civilization*, Chicago: Third World Press, 1974.

Williams, Richard, ed., *Textbook of Black Related Diseases*, New York: McGraw-Hill, 1975.

Wilson, Edward, *Sociobiology: The New Synthesis*, Cambridge, Massachusetts: Belknap Press of Harvard University Press, 1975.

Wilson, William Julius, *Declining Significance of Race*, Chicago: University of Chicago, 1978.

Wright, Bobby, "Menticide: Ultimate Threat to the Black Race," New Orleans: Southern University Press, 1978.

Wurtman, Richard, "The Effects of Light on the Human Body," *Scientific America*, July, 1975.

GLOBAL AFRICA IN FLUX: THE DIALECTIC OF DIVERSITY IN THE BLACK WORLD

ALI A. MAZRUI

In the heat of the debate about multiculturalism and diversity in the wider American society, one thing may so easily be overlooked — the increasing diversity within the African American community itself. Never has the Black population in the United States been as diverse as it is today. The richness lies in a wider range of sub-ethnicity, a wider range of religious affiliation, a wider spectrum of ideology, and a more complex class structure.

If Global Africa means people of African ancestry all over the world, the Black population of the United States is a microcosm of Global Africa. Today this Black population includes people from literally every Black country in the world—from every member of the Organization of African Unity, every member of the Organization of American States, and from other parts of the Black world as well. If there is indeed a microcosm of Global Africa, it is to be found within the shores of the United Sates of America—from Hutus to Haitians, from Baganda to Barbadians, from natives of Afro-Muscat to *desidens* of Afro-Mississippi. Black America is Global Africa in microcosm. The Black experience has a new dialectic of diversity.

In some cases there is a transition from the concept of "Africans in America" to the succeeding generation of "African Americans". Thus, while Ali Mazrui is still an "African in America," his children are already African Americans or are in the process of becoming so.

The geographic origins of the Black population in the United States have been diversified as a result of a number of factors. First, the immigration policies of the United States have been liberalized in the second half of the 20th century as compared with the first half—thus admitting more Black immigrants. Secondly, the racial situation within the United States has been desegregated enough to make the country more attractive to middle class Blacks from other lands. Thirdly, post-colonial problems in Africa and the Caribbean have created a brain drain to the Northern hemisphere, including the United States. Haiti has experienced the exodus not just of the intelligentsia but also of members of the poorest sectors of society (the Haitian boat people). For a while the problem of apartheid in South Africa also created a brain drain of refugees to Europe and North America. While many of these South Africans are now returning home, or planning to do so, a large proportion have become Americans and will remain in the United States.

Partly because of the stimulus of new immigrants, and partly for other reasons, the religious landscape of Black America has also become more diverse. Haitians have not only strengthened Catholicism; some of them have also arrived with residual "voodoo" culture of their own. More ancestral traditional religions directly from Africa have become more legitimate in some African American circles. Yoruba religious culture has been particularly influential.

Within the Protestant tradition there is also more diversity now in Black America than there was in the first half of the 20th century. Immigrants from Africa and the Caribbean have enriched Protestant diversity in the country, ranging from Anglicans from Nigeria to followers of Simon Kimbangu from Zaire. In addition, African versions of the Eastern Orthodox tradition are now better represented in the United States. The Ethiopian Orthodox Church and the Coptic Church now have stronger leadership in the United States.

The Rastafari movement from the Caribbean has also been part of the American scene in the second half of the 20th century. It is as much a cultural phenomenon as it is a religious one.

Black Jews are an older phenomenon in the United States. Sometimes these are basically Old Testament Christians who have become more and more Abrahamic. African American Jews have sometimes had difficulty being recognized by Israel under the Law of Return. The Black Jews of Ethiopia (the so-called Falasha) were also slow in gaining full recognition in Israel, but most of the Ethiopian Jews were at last moved to Israel in the 1980s under Operation Moses and subsequent transfers. A few Ethiopian Jews have migrated to the United States and become Americans.

Islam has wider pan-African implications. There are now virtually as many Muslims as Jews in the United States—but the Muslims are of course much less visible and much less influential than are the mainstream U.S. Jews. Islam provides some direct African American linkages with both Africa and the Middle East. But there are also areas of contrast between African Americans and West Indians in relation to both Islam and indigenous African religion. Let us look at the sociology of religion in the African Diaspora more closely.

BLACK RELIGIOUS ALTERNATIVES

Among Diaspora Africans of the Western hemisphere there are two routes toward re-Africanization. One route is through Pan-Islam, the transition chosen by Elijah Muhammed and Malcolm X. The other is the route directly through Pan-Africanism, the transition chosen by Marcus Garvey and the Rastafari Movement. Ras (Prince) Tafari were the title and name of Haile Selassie before his coronation as Emperor of Ethiopia.

One question which arises is why Islam has made much more progress among North American Blacks than among Blacks in the West Indies. The second question is why African traditional religion, or beliefs rooted in sacred Africanity, sometimes appear to be more visible in the Caribbean than among Africans of North America.

One major variable was the tendency of African Americans to equate Brown with Black. No sharp distinction was made in the Black American paradigm between Brown Arabs and Black Africans. Indeed, until the second half of the 20th century, almost all "colored people" in North America—whether they came from Africa or Asia or elsewhere—were treated with comparable contempt. When someone like W.E.B. DuBois argued that it was not Blacks who were a "minority" but whites, he had added up the teeming millions of Asia with the millions of Africans to give the colored races a massive majority in the *global* population.

If the transition from Brown Asian to Black African was so smooth in the Black American paradigm, the transition from Africanity to Arabness continues to be even easier. Of all the religions associated with Asia, the one which is the most *Afro-Asian* is indeed Islam. The oldest surviving Islamic academics are actually located in the African continent—including Al-Azhar University in Cairo. The Muslim Academy of Timbuktoo in what is today Mali is remembered by Pan-Africanists with pride.

In Nigeria there are more Muslims than there are Muslims in any Arab country—including the largest Arab country in population, Egypt. On the other hand, there are more Arabs in Africa as a whole than in Asia. Indeed, two thirds of the Arab world lies in the African continent.

Given then the tendency of the Black American paradigm to draw no sharp distinction between being Black and being "colored," Islam's Africanness was not too diluted by its Arab origins. Elijah Muhammed, Malcolm X and Louis Farakhan have sometimes equated Islamization with Africanization. North American Black Muslims have seen Mecca as a port of call on the way back to the African heritage, as well as a stage on the way back towards God.

Islam in the Caribbean, on the other hand, has been handicapped by two factors. Firstly, race consciousness in the Caribbean does not as readily equate Black with Brown as it has historically done in the United States. The Caribbean historical experience was based on a racial hierarchy (different shades of stratification) rather than racial dichotomy (a polarized divide between white and "colored"). Arabs in the Caribbean racial paradigm therefore belonged to a different pecking order from Africans. Indeed, Lebanese and Syrians were more likely to be counted as white rather than Black. Because of that, the Arab origins of Islam were bound to be seen as being in conflict with Islam's African credentials.

Moreover, the Caribbean has a highly visible East Indian population, a large proportion of whom are Muslims. When I gave a lecture in Georgetown, Guyana, in 1988, on the subject of "Islam in Africa," the overwhelming majority of my audience were not Afro-Guyanese (eager to learn more about Africa) but Indo-Guyanese (eager to learn more about Islam). In the Black population in Guyana and Trinidad, there is a tendency to see Islam neither as *African* nor as *Arab* but as *Indian*. The result is a much slower pace of Islamic conversions among Caribbean Africans than among African-Americans. Caribbean Blacks are unlikely to see the Muslim holy city of Mecca as a spiritual port of call on the way back to the cultural womb of Africa. On the contrary, Mecca is more likely to be perceived as a stage of cultural refuelling on the way to the Indian subcontinent.

In contrast, indigenous African religiosity has often prospered better in the Caribbean than in Black America. Why? One reason is that cultural nationalism in Black America is rooted in *romantic gloriana* rather than *romantic primitivism*. Gloriana takes pride in the complex civilizations of ancient Africa; primitivism takes pride in the simplicity of rural African village life. In the words of Aimé Césaire, the Caribbean romantic primitivist who coined the word *negritude*:

Hooray for those who have invented neither
powder nor the compass,
Those who have tamed neither gas nor electricity,
Those who have explored neither the seas nor the skies...

My negritude [my Blackness] is neither a tower nor a
cathedral;
It plunges into the red flesh of the soil.

While this idealization of simplicity can capture the Caribbean
mind, it seldom inspires the imagination of the African American.
The dominant North American culture is based on the premise of
"bigger, better and more beautified." Black rebellion against
Anglo-racism therefore seeks to prove that Africa has produced
civilizations in the past which were as "big and beautified" as
anything constructed by the white man.

In this cultural atmosphere of gloriana, African indigenous
religion appears capable of being mistaken for "primitivism."
Indigenous African rituals appear rural and village-derived. While
Yoruba religion does have an impressive following in parts of the
United States, and its rituals are often rigorously observed, the
general predisposition of the Afro-American paradigm of nationalism is afraid of appearing to be "primitive."

The Islamic option is regarded by African Americans as a
worthier rival to the Christianity of the white man. Parts of the
Qur'an seem to be an improvement upon the white man's Old
Testament. The Islamic civilization once exercised dominion and
power over European populations. Historically Islamic culture
refined what we now call "Arabic numerals," invented algebra,
developed the zero, pushed forward the frontiers of science, and
built legendary constructions from Al-Hambra in Spain to the Taj
Mahal in India. Black America's paradigm of romantic gloriana is
more comfortable with such a record of achievement than with the
more subtle dignity of Yoruba, Igbo or Kikuyu traditional religion.

There is a related difference to bear in mind. Cultural nationalism in Black America often looks to ancient Egypt for inspiration—perceiving pharaonic Egypt as a *Black* civilization. Caribbean Black nationalism has shown a tendency to look to Ethiopia.
The Egyptian route to Black cultural validation again emphasizes
complexity and gloriana. On the other hand, the Ethiopian route to
Black cultural validation can be Biblical and austere.

The most influential Ethiopic movement in the African Diaspora has become the Rastafari movement, with its Jamaican roots. Named after Haile Selassie's older titled designation, the Jamaican movement evolved a distinctive way of life, often austere. Curiously enough, the movement's original deification of the Emperor of Ethiopia was more Egyptian than Abyssinian. The fusion of Emperor with God-head was almost pharaonic. The ancient Kings of Egypt built the pyramids as alternative abodes. The divine monarchs did not really die when they ceased to breathe; they had merely moved to a new address. To die was, in fact, to change one's address and modify one's lifestyle. In this sense the original theology of the Rastafari movement was a fusion of Egyptianism and pre-Biblical Ethiopianism. The resulting lifestyle of the Rastas, on the other hand, has been closer to romantic simplicity than to romantic gloriana. In North America the Rasta style is still more likely to appeal to people of Caribbean origin than to long-standing African Americans with their grander paradigm of cultural pride.

Pan-Africanism and Pan-Islamism are still two alternative routes towards the African heritage. After all, Islam first arrived in the Americas in chains for it was brought to the Western hemisphere by West African slaves. If Alex Haley is correct about his African ancestor, Kunta Kinte was a Muslim. So Haley assures us in *Roots*. In reality the Haley family under slavery was better able to preserve its African pride than to protect its Islamic identity. Slavery damaged both the legacy of African culture and the legacy of Islam among the imported Black captives. But for quite a while Islam in the Diaspora was destroyed more completely than was Africanity.

But now Islamization and Africanization in North America are perceived as alternative routes to the cultural bosom of the ancestral continent. It remains to be seen whether the 21st century will see a similar equilibrium in the Caribbean as the search continues for more authentic cultural paradigms to sustain the African Diaspora of tomorrow.

BLACK IDEOLOGICAL ALTERNATIVES

Some ideologies are more secular than others. While religious diversity in the Black world has undoubtedly increased, has ideological diversity shrunk? Has the collapse of communism in the Soviet Union and Eastern Europe weakened the Black Left all over the world? Is socialism in serious danger of extinction in Africa? Is it already extinct in the Caribbean (outside Cuba) and in Black America?

There is little doubt that left wing movements all over the Black world have suffered a severe setback as a result of events in Eastern Europe and the apparent triumph of capitalism in the cold war with communism. But in Africa socialism is not dead. Indeed, its strongest hold may turn out to be South Africa under majority rule. It is unlikely that Marxists will be ruling South Africa after apartheid, but a strong socialist party in opposition is almost definitely on the horizon in the new South Africa.

In Black America the end of the cold war may *help* socialism rather than hinder it. For as long as the old Soviet Union was the enemy of the United States, to be a socialist in the United States came close to being "unpatriotic." There was a time when to be a Marxist like Paul Robeson was almost a form of "treason." Socialist thought in the United States, did not enjoy the degree of legitimacy it had in Britain, France, Italy or other Western European countries. Many Europeans have combined a commitment to socialism with a commitment to representative government and political pluralism. In the United States, on the other hand, socialism was not only a negation of capitalism. It was also regarded as a negation of democracy and of patriotism.

Now that the Soviet Union is dead, and international communism is no longer a military threat to the United States, the atmosphere for socialism may begin to improve fairly soon. It is almost certain that socialist thought of some kind (even if not communism) will begin to acquire a degree of legitimacy in American society. And more African Americans may be attracted towards it as disenchantment with the existing social and racial order in the United States persists relentlessly. There will almost certainly be many more ideological "Paul Robesons" in the America of tomorrow, an America more ideologically tolerant than it was during the days of the first Paul Robeson.

Paradoxically, on the other hand, *right wing* thought among African Americans is already becoming more legitimate. All the signs are that the Republican Party will increase its share of middle class Black voters. If both Judge Clarence Thomas and Professor Anita Hill were Republicans, they were part of a changing ideological configuration in the country. In the future the white Democrats will stop thinking that African American voters have nowhere to go but into the fold of the Democratic Party. And the white Republicans may try harder to win over Black voters through suitable policy adjustments. When Black electoral behavior becomes as *variable*, as Jewish electoral behavior, both major parties in the United States would stop taking the Black vote for granted.

In Africa ideological diversification has taken the form of pro-democracy movements from Angola to Algeria, from Zambia to Ghana, from Dakar to Dar es Salaam. Almost everywhere in Africa there are demands for a more pluralistic constitutional order. A liberal revival is clearly under way. In a country like Zambia and Tanzania the shift is from left to center. In countries like Kenya and Malawi the shift is likely to be from right to center. In Nigeria the transition is to be from military rule to a civilian two-party system. In Algeria the transition may one day be from a secular political order to a greater fusion between church and state (or, more appropriately, a fusion between mosque and state).

In secular politics in most of Africa, it has been the ideological *middle* which has been holding. The main beneficiaries of the pro-democracy and pro-pluralism movements in Africa have been center parties and tendencies almost everywhere. Center parties are of course different from *centralizing* parties. Parties of the center in Africa are opposed to a highly centralized economy and to excessive statism—but they still support a bigger role for the state than would be regarded as legitimate in the United States.

Ideology generally is inseparable from political culture. In the Caribbean that political culture has been a *trialectic* between American influence, the European imperial cultural legacy and the fundamental foundation of Caribbean culture itself. Americanization of Caribbean political culture has been increasing. The *British* legacy in English-speaking Caribbean is still strong, but declining in its hold. Caribbean proximity to Latin America has also had its impact on the sub-region's political culture.

The biggest foreign rivalry has not been between the old Soviets and the Americans, but between the Americans and the former European colonial powers in the Caribbean. The race has been between Americanization and residual Europeanization in the dynamics of Caribbean political enculturation. Can West Indian authenticity survive this cultural cold war between Western Europe and the United States?

A CULTURAL COLD WAR

Great Britain ruled parts of the Caribbean twice as long in duration as she ruled much of Africa. When the country of my birth, Kenya, became a British colony, Britain had already been ruling Jamaica for more than two centuries. Indeed, when Jomo Kenyatta was born in the 1890s Kenya was not yet a Crown colony. When Kenyatta died in 1978 Kenya had ceased to be a British colony. Kenyatta had lived right through the entire colonial period. He survived British rule by fifteen years, ruling Kenya himself as its first postcolonial president.

While British rule in Kenya was a matter of a single lifetime, British rule in Jamaica traversed the reigns of about ten British monarchs. By any measurement, therefore, Jamaica and much of the rest of the Commonwealth Caribbean are much more deeply Anglicized than almost any part of Commonwealth Africa.

The very success of cricket in the West Indies is itself a measure of comparative acculturation. In Africa cricket is a game still mainly of white and Indian immigrants. The only Black people who have been extensively converted to the culture of cricket are

West Indians. As C.L.R. James put it in his insightful book on cricket "Who should know of cricket who only cricket know?"

In spite of the deep Anglicization of the Commonwealth Caribbean, the question has lately arisen whether the Britannic factor in Caribbean culture is now declining. Is the deAnglicization of the Caribbean truly underway?

A number of factors may have contributed to such a process of de-Anglicization in the sense of declining *British* influence. One is the surprising phenomenon of Britain's cultural abdication. This is in sharp contrast to the missionary zeal of the French in the realm of culture. British commitment to cultural diplomacy is much weaker than that of France—both in Africa and the Caribbean. The United Kingdom spends the equivalent of only a fraction of the French budget for cultural diplomacy. The very success of the English language globally has reduced Britain's need to promote it in other lands. The fact that there is an English-speaking power mightier than Britain (the United States) has also helped to dwarf Britain's cultural role in promoting Anglo-Saxon culture.

The French language, on the other hand, is on the defensive against the devastating competition of Anglo- American cultural diffusion. Moreover, there is no French-speaking superpower the equivalent of the United States. France tries to play the cultural roles of both Britain and the United States fused into one.

But the United States is itself another reason why British influence in the Caribbean continues to decline. In the postcolonial era, the sheer proximity and size of the United States have been felt more directly than was possible under British imperial rule. American investment, American tourism, American television programs, American goods and services, and even Caribbean membership in the Organization of American States, have all played their part in tilting the balance towards Americanization in the Caribbean experience.

Then there is the phenomenon of American education as compared with British education. Here it is worth pursuing the comparison with Africa also more fully.

There was a time when Africans asked themselves whether being educated in the United States was a more radicalizing experience for a Black person than being educated in Great Britain. In the first half of the 20th century the evidence seemed to support that proposition. Kwame Nkrumah was mainly educated in the United States; his rival in Ghana, Kofi Busia, was educated in Great Britain. Nkrumah captured the torch of radical nationalism; and Busia moved further to the right.

In Nigeria the young Nnamdi Azikiwe (Zik) was the voice of nationalist militancy. He was American-educated. The leading British-educated Nigerians in the 1940s and even the 1950s were mainly to Zik's right in nationalist orientation.

If it was true that American education in the first half of the 20th century was a more radicalizing experience for Africans than was British education, what were the reasons at that time?

One factor in the first half of the century was that the United States was not only a much more racist society than Great Britain but American racism at the time was still highly institutionalized. African students in the United States were therefore more subject to humiliation and harassment than their counterparts in the United Kingdom. African students in American colleges were as a result more liable to get radicalized.

Also contributing to this radicalization was African inter-mingling with Black Americans and being exposed to a more intense pan-African experience. Indeed, African students in the first half of the 20th century were more likely to go to the historically Black colleges of America. Both Nkrumah and Azikiwe went to Lincoln University in Pennsylvania. At least for African students, being educated in Black colleges was often a politicizing experience. Kwame Nkrumah was later to declare that the most important ideological influences in his life were V.I. Lenin and Marcus Garvey—to both of whom he was first exposed during his years in the United States.

The comparative impact of American and British education on Caribbean Blacks, on the other hand, was often more complex than on Africans. This was partly because the more prolonged impact of British capitalism on Caribbean society had created an

indigenous Caribbean class structure which was more clearly strat-
ified than were classes in colonial Africa. Many of those Caribbean
Blacks who went to Britain for their education were from the more
privileged strata of society; many of those who went to the United
States were from the less advantaged ranks of Caribbean society.
Middle class Caribbean Blacks could go either way when highly
educated—they could move more decisively to the left (going even
Marxist) or become more eloquent defenders of the capitalist status
quo. Less privileged Caribbean Blacks educated in the United
States were more likely to go *nationalist* rather than
socialist—often emphasizing race rather than class, although their
own origins were often rooted in class disadvantages.

By the second half of the 20th century some of the most
eloquent voices of the socialist Left in the Commonwealth
Caribbean were British-educated. Even Eric Williams was initially
a product of British leftism. George Padmore flirted with communism and C.L.R. James was both highly anglicized and highly leftist
to the end of his days in England in 1989. He was in love with both
cricket and communism. Michael Manley (Phase I) and Trevor
Monroe are also products of the Neo-Fabian Legacy of London
and Oxbridge. Walter Rodney, the leftist martyr of Guyana, was
also British educated.

The greatest of the disadvantaged West Indians who became
nationalists (rather than socialists) was Marcus Garvey. His
primary theatre of action was of course the United States. A more
recent American-educated defender of the capitalist status quo was
of course Edward Seaga who served as Prime Minister. A younger
Jamaican product of American education, Rovan G. Locke,
combines hostility towards imperialism with ambivalence towards
capitalism. He is more nationalist than socialist.

One question which arises is whether the balance in influence
is shifting in the Caribbean in favor of the American-educated and
against the British-educated. At least in the sense that the proportion of Caribbean Blacks who have been American-educated has
grown, more positions in journalism, the bureaucracy, politics and
education are gradually occupied by the "Americanized" West
Indians. The statistics are shifting in favor of the American edu-

cated. But in reality they are only narrowing the gap between them and the more influential British-educated. The de-Anglicization of the Caribbean has not yet gone far enough to dethrone the Anglophiles in the Commonwealth Caribbean completely. After all, Manley is back in power—and Seaga is in the political wilderness in Jamaica.

For the products of the American experience it is too early for them to celebrate the following:

> The stream of experience meanders on
> In the vast expanse of Caribbean time.
> The new will come and the old be gone!
> Let's toast the fortunes of changing clime.[1]

The toast may be premature, but the de-Anglicization has truly started.

BLACK AMERICA: THE CULTURAL OPTIONS

As for the cultural options available to African Americans in the United States these are, in the final analysis, reducible to a range of three.

I. INTEGRATION: A fuller absorption into the mainstream of American society. This is what Dewayne Wickham has called "the litmus test of *inclusion*."
II. RE-AFRICANIZATION: A partial recovery of African culture and identity and a Pan-Africanization of perspective.
III. SEPARATISM: A sharper emphasis on the separateness of African-American identity and the pursuit of separatist economic and cultural policies. Opting out of the United States' electoral and political system could also be part of separatism.

The original impact of enslavement on American plantations was towards dis-Africanizing the identity of the slaves. The captives were called upon to forget that they were Africans. They were forced to renounce their African names, reject their African languages, and be ashamed of their African ancestry. On the other hand, the identity of the captives was also *racialized*. They were told that the most important thing about them was their race—which was in any case inferior. Their collective names became "Negroes" (or even "niggers")—a name based on the color of their skin. In short, the whole history of slavery and racism in the United States had one persistent refrain addressed to the captives:

> Forget where you came from
> > remember what you look like;
> Forget your ancestry,
> > remember your skin-color;
> Forget you are African,
> > remember you are black.
> Don't look at the map,
> > look at the mirror![2]

So successful was this policy that the collective name of the captives remained imprisoned within the pigmentational paradigm until 1988 when the Reverend Jesse Jackson Jr. recommended that we should switch at long last to the name "African Americans." Even the transition from the term "Negro" to the term "Black" had remained a prisoner of the pigmentational paradigm. Only when we switched to "African Americans" did we at last look at the map instead of the mirror.

Of course, we can never abandon the term "Black" completely for as long as the United States and much of the rest of the world remain racist and often anti-Black. This is one reason why the term "Black America" is still a meaningful intellectual and sociological currency. But from 1988 we look afresh at the imperative "Forget you are African, and remember you are Black." We decided to reject the first half about forgetting that we were Africans; but for the time being we still accept the second imperative about remembering that we are "Black."

Nevertheless, one can still be self-consciously African American and still opt for the strategy of fuller integration into mainstream United States, just as one can be self-consciously a Jewish American and still be part of the United States' political establishment.

The inclusive or integrationist school in "Black America" has indeed had a number of successes. African Americans have won elections as mayors of many major American cities, including at long last the city of New York. Douglas Wilder became the first Black governor of an American state, and quite surprisingly, Virginia. Clarence Thomas succeeded Thurgood Marshall as a Justice of the U.S. Supreme Court. Upward political mobility for Blacks has reached higher in the United States than in any other country where Blacks are a minority outside the Arab world. In the Arab world people with "Negro" blood like Anwar Sadat have risen as high as the presidency or its equivalent.

Upward *economic* mobility in "Black America" is less visible, but no less real. It is true that the Black underclass is, in size, as large as ever. In predicament it is *more* devastated than ever. We must now add AIDS and drugs to poverty and crime. On the other hand there is indeed an increase in African American millionaires and business tycoons. Although African American academic opportunities are shrinking, for the time being there are more distinguished African American professionals than ever. Black doctors, lawyers, professors, consultants, computer experts, scientists, are greater in number today than they have been in the last 300 hundred years of American history added together. The integrationist school of inclusion among African Americans seems to have a solid case behind it.[3]

But the re-Africanization of African Americans is also a tempting alternative option. Why cannot history be partially reversed? The Jews did it with the creation of Israel and the resurrection of what was previously the dead language of Hebrew. A partial resurrection of Jewish history occurred with the creation of Israel—certainly a revival of Jewish sovereignty, language and parts of Jewish culture. Can African Americans re-Africanize themselves?

Some of that revival is under way. When African Americans are being *religiously* Pan-African, they are drawn towards either Islam or *West African* religious traditions. As we indicated, Yoruba religion is particularly attractive to sections of African American opinion.

On the other hand, the most popular African *language* to African Americans is Swahili (or Kiswahili)—a language of *Eastern* Africa. Courses on Kiswahili language and culture at Ohio State University have sometimes attracted many *dozens* of African American students. The *Kwanzaa* celebration in African American culture (partly in competition with Christmas) is based on principles formulated in the Swahili language. Many African Americans have adopted Swahili (or Muslim) personal names for themselves. These include Rashida, Ali, Munira, Karim, Jemadari and others.

While West Africa was *religiously* inspiring, and East Africa *linguistically* stimulating, Southern Africa has been the special area of *racial* empathy for African Americans. The special extremities of *apartheid*, and the martyrdom of people like Nelson Mandela and Steve Biko, created a sympathy comparable to the feelings for those who were *lynched* in American history.

In North Africa African Americans were not looking for *religious bonds* (as in West Africa), or a *linguistic bond* (as in East Africa) or a *racial bond* (as in Southern Africa). With North Africa, African Americans were looking for a *civilizational bond*. And they found it in ancient Egypt. Cheikh Anta Diop helped them in his thesis that ancient Egypt was a Black civilization.[4]

What emerges from all this is that *linguistic* re-Africanization of African Americans would have to look mainly to Eastern Africa; *religious* re-Africanization would have to look more to West Africa; *racial* empathy would be drawn inevitably to Southern Africa; and *civilizational* celebration would turn its eyes northwards towards ancient Egypt.

The re-Africanization theme in the African American experience includes the struggle for multicultural education in the United States. There are demands for more attention to be paid to the African connection in the educational system. This would affect syllabus and curriculum in American schools, with a lot more attention to African history and culture in the classroom. Of course, multicultural education is for white students as well as for minorities.[5]

There are also subsidiary elements of re-Africanization. These include changes in dress culture, hair style, naming culture and the like. Choice of furniture and decorations in African American homes sometimes also reflects Pan-African tastes and aesthetics ranging from Yoruba sculpture to framed butterflies from Southern Africa. The trend is towards a deepening African consciousness and sense of identity.

We have already referred to Islam as an alternative route towards re-Africanization. But Islam has sometime been an alternative route toward Black separatism. The origins of the Nation of Islam was probably neither Pan-African nor Pan-Islamic but Black separatist. This was nationalist Islam rather than universalist Islam. The Black Muslims in the 1950s and early 1960s tapped the talents of Elijah Muhammed and Malcolm X in support of greater Black self-reliance at home in the United States—from Black schools to Black firms and factories. Nationalist Islam in the American context was a form of religious defiance, an assertion of religious separatism from the mainstream.

Under leaders like Louis Farakhan, nationalist Islam in the United States has forged more links with Muslims elsewhere and manifested greater Pan-Africanism. But the separatist tendency in Black Nationalist Islam is still quite fundamental, including the call for a separate Black economy.

Of course, not all forms of Black separatism in the United States have been associated with Islam. Separatist tendencies have ranged from the militancy of Black Panthers to the establishment of many Black Studies programs on American campuses—some of which have seen themselves as the vanguard of a Black intellectual and academic crusade. In so doing the Black Studies centers have often enriched the United States credentials as "Global Africa in microcosm." In no other country in the world is the totality of both the African and the Black experience studied on a wider scale and by more scholars than in the United States. No other country in the world has more courses taught about comparative Black experience than does the United States. The Black studies movement—inspired originally by separatist nationalist sentiment among African Americans—became a major contributor to intellectual and academic *diversity* on campuses.

A CONCLUSION

Of the three options open to African Americans—integration, re-Africanization and separatism—which one would be in the best interest of *Global Africa* as a whole? What Global Africa will ultimately need from African Americans is a *combination* of *integration* and *re-Africanization*. African Americans will need to become American enough to wield power and influence in the United States, and be re-Africanized enough to care deeply about what happens to Africa and to other people of African descent everywhere. Once again the precedent set by Jewish Americans is compelling. They are American enough to be immensely influential in the United States, but still Jewish enough to care deeply not only about Israel but also about Jews everywhere. They fight for Jewish causes without ceasing to be American patriots. One day more and more African Americans will fight for the broader interests of *Global Africa*—and still remain patriotic Americans.

Black separatism in the United States can only be defended as a short term tactical approach. Separatist sentiment sometimes works in mobilizing Black support for self-reliance. Separatism may also help to alarm the political establishment into making long overdue concessions to minorities. But the longer-term strategies for African Americans lie in a combination of integration and re-Africanization. African Americans need to counterpenetrate the citadels of American power, and get their fair share of American wealth. But African Americans also need to recover enough of their African pride and identity for the sake of their own children—and for the sake of Global Africa. The dialectic of diversity needs to be purposefully selective.

If a new world order is in the making, Global Africa should at last insist on a greater role than it had in the last 400 years. In that process of insistence, the voice of African Americans will be particularly crucial, fusing the moral power of Martin Luther King, Jr. with the vocal power of a latter-day Paul Robeson.

Notes

1. For articles about the Caribbean (including my own articles) this paper is particularly indebted to *Caribbean Affairs* (Port of Spain, Trinidad: Trinidad Express Newspapers) and *Caribbean Commentary* (Miami, Florida).

2. This issue is also addressed in Ali A. Mazrui, *The Africans: A Triple Heritage*, 9-part television series, (Public Broadcasting Service and British Broadcasting Corporation, 1986). A book of the same title is published by Little Brown (Boston, Mass: 1986).

3. See DeWayne Wickham, "New Litmus Test for Black Leaders, (Syndicated Column), *Press and Sun Bulletin* (Binghamton, New York), January 12, 1992.

4. See, for example, Cheikh Anta Diop, *The African Origin of Civilization: Myth or Reality* (edited and translated by Mercer Cook) [Chicago: Lawrence Hill Books, 1974).

5. See, for example, the Report of the New York Syllabus Review and Development Committee, *One Nation, Many Peoples: A Declaration of Cultural Interdependence* (Albany, NY: Department of Education, 1991).

This paper by Professor Ali A. Mazrui was presented at the International Symposium on the theme of "Will the Circle be Unbroken? Historical Perspectives on the African Diaspora" sponsored by the Smithsonian Institution, and held at the Carmichael Auditorium of The National Museum of American History, Washington, D.C., February 6-8, 1992.

Professor Ali A. Mazrui was kind enough to allow his text to be timely included in the current volume.

EPILOGUE
THE "NEGRITUDE CONFERENCE": A PERSONAL ASSESSMENT OF ITS IMPACT

FRANCENA THOMAS

It WAS a humid autumn day in Miami. The University dining room was almost empty. I had been sitting there for over an hour with the remnants of a chicken sandwich lunch. My mind was somewhere else that day when I was first to hear the word Negritude.

As I sat thinking, I saw coming up the path this beautiful, beautiful African, or so I presumed. His skin was a deep, velvet black. A shock of white hair crowned a surprisingly youthful face. With him was a lovely young woman. Her smooth cafe-au-lait complexion complemented his deep blackness. About the same height as he, she was so very slim she appeared to be a bit taller. They made a striking couple. I wondered who they were. What country in Africa did they call home? Where were they headed with such purposeful strides?

The man, though small in stature, carried himself with an air of power and resolve. He wore a two-piece garment of white sharkskin fabric. The collarless shirt loosely followed his body contours. His pants, straight without cuffs, were sharply creased.

Even in a town as accustomed as Miami to ethnic diversity in dress, his quietly elegant attire was riveting.

The couple came straight to me. He took my hand in his. "My sister, I've been looking for you. I've been trying for days to get in touch with you." I was completely dumbfounded. "This is Shawna, my wife. I am Carlos Moore," he said.

Who was this man? Why was he looking for me? His wife smiled at me with such warmth that I felt irresistibly drawn to her. Carlos' pleasure in having found me was evident from the salutation–"sister." He went on to say that he was about to convene a summit of World Black intellectuals. The theme of the gathering would be *Negritude*. The word jarred me.

NEGRITUDE AND ME

"Negritude"? The word was new to me. There was something in it which fell uncomfortably on my ears; it reverberated with powerlessness. There was no way I could bring myself to deal with anything that smacked of subservience. It seemed but one more "tude"– i.e., like servi*tude*. We had been America's servants. America's free labor pool. American's underpaid slum dwellers. American's last hired, first fired. America's incessant seekers of the promised land. Servitude was a prime ingredient of the economic and legal system that necessarily reduced black people to chattel.

There was the word inepti*tude*. The only time we were "allowed" to express ourselves in the arts was when we were acting like buffoons–rolling big white eyes in big black faces; laughing when we weren't tickled; scratching where we didn't itch. Whites thought the only thing we could be was funny, so every stereotype depicted us as being inept.

There was, also, grati*tude*. We were always told in one way or another that we must show our *gratitude*. Gratitude for things being "so much better" than they used to be. Gratitude that they didn't lynch us anymore! Gratitude that we were no longer murdered for trying to vote. Gratitude that they now let our kids go to school ten months of the year instead of five.

I know there are other "tudes" which have positive meanings. Like fortitude. Exactitude. But it was rare that we ever thought of ourselves in these terms. And just as servitude, ineptitude and gratitude were unacceptable to me, *Negritude* also rang with a demeaning sound.

MY MIAMI

Carlos was curious about Miami, my hometown. A city torn asunder by racial and ethnic cleavages. A city whose name evoked swaying' palm trees, soft ocean breezes and glittering lights. Beneath, Miami was a bubbling cauldron of racial strife which exploded from time to time. In 1979, over a ten-month period alone, six black men had lost their lives at the hands of white police officers. In almost every case, the officers implicated claimed that they had fired in self defense, so much so that blacks coined the phrase, "Death by Sudden-Move-Syndrome."

Each murder made the black community angrier, more hostile toward the police and elected officials. The rage was covered with a surface civility that job security and responsibilities required. But blacks were terribly disappointed with the politicians. Prominent when black votes were needed, none came forward to share the pain and anguish the black community was experiencing. The silence in high places was deafening. Had black officers killed six young white men "in the line of duty," we argued, the prosecutorial and judicial system would have responded with the brutal efficiency of a lynch mob.

How could I tell this man about Miami—my Miami without getting caught up in the painful feelings and memories dredged up from my childhood?

I came of age in the '50s, a time when every black person "knew" his place and for the most part accepted the "power differential" between blacks and whites. It was a time when Father Theodore Gibson, an Episcopal Priest and the President of the

Miami Chapter of the National Association for the Advancement of Colored People (NAACP), refused to hand over the membership rolls of the organization to the State Legislature, as he had been ordered to do. He was threatened with jail. Had he lacked courage or commitment to his followers in the struggle for equality, a lot of black and white people would have surely lost their jobs and their homes, and burning Ku Klux Klan crosses would have lit up their neighborhoods.

It was a time when blacks had to have picture I.D. cards to work on Miami Beach and had to be back in their black communities by 6:00 P.M. If there was a reason to work late, the "boss" had to call the police to let them know when his black employee would be leaving. I had to carry one of those cards with me when I worked at the now defunct Carillon Hotel on Collins Avenue. I remember the big red-haired cop who would board the bus each day to check the I.D. of blacks on their way to work. If you forgot your I.D. card you would have to get off the bus and miss a day's pay.

It was a time when the toilets and water fountains were labeled "White" and "Colored;" when every black male, whether old or young, whether doctor or elevator operator, was called "boy." (Even today, many policemen employ "boy" to provoke young black men to anger when stopped for a traffic offense, or for no reason at all.) A time when my own mother, a domestic, was called "Lou Ella," her first name, by a three-year-old white boy. That was the tone and tenor of black life in the '50s, when I was growing up in Miami.

Nonetheless, a few good things were carved out of our separate and unequal existence. For instance, the 2nd Avenue business corridor was dubbed "little Broadway." Its swanky hotels–Mary Elizabeth and Sir John were the showplaces and lodging for famous black entertainers who were not allowed in Miami Beach hotels and clubs. The "power differential," however, designed the I-95 Expressway to slice through our unique black economic oasis. So that by the late '60s, the dazzling bright lights of N.W. 2nd Avenue, and the wonderful jazz music of the black bistros and restaurants, were no more. The real Overtown, as we had known it, was dead. In its stead, there were now abandoned buildings. Empty stores. Desolate, dangerous, alleys. Homeless people. And new high rise apartment buildings had mushroomed around a new Sports Arena, designed to attract "Yuppies" and a few "Buppies" to another Overtown. One without the soul of our people! (During the Negritude Conference, black homeowners in the northern end of the county were again battling local government and wealthy white developers with designs on transforming their communities into another sports playground.)

FACING RACISM

From the time I was able to understand words, my mother taught me the poetry of Paul Laurence Dunbar. He was my literary talisman. When I went to the library, I took Paul's lyrical poems with me, in my heart, and my soul. I began going to the library when I was in elementary school. It was the only library in my little world where black people could go. It was run by two lovely ladies, Olive B. Alexander and Zilpha Sawyer, who read a few stories to us about black people. But there were so very few of them!

The little wooden frame building sat on the corner of 15th Avenue and 65th Street. The books on the shelves had been donated by "good, decent, caring white people" to help the "Colored" children. The library was my second home; my love for reading drove me there. I could always find stories about the Bobbsey Twins or Brenda Starr, and I read them eagerly. But even then, there was something missing. Even then, I wanted to read stories about people who looked like me.

That little library handed me my first big racial trauma. One that I would carry with me all of my life. I had never felt so worthless and angry as when I read the definition of "Negro." It said that Negroes were "dirty, poorly educated, untrustworthy and lazy people." Those words were in a huge book that served as a tool in the education of *white* children. It had found its way into our little library through some "generous" spirit who made it a gift to be used by Black children. It was such a lying, degrading, demeaning definition of *me* and what I knew myself and my family to be! I felt real anger against an unknown entity and for the first time in my life, I felt totally powerless. I wanted to hit someone or something. But whom or what would I hit? Whom or what was responsible for these vile lies about my people?

I was so traumatized that I rejected that book and, along with it, everything white people stood for. Thereafter, whenever I heard a white saying anything, I assumed it was a lie. Looking back I can see I was becoming as racist in my thinking as were those cruel uncaring people who wrote that definition. I never went back to that library. Some mean-spirited evil "thing" had invaded my happy space and brutally slammed the door on my happy, golden childhood days. I was angry at white people.

There was one more incident that, when coupled with the experience in the library, changed me from a loving, trusting child to an angry, raging, skeptical young woman of twelve. I read Kyle Onstott's *Mandingo!* Others may have read this powerfully vivid description of some of the most dehumanizing facets of American slavery as a piece of fictionalized history. For me every word was true. Particularly since I already knew that my paternal great, great grandfather had been killed by a group of white men who threw him bodily across the stump of a tree and broke his back. He had tried to stop them from fondling his wife. He was a freed slave. She was a Blackfoot Indian.

For the next eight years, I had little love for white people and no trust at all. I never let my mother know how I was feeling, because mom's attitude was that God had made white people too. Who were we, then, to behave as though God had made a mistake? We didn't have to lower ourselves in the eyes of God by hating them because of the color of their skin, she told me. My mother wrote fiery poetry that showed her militancy, but she was deeply religious as well. Not one word of her poetry expressed hate, or violence, as a way to respond to racism.

More than ever before I began to feel my "Negro-ness." It was a feeling that told us that we were *different* and that though we might feel pride in our own communities, we could not really compete with white folk. We were told that was why it was to our advantage to stay segregated. Separate.

Our parents taught us a new, stand-up-and-fight credo that was repeated so often on so many occasions that it became our catechism. "Darling," my mother would say, "it's always been true—you can't be only as good as they are; you've got to be *better* in every way. You've got to be *twice* as good to get half as much as they have." This little catechism of survival or self-preservation took me through high school and eight years of college.

FACING MY IGNORANCE

Meeting Carlos, hearing him talk about the diaspora and events I knew nothing about, did shock me. How in the world, in my twenty years of study, which had earned me double masters, had I never heard of this? I had finished college and the survival catechism of my childhood had served me well. It had protected my ego and personhood from whites. But what could I use to protect myself from me? How could I have gone through four years of a black state university and never learned anything about other Blacks? About the Black Diaspora? About our universal roots? About Blacks being everywhere and not just in the one little place where I grew up?

Eight years of college had taught me *nothing* about people in Brazil, Ecuador, Peru and so many other countries of the diaspora. What I knew about black people, I had learned from my mother, or from *Encore Magazine* and *Ebony.* I had read about a few outstanding blacks. But *Black History,* as such, was a set of obscure facts about cardboard personalities. Nat Turner, Denmark Vesey, and other blacks of a militant bent, had yet to come into my consciousness. Information about great black scholars, fighters, intellectuals may have been marginally available. But how many of us were even informed enough to ask? We had never heard the names. Our curiosity had not been nurtured anywhere. Every voice on radio was white. Every face on TV was white. We were indeed invisible everywhere. Sometimes even to ourselves.

It was this literate, competitive, capable woman with the wounded child in her breast that Carlos told about Negritude.

WHITE CUBANS ARRIVE!

In the early days of the Cuban airlift to Miami, *white* Cubans were not perceived as being anti-black I just saw them as being "pro-Cuban." To me, there was nothing wrong with that. Of course, the economic conditions for blacks soon began to decline in direct proportion to the upward economic mobility of the white Cubans. But few of us at the time had detected the correlation between those facts.

Miami's economy was based on the tourism industry. From the City's earliest origins, blacks had held jobs as waiters, maids, bus boys, counter girls.... The tips were good. Black men and women raised families, bought homes, sent their children to college, on tips. Then, suddenly, surprisingly, those jobs vanished. How? Why? Cubans seeking a toehold in this new land were willing to work for less pay than blacks. There was no opportunity for negotiation over this issue. White businessmen saw a double bonus in hiring Cubans and moved swiftly to take advantage of it. First, they would pay the Cubans less. Second, they were getting *white* employees. In fact, for a short while, Cubans were even thought to be America's new "niggers." But this illusion proved to be short-lived. At best, it was an expensive miscalculation on the part of the hotel owners and Miami Beach merchants. After the new, non-English speaking white Cubans became securely positioned in all the jobs formerly held by blacks–waiters, bellhops, maids and bus boys–they organized into an exclusive union. The Cubans demanded higher pay and when their demands were rejected, they went on strike. Needless to say, black employment in that part of the tourism industry was never the same.

As blacks continued to feel the erosion of their economic base, the white Cubans continued to rise. The schism widened when it was noted that *there were few black Cubans advancing,* though there were many here. The idea that language was a barrier to employment lost legitimacy. Blacks were unionized, but their unions were not big enough, or strong enough, to strike.

Perhaps the most shocking and devastating aspect of the Cuban immigration was that it totally abrogated the unwritten understanding and tacit agreements about work between blacks and whites. Throughout our travail in this land called America, there had always been a tacit understanding about a "racial division of labor." There were jobs for whites: president, boss, manager, accountant, broadcaster, movie star, etc. There were jobs for blacks: janitor, yardman, waiter, maid, cook....We, blacks, could not believe that a *white* refugee would permanently want a menial "black" job.

Everywhere else in the south there was a simple two-way power split between blacks and whites. In Miami we now found ourselves sitting on a three-legged stool with one leg shorter than the others. Over a period of some 26 years, Dade County had absorbed over 800,000 predominantly white Cubans. Their sheer numbers alone caused their culture to spill all over the County. Their aggressive style, their aggrieved sense of betrayal at the Bay of Pigs, made these foreigners a formidable single-purpose force to be dealt with in the marketplace!

Unfortunately for Miami Blacks, the Cubans came in 1960, exactly three years after the Montgomery bus boycott, at what was then the height of the Civil Rights Movement. Blacks and whites in other parts of America were being forced into a dialogue, but Miami would get a reprieve from such deliberations because the "poor" Cubans who lost their homeland to Castro and Communism served as a welcome buffer. Elected and appointed officials found it easier to welcome 800,000 Cubans fleeing Communism and Castro than address the legitimate grievances of 250,000 African American citizens. It became politically more palatable to vilify Castro and Communism than to confront the racism inherent to black-white relations in Miami.

The Cuban refugees were said to be seeking freedom. However, these white Cubans had three major advantages over American Blacks. First, most of those who came in the '60s had *white* skin in a land that had historically welcomed white refugees.

Second, they arrived in the United States with the firm purpose of "getting back" what they had lost materially and psychologically in their homeland. Third, they were the former business and political leaders in Cuba who brought with them experience, money and connections. American Blacks, on the other hand, were trying to "catch up" and to maintain what little we had gained materially, while keeping the focus on the black-white inequalities still extant in this "free" society.

The massive white Cuban, anti-Castro influx had the effect of putting a brake on the embryonic Civil Rights and desegregation drive. Miami could thereafter boast the dubious distinction of being the only part of the southern United States which was not sensitized by the Civil Rights clamor of the '60s.

CONDITIONS IN THE '70S AND '80S

In December 1979, a Black insurance man named Arthur McDuffie was involved in a late-night, high-speed chase with County police officers. After a minor traffic infraction, McDuffie had failed to pull over when ordered to do so. His life was taken as a result; beaten by police officers who behaved as a mindless mob. All of the officers involved in the killing were *white* and many of them had Spanish names. It was clearly a case of vicious homicide; the brutal murder of an unarmed civilian.

McDuffie's death on December 17, 1979, was for the black community one more soul-numbing experience to absorb. One more sign that black people did not count. Still, the senseless, inexplicable assault on this lone black motorist provoked no riot on December 17. The black community simply withdrew inward, to their churches, their clubs, their living rooms, where blacks consoled each other. One question was on everybody's lips: Why had not a single white elected official uttered a word of comfort?

It was a white police officer who first began to peel away the layers of deception that had begun to envelop the McDuffie killing. Then, Edna Buchannan, a *Miami Herald* reporter, wrote the first true account on the circumstances of McDuffie's death, relying mainly on the medical examiner's report. McDuffie's skull had been cracked by one blow from a heavy, blunt object. It was later revealed that the "heavy, blunt object" was a Kell light, the long, heavy flashlight police officers use for crowd control.

On May 17, 1980, the four officers charged with the killing of McDuffie were acquitted. Blacks went on a rampage. It started with a peaceful protest march on the Justice Building. Then someone threw a rock and hell broke loose. There were dock workers, doctors, lawyers, teachers, maids, bankers, waiters, janitors, students and black people from every walk of life in that crowd. Blacks from every corner of Miami had come to march in protest, and when police managed to disperse them from the Justice Building, they all rioted. Anger spread to Liberty City. Overtown. Coconut Grove. Richmond Heights. Opa Loch. All places with high concentrations of blacks. Cars were overturned. Fires were set. And what followed were the bloodiest, most terrifying days in the history of Miami. When it was all over, *twenty-six* people had been killed. Fourteen blacks, twelve whites. One hundred million dollars worth of property had been destroyed.

Not much has changed since then. In 1983, another young black man, Neville Johnson, was killed while in a poolroom playing a video game. The people rioted. The officer incriminated had, again, been acquitted, pleading "self-defense." How in the world could a summit of the world's leading black scholars and intellectuals be convened in such a city? In such an *anti-black* environment?

RACIST MIAMI: THE WRONG CITY

One day Carlos sat me down in my office. "My sister, what is wrong? Do you *really* understand what we want to do?" It was then that I confessed my distaste for the word Negritude; my opposition to such a grand conference being held in such a citadel of racism as Miami; in such a university as Florida International University. In the eyes of the black community, the host institution—Florida International University—was unworthy of the honor being bestowed upon it. An institution of some 15,000 students, where only 6% of the student body was black. A state-funded university of some 435 faculty members where only 8% of the faculty were black. Mostly non-American blacks at that!

Looking back today I wish I had taped the talk Carlos gave me that day. It lasted almost two hours. "My sister, why didn't you tell me how you felt? How can you convince others to join you in a project you yourself are unsure of?" Negritude, he explained, was not a new concept; it was over 50 years old. In fact, it was a child of the Harlem Renaissance. But most important, it was not a "tude" which white folks were responsible for or had given us. A black man had *deliberately* coined it to, signify black awareness and a collective self-consciousness linking New World Africans with those Africans on the continent. Aimé Césaire, the man in whose honor the conference had been convened, had fathered the word *Negritude.*

Carlos spoke about Aimé Césaire, Léopold Sédar Senghor, Léon Damas and about his (Carlo's) personal mentor, Cheikh Anta Diop, the Senegalese scientist. The deep love and respect felt for each of them came through in his voice.

Aimé Césaire had first used the word *Negritude,* in 1939, in his 70-page epic poem, Notebook of a *Return to the Native Land.* The three founders of what came to be known as the "Negritude Movement" had urged blacks worldwide to take pride in their heritage and to cast off the self-deprecating shackles of assimilationism. They were uncompromising in their stand on colonialism. "Today Negritude is perhaps the closest to being a universal concept among those whose roots are in Africa," Carlos argued. "It is *African* consciousness."

As he talked, I began to experience shifts in my perception. He spoke about the Black Diaspora. He pointed out that Negritude had been spread throughout most of the Black world. "Negritude was born right here in America with the works of W.E.B. DuBois," he stated. To my objections to bringing our foremost intellectuals and scholars to Miami for this conference, he argued: "My sister, it is *precisely* because of the conditions here that Miami is the best place for *this* conference. You will see that this is the right time, the right place and the right way."

Today, looking back, I admit that such an assessment was rooted in facts that were not so apparent at the time. Facts which perhaps only a total foreigner could have discerned so perceptibly. What Carlos Moore had seen–or sensed–was the dormant potential for *mobilization* in the Miami African American community. That potential first showed itself in the type of warmth with which *all* of black Miami embraced what everyone began to call the "Negritude Conference." Four years after, that capacity for mobilization would burst forth with the City Boycott, led by Attorney H.T. Smith. Although fueled by longstanding grievances of police brutality, political impotence, and employment discrimination, the triggering event was a disrespectful slight by the white establishment of South Africa's Nelson Mandela.)

I was now eager to hear more. About Césaire, Senghor, and all the others. I began doing some research of my own. At one point, I had become so caught up in this event that I would have willingly paid for the opportunity to be a part of it!

THE BLACK COMMUNITY'S RESPONSE

The truth is that nobody could have anticipated the overwhelming response from a black community which, until this time, had been lethargic and apathetic. And respond it did. People began to come from everywhere seeking to be involved in some small way in what they sensed would be a life-changing event. Young people. Senior black women. Men. Middle class. And Just ordinary folks. The *Miami Times*, a weekly African American newspaper, must be credited for having made the conference, its underlying concepts, a household property. The newspaper published story after story about the forthcoming conference. It listed the names, and provided background data on some of the national and internationally known personalities who would be present (Alex Haley, John Henrik Clarke, Maya Angelou, Abdias do Nascimento ...). Soon, a large segment of the City's black populace could boast of some form of involvement. Some people offered their homes to receive visitors. Others offered their services as chauffeurs, guides, interpreters....

Felicia Lee, presently with the *New York Times*, was then a reporter for the *Miami Herald*. She wrote a very moving, insightful, piece about Aimé Césaire, Léopold Sédar Senghor, Negritude and Carlos. As I wrote this piece, I felt compelled to talk to Felicia, four years later. "The Negritude conference was a transcendental experience," she said. "In bringing together black intellectuals from around the world—each anticipating their unique, yet common, experience of racial oppression—the terms 'diaspora' and 'Negritude' became real. The pain and power of the speakers, and the need for blacks to acknowledge their history and envision a future, has rarely found voice in such a gathering. As an African American journalist who covered the event, I came away with a fresher, more textured, understanding of myself and my people."

BLACK MIAMI PRIDE

For Miami's black community, the Negritude Conference was a feast for the eyes, the ears, the senses. For once the spot light was on Miami's blacks. Not on Fidel Castro, Cuba, or Communism. We were the news. Not as rioters, thugs, criminals, pimps, prostitutes, or welfare recipients. We were *the* news in terms of what we had always known that we were: *a dignified community!*

Pride swelled in black Miami as more national and inter-national attention focused on the Negritude Conference. *Sbinbua*, China's News Agency, *Reuters* and *Associated Press*, *The New York Times*, *Agence France-Presse*, *Le Matin (Paris)*, *Le Soleil of Senegal*, Jamaica's *The Daily Gleaner*, *France-Antilles* of Guade-loupe, Martinique and French Guiana and Latin America's continent-wide *Vision* had joined *the Miami Times* and the *Miami Herald* in a chorus.

Statements of admiration and support began streaming into Carlos' little office at FIU from U.S. officialdom (Rep. William

Gray, Mervyn Dymally, Dante Fascell, Sen. Bob Graham...), and from presidents of more than 50 African American universities and colleges which by then would have gladly swapped places with Florida International University. Known only to a few of us—whom Carlos had dubbed the "Shadow Cabinet"—a number of these institutions were on a standby. Particularly when, three weeks prior to the conference's scheduled opening, the attacks from the white Cuban exile radios had become most virulent. *"Nobody* is going to be allowed to sabotage *this* conference!", Carlos told us one day in his office, in quite a somber mood.

MEETING SENGHOR AND CÉSAIRE

The day President Senghor arrived in Miami–a day ahead of Aimé Césaire–I had read enough, heard enough, and understood enough to become a full-fledged proponent of everything implicit in the term Negritude.

At the airport there was quite a hubbub all around us. Security people were running around with walkie-talkies. Certain areas had to be cordoned off to keep unauthorized persons from accidentally wandering in. We were a select group of some twelve to fifteen university representatives. All of us had been deeply involved in the planning of the conference. We huddled at the door through which President Senghor would enter. We were standing there with our badges and tags indicating that we were the official welcoming party for a major dignitary. My heart was beating at a very rapid pace. Butterflies were having a convention in my stomach.

At last the waiting was over. President Senghor now came into our midst, led by a Secret Service Agent. He was remarkably youthful-looking for all of his eighty-two years. He carried himself with grace, his lovely wife with elegance. I must admit surprise at the fact that his wife was a white woman because I knew so much about Senghor at this time, and had read some of his poems as well, particularly, his "Black Woman." No man had ever paid greater homage to black women than Senghor in that poem:

Naked woman, black woman
Clad in our color that is life, in your form that is
    beauty!
I have grown up in your shade, the sweetness of
    your hands bound my eyes.
And now in the heart of summer and noon, I dis-
    cover you, promised earth, from the tower of
    your sun-scorched neck.
And your beauty smites me to the full of my heart
    like the flash of an eagle.

I was puzzled, though not disturbed. For I had come to know him on an intimate basis through his writings. I knew that Senghor, unlike Césaire, had pleaded for a more "accommodating" relationship between the races, while denouncing the terrible effects of racism worldwide on Africa's children.

President Senghor smiled warmly. He embraced Carlos and Shawna as would a *father*. He shook each person's hand with a firm grip. "And how are you, my sister?" All I could stammer out as he greeted me was, "It's a moy to jeet you, sir" (translation: "it's a joy to meet you, sir"). After that dazzling demonstration of poise and verbal fluency, I was ready to disappear under the carpet.

When we arrived at the Sofitel Hotel, a few of us were invited to spend some time with President and Mrs. Senghor. Small in stature, Senghor had a commanding presence. Of a man of his extraordinary accomplishments, one would have expected some form of snobbishness. To the contrary, he made us all feel at ease. The way he greeted us indicated that he was an open, warm and loving person. He spoke softly. He inquired about the riots which had rocked Miami.

We were about to take leave of him when I explained that I was from a large, loving family. When good things happened, such as when a family member returned home after a long absence, he would be greeted with tears and kisses. I felt tears welling up. I was filled with wondrous emotions as the tears actually began to fall. I asked Senghor if I might give him a welcoming family hug.

"Oh come, my little sister," he said. He reached out to hug me as eagerly as I him.

Today, years after, I still get goose bumps when I remember that up-close-and-personal meeting with Senghor. Tears still come unbidden. Our embrace had expressed what many African Americans would have wanted to, had they had the same good fortune to be in his company. I do believe there is a universal "diasporan" desire to be welcomed by somebody. To be understood by somebody. Respected. Appreciated. This gentle poet's embrace was that of the father from whom we had been kidnapped. The father who, despite the centuries, had never forgotten his child. The father who had kept a place for you at the family's table. The one who had searched for you, prayed in the darkest of times, and finally one day had found you! I was safe and strong again, though tattered and torn from my long, lonely terrible ordeal.

Hugging President Senghor the way I did, may have broken established rules of protocol, but I had honored the unwritten covenant of brotherhood that supersedes the petty rules of our "soulless" society. Senghor and I were brother and sister, father and daughter, and had recognized one another as such. Were not the people of the African diaspora the brothers and sisters of those who had remained on the continent? Negritude was a validation of that claim.

At the airport, security for Aimé Césaire was even tighter than it had been for Senghor. I would not learn why until the last day of the conference: White Cuban exile groups had threatened to disrupt the gathering. Carlos took no chances.

As we waited for Césaire's plane to land, I thought about all which I had read about this eloquent, lonely, volcanic man. Known to be a very polite, shy man of great dignity, it is in his poetry and prose that his rage against racism, his fierce pride in his blackness, suddenly erupts. In his Notebook of the Return to the Native Land, a 70-page epic poem, the poet-philosopher cries out:

> My Negritude is not a stone,
> Its deafness hurled against the clamor of the
>   day...

My Negritude is neither tower nor cathedral.
It takes root in the red flesh of the soil.
It thrusts into the warm flesh of the sky.
It digs under the opaque dejection of its rightful
    patience.

Negritude as a concept, for Césaire, was but the common
ground for communication between all of Africa's stolen legions.
In hot, cutting lines, he shouts:

My name is Bordeaux, Nantes, Liverpool, New
    York and San Francisco, Virginia, Tennessee,
    Georgia, Alabama.
A monstrous putrefaction of results coming to
    nothing.
Putrid marshes of blood ... lynching in America ....
Red earth, brother earth,
Blood-Brother earth ....

Césaire's plane had arrived. Despite the heavy security, we
were permitted a few delightful moments to greet him, then he was
frisked away.

A BLACK INTELLECTUAL FEAST

On February 27, 1987, the "Negritude Conference" had opened
movingly with a black high school choir bringing tears to many
eyes as they sang "Oh Freedom." Over 2500 people had come
from as far as Zaire, Paris, Senegal, Haiti, and the West Indies to
Miami to attend the "Negritude Conference." Many more would
have converged on the city had the organizers not dissuaded them.
There was simply nowhere to put them. The first day session was
intended to be by invitation only. But the people ignored that.
Overflow rooms had to be set up, and still, all outside the
auditorium, people were standing at doors, crowded together trying

to hear what Senghor and Césaire were saying. Or to even get a glimpse of them.

A healing balm could be felt. We were at a Family Reunion of the Diaspora. Not at a formal and cold conference! The black family was ... reunited. There was a bonding going on. There was a reaching out going on. Something *special* was happening! People were walking differently. Talking differently. Smiling differently. They were even *dressed* differently.

The conference organizers made sure that the quality of black women representation was as multi-faceted as was the nature of black women the world over. That "little detail" became evident on the second day's afternoon session, appropriately titled: *"Inequality. Within Inequality! The Situation of Afro Women in the Americas."*

Maya Angelou, the high priestess of African American, womanhood, had fired the opening salvos. Not salvos of aggression. But of salvation. She brought tears to the eyes of the strongest. What was exploding over our heads were loving thunderbolts. A pressing call for *companionship* and respect between African men and women. A compelling cry for mutual understanding rooted in a past togetherness.

We had heard the wise men. Maya's words were good old black woman wisdom! The counterpart to the wisdom of Césaire and Senghor. A wisdom born out of an equally horrifying experience. Deracination. The Middle Passage. Centuries of slave labor *alongside* black men in the cotton, tobacco and cane fields of the Americas. And throughout, the unspeakable experience of centuries of physical *rape*; the defilement of the body but also of the soul. Did black men *really understand* what physical rape was? Many of us shed quiet tears.

The women presenters brought new perspectives from all angles. Lelia Gonzalez, the Brazilian, graphically painted a picture of black womanhood in so-called "Latin" America: domesticity, mass unemployment, prostitution ....

Iva Carruthers, Betty Parker-Smith, Mari Evans–all African Americans—spoke to the issues of evolution of racism into the 21st century; the seemingly "impossible-to-resolve" conundrum

be-tween the "Diasporan" African Man and Woman; the dysfunc-
tional socializing practices within the black family....

The Peruvian, Victoria de Santa Cruz, insisted that male/fe-
male bonding without firm cultural moorings and profound
spirituality, could spell but failure....

Aulana Peters, African American, spoke to the opportunities
for the growth of black businesses. African women, she implied,
would have to play greater entrepreneurial roles in black economic
development if those efforts were to succeed....

POMP AND CIRCUMSTANCE

The pomp and circumstance surrounding this event was sure to
come. We recognized our royalty. For surely Aimé Césaire and
Léopold Sédar Senghor are the uncrowned royalty of the African
diaspora.

A highlight in the State Dinner came when Carlos broke down
in tears in praising his mentors; his love, respect, appreciation for
what these two old warriors had accomplished. Unknowingly, he
had expressed what each one of us felt in our innermost souls.
Plain "gut" emotions now overcame us all.

As I look back and remember those three wondrous and
impossible-to-describe days, it is clear to me that we had all been
involved in much more than a conference. It was a moment of
catharsis. A moment of our lives when each one of us would have
given all that we had for it not to have ended. A rare moment
when, unashamedly, we had *truly embraced... ourselves!*

CONTRIBUTORS*

Maya Angelou (USA) Woman of Letters, Professor of Literature, poet, Ms. Angelou won international acclaim for her best selling autobiographical novels (*I Know Why The Caged Bird Sings*, etc.) A leading personality in African American cultural and civil rights circles since the late 1950s, Ms. Angelou belongs to the avant-garde of African American women writers who began re-shaping the landscape of American letters in the 1960s.

Justo Arroyo (Panama) Poet. Professor of Literature, literary critic and essayist, Mr. Arroyo is a former director of Cultural Affairs and former Ambassador of Panama.

Roy Guevara Arzu (Honduras) Economist. Advisor to the Ministry of Economic Planning of Honduras. Mr. Guevara Arzu is currently president of the National Black Brotherhood of Honduras (OFRANEH).

Antonio Preciado Bedoya (Ecuador) Poet. Professor Preciado Bedoya is currently president of the Technical University of Esmeraldas in Ecuador. He is author of several collections of poetry, heavily influenced by the Negritude writers of the 1930s and 1940s.

Iva E. Carruthers (USA) Sociologist. Professor and former chairperson of the Sociology Department at Northeastern Illinois University. Ms.Carruthers is a specialist on questions relating to biostatistics, racial prejudice and the conceptualization of racism.

Bassette Cayasso (Nicaragua) Medical Doctor. Dr. Cayasso was associated with the Sandinista movement that came to power in 1979. He became progressively disenchanted with the new regime's racial policies (particularly Managua's efforts to civilize the African coastal communities) and eventually fled to Costa Rica where he ministered to the needs of Nicaraguan refugees. He now lives and works in Managua.

Aimé Césaire (Martinique) Man of Letters. Together with Léopold Sédar Senghor of Senegal and Leon Damas of French Guiana, Cesaire is the legendary co-founder of the Black Awareness Movement known as Negritude. An acclaimed poet, playright, literary critic and philosopher, Césaire is also a political pioneer in his own right. He was Mayor of Fort-de-France, Martinique, over three decades, a deputy in France's National Assembly and by far the most powerful political voice in the French West Indies. Currently Mr. Césaire devotes most of his time to writing. His opening speech in Miami at the conference on "Negritude, Ethnicity and Afro-Cultures in the Americas" in 1987 is widely considered to be his definitive statement on Negritude.

John Henrik Clarke (USA) Historian. Professor Emeritus of African American History, Hunter College. Mr. Clarke is the author of numerous books, and a frequent lecturer at American campuses. Along with St. Clair Drake and John Hope Franklin, Professor Clarke is an outstanding Elder scholar of African American academia.

Jean Crusol (Martinique) Economist. Professor of Economics at the University of the French West Indies (Martinique), Mr. Crusol is an economic advisor to the Regional Council of Martinique. He is an authority on insular Caribbean economies.

Quince Duncan (Costa Rica) Writer. Professor of Literature at the University of Heredia in Costa Rica, Mr. Duncan is the most prominent African Costa Rican man of letters. He is the author of more than 15 essays, collection of story tales and novels including his much acclaimed *Kimbo*.

Mari Evans (USA) Poet, playright and literary critic. Ms. Evans is a former distinguished writer and Assistant Professor of African

Studies and Research at Cornell University and the State University of New York at Albany. She is the author of several works, including collections of poetry and her acclaimed *Black Women Writers: 1950-1980*.

Lelia Gonzalez (Brazil) Sociologist. Professor at the Pontifical Catholic University of Rio de Janeiro, Ms. Gonzalez is a co-founder of the Unified Black Movement of Brazil. In 1981, as a cultural and political activist, she became the first African Brazilian woman elected "Woman of the Year" by the National Council of Women of Brazil. She died of a heart attack in July 1994 in her native Rio de Janiero at the age of 56.

J. Edward Greene (Guyana) Political Scientist. Pro Vice Chancellor of the University of the West Indies and director of its Institute for Social & Economic Research (ISER). Professor Greene's works have centered on questions of political dominance and economic stratification in the English-speaking Caribbean. He is regarded as one of the area's avant-garde scholars.

Ruth Simms Hamilton (USA) Sociologist. Professor at Michigan State University and director of its African Diaspora Research Project, Ms. Simms Hamilton is at the forefront of a new generation of African American scholars who have successfully extended the scope of African diaspora studies to include Asia, the Near and Middle East. She is the author of numerous monographs on Africans in South and Central America.

José Carlos Luciano Huapaya (Peru) Sociologist. A representative of the new generation of Africa-oriented scholar/activists in South/Central America, Lucinao Huapaya is a co-founder of the Centro de Estudios Afro-Peruanos. His sociological works are centered on the African family in Peru and the role of the woman as the transmitter of ancestral traditions.

Richard Long (USA) Man of Letters. Professor of Literature

(Emory University) and former director of the Center for Afro-American Studies of Atlanta University. Mr. Long is founder and permanent chairperson of Symposia on Traditional African Art. Author of numerous works on the Harlem Renaissance, the Negritude Movement and the history of African art, Professor Long is one of the most influential Elder statesmen of African American culture.

Ali A. Mazrui (Kenya) Political Scientist. Professor of Political Science and African Studies at the University of Michigan, Professor Mazrui has written numerous books and articles, has lectured on five continents and has served as vice president of both the International Congress of Africanists and International Political Science Association. Professor Ali Mazrui has been described as "Africa's most independent thinker."

Val T. McComie (Barbados) Career diplomat. A former professor of history in West Africa, Ambassador McComie is a former Assistant Secretary General of the Organization of American States. He is an authority on pre-and post-federation politics in the English-speaking Caribbean.

Carlos Moore (Cuba) Political Ethnologist. Specializing in the study of the impact that racial/ethnic dynamics bear upon domestic and international politics. Mr. Moore is the author of *Castro, the Blacks and Africa,* the first comprehensive analysis of race relations in post-revolutionary Marxist Cuba.

Abdias do Nascimento (Brazil) Man of Letters. Professor do Nascimento is a former director of the Puerto Rican Studies and Research Center of SUNY at Buffalo. Playright, poet, essayist and painter, do Nascimento has been the foremost spokesperson for the African Brazilian community since the 1930s when he founded the Black Experimental Theater. He is currently president and co-founder of the Congress of Black Cultures of the Americas, and a member of the Federal Parliament of Brazil.

Rex Nettleford (Jamaica) Writer and choreographer. Pro Vice-Chancellor of the University of the West Indies and director of its Institute for Extra-Mural Studies. Professor Nettleford is founder and principal choreographer of the internationally acclaimed National Dance Theater Company of Jamaica. Literary and social critic, essayist and cultural historian, Mr. Nettleford is widely regarded as one of the Caribbean's most influential intellectuals. He is currently a member of the UNESCO Executive Council and an advisor to CARICOM.

Manuel Zapata Olivella (Colombia) Writer. Professor Zapata Olivella is the foremost novelist and essayist in South America as well as an early proponent of Negritude. A medical doctor by profession, he has published more than 15 novels. In 1977 he convened the First Congress of Black Cultures in the Americas, at Cali, Colombia. Since 1940 Dr. Zapata Olivella has been in the forefront of the struggle for the social uplift and political/economic emancipation of Afro South Americans.

Léopold Sédar Senghor (Senegal) Man of Letters and former Head of State. Along with Aimé Césaire of Martinique and Leon Damas of French Guiana, Senghor is co-founder of the Negritude Movement. A poet, historian, literary critic and philosopher, Senghor became Senegal's first president in 1960. In 1980 he became the first African head of state to have voluntarily resigned his post. He retired from politics altogether and joined the prestigious Academy of France, devoting most of his time to writing "Negritude and the Civilization of the Universal," which was the theme of his presentation at the 1987 Conference in Miami, and stands out as his definitive statement on the subject.

Adrienne Shadd (Canada) Historian. Ms. Shadd is one of a handful of budding African Canadian scholars whose research work is contributing to dispel the widespread ignorance regarding African experience in Canada. "The Long Journey: A History of Black

Women in Canada," presented here, was secured after the Miami Conference and was prepared with assistance of Professor Frederick Case and Ms. Ayanna Black.

Bettye J. Parker Smith (USA) Writer. Professor of Literature and critic, Ms. Parker Smith is currently a Vice President at Tougaloo College in Mississippi. She co-authored the seminal study *Sturdy Black Bridges: Visions of Black Women in Literature.*

Francina Thomas (USA) Writer and Public Relations person. Ms. Thomas served as public relations and community liaison person for the conference on "Negritude, Ethnicity and the Afro Cultures in the Americas" held in Miami on February 26-28, 1987.

---

* The contributions presented in this volume represent roughly half of the 52 papers presented at the Miami Conference (Feb. 1987). They strictly reflect the views of the individual contributors.